JOAN
SUTHERLAND

JOAN SUTHERLAND

Norma Major

Introduction by Dame Joan Sutherland

Macdonald
Queen Anne Press

To my family

A Queen Anne Press BOOK

© Norma Major 1987

First published in Great Britain in 1987 by
Queen Anne Press, a division of
Macdonald & Co (Publishers) Ltd
3rd Floor
Greater London House
Hampstead Road
London NW1 7QX

A BPCC plc Company

Jacket — Front: *Esclarmonde*, Covent Garden, 1983. Photograph
Reg Wilson. Back: *Lucia di Lammermoor*, Covent Garden, 1985.
Photograph Clive Barda.

British Library Cataloguing in Publication Data

Major, Norma
  Joan Sutherland.
  1.   Sutherland, Joan   2.   Singers ——
  Australia —— Biography
  I.   Title
  782.1'092'4   ML420.S96

ISBN 0–356–12693–5

Printed and bound in Great Britain by
Hazell, Watson & Viney Ltd
Member of the BPCC Group
Aylesbury, Bucks

Contents

ACKNOWLEDGEMENTS

The help of many people who supplied me with information on various stages of Sutherland's career has been much appreciated, and for their generous contribution I would particularly like to thank Norman Ayrton, Sylvia Holford, John Copley, Graham Newell, the Earl of Harewood, Sir William van Straubenzee, M.P., Mrs Isobel Hall, Mrs Ailsa Hargreaves, Dorothy Jordan, Phyllis Abbott, Gerald Moore, Peter Gellhorn, Bryan Balkwill, Elizabeth Allen, Nicholas Goldschmidt and Emanuel Young.

The catalogue of Sutherland's performances has been assembled from opera house archives and the indispensable help of friends, too numerous to mention, who sent me programmes from around the world — each one fitting a valuable piece into the jigsaw of Sutherland's performing life. However, very special thanks are due to John Rosonakis and Robyn Simms in Sydney; Betty Weiser, Mrs Lester C. Osborne and Fr. Matthias Montgomery in America; Anne Roughley, Tessa Trench and Darlene Neuman wherever they happened to be and without all of whom the catalogue and much more would not have been possible.

My grateful thanks are also due to Evelyn Klopfer at the Sydney Opera House Trust Library, the State Library of New South Wales and the Victorian Performing Arts Museum; Boris Skidelski and Francesca Franchi for allowing me access to the Covent Garden Archives; the assistance of the British Newspaper Library, the Royal College of Music, the BBC Archives and St Catherine's School, Waverley, Sydney where Sutherland's early life and career forms part of the first-year history syllabus; the Decca Record Co. Ltd, and in particular, Raymond McGill for help in compiling the discography; also to class 2W at Hemingford Grey County Primary School and James and Elizabeth Blatch for painstaking work on the index.

For permission to quote extracts from reviews of Sutherland's performances I am indebted to *The Times*, the *Daily Telegraph*, the *Guardian*, the *Financial Times*, the *Daily Express*, the *Observer*, the *Edinburgh Evening News*, the *Glasgow Herald*, the *Birmingham Post*, *Opera Magazine* and *Music & Musicians*; the *New York Times*, the *Saturday Review*, the *Chicago Tribune*, the *Seattle Times*, the *Vancouver Sun* and *Opera News*; the *Sydney Morning Herald*, the *Bulletin* and the *Australian*.

I will always fondly remember the many friends who helped more than they could possibly know by merely listening and encouraging; also Sara Wheeler, my editor, who led me by the hand through the intricacies of publication with great patience and constant reassurance, and Suzanne Williams who tracked down hundreds of photographs and helped with the painful task of selection and rejection.

I cannot conclude these acknowledgements without expressing my gratitude to Dame Joan and Richard Bonynge for giving their blessing to the project and for their help and interest ever since, but especially for reading the manuscript and making valuable suggestions. And last, but by no means least, to the tolerance of my family as a little indulgence became a viable proposition. I am sure they will not mind if they never see egg and chips or spaghetti bolognese again.

Introduction by Joan Sutherland

As I approach nearly 40 years of singing before the public and 34 years since my Covent Garden debut, I am quite incredulous and profoundly grateful that I was able to accomplish such an amount of work. When I look at my record shelves at home I am amazed at the ever-growing bulk of recordings I have made, not to mention the number of public performances.

I was the fortunate choice for this wonderful life — I have loved it and it has brought me rich rewards in every sense. I confess that the thought of continuing too much longer is a daunting one and I must soon leave the field to younger artists: and yet I never tire of singing — only travelling and some of the 'carry-on' that goes with any career. My voice was obviously God-given and I have tried to give of myself honestly. I shall always be grateful for the loving response of my public and of many wonderful colleagues and friends throughout the years, and I hope they will all enjoy Norma Major's book. Norma's diligence and stamina in accomplishing such an enormous project have been admirable.

I was recently suffering from a severe ear infection and forced to make one of my infrequent visits to the doctor. He made me rest for a period but told me that my vocal cords were in such a pristine state that I would sing for easily another 15 years. I said to him, 'Please don't tell my husband!'

March 1987

On 12 December 1946, Bach's *Christmas Oratorio* was performed in Sydney Town Hall by the newly formed Bach Choral Society under the baton of Henry Krips. The following day the music critic of the *Sydney Morning Herald*, after commenting on the performances of the soloists, reported: 'There was another soloist, a mysterious young lady who rose from behind the orchestra and gave some of the best singing of the evening, but her name was not even included in the programme.'

The music critic did not know that this young lady inherited her voice from her mother, nor that as a child what she most wanted to do was to become an opera singer. She had waited a long time to fulfil a childhood ambition to sing in the Town Hall — an achievement which was to be the bottom rung of a long ladder to international success. She was to remain neither mysterious nor anonymous. She was making her public debut, she was just 20 years old and her name was Joan Sutherland.

1
A Big Fish in a Small Pond

William McDonald Sutherland was the youngest son of a Scottish fisherman. He was born in Portskerra on the north coast of Sutherlandshire, close to the border with Caithness, on 4 November 1869, although subsequent birthdays were celebrated on the ninth, the date on which his father registered the birth. Growing up with little prospect of learning about anything other than fishing, which did not appeal to him, he turned his attention to the town of Thurso where he worked for a short time as a mercer. From there he went to Glasgow to begin a tailoring apprenticeship with the family firm of R.W. Forsyth, and then to London to continue his apprenticeship in Bond Street. Since his native tongue was Gaelic, he studied English in the evening and at the age of 22 extended his horizons considerably further afield, emigrating to Australia, never to see his parents nor Scotland again, but remaining staunchly loyal to his Scottish ancestry.

Emotional farewells and a long uncomfortable sea voyage did not crush his spirit, nor did the discovery that Sydney offered him no opportunity to practise his trade. However, his uncle had earlier emigrated from Scotland and set up a large country store in Crookwell, New South Wales, and it was here that William Sutherland worked, and in 1901 he married his cousin Clara McDonald. They joined the tail-end of the gold-rush to New Zealand, returning to Australia when prospects for resuming William's chosen career were more hopeful. He found employment with a tailoring firm and subsequently as a cutter in the tailoring room of David Jones, now one of the largest department stores in Sydney. He then established a partnership with a friend, called Sutherland and Gamble, before finally setting up his own bespoke tailoring business in the centre of Sydney. He earned himself a solid reputation and a large clientele, and the business flourished. The Sutherlands now had three daughters, Heather, Ailsa and Nancye, and they were eventually able to set up home in an imposing residence at Point Piper, an up-market suburb of Sydney, with a splendid view over the Harbour. It was a happy, secure family with a position of considerable social standing, for

William Sutherland channelled his energies in many directions and involved himself thoroughly and conscientiously in everything he undertook. A strict Scots Presbyterian, in due course he became an Elder of the Presbyterian church in Phillip Street, President of the Council of the Highland Society, a Freemason and President of the Master Tailors' Association. In 1917 Clara gave birth to a son, James, and there was nothing to touch the peaceful tranquillity of life in the Sutherland household until Clara died in 1919, a victim of the influenza epidemic that swept the world after the Great War.

In 1921 William Sutherland married again. Muriel Alston was also a Scots Presbyterian, but 15 years younger than her husband, and taking on a ready-made family of three grown-up daughters and an energetic toddler was no easy task. Heather was capable of running the home herself and inevitably this close-knit family resented the intrusion of a young stepmother. To some extent the task of integration was mitigated by the arrival of Barbara in 1922, upon whom Muriel doted. When Joan was born on 7 November 1926 the older girls could not fail to notice that the children of this second marriage were being indulged in a way denied to them. Father was mellowing in middle age, and Joan, who had become the apple of his eye, was extremely spoilt.

Music played an important part in the Sutherland household. Clara was an accomplished pianist and Heather followed in her mother's footsteps. The family had a fairly catholic taste in music, and between them and their friends there was enough talent to provide regular home entertainment in pre-radio days. Although William Sutherland was tone deaf, he did appreciate the value of good music, discouraging his daughters from the latest 'pop' to such an extent that they were obliged to take their wind-up gramophone to the boathouse to listen to the latest ragtime and jazz. When Muriel Alston joined the family there was serious competition for the piano-stool, for she was a talented singer with a glorious mezzo-soprano voice compared, by those who heard her in later years, to Ebe Stignani. Mrs Sutherland had been taught by the distinguished Burns Walker, a former pupil of Mathilde Marchesi, Nellie Melba's teacher. Burns Walker continually urged her to go to Paris or London for further training, but she was too nervous. Instead she found satisfaction in recitals and musical evenings with friends. Yet she had sufficient application to continue her vocalises, the voice studies written out by Marchesi and Vaccai, and had been known to be so preoccupied with her singing that she left an afternoon gathering and forgot to take Joan, who was playing in the hostess' garden.

Joan, a chubby, undemanding baby, grew into a plump little girl with a sunny disposition who was never any trouble to anyone. Often obliged to play alone, she would talk to the flowers, and sing to Tommy, an inattentive tortoise she had tethered with father's pyjama cords to the camphor laurel tree. But most of all she liked to sit under the piano when her mother practised her singing. Subconsciously Joan absorbed what she heard at these sessions and before long she came from under the piano to sit precariously on a stool beside her mother, copying the sounds she made, and the way she breathed, and singing her favourite songs. Mrs Sutherland's passion for bel-canto was strangely out of gear at a time when everyone was singing Puccini and Wagner, but there was nothing narrow about her taste in music. By the time she was three Joan was as familiar with the Page's aria from *Les Huguenots*, and the Brindisi from *Lucrezia Borgia* as 'Take a Pair of Sparkling Eyes' and 'Daisy, Daisy'.

Before she was six, Joan was self-consciously aware of heads turning in church. While her father sang with toneless gusto, and her mother and Barbara sang in the choir, Joan, hating to be in the least conspicuous, struggled to control her voice — suppressing the high notes and singing only the low parts.

Storm clouds were now gathering on their personal horizons: the Depression was beginning to bite and William Sutherland's business was not immune to the prevailing economic climate. Refusing to cut corners, he continued to use the finest materials to make suits for clients who were no longer able to pay. The obvious solution was to sell the house in Point Piper — a prime property — while the market held, and move with his youngest children into one of the houses owned by the Alston family. But William Sutherland was a proud man; and in true patriarchal fashion he kept his financial problems to himself and discreetly took out a second mortgage on the house.

Since the house overlooked the harbour and had its own harbour-side beach, Mr Sutherland regularly took Jim, Barbara and Joan for an early morning swim. On Joan's sixth birthday, while climbing the long flight of steps back to the house, he collapsed and died. It was just two days before — or three days after — his sixty-third birthday, and without a doubt the increasing financial burden contributed to the heart attack which killed him. His death was noted with respect in the minutes of the Board of the Scottish Hospital to which he had been appointed by its Founder in 1926:

Mr Sutherland held a worthy position in the community as an honourable and upright man and a loyal citizen. In a variety of ways he sought to serve his day and generation, but particularly in all things connected with the Scottish community. He was one of the original directors of the Scottish Hospital, and took a keen interest in its welfare, bringing a clear mind and enthusiastic service. . .

He died intestate with the business far from solvent; added therefore, to the shock of his untimely death was the need to sell the house in Point Piper and for the two families to go their separate ways. Heather, Ailsa, Nancye and Jim took a flat of their own, and Mrs Sutherland took Barbara and Joan back to the home of her maternal grandmother in Woollahra, and into the company of her elder sister Annie Ethel — known as Blos — and her eccentric brother Tom.

While the composition of the new household offered different diversions, the musical evenings remained constant. Mrs Sutherland indulged her love of bel canto, and Uncle Tom added a new dimension to Joan's musical education, launching with great spirit into his rather vulgar Edwardian repertoire with 'My Old Woman's an Awful Boozer', and "Twas only the Leaf of a Rosebud, but it Changed the Whole Course of My Life'. Mrs Sutherland's cousin John had a more salubrious taste in operatic music. He was a regular visitor to Woollahra, bringing with him a selection from his large collection of gramophone records. As Joan listened to the voices of Melba, Galli-Curci, Caruso and Lily Pons, he fed her imagination with tales of gossip and backstage intrigue. Joan was impressionable, and as most little girls love to dress up, she loved to sing, and sitting on the swing in the camphor laurel tree she would sing to the birds and dream dreams. Dreams of one day getting to play the fairy instead of the giant in the school play; of looking and sounding like Grace Moore and Deanna Durbin in the romantic musical films which she adored; of becoming an opera singer and singing in Town Hall; of becoming a prima donna.

Joan confided this ambition to her mother, and although Mrs Sutherland did not burden Joan with her doubts there were some fairly overwhelming impediments. She was never mollycoddled, and neither was her sister Barbara (the unfortunate victim of periodic attacks of epilepsy), but from an early age Joan had learnt to put up with the pain and discomfort of blocked sinuses and chronic earache with a fortitude rare in a child so young. Stoicism, however, would not be enough when her career was dependent on a completely healthy throat and respiratory system. Barbara was beautiful, but highly strung, and while her sister Ailsa refutes the accusation that Joan was ever considered an ugly duckling, she was large and ungainly and had an almost paranoid fear of drawing attention to herself.

Since 1934 Joan and Barbara had attended St Catherine's School, Waverley, the oldest girls school in Australia. The school had been founded in 1856 by Jane Barker, the wife of the Bishop of Sydney, as a school for the daughters of the clergy. Inspired by Casterton School in Westmoreland, England, Mrs Barker had not been aware that the latter was also the model for the grim educational institution in *Jane Eyre*. But St Catherine's bore no resemblance to the school that inspired it, and by 1934 it had undergone many changes and much expansion, though still prided itself on small classes with a high degree of individual care for the child, a factor of some consideration to Mrs Sutherland. Joan did well at St Catherine's, participating fully in the life of the school and earning several prizes. She was conscientious, cooperative, good-natured and generous, even to the point of allowing tardy classmates to copy her homework. She sang in the annual school concert, although not in the choir as she tended to drown everyone else, and Mrs Sutherland's wish that her voice should be exercised as little as possible was respected. There was no sign of any great talent however, and when she spoke of her ambition to sing at Covent Garden she was regarded with incredulity by her friends and compassion by the staff.

Joan achieved good results in her Intermediate Examinations at 15, with an A in six subjects, but she dismisses the idea that she left school at 16 because of her health and a doctor's advice that it might be unwise to subject her to the added pressures of the School Leaving Certificate. She insists it was purely a question of economics: the Freemasons had generously paid the fees to St Catherine's for both girls and Mrs Sutherland did not feel she could take advantage of their benevolence a moment longer than necessary.

The world was at war and careers for girls strictly limited. Barbara was training as a nurse and Joan spent the final year at school preparing for Business College where she would train for a routine office job. In 1942 she went to college, qualified as a shorthand typist and took a job with the Council for Scientific Research at Sydney University which involved the rather mundane task of typing endless weather reports. Ever practical, she also took a part-time course in dressmaking.

At this time Joan auditioned for an amateur entertainment, *The National Standards Laboratory Radio Physics Review*. The competition was strong, and although the producers, Ernest Adderley and Bob Coulson, thought she had a sweet voice, her brand of entertainment was not quite what they were looking for. As a gawky, self-conscious teenager she was too lacking in sex-appeal to be ideal review material, but Messrs Adderley and Coulson were later to mourn the fact they had missed the opportunity to be the first to present Sutherland on stage.

Joan enjoyed the job at the University, but she realized that if she did not put her shorthand to greater use it would grow stale. So she moved to a firm of farming equipment specialists where she worked conscientiously among the rabbit-traps and combine harvesters but without any real sense of vocation. She had not shrugged off along with her school uniform her school motto 'We attain by attempt', and in spite of the difficulties there was now no doubt in her mind that what she most wanted to do was become an opera singer. At school Joan had preferred to stay in the grounds rather than go out with the other girls and face the taunts of rude boys calling her 'fatty'. She was gauche and overweight and painfully self-conscious because of it. Surprisingly nimble on her feet, she had played basketball at school with some success, but now she loathed sport and shied away from social activities of all kinds. Lonely and introverted, she concentrated more and more on her music until it became her sole preoccupation outside of her job. Should she fail in her bid for an operatic career, she could fall back on her secretarial qualifications, and in the meantime it was essential that she earned her own living while she trained.

Hitherto this training had been in the hands of Mrs Sutherland, who held strong views about the damage that could be done through the overworking of immature voices. At 18, therefore, Joan's only teacher was her mother, and Mrs Sutherland worked on the basis that her daughter's voice was the same as her own — that of a mezzo-soprano. So the time was right, one morning in January 1945, when an advertisement in the *Sydney Morning Herald* attracted her attention. It offered a two-year scholarship for an untrained voice to the winner of a vocal competition to be held by John and Aida Dickens. The Dickens' were formerly on the staff of the Melbourne Conservatorium and John Dickens' musical antecedents stretched back to his grandfather Otto Vogt who had taught Nellie Melba to play the organ. John, a singer trained by Clive Carey, was now more interested in the technique of voice production than a singing career; his wife had both sung and played professionally during her career. It was an opportunity for potential free tuition that Joan, along with 40 other aspiring singers, could not afford to miss. She arrived at Palings Studio in Sydney on a typically humid summer's day, accompanied by her mother. Her appearance was not impressive for her skill with the needle was not matched by a flair for fashion, and she could not disguise her shyness. She sang one of her mother's favourite arias, 'Softly awakes my heart', and although the Dickens' reaction may not have been as spontaneous as Marchesi's cry to her husband on hearing the young Melba for the first time (*'Salvatore, j'ai enfin une étoile!'*), they awarded her the scholarship with hardly a moment's hesitation.

The quality of her voice, with its rich, full middle register had astonished them. John Dickens was not slow to point out, however, that although she showed exceptional promise, she was singing in the wrong register. She was forcing her low tones — after all she had been trying to keep her voice 'down' since she was six years old — and she was not, in fact, a mezzo-soprano, but a dramatic soprano, an opinion he holds to the present day. To Joan the whole idea was anathema, yet despite her resistance and Mrs Sutherland's disapproval, the process of lifting and developing the Sutherland voice had begun.

Joan had a capacity for work which astounded the Dickens', and they liked her sincerity and wonderfully gentle nature. To Joan, however, John Dickens was not a sympathetic personality and she found his military bearing and brusque manner somewhat intimidating. In fact, Joan was so placid and laid-back that the only way to galvanize her into action and thereby get the best from her was to bully her a little. He pushed her and relentlessly she practised, to the exclusion of all else, only too pleased to fill with work the time the other young girls filled with parties and boyfriends. She had, however, become a member of the Affiliated Music Clubs of New South Wales where she found friendship through a common interest, and she was appreciated more for her musical ability than for her social talents. It was at the Queen Victoria Club that she first met Richard Bonynge, four years younger than she and a student at the Sydney Conservatorium. Joan sang as the ladies of the Club sipped their tea, and Richard accompanied her at the piano.

Born at Bondi on 29 September 1930, the only child of Carl and Beryl Bonynge, Richard was something of a musical prodigy. He played the piano from an early age, picking out thirds and sixths without being taught, and he was barely five when it became apparent that he knew more about playing the piano than his mother did. When one day he looked up from his trains to admonish her for playing sharps instead of flats, the time had come for him to be professionally trained. His first teacher, Mrs Florence Crocker, used to crack him across the knuckles at the least provocation, but she was excellent at her job and gave him a thorough grounding for which he would always be grateful. By the age of 12 she had taught him all she could, and he won a scholarship to the Conservatorium where he played for Lindley Evans who had already expressed himself willing to teach Richard free of charge. Evans had been Melba's accompanist on her last Australian tour and was much loved by children of all ages for his presentation of a *Children's Hour* broadcast as 'The Melody Man'. Richard was greatly in awe of him, and while he might be tempted to skip the classes on counterpoint and harmony he never missed a class with Lindley Evans.

Richard's father no longer cherished hopes of a career in the Diplomatic Service for his son. A facility for languages had made the Diplomatic Corps a possibility, and he was capable of exercising a great deal of charm, but in his early teens it was the concert platform that beckoned. He was already familiar with all the basic orchestral repertoire and at 14 played Grieg's Piano Concerto with the Sydney Symphony Orchestra in the Town Hall. At this stage, however, his experience of operatic music was limited to Gilbert and Sullivan — although he has an early recollection of accompanying a cousin who sang with the opera company in Melbourne at the tender age of seven — until one day at the Conservatorium the opera class found itself without an accompanist. The Director, Eugene Goossens, asked Richard to come to the rescue and he made a good enough impression with the second act of *Figaro* to be asked to become a regular accompanist. The die was cast, and his growing interest in the vocal art was lovingly fostered by Lindley Evans, thus laying the foundation for the love and knowledge of eighteenth- and early nineteenth-century music which was later to play such an important part in Joan's career.

For the moment, as he and Joan performed under the auspices of the Music Clubs, her physical shortcomings were compensated by her voice, which Richard found a large, strong instrument, although as yet cold, hard and utterly lacking in the flexibility and timbre which were to make it such a distinctive sound. Her upper limit, by virtue of the Dickens' having extended her range, was a nervous high C and many of her arias were the big dramatic ones from *Aida*, *Tannhäuser* and *Tristan und Isolde*, which she sang as much like Kirsten Flagstad as possible. Dreams of romantic roles having given way to heroic visions of breastplates and winged helmets, Joan now saw herself as a Wagnerian soprano. Once she had stopped modelling her voice on her mother's, Flagstad had become her idol.

Meanwhile her music was encroaching more and more upon her working life. In quiet moments she would pull a score out from under her desk, but any time she took off had to be made up, which often meant sacrificing precious Saturdays. In due course she moved to another firm of agricultural suppliers only a stone's throw from Palings Studio where an added bonus was the keen interest her new boss, 'Pop' Clyde, took in her music. Always threatening to take it out of her holidays, he gave her time off whenever she needed it, and never kept count.

Joan had found a friend in Elizabeth Allen, a contralto whom she had met at an Eisteddfod. They took it in turns to spend their lunch-hour queuing for the cheapest seats to concerts, musical comedies and visiting opera companies. They also entered many of the singing competitions which abound in Australia, trying all fields of the vocal art from oratorio, through art songs to musical comedy. Winning, as Joan often did, helped her shaky confidence immeasurably. In an attempt to build up this confidence, the Dickens' had sent her to the Rathbone Academy of Dramatic Art, where Judy Rathbone Lawless recognized that much of Joan's self-consciousness sprang from embarrassment about her height and size, and tried to persuade her that far from being a negative factor, her statuesque physique would be an asset on stage. At this time, however, Joan was not convinced of this, nor the validity of the rest of the tuition Miss Lawless offered, and she resented her undisguised contempt for her Australian accent.

Joan at last made her public debut in December 1946, singing from the chorus in Bach's *Christmas Oratorio*. This was a notable event for it brought her to the attention of Henry Krips, and in March the following year he invited her to take part in a Wagnerian concert. Notwithstanding the rehearsal atmosphere created by the piano accompaniment, the music critic of the *Sydney Morning Herald* (apparently not connecting Joan's name with his 'mysterious young lady' of a few months earlier) described how she caught the tense mood of Senta's Ballad from *The Flying Dutchman* and 'filled it with compelling speech'. A few months later she made her solo debut in a concert performance of Handel's *Acis and Galatea*, followed by a rather more distinguished debut at Town Hall as Dido in Purcell's *Dido and Aeneas*.

Her scholarship had been extended, and with her sights firmly fixed on Covent Garden she worked hard to swell her account at the Commonwealth Bank. For three guineas she sang at weddings and from all accounts was more than generous with her services, on one occasion singing '*Panis Angelicus*' and '*Ave Maria*' in the church and several arias at the reception, and taking the time afterwards to write to the bride's mother to say how much she had enjoyed the wedding. For seven guineas she sang for the Australian Broadcasting Corporation, competitions brought financial rewards, and in 1949 she decided to compete for the big prize in the newly instituted 'Mobil Quest'.

Convinced that Australia had a wealth of untapped musical talent, the Vacuum Oil company initiated a nationwide commercial radio programme to find the best voice in Australia. The organization was of marathon proportions with almost 2,000 entrants for the 54 places in 18 heats. Joan reached the last six and travelled to Melbourne for the final round. However, with her performance of Elsa's Dream from *Lohengrin* and *'Ritorna vincitor'* from *Aida*, she only won fourth place and the much coveted first prize of £1,000 (Australia had not yet converted its currency to dollars) went to Ronal Jackson.

Joan may have been lacking in confidence, but it was not in her nature to be despondent for long; besides, she had recently won the Sun Aria, the biggest vocal competition in her home state, having reached only the semi-final the previous year. From her family, always supportive, came nothing but encouragement. Barbara's faith in Joan's ability was almost fanatical and cousin John promised to double the prize money should she win at the next attempt. Sadly, Joan's view that all was for the best in the best of all possible worlds was not shared by Barbara. Mrs Sutherland found Barbara moody and difficult in comparison to her placid, easy-going younger daughter, and although Joan was very close to her sister, when it came to helping with her complex emotional problems she was out of her depth and could offer nothing but sympathy for the fears that assailed her. One day, in the grip of a black depression and convinced that she would never be able to live a normal life, Barbara took a bus to The Gap, Sydney's equivalent to Beachy Head, and jumped to her death.

The family were stunned by the tragic way in which she had died and their inability to prevent it. Joan was preparing for a recital, but her music held no joy for her, and she had never felt less like singing. Persuaded, however, that to give up would be a betrayal of her sister's faith in her ability, she fastened her mind on the Mobil Quest of September 1950 with a determination that more than compensated for a lack of genuine competitive spirit. She gave up her job and turned her undivided attention to her singing. Her boss received the news with the retort: 'Good, I'd have sacked you, if you hadn't', but she found comfort in Pop Clyde's assurance there would always be a job for her should she need it.

Spurred on therefore by the memory of Barbara, the promise of £1,000 from cousin John and with a four-leaf clover inside her long white glove, she won the Mobil Quest in Melbourne with her singing of *'Voi lo sapete'* from *Cavalleria rusticana* and *'Dich teure Halle'* from *Tannhäuser*.

Once, the pinnacle of her ambition had been to sing in Sydney Town Hall. Now she achieved the grand slam of singing in every state capital and major city throughout Australia, since the terms of her contract with the Vacuum Oil company included a gruelling interstate recital tour.

Joan and Mrs Sutherland were now making positive plans to go to England, for although there was no shortage of work, Australia had little more to offer towards the development of an operatic career. It was time to go to London, to complete her studies and widen her experience as other Australian singers had before her. Displaying a confidence in her continued success the Vacuum Oil Company joined forces with Associated Press to sponsor a Farewell concert in Sydney Town Hall.

> Joan Sutherland, who has disciplined and matured her soprano voice considerably since her last public recital, provided some stylish and attractive singing ... Although there was still a brittle quality to her voice, and she still found difficulty in holding her strong tone in check once it touched forte, she also achieved unexpected restraint and delicacy of phrasing in a group of Lieder by Schubert, Liszt and Wolf. At such times her tone had truly a delightful sheen upon it. But as a whole her voice lacked variety and richness: she did not achieve the glowing passion of Isolde's *'Liebestod'*, nor the intimate warmth of 'Margaret at the Spinning Wheel' and 'The Secret' of Schubert. Interpretatively, also, she was inclined to pay attention to the surface polish than to the essential matter of the song. Her best achievements were with Verdi's *'Pace, pace'*, and Liszt's *'Die Lorelei'*, wherein she used her vocal equipment effectively without it being regarded as an end in itself.
>
> *Sydney Morning Herald*, 21 April 1951

She had still not made her debut in a staged operatic production and it came as something of a surprise (since she had not studied at the Conservatorium) when Eugene Goossens asked her to sing Judith in the Australian première of his one-act opera. Judith was a dramatic soprano role, but privately Joan thought it unlikely that she could turn in a dramatically convincing performance with a plot that hinged on a grand seduction scene. But Goossens thought she could convey all he required by vocal means, and Joan was enormously encouraged by his confidence in her and by the personal interest he took in the progress she was making.

Joan was considered to have handled all the declamatory vocal writing 'freshly and well', but the production was described as hesitant and unimaginative, the poor stage direction exaggerated by cramped scenery. It was also Joan's first experience of an on-stage crisis, for Judith, having decapitated the sleeping Holofernes and holding aloft a grisly papier mâché head, was horrified to see him slipping off the couch. As the curtain fell, Joan rushed to his aid, but it was too late to prevent the exposure of Holofernes' highly inappropriate orange socks.

It was a worthy debut by local standards, though not disposed to point the way to a future of international status. However, disregarding the advice of Neville Cardus to stay in Australia and be a big fish in a small pond, Joan and Mrs Sutherland sailed from Sydney in July 1951. Festooned with streamers, the liner Maloja moved through the harbour, past the red-brick tram depot at Bennelong Point, the site of the Opera House that was to take over from Harbour Bridge as Sydney's most famous landmark. At the rails, Joan, with letters of introduction to the Royal College of Music and the Royal Opera House in her handbag, was embarking on a long and difficult journey in pursuit of a career that would far exceed her modest dreams.

2
With Work Might Do Better

Arriving in Southampton, Joan and Mrs Sutherland were driven to London in a limousine provided by the Vacuum Oil Company. They booked into a small hotel and among their first visitors was Richard Bonynge, who had arrived the previous year with a Teaching and Performing Diploma and a Scholarship to the Royal College of Music. Anxious to introduce Joan to the delights of the capital he whisked her off on a crash course on England's heritage which included five art galleries in one day. Joan therefore not only had to contend with a freshly-broken tooth but with an acute attack of cultural indigestion as well.

Richard also wasted no time in acquainting her with his opinion of the Royal College of Music, where he was studying piano with Angus Morrison. The College had refused to allow him to take up conducting as his second subject, insisting that he learnt piano accompaniment, which he thought he knew all about. Despite Richard's disenchantment with the College, Joan was determined to seek an interview with the Director of the Opera School, Clive Carey, a former co-director of the Melbourne Conservatorium and pupil of the great Jean de Reszke. Professor Carey was much impressed by what he heard when Joan sang for him. He recognized a big natural voice which needed developing; he liked its mezzo-quality, found her breath control remarkable, but noticed that she was not entirely at ease with her top notes. He suggested that if she were to contemplate getting into Covent Garden she should study for at least a year at the Opera School.

The first hurdle had thus been crossed, and Joan calculated that if she was careful her finances were sufficient for her to stay in London for two years. With no academic or residential qualifications to entitle her to a grant to study at the Opera School, allowance had to be made for her fees as well as for living expenses, so the Sutherlands bought an upright piano that had seen better days and moved out of the small hotel into a chilly bed-sitter in the attic of a house in Pembridge Crescent, Notting Hill Gate. Sharing a kitchen and bathroom and including a change of sheets every fortnight it cost £3 a week. In the flat below lived

Dorothy Jordan and Phyllis Abbott, fortunately music-lovers, who were to become staunch admirers of Joan. Mrs Sutherland filled in the football pools and urged Joan to continue her shorthand and typing in case she was obliged to return to Pop Clyde.

In the meantime Joan saw no harm in applying for an audition to Covent Garden, enclosing a letter from Eugene Goossens to the General Administrator, David Webster:

> The bearer of this letter has a magnificent dramatic soprano voice, and has done excellent work here (Australia) in concert and operatic performances. Her voice is in the true Austral tradition, and she made quite a sensation here recently in her creation of Judith in my opera of that name. Her departure for Europe will be a great loss to Australia for such grand natural voices as hers are all too rare nowadays.

By the middle of October she had secured an audition for Covent Garden at Wigmore Hall, after which Sir Steuart Wilson, the Deputy Administrator, noted: 'Starts with a good ring in the voice. Very little stage experience or gifts by nature.' He suggested that she apply again in six months time. Had Joan seen the report it would have come as no great surprise, for she was finding life at the Opera School difficult and depressing. Surrounded by students with infinitely more poise than she felt she would ever possess, she was once again reminded of her physical shortcomings. She was out of tune with the 'in' talk and sophisticated ways, and she found the ballet class an ordeal and the drama class an embarrassment. She had no facility for learning by rote and chunks from Shakespeare did not come easily to her. Even with her singing, which was the only thing she approached with anything like confidence, she was so nervous at her first session with Alexander Gibson, then a student *répétiteur*, that she was unable to read the music.

Outside the College and her lessons with Professor Carey she was spending more and more time with Richard Bonynge. He had now abandoned his scholarship and was going for private tuition to Herbert Fryer, but he was growing increasingly out of sympathy with the piano. He had no patience for the endlessly repetitive exercises to improve his technique, and in London he was drawn towards the theatre in general and operatic music in particular. Fed up with the onerous practice, he would play through an operatic score. He taught piano, but since he was fascinated by the human voice he coached singers as well, and one of them was Joan.

As Richard heard her trilling carelessly around the flat, demonstrating a greater flexibility than when she worked, he felt sure that she had the kind of voice — all too rare — for the romantic roles of the nineteenth-century bel canto repertoire. He had been captivated by the first recordings of Maria Callas, which included '*Qui la voce*' from Bellini's *I puritani* for which he already had a great affection, having discovered an old score in a junk shop at the age of 13. He pleaded with Joan to try them, to veer away from the heavier roles on which she was concentrating, and to apply this obvious coloratura ability to her work instead of confining it to the bathtub or the kitchen sink.

The way he tricked her into extending her range above the stave has now passed into operatic mythology. Neither Joan nor her mother have perfect pitch: while Joan thinks she is singing in C major, she might well be in E major, a third higher. Richard took advantage of this. He played for her when she went to Carey for lessons and at home when she practised her vocalises. He persuaded her to move around as she sang, and when she could no longer see the keyboard he would begin the vocalises much higher than she expected. If she found it a struggle, she thought it was because she was tired, but she would follow him unwittingly up the scale — once to an astonishing F sharp in altissimo.

It may have won him the argument but he was a long way from winning the battle, for Joan's problem was a psychological one. She listened to the recordings of Melba and Galli-Curci and to her mind her voice did not have that quality at all. Callas was not exactly slight of physique, but Joan felt physically unsuited to the frail heroines of the operas Richard was advocating. Having accustomed herself to the idea that she was not a mezzo-soprano, she was looking to the day when, like Marjorie Lawrence, she might leap onto a horse and ride into Siegfried's funeral pyre! She had not seen enough Wagner on stage to appreciate that her voice was neither big enough nor powerful enough to sing Brünnhilde.

Neither did Richard find an ally in Mrs Sutherland, for in spite of her great fondness for the bel canto repertoire she did not think Joan would fit into it in quite the way Richard had in mind. He was not technically qualified to mastermind her vocal development, and she constantly complained that he was learning his trade at the expense of the voice she had so carefully nurtured. Long, acrimonious arguments were commonplace with Richard frequently disparaging her knowledge of music. One day Mrs Sutherland picked up the music for '*O don fatale*', and waved it at him saying, 'If you can play it, I can sing it'. Standing like a diva with the awe-inspiring dignity of Queen Mary she delivered the difficult aria with a sense of style that made Richard gape. It was to be a long time before they were to see eye-to-eye on the matter of Joan's voice but he never cast doubts on her mother's musical intellect again.

Mrs Sutherland, however, could not fail to be aware of Joan's growing affection for him, although she would never become accustomed to the way in which he bullied her, nor the easy way in which Joan accepted it. After much ranting and raving from Richard: 'How do you know what you can do until you try?' and excuses from Joan: 'I can't sing this canary stuff', or 'I have the washing — or the ironing — or the dishes to do', he persuaded her to learn '*Qui la voce*' from *I puritani*. Having mastered this difficult aria to Richard's satisfaction — and her own surprise — she tried it out on Clive Carey, who did not know what to make of this girl he thought was a heavy dramatic soprano who now tossed off elaborately adorned fiorture in a manner read about but never heard.

In due course Joan applied for her second audition at Covent Garden, also at Wigmore Hall, for which she had prepared a selection including coloratura arias she had been working on with Richard. On this occasion the panel were more impressed, but at the same time confused, for she had sung '*Dich teure Halle*' before '*Qui la voce*'. A remarkable thing, for most singers would fear a loss of flexibility having sung the heavy Wagnerian piece first. Yet she had tossed off the hellish coloratura with great aplomb and apparent ease. Joan had already discovered that her voice tended to bewilder people since it did not fall readily into any of the stereotyped categories, and the audition report reflected this:

> A voice of unusual solidity. Not very easy to place this type. She sings mezzo-coloratura then rips up to an E flat in alt. One thinks it will be a dramatic soprano, but will it? This shows a really solid middle and much better top. Ought to be an asset in time for parts like the Marschallin and Countess . . .

Peter Gellhorn, Head of the Music Staff at Covent Garden, was immediately struck by the fact that she had taken the trouble to learn to sing before presenting herself for audition — a rare, if somewhat basic, prerequisite in his experience.

Confusion does not inspire confidence, but she was invited to sing again the following month, this time on the stage of the Opera House and before the General Administrator. Accompanied by Richard she repeated the '*Non mi dir*' from *Don Giovanni*, shirking none of its difficulties, and followed it with '*Ritorna vincitor*' from *Aida*, an opera in the current Covent Garden season. This time the consensus was that although she lacked temperament, her voice was large, pure and flexible, and she could probably become a useful member of the company and understudy Sylvia Fisher, also a dramatic soprano and fellow Australian. But with characteristic foresight, David Webster commented: 'With work, might do better than that'.

Yet no decision was taken and her only consolation lay in the fact that at least she had sung from the Covent Garden stage. Broadcasts were easing the financial strain — with one series, *May I Introduce*, classifying her as a contralto — but with her year at the Opera School drawing to a close, she was beginning to wonder where she went from here. She had appeared in excerpts from several operas in the College's Parry Theatre, singing Pamina in *The Magic Flute*, Elisabeth in *Tannhäuser* and Donna Anna in *Don Giovanni*, and in the end of year production of *Il tabarro*, Joan sang the soprano role of Giorgetta.

The performance was attended by Opera House representatives, always on the lookout for potential talent, and a review in *The Times* had suggested that if she could develop a greater freedom of tone production, she should, before long, make a useful recruit to professional opera. A week later Joan was asked to attend her fourth audition, and along with the Wagner she sang '*Ah, non giunge*' from Bellini's *La sonnambula*. 'Stylish singing', noted the report, 'very good diction . . . sympathetic personality, but is it a proposition for the theatre?' Sir Steuart Wilson thought it was, offering her a contract for the 1952/53 season at £10 a week in London and £15 on tour. She was advised to look at the First Lady in *The Magic Flute*, the High Priestess in *Aida* and Clotilde in *Norma*. Meanwhile, of the performance of *Il tabarro* Arthur Jacobs had written in *Opera Magazine*:

> The most arresting portrayal came from Joan Sutherland's Giorgetta; here is a dramatic soprano of high quality and well controlled dramatic power. Doubtless Clive Carey has assisted Miss Sutherland to develop her considerable stage presence and one may confidently look forward to hearing more from her.

3
A Reliable Trouper

Joan found the activity at Covent Garden just as disconcerting as
the Opera School. Never having been stage-struck, she was not
immediately caught up in the magic of the place: she found it
confusing and was constantly getting lost in the rabbit warren of
backstage corridors. Contrary, however, to what she might have
expected in the aggressive world of show business, she was delighted to find everyone kind and friendly towards her, and she
readily accepted advice from all who gave it. There was no need
for other performers to regard her with jealousy for although she
had a good voice and a place on the soprano roster with Adele
Leigh, Sylvia Fisher and Blanche Turner, it was impossible to
believe that somewhere, albeit dormant as yet, was that indefin-
able something known as 'star quality'.

Joan's dedication to her work was total. She worked at the
Opera House with *répétiteurs* on such roles as the Marschallin and
Chrysothemis, at home she practised with Richard and she continued private lessons with Clive Carey. At a Promenade Concert
in the Albert Hall in August, understudying the mezzo role of
Jocasta in Stravinsky's *Oedipus Rex*, she had been filled with
dread at the thought of actually having to go on, and was para-
lysed with nerves as she prepared to face her first Covent Garden
audience as the First Lady in *The Magic Flute*. In the stalls Mrs
Sutherland and Richard painfully clasped hands in mutual excitement and anxiety, and in spite of her nerves her debut did not slip
by entirely unnoticed. For example, Philip Hope Wallace wrote
in the *Manchester Guardian*: 'Among the small parts, Joan
Sutherland as the First Lady was noted.'

A few nights later she sang the offstage High Priestess in *Aida*
and among those who took notice on this occasion was Lord
Harewood, soon to take up his position as Assistant Administrator. He was not alone in thinking her the finest Priestess he
had heard. Notice was also taken of her first Wigmore Hall
recital, but reference to Joan's physique and the heavy Italian

and Wagnerian roles did nothing to strengthen Richard's bel canto crusade:

> This young Australian has a voice and physique to make her a dramatic soprano capable of tackling either the heavy Italian or Wagnerian roles. At present she is inclined to spoil the vocal line in the middle and lower registers by throwing her tone back into her mouth, but at the top there is flexibility, power, brilliance and beauty of tone. She has much yet to learn about style — Gluck, Mozart, Bellini and Liszt are all much of a muchness to her and likely to remain so until she attends to her words. At the moment she is fully occupied with the mechanics of singing and though her programme ranged widely she appeared to have given no thought to her interpretation. Attention alike to the significance and articulation of words is now required if she is to become the great singer that, on the strength of her voice, she might hope one day to be.
>
> *The Times*, 10 November 1952

Her distinguished accompanist, Gerald Moore, recognized her professionalism and musicianship, but at that time he thought she was a mezzo-soprano, and there was little evidence of what he described as the 'marvellous soprano that was destined to thrill the world'.

At that moment another soprano was thrilling the world, and the prospect of singing on the same stage filled Joan with much excitement. Maria Callas was making her Covent Garden debut in the first production of *Norma* since 1930 and Joan was singing the small role of Clotilde. The opera was of special interest to Richard for it epitomized the early-nineteenth-century romantic Italian opera he adored, and the title role was one he was sure Joan would one day be able to sing. 1952 was a year of unparalleled success for Callas, her portrayal of *Norma* already a legend. While very much in awe of her, working with Callas dispelled any preconceptions Joan might have had about the temperament of a prima donna. Driving herself to the point of exhaustion in her constant striving for perfection — and expecting the same from those with whom she worked — Callas was an inspiration to any young singer. In the wings, as she listened to the torrent of applause for Callas after each performance, Joan dared to wonder if she might ever be on the receiving end of such acclamation. With Richard's exhortations in mind she even ventured to express to the great diva the hope that she might sing a coloratura role. It would be hard work, Callas replied, but, 'why not?'

Why not, indeed? Here was a dramatic soprano of comfortable proportions enjoying an enormous triumph in one of the most difficult bel canto roles. If Callas could do it, so could Joan. This carried no weight with Mrs Sutherland, who still genuinely believed that the best Joan could hope for was a career as a good second-rank Wagnerian singer, and Joan herself was still fiercely resisting Richard's attempts to turn her into a coloratura soprano. It was also plain that the Opera House did not subscribe to his views either, for at six hours notice Joan was asked to sing Amelia in Verdi's *A Masked Ball*. A succession of guest artists had fallen ill, and if the performance was not to be cancelled, Joan was Covent Garden's only substitute. She was in a precarious position. She had coped with a *sitzprobe* with a score in her hand, but had by no means mastered the role. She was terrified that if she refused to sing her contract might be terminated, yet making a shambles of a public performance could have the same result. Richard thought otherwise, but, deciding she had nothing to lose, she agreed to do it. Edward Downes, her *répétiteur*, was far from being one of her advocates. Although she did not know it, he had already attempted to remove her from the company. He thought she was a clumsy, awkward lump without much promise. She was a slow learner with an appalling memory and there seemed little likelihood of her being word- or note-perfect, and worse, she did not fully understand her own role in the context of the whole opera: 'What's all this business with the gypsy?', she pleaded, and his heart sank. In spite of an acute attack of stage-fright, she coped better than either of them could have hoped with the complexities of a difficult soprano role, picking up her cues well and efficiently disguising lapses of memory with strategic stage movements. As a first performance in a leading role it could not be counted a resounding success, but neither was it a failure. It was moderately well received, and Downes congratulated her and helped and encouraged her from then on.

Notwithstanding the grudging acceptance of some of his colleagues, Joan from the outset had a firm supporter in David Webster. He had come to the Opera House via the unlikely route of work in the John Lewis Partnership, and had been General Administrator since 1946. From the start he demonstrated an uncanny instinct for spotting operatic talent, and was especially energetic in championing the cause of British singers. In his view there was nothing to prevent the country from producing a first-class opera company largely of British artists. Webster was always optimistic about Joan's potential, and Lord Harewood recalls it would be quite wrong to think that she was unregarded in those days. The talent was obvious; the problem was what to do with it. She was a tall, strong girl whose voice did not contradict her physique. Should she learn Octavian or Brangäne? Would she be Eva in *Die Meistersinger* or one of Verdi's Leonoras? In his view she was a superb musician, but in spite of her year at the Opera School she was still horribly ill at ease on stage. As she was usually second or third cast she had to rely on whatever she could pick up watching others at work, and the overworked producers had no extra time to give her. It was obvious to Harewood and Webster that this approach was not positive enough for Joan, and that the Opera House should do more to help her. So they arranged for her to go for extra dramatic coaching to Norman Ayrton's studio in Paddington Street.

Norman Ayrton trained at the Old Vic Theatre School and had been a member of the Old Vic Company since 1948, only recently opening his own teaching studio. As Joan battled her way through the dustbins in the alley leading to it for the first time her attitude was not one of enthusiasm. She had not enjoyed her sessions at the Rathbone Academy in Sydney nor the drama classes at the Opera School. She saw no reason to suppose these would be any different. Norman Ayrton was only two years older than Joan. Behind his English reserve lay a marvellous sense of humour, a sharp eye for detail and an enviable self-assurance. He contemplated her pessimistically, for she was still singularly disinterested in her appearance and her rather nice ankles scarcely detracted from an unflattering hat which almost covered an equally unflattering hairstyle. He recalled that she had caught his eye — but not his ear — in *Norma*, Clotilde being a spit and cough of a role, but Webster said they had this large Australian girl with international potential and could he please do something about her acting.

Joan, oblivious to this 'international potential', was preparing the role of Agathe in Weber's *Der Freischütz*. She was to understudy Sylvia Fisher in a new production scheduled for the 1953/54 season and sing it in her own right on the spring tour. Since it was the first major role to be assigned to her, it seemed a logical basis for Ayrton's coaching sessions. He was captivated by her voice as she sang the main aria, yet it was glaringly obvious that she knew virtually nothing about acting and apparently had no natural instinct upon which to build. Callas had seen to it that the days were gone when operas were little more than concerts in costume, and all that was required of a singer was to stand and deliver. Unless he could help her express herself in dramatic terms there would be no place for her on the operatic stage. Joan, however, had not come this far to give up without a struggle, but when he asked her to get a pair of slacks she feared the worst. He propounded theories of acting which, although relevant, were utterly beyond her, and made her do exercises at the *barre* wearing the slacks (which she loathed) to make her more aware of her body. But Joan was only too aware of her body: she hated it, and she hated him.

Temporary reprieve came, however, in the form of her first provincial tour. In the freezing February of 1953 the Company travelled to Glasgow via Cardiff and Edinburgh, and back again via Liverpool, Manchester and Birmingham. In each city, the digs she was able to afford were worse than the last. She was always cold, and seemed constantly to have a cold. Her ears ached and her antrums were blocked. Nevertheless, with her strong sense of loyalty to the company she ᴄontinued to stand in for indisposed Amelias and was gaining a reputation as a reliable trouper, as the reviews indicate. For example, in Glasgow:

> Joan Sutherland's Amelia may not have been quite consistent as a dramatic performance, although there were some very effective moments, but her singing was lovely in quality. There is a natural warmth in her voice which makes her a sympathetic character.
>
> *Glasgow Herald*, 12 March 1953

In Manchester:

> ... Joan Sutherland sang pleasantly and accurately and managed the *Traviata*-like fioriture very comfortably. Her performance last night was not very free, nor big, but it suggested she will grow in the part given the chance, and she has the makings of a first-rate dramatic soprano, if her voice can develop properly.
>
> *Manchester Guardian*, 31 March 1953

In Birmingham:

> Her voice was fresh and firm and most skillfully used, her diction was remarkably clear and her acting was adequate.
>
> *Birmingham Post*, 14 April 1953

In Edinburgh she made her debut as the Countess in *The Marriage of Figaro* to no particular acclaim, and at the Free Trade Hall, Manchester, sang the mezzo role of Brangäne in a concert performance of Act II of *Tristan und Isolde* conducted by Sir John Barbirolli. Edward Downes had suggested Joan for the part and demonstrated his new-found faith in her by helping her to learn it in record time. The *Manchester Guardian* reported:

'Her tone was maturer than her singing of Amelia last week ever hinted at, enriched by just sufficient vibrato to give it the sensuous beauty in which it was then deficient.'

It was the middle of April when the Company returned to London, by which time Joan had lost five inches all round, the first attempt at improving her public persona, but her sinuses were infected. In Australia she had been plagued with sinusitis and tonsillitis, but when a specialist had been consulted he had refused to remove the tonsils for fear of damaging the most perfect vocal cords he had ever seen. Thus, still in possession of her tonsils, in the deadly atmosphere of London smog she was particularly susceptible to sore throats and sinusitis. In December the worst pea-souper in living memory had penetrated the Opera House and swirled around her feet as she sang. Visits to Mr Ivor Griffiths, the Opera House laryngologist, in Upper Wimpole Street to have her sinuses drained were a matter of routine: a painful ordeal one might expect to follow with several days rest. But Joan would take the tube back to Covent Garden and sing.

The tour to Rhodesia for the Rhodes Centenary in 1953 was a much more comfortable experience, not least because of the climate, the gum trees and the jacaranda blossom, which reminded Joan of home. In a converted Nissan hut on the outskirts of Bulawayo she sang Lady Rich in *Gloriana*, the new opera Benjamin Britten had composed for the Coronation. The critics praised her performance and Lord Harewood recognized elements of stardom in her portrayal. Joan, however, found the offstage Priestess more to her liking even though Sir John Barbirolli conducted with such consistency of tempo that her entrance each night coincided with the shrill whistle of an express train as it approached a nearby level crossing — much to the amusement of the company. At later performances Emanuel Young took pity on Joan and the tiniest liberty with the score, thereby bringing her in before the train and earning her undying gratitude.

On her return, Richard found himself with the alien task of coaching Joan as a Valkyrie in *Die Walküre*, and although he was thorough and conscientious, Joan was not encouraged by his obvious disapproval. When she added the role of the Overseer in *Elektra* to her repertoire he had expressed his distaste quite forcefully, though mercifully the role was short and they could leave the theatre as soon as Joan had finished! Likewise when she made her debut as Frasquita in *Carmen* his opinion that Micaela would have been preferable was voiced loudly and clearly. He hated her in the black wig, and thought the excuse that it was inappropriate for Micaela to be bigger than Carmen was a flimsy one. Nothing would have pleased him more than for Joan to turn down the roles for which he considered her voice unsuited and he increasingly felt that she was being fobbed off with roles not suited to anyone else. He never missed an opportunity to steer her away from the heavier soprano roles towards the Italian bel canto for which he now had an all-absorbing passion, but she could not take him seriously when he suggested that she could become as great a singer as Callas and Tebaldi. She had no ambition to be the greatest anything; indeed, she had no long-term view of her own career at all. She knew her contract depended upon taking the roles that were offered even if they were the leftovers.

Meanwhile Mrs Sutherland had returned to Australia temporarily and Joan, after consulting David Webster about her prospects, used some of cousin John's £1,000 to take a lease on a house in Aubrey Walk, Campden Hill. For the sake of convenience Richard lived there as well and now she worked at home with him instead of with the Opera House *répétiteurs*. There was no objection to this arrangement as Joan was demonstrating time and again the thoroughness of his coaching, although the best results were only achieved by a lot of nagging. She was not intrinsically afraid of hard work, but because she found the learning process so difficult she was apt to underestimate her capabilities and was easily distracted. As a naturally domesticated person it was almost impossible for her to separate herself from household affairs and give her undivided attention to her work. She was more likely to be thinking about what to have for dinner than the motivation behind the part she was learning. With her mother away responsibility for the housekeeping was entirely hers, so Richard was constantly dragging her away from the washing or the ironing. Her lack of concentration was also Norman Ayrton's main bone of contention. During one ill-advised session at home, frustrated beyond endurance by her inability to keep her mind on the matter in hand, Ayrton stormed out of the house vowing he would have nothing more to do with her. Happily, however, their differences were resolved, and a working relationship developed into a life-long affection and professional alliance.

She had now studied the role of Agathe scene by scene, and she was beginning to see modest results from her labours at the *barre*; her movements gradually lost some of their awkwardness and she no longer felt she had twenty hands and feet. When she sang Agathe for the first time at Covent Garden the music critic of *The Times* described her as the epitome of the demure country maiden, and although the production as a whole was not highly praised Joan's performance was referred to as 'big with promise'.

In *Opera Magazine*, Cecil Smith wrote:

> With a competence as impressive as it was modest, she established herself as one of the whitest hopes of the coloratura department. Her voice is a true operatic lyric soprano. . . It is large enough to carry across the orchestra in all its registers. Her A flat in '*Und ob die Wolke*' was as enchanting in texture as any tones we have heard all year. As yet she had not the flexibility to take all of Agathe's earlier scena at a desirable pace but there is nothing about her basic method of singing that should keep her from developing all the flexibility in the world. Her characterization was somewhat unformed. . . but whatever she did was honourable and right.

It was sung in English, as was most of the repertoire at that time, but, more significantly, it had spoken dialogue — the very thought of which made Joan cringe for fear of making a fool of herself in a broad Australian accent. Ayrton had unsuccessfully tried to stem her anxiety, but in the event she had not been over conspicuous among the polyglot accents of James Johnston, Geraint Evans and Otakar Kraus, and had delivered her famous line, 'Don't shoot Max, for I am the dove', with great fervour.

Richard found her singing of Agathe breathtakingly beautiful, and Lord Harewood, prevented by official duties from seeing her complete performance each night, made a special point of going in to hear the last act and her incomparable singing of '*Und ob die Wolke*'. It was Joan's performance in *Der Freischütz* that finally convinced him that given ordinary luck and proper management, she could become a star.

On 16 October 1954 Joan and Richard were married by special licence at a Methodist Church in Ladbroke Grove. Unable to keep their secret plans totally to herself, Joan had confided in Elizabeth Allen, now in London studying with Richard having won the 1953 Mobil Quest. Wearing a red velvet dress and carrying a bouquet sent by David Webster, Joan was given away by Clive Carey and one of the witnesses was a pupil of Richard's who had arrived for a coaching session he had forgotten to cancel. They were expected by Joan's half-sister Ailsa for supper the same evening, and the unexpected news of their marriage caused much excitement. Two other guests rushed out in a futile quest for a cake, but returned with champagne, and Joan and Richard cut with ritual ceremony into a home-made apple teacake.

Mrs Sutherland, on her way back from Australia, received the news by cable and when the ship docked Joan and Richard were at Southampton to meet her. Mrs Sutherland had hoped for a son-in-law with a more reliable profession, hence the secrecy, and although Joan was somewhat tearful about it they thought it would save a lot of trouble to present her with a *fait accompli*. By the time they arrived at Aubrey Walk, where Ailsa had prepared a meal, eyes were dry and recriminations more or less forgotten.

Richard now became even more proprietorial with regard to Joan's voice and the proper management of it. They had few close friends and were not particularly sociable, but they went to parties which gave Richard the opportunity to convince others of the path her career should take. Joan had already made tentative approaches to David Webster about the possibility of a dramatic coloratura role, and she was delighted when he offered her the consumptive singer Antonia in *The Tales of Hoffmann* — even if only second cast to Elsie Morison. As it happened, she took over sooner than expected when Elsie Morison was indisposed, and according to Lord Harewood the brilliance of her top notes and flourishes was astounding. Later, on tour, she sang the courtesan Giulietta and Aida on consecutive nights, and eventually the purely coloratura role of the Doll, Olympia.

Richard had been suspicious of Webster's motives, for there was a cautionary tale of another soprano who had whined for more roles, over-sung herself and rapidly faded from sight. But Joan had delighted the critics in all three *Hoffmann* roles, and Richard at last felt she was singing the kind of music to which her voice was best suited. He pleaded for more of the same, but there were no works in the current repertoire that fitted the bill apart, that is, from the rather ambivalent one represented by Michael Tippett's new opera *The Midsummer Marriage*. Joan was to create the soprano role of Jenifer, one of the spiritual lovers, and Tippett was encouraged to elaborate the vocal line with her in mind. Joan, however, had no difficulty with the fiendish coloratura, but along with the rest of the cast she found the symbolic and allegorical nature of the work quite incomprehensible. When in desperation she appealed to the composer to tell her what it was all about, he replied cryptically: 'It was something inside me that had to come out.' It was not an experience that endeared her to twentieth-century opera.

In the same season she sang a few more performances as Aida, all conducted by Emanuel Young, took part in two cycles of *The Ring*, and did a considerable amount of work for the BBC. The 1954 season began with her first joint recital with Richard at

Wigmore Hall, for which she wore a borrowed dress and he a borrowed dinner jacket, but it was not the sell-out occasion their recitals were later to become. The same month she sang Micaela in *Carmen* with a purity of tone and beauty of phrasing only marred by her far too mature and sophisticated bearing.

She had been praised for her demure, maidenly appearance in *Der Freischütz*, but it was somewhat harder to achieve now that she was five months pregnant. Wakhevitch's voluminous costumes and the ingenuity of Gertie Stelzel, her dresser, contrived to provide camouflage, but her pregnancy effectively put paid to plans to sing the Queen of Shemakhan in Rimsky-Korsakov's *Le coq d'or*. She took a few weeks maternity leave before Adam was born on 13 February 1956 (ironically, Wagner's birthday), and Joan was now sufficiently respected as a singer to be referred to in reports of the birth as the 'celebrated' Australian soprano.

She was back on stage again in April as Antonia, and of her performance as the First Lady Andrew Porter wrote: 'Her sweet pure tone and delicate sense of phrasing afforded the only really positive vocal pleasures of the evening.' In July she made her debut at Glyndebourne to become the first English-speaking Countess in *The Marriage of Figaro*. She followed Elisabeth Grümmer in the role — not an easy task, for Grümmer was an experienced Countess and not new to the Festival — but gave a radiant and dignified performance and satisfied the demands of a difficult role. Although Joan was a prime candidate for Mozartian opera, on this occasion Lord Harewood found her disappointing. He thought she was incompatible, physically and vocally, with the tiny auditorium, and Richard had already noticed that the bigger the theatre and the more space there was around the voice, the better it sounded. It was also apparent in these intimate surroundings that she had bad teeth, and via Joan Ingpen, her agent, came the message that unless she had something done about it Glyndebourne would be unable to engage her again.

Joan, therefore, sought a consultation with Henry Pitt-Roche, a highly respected dental surgeon. The estimated cost of having all her teeth capped was £700, and it was an uncomfortable and painful process taking almost a year to complete. During these lengthy sessions Pitt-Roche worked to the accompaniment of orchestral music, and to this day Joan has an almost Pavlovian distaste for some of the music he played. Eventually she took along a selection of her own, heavily biased towards Maria Callas, and was vastly amused when Pitt-Roche confessed to having very little liking for the human voice.

Harold Rosenthal was now writing optimistically about her

performances in *Opera Magazine*, even suggesting that 'she was one of *the* singers of the day'. As Antonia she produced some of the most ravishing sounds heard for a long time and when she made her debut in December 1956 as Pamina in *The Magic Flute*, a role notorious for highlighting deficiencies in vocal technique, he wrote:

> Joan Sutherland, for whom the music of Pamina holds not the slightest difficulty, enchanted the ear with her pure silvery tone and lovely top notes; she only needs to cultivate a ravishing piano tone to become a first rate interpreter of this role. She looked and moved on stage with far greater assurance than in the past.

When she undertook the role of Eva in a new English production of *Die Meistersinger*, he thought she rode the quintet with ease and beauty, although he had reservations about her characterization. Personally Joan disliked it. It was Rafael Kubelik's first *Meistersinger*; orchestrally it was too loud and she saw no virtue in striving for perfection if no-one could hear her. She had turned down Elsa and Sieglinde which would inevitably have lead to Brünnhilde, for she was now convinced that her career was not heading in that direction.

While Covent Garden continued to scratch only the surface of Joan's capacity for florid singing, the fledgling Handel Opera Society asked her to sing Alcina in the first British performance since 1737. Joan's reaction was to plead pressure of work and decline, but here was the opportunity Richard had been clamouring for: a dramatic coloratura role that would demonstrate Joan's talent to perfection.

Handel composed *Alcina* for Covent Garden when Italian *opera seria*, with the stress on the singer, was all the rage. Strict operatic conventions had evolved whereby the opera was dominated by the da capo aria — an aria in three parts, the last being a repeat of the first allowing for a showy display of virtuosity — linked by recitative with very little in the way of ensemble or chorus. Castrati, adored and idolized, were still very much in evidence, although they now appeared alongside female singers, competing with each other for vocal supremacy. Both groups were capable of some fiendishly difficult bravura and mellifluously smooth melody.

Handel's work for the English stage attracted huge audiences. Although bound by conventions which stretched credulity to the utmost, Handel had an individual vocal and instrumental style, a genius for beautiful melody and a gift for bringing his characters vividly to life through the music. *Opera seria*, however, was eventually dealt a death blow by the rising popularity of *opera buffa* in the wake of John Gay's *The Beggar's Opera* — a satire on what Dr Johnson characterized as 'an exotic and irrational entertainment'. Disillusioned, Handel retired from the theatre and devoted the rest of his life to the composition of oratorio.

Charles Farncombe took a great risk when he ploughed his war gratuity into the formation of the Handel Opera Society. Modern revivals presupposed the existence of singers proficient in the style and technique of *opera seria*, and that a modern audience, unaccustomed to its conventions, would accept Handel for the consummate musical dramatist he is. Somewhat to Farncombe's amazement the first two productions of *Deidamia* and *Hercules* had been appreciatively received and *Alcina* was even more successful. They gave two performances in St Pancras Town Hall to an enthusiastic audience and the press warmly praised Joan's command of Handel's style and technique:

> Now that in Miss Sutherland we have a first rate Handelian soprano who phrases and flourishes, trills and embellishes with lovely tone and exquisite art, we must have Handel added to the national repertory.
>
> Andrew Porter, *Financial Times*, 20 March 1957

Joan had found the music of her six great arias compatible with voice, giving a performance of ease and assurance such as to win over those previously uncommitted to her voice or personality. Notwithstanding a costume adorned with pieces from a cannibalized chandelier she felt comfortable on stage for the first time, and in his uncompromising way Richard immediately announced that she had the potential to become the greatest exponent of Handelian opera.

Alcina undoubtedly marked a watershed in Joan's career, and privately Covent Garden were beginning to reassess her prospects and recognize that her facility for Italian coloratura roles might be worth exploiting. Harewood and Webster needed no convincing that given the right opportunity Joan would exhibit all the star quality they were confident she possessed. But they had to persuade a Board of Directors not overburdened with musical knowledge nor expertise, and there was still much public opposition to the Arts Council subsidy, which meant that everything had to be carefully justified. The risk inherent in mounting a new production for Joan's blossoming talent was enormous. Tentatively they suggested an ideal vehicle might be Donizetti's *Lucia di Lammermoor*. On the debit side, it was not an opera familiar to Covent Garden audiences: Melba had made an inauspicious debut as Lucia in 1888 and when it opened a season of

Italian opera in 1925, with Toti dal Monte making her Covent Garden debut, it had survived only one performance. On the other hand Maria Callas had done much to reawaken interest in the neglected field of bel canto, and a recent programme poll put *Lucia di Lammermoor* high on the list of operas the audience most wanted to see.

The Board discussed the costs involved with a new production, the extraordinary complexity of the title role, and the extent to which the success of the opera depended on the singer of that role. The Board and members of the music staff did not see Joan as another Callas, and saw no reason to suppose she could succeed where others had failed. They offered her Charpentier's *Louise* instead, and grudgingly Joan and Richard agreed to look at the sets, in storage since 1914, before turning it down.

Unable for the moment to sway the Board, Webster never faltered in his determination to mount *Lucia* for the 1957/58 season, and to this end commissioned an English libretto from Christopher Hassell. Then came news that a visiting Italian company had *Lucia* in its repertoire for its annual visit to the Stoll Theatre in May 1957; this was a crushing disappointment to Joan, for it was now out of the question for Covent Garden to mount the opera the next season. In the meantime her astonishing success in *Alcina* added weight to Webster's arguments; now more than ever *Lucia* seemed the ideal vehicle, but even with all thoughts of an alternative discarded, no decision was made.

Joan now had a considerable personal following, and each new role she undertook was awaited with interest. None more so than that of Gilda in the 1957 revival of *Rigoletto*, which happened to coincide with *Lucia* at the Stoll:

> Miss Sutherland's *'Caro nome'* was vocalized with high accomplishment and called forth rapturous applause, too. Phrases indeed were bewitching, but there was, forgivably enough, a certain self-consciousness about this first performance of this difficult scene . . . the soprano line of the quartet, a floating silvery *'Lassù in cielo'*, were not only exquisite, but expressive within the dramatic context. Miss Sutherland seldom seems to get onto easy terms with her roles; one wishes that she would relax a little, confident that her actual singing is going to be alright.
>
> Andrew Porter, *Financial Times*, 9 May 1957

Gilda had certainly been one of her more congenial roles, and she had studied it exhaustively with Richard, working and re-working every phrase until it was exactly right. They had evolved a whole new vocabulary of terminology that was uniquely personal, and their working relationship had developed into a mutual pursuit of romantic nineteenth-century Italian opera.

Richard's collection of scores extended to an insatiable appetite for theatrical memorabilia of all kinds, and the walls of their Kensington flat were covered with prints of nineteenth-century prima donnas. But with Covent Garden unable to come to a definite decision about *Lucia* Joan was still two seasons away from emulating these legendary ladies, although she did give an accomplished performance of Madame Hertz in Mozart's *Der Schauspieldirektor* at Glyndebourne, displaying her new teeth and top Fs!

From May 1952 Joan had featured regularly in broadcasts on the BBC Third Programme, and many of the operas in which she appeared were broadcast 'live' from Covent Garden and Glyndebourne. The BBC offered valuable experience in a wide diversity of vocal music. She sang all the soprano music from *Madama Butterfly* and *La bohème* in a series of illustrated talks; she sang in studio broadcasts of Piccinni's *La buona figliuola* and Scarlatti's *Mitridate Eupatore* and the soprano part in the première of Frank Martin's twentieth-century oratorio *Golgotha* 'live' from the Festival Hall. She broadcast a programme of arias associated with the English soprano Elizabeth Billington, whose career had been carefully documented by Richard and whose portrait dominated their sitting room, and from time to time songs and arias popped up which were to form a regular part of Joan's concert and recital repertoire.

When the score for one of Donizetti's earliest operas, *Emilia di Liverpool* came to light Joan was the BBC's natural choice for the title role. The recitative was replaced by a narration written and spoken by Bernard Miles, who with dry humour described the opera to radio listeners as 'a tale of passion, intrigue and high drama set on a mountain top outside Liverpool, somewhere between Brownlow Hill and Limestreet Station'. John Pritchard conducted this Donizetti rarity and recalls Joan singing the final scena with such authenticity of style that observers were already predicting her complete takeover of the Donizetti and Bellini heroines. Later, when she recorded the cavatina and rondo finale (under very primitive conditions), the now distinctive Sutherland sound was instantly recognizable: a tantalizing foretaste of what was to come.

In the wake of Virginia Zeani's tremendous success as Lucia at the Stoll Theatre, the Covent Garden Board were again considering whether a production with Joan was a viable risk. They had capitulated to Webster's arguments, now backed by substantial evidence, on condition that the great Italian maestro Tullio Serafin could be engaged to conduct. The opera would therefore be sung in Italian, in keeping with the Board's policy to forge ahead with opera in the original language. This was not entirely to Webster's liking because, above all, he wanted his opera house to be popular and was worried such a move would frighten people away. The ultimatum, however, was a great comfort to Joan. There was no need now to tell Webster — after all his efforts on her behalf — how reluctant she was to sing in English, and it would be her first opportunity to sing a major role in the original language. Christopher Hassell's libretto was set aside and the performance was scheduled for February 1959.

Meanwhile the current season was underway with the inevitable Ring Cycles, the now familiar role of Antonia, and Micaela in performances of *Carmen*, remembered today as much for the battle of wills between Joan and the Musical Director, Rafael Kubelik, as for the Covent Garden debut of Regina Resnik. Joan's dislike of dialogue was well known, and when she first sang Micaela under Edward Downes it was accepted that she would sing as recitative the lines traditionally spoken as dialogue before her aria in Act III. Kubelik, however, subscribed to the view that *Carmen* should be performed as Bizet wrote it and whatever the precedent had no intention of deviating from it to accommodate Joan's foibles, while Joan, accustomed to singing recitative, had no intention of changing it for Kubelik, Bizet or anyone else. The situation had reached a hostile impasse until Webster intervened, and in the end Joan *did* sing her recitative. The company had watched while unassertive Joan stood firm on a matter of principle. To his credit Kubelik did not bear her a grudge, and ironically he had been one of the few music staff who supported her claim to sing *Lucia*.

At the end of November 1957 Harold Rosenthal asked Joan to illustrate a lecture he was giving to the Friends of Covent Garden on the history of the Opera House, and Joan gave a brilliant performance of Lucia's aria and cabaletta '*Regnava nel silenzio...Quando rapita*' before a rapt audience. Afterwards, in contrast to Eugene Goossens who hailed her as Florence Austral's logical successor, Rosenthal recognized in her a worthy successor to that other formidable Australian diva, Dame Nellie Melba. Three weeks later Joan enjoyed an unqualified personal success in one of Melba's favourite roles, when she made her debut as Desdemona. In rehearsal, however, her lack of affinity for the role had not filled Norman Ayrton with hopeful anticipation. She had no real sympathy for Desdemona's plight: 'It was all her fault. She should have known something was wrong, and not gone on talking about Cassio and handkerchiefs', and wept tears of frustration into her lunchtime beer. It was Ramon Vinay, whom many regarded as the finest post-war Otello, who finally did the trick, hurling her across the stage in a most convincing jealous rage. Joan crashed against a pillar and turned to face him, eyes blazing, face flushed, every inch the wronged and misunderstood woman. Ayrton rejoiced. No matter that this was for real rather than an inspired performance. What she needed was motivation, and while he had helped shed some of her inhibitions, she had not entirely overcome the embarrassment of attempting something new and original for the first time. Once accomplished, however, Joan seemed to have no difficulty repeating it.

She gave an exquisite performance of Desdemona, sung with persuasive purity and simplicity, and Andrew Porter considered it her greatest success so far:

> Miss Sutherland could quite easily make her assumption more patently effective in the short run by sacrificing purity and power, by forcing the note of despair, by launching into chesty tones. But this is not her way; and five years on we shall bless her for not endeavouring to be 'exciting' but, instead, lyrical and beautiful. This is not to say that the note of passion was missing, only that it was never forced. We note too she has accepted her height for the virtue it is and moved gracefully and with dignity without awkwardness. Also, that especially in conversational exchanges, a new timbre has come into her voice — one that recalls surprisingly Toti dal Monte's in seeming to fall right from the lips, warm and ripe.
>
> Andrew Porter, *Financial Times*, 31 December 1957

In only three performances she demonstrated a capacity to refine and mature a role, already showing signs of qualifying for a place among the finest contemporary Desdemonas of Tebaldi, Rysanek, Jurinac and Brouwenstijn. It was much to be regretted that apart from two performances in Vienna at the end of 1959 Joan did not sing Desdemona again until much later in her career.

In sharp contrast to *Otello*, January 1958 saw the first British performance of Poulenc's *The Carmelites*, based on Georges Bernarnos' stage play of the French Revolution. Margherita Wallmann, who had staged the première at La Scala in 1957, was also the producer on this occasion and Poulenc was at Covent

Garden to keep a proprietorial ear on the musical preparation. Joan was agreeably cast as the New Prioress, Madame Lidoine — a baker's daughter — which suited her unworldly personality, and she brought a graceful serenity to the role. Apt to turn compliments aside she was nevertheless greatly touched when Poulenc offered congratulations on her performance.

The season continued with Joan singing Gilda, a delight to the ear with its radiant purity of tone and expressive phrasing, and using coloratura skilfully as a legitimate means of dramatic expression she made 'Caro nome' into more than just a coloratura show-piece. During her last provincial tour she sang Madame Lidoine and Gilda to an even more enthusiastic reception and at Covent Garden in April, after another memorable performance, the music critic of *The Times* claimed she had all the potential of another Melba or Galli-Curci.

This was not the first time, however, that Joan had given a superlative performance against the most appalling odds, for in Manchester she had developed abscesses in both ears — not an uncommon occurrence and one she normally took in her stride. It was not unknown for her to sing almost deaf to the orchestra, her eyes glued to the conductor, and afterwards to take the tube home. It hardly occurred to her to see a doctor. A friend recalls visiting to find Richard frantically cleaning the remains of tomato soup and scrambled eggs from the cooker, with Joan sitting up in bed, score propped in front of her, and a Kotex clasped to an ear in which an abscess had burst. This time she could not shrug it off. Injections of penicillin enabled her to complete the tour, but she returned to London with her legs so painfully swollen that she was unable to kneel or get into the breeches required for the last act. She wrapped herself in a voluminous cloak and hoped no-one would notice.

Secretly afraid that she had elephantiasis, she delayed seeing a doctor for fear of being confined to bed and thereby missing her first significant recording session: two arias from *Alcina*. Sitting on a conductor's stool and in considerable pain, she accomplished the recording, after which she was not only ordered to bed, but to hospital where she stayed for an anxious three weeks. Exhaustive tests revealed nothing conclusive, but a specialist, for want of any rational explanation, suggested her newly capped teeth were the cause of her condition, and that they would all have to come out. But the teeth were not even paid for yet, and panic-stricken Joan dragged herself to the telephone to send an SOS to Ivor Griffiths. He vetoed the decision and the teeth stayed in, for it appeared her abscessed ears, constant catarrh and what seemed to be an acute arthritic condition were all the direct result of the shocking state of her sinuses. Joan was relieved by this diagnosis, for she was quite used to the routine visits to Wimpole Street to have her sinuses drained. But this treatment was no longer enough: a much longer, more delicate operation was necessary and Joan was left in no doubt of the risk to which such an operation would expose her voice.

Such a crisis could not have come at a worse time. Arrangements were already in hand for her to go to Italy to study *Lucia* with Serafin, and her first international engagement was only months away. Nicholas Goldschmidt had heard her in *Der Schauspieldirektor*, and invited her to sing Donna Anna at the first Vancouver Festival. It was a golden opportunity to extend her horizons, for although she had built quite a reputation at home, she was totally unknown elsewhere. Reluctantly Griffiths agreed to delay the operation, but she went away with the gloomy prognosis that without it she could become a permanent invalid within five years.

Richard had not restricted his promotion of her career to her vocal development. Her greatest fan and severest critic, he also endeavoured — with varying degrees of success — to superimpose upon her homely personality his image of the grand diva. She indulged him in some of his fantasies. He steered her in the direction of a good dressmaker, not always with happy results, and encouraged her to cultivate a more reserved manner, although in the long-term any aloofness was cultivated in the interests of retaining some privacy. By nature she was open and friendly — it was her instinct to sign her autograph with fond or affectionate wishes, while Richard thought more formality appropriate — but his biggest obstacle was her total lack of personal vanity or pretension. When she left for Vancouver in July, however, a few dramatic changes were evident. Her smile was still intact and she was very much slimmer. After much experiment she had the red hair soon to be regarded as the Sutherland hallmark, and she wore a wide-brimmed hat infinitely more glamorous than those she had favoured in the past. Much to her surprise she was treated as a celebrity, but without Richard to keep a watchful eye on her dignity it seemed quite natural to sit on the steps of the Orpheum Theatre eating hot-dogs with the rest of the cast.

For the first time outside Norman Ayrton's studio she was the centre of a director's undivided attention, and Gunther Rennert's vitality and eye for detail filled her with confidence. Among strangers who regarded her as a star she shed more of her inhibitions and as a result the critics were able to write glowing reviews:

> Miss Sutherland's pure soprano voice rang out with definite purpose and direction. Her tonal production was flawless from one end of the scale to the other, whether singing coloratura or long sustained passages. At times it was coloured with passion and conviction and made her portrayal of Donna Anna a woman of flesh and blood. Her voice is one of the finest heard here for many long years.
>
> *Vancouver Sun*, 28 August 1958

Bruno Walter, who at the age of 82 came out of retirement to conduct two concerts for the Festival, attended the dress rehearsal and told Goldschmidt: 'She is the best Donna Anna I have ever heard.'

If Joan had let this first flush of international success go to her head, her ego would soon have been crushed, for returning home via New York, George London, who had sung Don Giovanni in Vancouver, persuaded her to audition for the Metropolitan Opera. She sang Gilda's '*Caro nome*' in English, as was her custom, but unlike her London critics the Metropolitan was not impressed and clearly not going to offer any short-cuts to fame.

Home again she contributed her Rhinemaiden and Woodbird to the 1958 Ring Cycles and went to Leeds with the company for the first Covent Garden performance of Handel's dramatized oratorio *Samson*. Every night for a week and twice on Saturday Joan stole the show with the Israelite Woman's single aria 'Let the bright seraphim'. *Samson* is full of high spots, but none sparked off such spontaneous enthusiasm as this shimmering piece. When she sang it again at Covent Garden the following month it had much the same effect, arousing the audience to a frenzy of applause and confirming Richard's opinion that she was an expert and stylish Handelian.

At the end of the year Noël Goodwin, who had followed her career with great interest since her first Gilda, predicted that within five years Joan would be as internationally famous as Callas was then. She had not squandered her vocal resources by taking on too much too soon, but developed from role to role in an artistic progression based on sound technique. The indicators had been there, few but decisive: Antonia, Olympia, Pamina, Alcina, Gilda, Madame Hertz, Desdemona and now the Israelite Woman. If she should carry off *Lucia di Lammermoor* with the same sense of style and technique her success would be assured.

4
Lucia di Lammermoor

Rudolf Bing at the Metropolitan Opera House thought the majority of audiences loved only those operas they knew by heart. The undying popularity of operas such as *La bohème*, *Tosca*, *La traviata* and *Carmen*, all of which, like *Hamlet*, are full of quotations, testify to this. But new productions represent the life-blood of an opera company by maintaining interest and attracting audiences, although each new production is a risk in itself, and to mount an opera like *Lucia di Lammermoor* was a brave step to take without a famous guest artist.

During her six seasons at Covent Garden, Joan had appeared in the opening night of 11 of the 29 new productions, but only two of these could be classified as major roles: Jenifer in *The Midsummer Marriage* and Eva in *Die Meistersinger*. Ironically she been happy with neither of them, and if she should fail in *Lucia* the opportunity might not present itself again.

Donizetti was a prolific composer, popular with audiences and singers alike. He wrote music which appealed to the public, which was accommodating to the voices of their favourite singers, and could be relied upon to fill the theatre. Not surprisingly he was much in demand by impresarios, and *Lucia di Lammermoor* was one of four operas commissioned for the San Carlo, Naples in 1835. Donizetti's contract stipulated that after each libretto had been approved by the censors he had four months in which to compose the music until the date of the first performance. The time was often a good deal less in practice and the path far from smooth, but Donizetti was accustomed to working in haste and soon recognized 'Often the accusation of carelessness is made against the music that cost me the most time'. His motto was therefore *'Presto'*, and he completed *Lucia* in six weeks.

Based on Sir Walter Scott's romantic novel *The Bride of Lammermoor*, *Lucia* was the first and by far the most successful of the eight operas Donizetti composed in collaboration with the librettist Salvatore Cammarano. With Fanny Persiani in the title role, Gilbert Duprez as Edgardo and Domenico Cosselli as Enrico, it was also one of the greatest successes in the history of the San

Carlo. Much to Donizetti's amazement it was listened to with rapt attention — unusual in Italy where the audience, although rivetted by the display arias, duets and ensembles, took the linking passages as a cue to gossip, gamble and eat. With characteristic modesty, in a letter to his publisher, Ricordi, Donizetti wrote: 'It pleased, and pleased very much if I may believe the applause and compliments received.'

It continued to please after more than a century when all but a handful of his operas faded into limbo, extending its popularity beyond Italy with its first performance in Vienna in 1837. The following year it was given at Her Majesty's Theatre in London, and 10 years later at Covent Garden. On each occasion the role of Lucia was sung by Fanny Persiani, who was noted for her brilliantly inventive ornamentation and the perfection with which she delivered it. Such ornamentation was a *sine qua non* of the bel canto style, which at its most simplistic can be defined as a very highly schooled method of voice production, involving a long and rigorous training and a musical style in which the melody is paramount and the emphasis is on the vocal line.

During this period of operatic evolution it was the custom of the composer to tailor his score to the resources at his disposal, and since no singer worth her, or his, salt would miss an opportunity to decorate the vocal line, the composer would indicate in the score where such cadenzas and embellishments might be interpolated. No score was regarded as sacrosanct. In order to accommodate a variety of exponents the composer was obliged to transpose up, or down, and to put up with the fact that his music could be, and often was, added to and subtracted from, and it was permissible for a singer to introduce a favourite aria of her own, which might even be the work of another composer. It was Fanny Persiani's practice to replace Lucia's first act aria and cabaletta with another lifted from Donizetti's *Rosmonda d'Inghilterra*, a role which she had also created. It mattered little since the words expressed similar sentiments but were technically more difficult than '*Regnava nel silenzio*' and so showed off her voice to better advantage. Having set the example, other singers of the role followed her precedent and it was often referred to as the well known air from *Lucia*. It therefore came as something of a surprise to audience and critics alike when Adelina Patti sang Lucia for the first time at Covent Garden and restored '*Regnava nel silenzio*' to its proper place.

Good taste, however, did not always go hand in hand with vocal superiority, and sadly over-indulgence in excessive ornamentation was, to a degree, responsible for bringing the genre into disrepute faster than the changing fashion for Wagner and the verismo school dictated. By the 1920s it had become associated with a rather lightweight style of singing, denigrated as 'canary fodder' — singing for its own sake at the expense of the drama. It was the artistry of Maria Callas in the early 50s, with her understanding of the bel canto style and technique and her instinct for the drama, which redressed the balance and gave impetus to the upsurge of interest in many of the late-eighteenth- and early-nineteenth-century operas. With her recordings of complete operas, among them *I puritani*, *Norma* and *Lucia di Lammermoor*, she had been able to reach an even wider public, revealing to a whole new generation of opera lovers the glories of these mostly unfamiliar works. The seed had been sown and there was a rich harvest to be gathered, as Joan and Richard discovered as the latter intensified his research, expanding his collection of old scores and exploring music that would show off Joan's voice to its greatest advantage.

For months Joan had been studying the score and libretto of *Lucia* in minute detail, and Richard was in his element coaching her for the kind of bel canto role he had for so long been advocating. He translated the libretto word for word so she had a total understanding of what she was singing about, and with his facility for languages he polished and corrected her Italian pronunciation. With reference to the different performing traditions, they worked on authentic cadenzas, arpeggios and trills, ever conscious of the delicate balance between good and bad taste. *Lucia* completely invaded Joan's life. Scott's *Bride of Lammermoor* became bedtime reading, the libretto accompanied every meal, while the music dominated her practice sessions and disturbed her sleep. Then they went to Venice to study with the maestro without whose love and understanding of the bel canto literature a revival would have been impossible.

Tullio Serafin, the last of the old-school Italian conductors, was now in his 80s. He had been closely associated with Puccini and Toscanini; his life had been dedicated to the theatre and as a conductor of Rossini, Bellini, Donizetti and Verdi he was without equal. His influence on the early career of Maria Callas cannot be overestimated; Gobbi described him as an infallible judge of voice and character; Rosa Ponselle, whom he coached for her first performance of *Norma*, referred to his ability to draw the highest response from all who performed under his baton as 'a divinely inspired gift'. For Joan, working with him was inspiring and encouraging. He was greatly impressed by her technique and mastery of the role, a tribute to Richard's coaching and a joint single-mindedness. Serafin was delighted to find a non-Italian singer who not only had a beautiful voice, but who could also interpret such a long and exacting role so completely. They worked together every day on *I puritani*, *La sonnambula* and *Norma* as well as *Lucia*, and Serafin's confidence in Joan's ability was secure.

Franco Zeffirelli, however, faced a far more daunting task. Zeffirelli, a pupil of Visconti, had been designing and directing opera at La Scala since 1952, but first came to prominence in 1954 with a production of Rossini's comic opera *Il turco in Italia*, in which the role of Fiorilla was sung by Maria Callas, whom he had grown to love and idolize. It had been no easy matter to turn the classic tragedienne, with her limited experience of 'fun', into a comic actress, but he achieved this to such striking effect that many critics endowed Callas with an untapped talent for comedy. With Joan, Zeffirelli was to experience the opposite difficulty of transforming Joan, with her innate sense of humour and a disinclination to take herself seriously, into a tragic actress. He succeeded with her as he had with Callas, and after the first performance of *Lucia* it was immensely satisfying to read Desmond Shawe-Taylor's reference to 'the previously unknown creature — Joan Sutherland, the tragic actress'.

Before this could be achieved, however, there was a long way to go. He had been warned that she was large and cumbersome, that she had very little dramatic instinct, and that she still did not regard the stage as her natural habitat. In fact she was not as large as when she first began her apprenticeship at Covent Garden. Norman Ayrton had taught her to move with grace and freedom, and how to overcome the traditional problem engendered by self-consciousness in one who is being looked at — what to do with her hands. She may not have had a natural flair for acting but she responded to firm direction and regarded it as an essential tool for the job.

Her first meeting with Zeffirelli was not an auspicious one. Joan, with the inevitable cold, huddled warmly in layers of sweaters, was looking and feeling far from her best. Zeffirelli's dynamic personality and quicksilver mind quite overwhelmed her, and his Italian effusiveness made him incapable of communicating without touching her. A few months into her Covent Garden career, Geraint Evans, slipping an over-friendly arm around her as sweater and skirt parted at the waist, had his face soundly slapped, and Joan still blushes at the memory. Now as she shrank in embarrassment from Zeffirelli he was obliged to explain: 'I am sorry Joan. I am Italian. I have to communicate with my hands because my English is not that good, and I want to feel the people I am shaping my life and work with.' Until she knew him better, she found his demonstrative manner hard to accept.

Zeffirelli has a genius for inspiring singers to act, winning their confidence by a blend of psychology and cajolery. Guiding his principals decisively but without too much minutiae, he seizes upon any spontaneous initiative and develops it. This creates a natural and individual characterization which springs instinctively from within and is thus essentially tailor-made.

It was concentrated production such as Joan had never before experienced, and Zeffirelli succeeded in persuading her to attempt what she had hitherto thought impossible. Encouraged by her achievement, her confidence in him grew, until, trusting him completely, she was prepared to try almost anything he suggested. He was staggered, as Serafin had been, by her mastery of the role, and vocally she seemed capable of anything. When he discovered that she could move around the stage as she sang, and without loss of vocal power or agility could run as well, Zeffirelli had found the master-stroke to make the long and difficult mad scene theatrically spectacular and dramatically convincing.

A realistic, albeit romantic approach to design and the premise that each production must have a focal point are Zeffirelli's hallmarks. The focal point in *Lucia* was obviously the famous mad scene. The complicated fioriture Donizetti composed to convey Lucia's madness had long been a victim of coloratura over-indulgence and had thus been robbed of all dramatic significance. Joan was about to redress the balance. Not for Zeffirelli, Scott's drivelling Lucy, gibbering in the inglenook. He dressed Joan in a nightgown liberally splashed with blood, and she darted hysterically round the stage, cringing from hallucinations, play-acting her demented memories, the wedding guests recoiling in horror from her madness. He also capitalized on a rare moment of Sutherland ingenuity. As she knelt, head bowed, draped in her bridal veil and living in her lunatic imaginings her marriage to Edgardo, the notes of the flute came to her. As though hearing phantom noises, she instantly jerked her head up, and like an echo repeated them. It may have been a moment of inspiration or, as one uncharitable observer suggested, twitching away from a fly, but it was to become an integral part of the Sutherland performance, bringing to this one section of the long *scena*, always in danger of becoming a vocalise, obvious and convincing signs of madness.

Zeffirelli had to argue his corner with Serafin for the blood-stained nightgown for the latter was appalled that art should need such crude devices. But Zeffirelli felt that Joan needed these macabre trappings, and the visual and vocal effect was sensational. His costumes were a *pièce de résistance* in greens and blues to enhance her complexion, and he added ringlets to her own titian hair to soften her jaw, and long curling lashes to her striking green eyes.

Joan no longer found the Covent Garden stage such a vast and intimidating place, and she was less conscious of her height. Zeffirelli contrived to look down at her when he spoke to her, constantly telling her: 'You're a star now, stand up straight', which obviously appealed to her far more than Norman Ayrton's exhortations: 'Stand up straight, you're not a bloody camel.' She had abandoned flat ballerina shoes since they made her walk and stand badly and she was about to stop worrying about her own height in relation to the invariably short tenors opposite whom she sang: 'If they're short, that's their problem, not mine.' But above all Zeffirelli had achieved the impossible, by making her look and feel beautiful.

As the opening night drew near, there was an air of confident expectation that something spectacular was about to happen. Word of this excitement reached the ear of Callas, in London to record her second *Lucia*, and she called David Webster to ask if she might attend the dress rehearsal. While Bill Beresford, the Opera House Publicity Manager scurried around in an attempt to gain the maximum publicity from this impromptu visit, Callas, not renowned for watching the performances of other singers, sat with the Earl and Countess of Harewood, Elisabeth Schwarzkopf and Walter Legge in the grand tier, a solicitous Webster at her side. Callas apparently needed only a little prompting to recall that Joan had sung Clotilde to her Norma, and that they had both appeared in the same Gala Performance as recently as June 1958. On that occasion Callas took the honours with the mad scene from *I puritani*, while Joan and John Lanigan sang a duet from Balfe's *The Bohemian Girl*, heavily cut at the last minute because the programme was too long. As the rehearsal progressed with applause from the orchestra and the auditorium filled with opera house personnel — a rare occurrence — Callas grew more impressed. So astonished was she at the physical and vocal virtuosity of the mad scene, that she was heard to comment: 'That is not good.' Surprised, her companion asked what was bad about it. 'It is too good', came the reply, a sense of professional insecurity asserting itself.

Bill Beresford had succeeded in summoning a bevy of Fleet Street photographers, and with a graciousness that did not come easily to Callas she agreed to be photographed with Joan. Immaculately groomed, she burst into the dressing room she had so often occupied to find Joan, in her dressing-gown, make-up streaked and her hair damp with perspiration. But bubbling over with excitement and exhilaration, her adrenalin ran too high to be overawed by the great diva. The next day newspapers carried a rare photograph of Callas and Sutherland together; Callas was the bait, but the next time the press fell over themselves to photograph Joan it was as the star of a performance which was to be marvelled at for nearly three decades.

The morning of the first performance was bleak, grey and damp — a typical February day. As luck would have it Joan was incubating a cold, and had a persistent tickle in her throat. She was tormented by the theatrical bromide that a bad dress-rehearsal means a good performance. Did the opposite apply? It was no comfort to learn that Kenneth Neate had been whisked over from Paris to replace Joao Gibin, her Edgardo, who had withdrawn with a throat infection, and there would be no time for a rehearsal. The responsibility facing her was enough to overwhelm the toughest of spirits, and she was in an acute state of nervous anxiety. Her once modest ambition had been stretched by the faith of others, and she had a driving determination not to disappoint them. It was Franco Zeffirelli's first bid for recognition on an international basis, and he had spared nothing to bring out the best in Joan. It was an act of faith on the part of David Webster and Lord Harewood, who had energetically championed her cause. It was confirmation of Richard's judgement of her genius and the readiness of the public to accept and enjoy bel canto opera. For operamanes following her career with propri-etorial interest, it was more than just another night at the opera.

On the night of 17 February 1959 success was absolute for Joan, Richard, Zeffirelli and Donizetti. For Joan it was a personal triumph beyond anything she could have anticipated, and it surpassed the achievements of any British singer at Covent Garden since the war. She concluded her opening aria and cabaletta to thunderous applause which was repeated at the end of the act, and after the famous sextet she took curtain-call after curtain-call. But as Zeffirelli had intended, it was the mad scene that was the crowning glory of the performance, bringing the audience to its feet in a riot of cheering and applause more in keeping with a football stadium than the decorous ambience of an opera house. Unused to such extravagant acclaim, she accepted the ovation with genuine humility, blowing kisses which stirred the house to renewed frenzy.

Afterwards in her dressing room, crammed to its limited capacity with friends and colleagues sharing the unprecedented excitement, Joan mopped her face on Lucia's wedding veil and drank champagne from glasses stained with Ribena.

Joan had sung with greater freedom and power than ever before and her voice had gained in richness and colour and showed a remarkable fullness in the upper register. She brought a new dramatic intensity to her performance which was a revelation, and replacing her former diffidence there was a new expressiveness in gesture and bearing. Transformed physically and vocally she had emerged as a creditable actress with a total command of the bel canto technique, vindicating the choice of *Lucia di Lammermoor* as the vehicle for her graduation to the international class:

> Her singing was exquisite; particularly notable were the sustained notes, followed by an octave drop. Her decorations were tastefully and justly conceived and beautifully executed. Arpeggios were delicate and lovely, trills were confident. But beyond this there was a meaning in everything she did. A singer who can make florid bursts in sixths with the flute heart-rending in effect has understood the secret of Donizetti's music.

Andrew Porter, *Financial Times*, February 1959

A star was born and there was not an opera manager in the world unaware of it. Signor Oldani from La Scala was in the audience and the presence of Serafin and Zeffirelli ensured that news of it reached the Italian press. Walter Legge, a director of EMI, had not waited until the mad scene clinched her success before coming to the dressing room to promise an exclusive recording contract. The BBC adjusted its schedule to relay a 'live' performance and before long opera houses around the world would be clamouring for her services.

She sought relief from the euphoria by arranging baths full of flowers and in the mundane housewifely chores neglected in the weeks preceding *Lucia*. Fan letters arrived by the sack, and helped by a friend she insisted on responding to them all — even to those who had belittled her ability and, anxious to jump on the bandwagon of success, now professed lifelong devotion. And before any attractive contracts could be taken up there was still the sinus operation to be attended to, the need for which had become no less urgent. Indeed, as the series of *Lucias* ran its course her cold had developed into acute sinusitis, and since lying down exacerbated the condition she slept for several nights propped up by cushions in an armchair. With an international career so enticingly within reach, the risk of the operation seemed even greater. Logically the condition was such that she should have no singing voice at all, let alone a unique one. There was no way of knowing what effect a 'clean up' would have on the resonance of the voice and the distinctive Sutherland sound. The best that could be offered was a semi-permanent treatment rather than a guaranteed cure, but without it the prospect for her future well-being looked bleak. Having exhaustively discussed the pros and cons, the decision was made to go ahead, but the name Welitsch loomed large. Lubja Welitsch had been a sensational Salome and had undergone a similar operation from which she tragically emerged with only half a voice.

Ivor Griffiths performed the operation at the London Clinic at the beginning of March. Well-wishers sent cards and telegrams, friends brought flowers and grapes, and Richard brought her operatic scores. Instead of talking she wrote on a large sketch pad and at the end of the week she left with Richard and Adam for a holiday in the South of France. Griffiths advised her not to sing for a month but when she tried to sing again the horrible, dry sounds she made sent her back to him in a panic. Griffiths was unable to give her further treatment or a reasonable explanation. Secretly afraid her voice had gone for ever, he calculated that if he told her to go home and put in some concentrated practice, she would have nothing to lose. Several days later, after excruciating sessions with Richard during which they both feared the worst, she returned joyfully to Griffiths with the news that she was singing better than ever. The future looked rosy, but she was not slow to perceive that life would never be quite the same again.

5
La Stupenda

It was June before Sutherland sang publicly again. The Opera House was full to hear her crown a performance of *Samson* with 'Let the bright seraphim', and for the Handel Opera Society, which continued to go from strength to strength, she scored a striking success as Rodelinda, glorying once more in Handel's elaborate and taxing vocal style:

> The brilliance and beauty of her coloratura are matchless. But no less notable is the exquisitely drawn phrasing of the slow melodies and recitative, the subtle and intricate line and play of tone colour by which she gives Handel's music such meaning and eloquence.
>
> Andrew Porter, *Financial Times*, 25 June 1959

In the same week Peter Heyworth wrote in the *Observer*:

> ... in three months in Italy I heard nothing to equal the musicality and precision, the brilliance and beauty of her singing.

She was now at the end of her current contract at Covent Garden, and in excellent voice she closed the season with a superb performance in *Lucia*. Her engagement diary was rapidly filling up. In June, accompanied by Bonynge she gave a recital at Australia House which included '*Qui la voce*', and when she sang the same *scena* under Sir Adrian Boult for a charity gala, *The Times* described it as a superlatively stylish performance which the Golden Age of singing could not have bettered. She had immediate invitations to sing Donna Anna and Desdemona in Vienna, Zeffirelli persuaded the Fenice in Venice to mount *Alcina* and her Lucia was in demand almost everywhere. For the present this suited her very well, as she and Bonynge mapped out the immediate future, frantically wondering how they would find time to learn the new roles to be added to her repertoire. Webster had asked her to sing *La traviata* at Covent Garden early in 1960 with *La sonnambula* later in the year, and she had been engaged to sing *I puritani* for the 1960 Glyndebourne Festival.

The Vienna Staatsoper was therefore the scene of her first

international engagement as Donna Anna, and with only two days to prepare she discovered that since she was recognized as a 'star', she was not expected to rehearse. There was nothing unusual in this. Singers were expected to fit in to a fairly stereo-typed and often unimaginative production, and in unfamiliar surroundings with a mostly unfamiliar cast, Sutherland was grate-ful to be able to fall back on the production Rennert had given her in Vancouver and hope that all would be alright on the night. She had sung Donna Anna and Desdemona to outstanding acclaim before, and she repeated this success in Vienna where parallels were drawn between her and Lilli Lehmann, and it was said that no future Mozart Festival would be complete without her.

By the New Year, however, there were signs that the honey-moon was over, her triumphal progress suffering an unexpected set-back when her debut as Violetta proved a great disappoint-ment. Before Christmas she had written anxiously to Webster:

> This is a colossal role and my memory is bad — worse when I am pressed for time ... You understand that since my very sudden 'rise to fame' things have become very complex for me — it will take a little time to adjust myself and to learn that I cannot sing too many new works at once.

For *La traviata* Verdi scored music of great beauty and dramatic depth which was to immortalize the play that inspired it — Alexandre Dumas' *La dame aux camélias*. Verdi saw the play in 1852 in Paris, where it was enjoying an immense if somewhat notorious popularity. He had already been commissioned to write an opera for the Fenice, and Dumas' play provided the perfect story. For the first time, Verdi was dealing with the bourgeois society of the present day, and he intended to give it a genu-ine contemporary flavour and perform it in modern dress. The Fenice, however, were aghast at the prospect, fearing such a setting might give offence to the audience, so the rather avant-garde nature of the work was softened by back-dating it to the period of Louis XIV. Verdi had grave misgivings about the pro-duction and in the event his worst fears were justified. The cast was not ideal: the tenor was in poor voice, the baritone disinter-ested in the work, and the soprano, Fanny Salvini Donatelli, a stout, unattractive lady, defied all attempts to make her convinc-ing as the consumptive courtesan, Violetta. Verdi related the sad news in a letter to his music publisher, Ricordi: 'I cannot conceal the truth from you. *Traviata* was a fiasco. Don't try to work out the reason, that's just the way it is.' He wrote to his pupil Emanuele Muzio in the same vein, adding: 'Was it my fault, or the singers? Time will tell.'

A year later, also in Venice, but at the Teatro Gallo, it was given another chance with a first-rate cast under the supervision of the librettist Francesco Maria Piave, and it was an overwhelming success. In London, with Maria Piccolomini as Violetta, the press excited public opinion as to the merits of her performance and the daring nature of the opera itself, arousing such curiosity that everyone wanted to see it. *La traviata* was to become an enduring favourite with a place in the staple repertoire of most opera houses.

The production which awaited Sutherland at Covent Garden, however, did not serve her well. It was old and unimaginative, and her costumes, designed by Zeffirelli, did not blend with sets that were past their best. The direction was so lacking as to warrant no credit in the programme and to send Sutherland frantically to Norman Ayrton for help. Under pressure she was experiencing more than the usual difficulty learning the words. Rehearsing all day at Covent Garden and half the night with Ayrton, she grew tired and unwell. By the first performance she was deaf, her throat was sore and she was vocally insecure. Her acting carried none of the conviction that epitomized her Lucia and except for those of '*Addio del passato*', which Ayrton in desperation pasted to the top of the dressing-table, she forgot her words. Catcalls and audible attempts to silence the helpful prompter did nothing to increase her confidence and during an interval she was given an injection to calm her ragged nerves and ease the strain on her vocal equipment.

Understandably she was mauled by the critics, though they were generous in offering excuses for a performance of the kind best forgotten. They acknowledged how difficult it was to follow such an astounding triumph as *Lucia* which had not been seen recently at Covent Garden, with a masterpiece like *La traviata* which had Callas as its most recent exponent; they acknowledged the undistinguished production, the negative direction and the insensitive conducting of Nello Santi. Others noticed Sutherland's apparent vocal distress which manifested itself in a virulent attack of tracheitis. The second performance was cancelled and the following two sung by Virginia Zeani.

With her voice and therefore a little of her confidence restored, Sutherland sang Violetta again later in the month, and while some did not consider it improved beyond all recognition, Andrew Porter saw and heard a brilliantly successful performance:

> The delicate portamentos, the subtle and supple phrasing, took on a dramatic significance. There was a glitter, not merely vocal, which made one believe in a Violetta who had

all Paris at her feet. And there was a consistent dramatic progression. The warmth of feeling and passionate outbursts were vividly conveyed. In Act II, loving with Alfredo, dignified with Germont, Miss Sutherland seemed again to realize in phrase and gesture the creature of Verdi's imagination. The dramatic intensity of the next act was remarkable. The little shudder of dismay as she perceived that Alfredo was there too, her agony as he forced her to avow love for Duphol, the gesture with which she tried to silence his outburst — all these were beautifully handled. And in the final act she found not only the pathos of resignation, but also moments of fierce defiance, of will to live followed by the bitter realization that it was indeed, too late.

Opera Magazine, March 1960

She had redeemed her reputation and was on top form for another handful of *Lucias* with her voice, in Rosenthal's opinion, freer and fresher than when she first sang it and with greater depth to her characterization. To a broad spectrum of opera lovers, however, her portrayal of Violetta was a flop, but she and Bonynge had learned a timely lesson. Never again would she appear in a production without first knowing who was to conduct it, design it, sing in it, and above all direct it. To Sutherland, Zeffirelli had become the epitome of operatic production, as much a source of inspiration and security to her as Visconti had become to Callas, and she was to work with him again when she made her Italian debut at the Fenice in *Alcina*.

Although the origins of *opera seria* could be traced back to Venice in the eighteenth century, Handel had come to England to develop and refine the genre. In Italy, Handelian opera was still uncharted territory and *Alcina* had seemed a doubtful choice for such an important debut. But the Fenice had a long history of notable debuts and Callas virtually launched the bel canto revival there with an unexpected performance of *I puritani* in 1949. Zeffirelli had been attracted by the strong musical and visual appeal of *Alcina* and with no precedents to inhibit him he devised an extravagant baroque production staged as a court entertainment, with an on-stage 'audience' of royal guests. It was all very much in keeping with an auditorium widely regarded as one of the most beautiful in the world.

Rehearsals were intensive, and costumes still held together with safety pins on the opening night; Bonynge played the harpsichord on stage in eighteenth-century costume because Zeffirelli had been unable to persuade the Fenice's harpsichord player to do it. If in its concept it had nothing to do with what Handel intended — such as the inclusion, as a kind of party-piece, of 'Let the bright seraphim' set to an Italian text — no-one seemed any the wiser, and no-one was more surprised than Sutherland, sceptical from the outset, at the rapturous reception it was given. In an excess of enthusiasm for which the Venetians have a word — *fantasimo* — they tore down the garlands of pink carnations that festooned the auditorium and showered them onto the stage. But the final accolade from this city which had dubbed Callas *La Divina* came when they hailed Sutherland as *La Stupenda*.

Franco Abbiati in *Corriere della Sera* praised her technique and expressiveness, referring to her as a 'faultless artist'. Giuseppe Pugliese in *Il Gazzettino* recognized her as an artist of 'rare value', while Mario Messenis in *Venezia Notte* acknowledged her as one of the great singers of our time.

Sutherland followed *Alcina* with performances of *Lucia* in Palermo, which were greeted with 'violent enthusiasm', and in April 1960 she made her debut at the Opéra in Paris, a debut essential in establishing her European reputation, and where success would provide further confirmation of her international status. The French are nationalistically sceptical of any achievement that is not home grown, but Sutherland's portrayal of *Lucia* was already becoming a legend and the press, at least, were intrigued by this Australian prima donna who was placid and unassuming and who reputedly reserved her artistic temperament exclusively for the stage.

She had by now sung *Lucia* a score of times and was thoroughly at home in the part. She felt comfortable with the production, an almost exact replica of Covent Garden's, and secure because it was to be directed by Zeffirelli. She was not particularly disturbed by the incongruity of the chorus singing in French while the principals sang in Italian, and she was highly flattered to learn she was to use Fanny Heldy's famous dressing room, a privilege she shared with Renata Tebaldi, who was adored in Paris. Fanny Heldy, a Belgian soprano much loved at the Opéra, had been given the right to decide, on her retirement, who should use her dressing room thereafter. Its Louis XVI opulence had remained unaltered since she occupied it herself: the ceiling was a canopy of pink silk, the walls draped in blue, Persian carpets covered the floor and a glittering chandelier hung from the ceiling. It was a veritable oasis in the depressing backstage gloom, and a far cry from the functional austerity of Sutherland's dressing room at Covent Garden. She was greatly honoured to occupy it, especially as Madame Heldy had denied its use to Callas.

The Parisian audience welcomed Sutherland with unusual enthusiasm, although a large contingent of British opera-goers, bursting with pride, had been loudly shushed into silence when they had the audacity to applaud mid-scene. Such philistine behaviour was unheard of at the Opéra, but the ovation after the mad scene was nothing short of tumultuous. *Lucia di Lammermoor* was not a great favourite with the French, and some critics made no secret of this fact, but they marvelled at Sutherland's ability to create a dramatically convincing character from music of extreme virtuosity:

> If anyone had told me last week that I would listen again to *Lucia di Lammermoor* not only without a moment's boredom, but with the kind of emotion one feels when confronted with the greatest lyric works, I would not have believed them.
>
> Marc Pincherle, *Les Nouvelles Littéraires,* 5 May 1960

> The famous florid singing had nothing in common with the vocal acrobatics that this scene [the mad scene] used to be ... Sutherland's voice in all its purity was simply Lucia's language.
>
> Maurice Tassart, *Music and Musicians*, June 1960

In *Le Figaro*, Bernard Gavotty was not so much impressed by the quality of the voice, which he thought beautiful but not incomparable, as much as by her extraordinary ability to convey emotion. Sutherland had scored a personal success greater than any at the Opéra for a very long time. She was even paid the doubtful tribute of a visit from Elsa Maxwell, the international socialite and gossip columnist, renowned as a collector of the rich and famous. But when *France Soir* acclaimed her the equal of Callas and Tebaldi, and Jean Mistler in *L' Aurore* went so far as to say that as Lucia she was better than Callas, Sutherland's cup runneth over.

The revival of interest in the works of Rossini, Bellini and Donizetti was becoming a significant trend, and Sutherland made her first of many excursions into the operas of Bellini with Elvira in *I puritani* at Glyndebourne. For a presumptive leading exponent in the field of bel canto it was a perfect role. The opera was a great favourite with Bonynge and it had been Sutherland's singing of '*Qui la voce*' that so astounded Clive Carey, who thought of her as a dramatic soprano more suited to the heavier roles, and the audition panel at Covent Garden who had not known quite what to make of her.

I puritani was Bellini's last opera, commissioned for the Théâtre Italien in Paris by Rossini, who was the Director. It was a product of that most splendid period when the voice was all important and when it was customary to write for the special talents of a particular singer. Verdi's French biographer, Camille Bellaigue, described Bellini rather indelicately as the composer who thought of 'nothing but his singer's gullets', but in the case of *I puritani* Bellini had been promised a much respected quartet of gullets: Giulia Grisi (who created the role of Adalgisa in *Norma*), Giovanni Rubini (to Rossini's mind, incomparable), Luigi Lablache (Queen Victoria's singing teacher), and Antonio Tamburini (a great bel canto baritone). His librettist though was less ideal, for having fallen out with his favourite poet, Felice Romani, Bellini turned to the theatrically inexperienced Count Pepoli whose libretto was no match for the score.

At its première in 1835 the opera was received with almost hysterical enthusiasm and Bellini was called onto the stage even before the end of the performance. His peculiarly characteristic style was one of infinite tunefulness and *I puritani* contained a more prolific outpouring than most. He wrote dramatically strong recitative, and having an innate sense of theatre, knew how to build the work to appropriate climaxes so that every curtain was guaranteed to bring the house down. He died in the same year, leaving a legacy of 11 essentially romantic, almost always tragic operas.

The role of Elvira required a large voice to ride the ensembles and cope with strong competition from tenor, baritone and bass, a solid and flexible middle register with a low range as well as a coloratura top, staggering breath control and great beauty of tone. Sutherland fulfilled these requirements with a technique that was practically flawless, singing with all the agility and accuracy of the bel canto tradition, moving the house to a cheering, stamping ovation. Peter Gellhorn thought it was her finest performance to date, and she had done nothing to disillusion Rosenthal of the opinion she was without equal in this field:

> Joan Sutherland's performance of this celebrated cabaletta ('*Vien diletto*') was perhaps the most lovely piece of vocalism of the whole evening, though her exquisite singing and shaping of the top line in the Act I finale '*Ah! vieni, t'affreta, o Arturo*', still rings in my ears. Perhaps the slow section of the mad scene was overcharged with emotion, but on the whole the ease and beauty with which she invested most of her music was sheer enchantment. The tall soprano looked and moved well, and as the season progressed, and she got well

into the skin of the role, her whole interpetation became more and more assured.

> Harold Rosenthal, *Opera Magazine*, August 1960

Many of the critics, however, were inclined to dismiss the opera itself as too trivial and insubstantial to warrant a production at all. Nevertheless she was to have ample opportunity to prove otherwise, for Elvira, along with Lucia, was to become one of her most memorable characterizations. Sutherland also appeared at the Festival as Donna Anna in *Don Giovanni*, an opera the critics found infinitely more satisfying.

La sonnambula, like *I puritani*, is a classic bel canto work, and David Webster's invitation to sing Amina at Covent Garden had been an irresistible one. The role had been created by Giuditta Pasta; Giulia Grisi and Maria Malibran performed it; Emma Albani and Adelina Patti made their London debuts as Amina, and Jenny Lind sang it 98 times in her short career. In recent years Callas had had a notable success and obviously Bonynge wanted Sutherland's name added to that distinguished list. It is a gentle, pastoral opera loaded with romanticism and beautiful melodies and one in which, for once, everyone lives happily ever after. It was Bellini's seventh opera, and his librettist was Felice Romani. He wrote it in two weeks, largely by virtue of using some music written for a discarded work, and it was premièred with great success at the Teatro Carcano, Milan in 1831 with Pasta, Rubini and Luchiani Mariani. Later the same year it was performed in London and Paris, and in 1833 it was presented at Drury Lane — in English — with Maria Malibran as Amina. It was here that Bellini heard her for the first time, and he worshipped her from that day. Its popularity remained almost to the end of the century, when it faded from the repertoire with the changing taste in operatic fashion, and its last performance at Covent Garden was in 1909 with Luisa Tetrazzini.

The performance on 19 October 1960 was a Royal Gala for the State Visit of the King and Queen of Nepal. As befitted the occasion it was a new production and Sutherland rose to it with a performance as inspired as the first *Lucia*. Two days later, however, when she made her debut before the public and the critics, she had a cold, a sore throat and very little voice. To cancel a performance, especially one such as this — the official opening of the season, with the house sold out on Sutherland's reputation, was unthinkable. Yet with the ill-fated *La traviata* not forgotten, there was a sense of *déjà vu* about the situation. Sutherland knew there was no understudy and there was no question of letting Webster down. He had stuck his neck out on her behalf many

times and she felt a tremendous sense of obligation for his un-
wavering support — support without which she would not now
have the honour of opening the new season in a new production.
The show had to go on, an unpalatable fact she had learned very
early in her career.

David Webster always accepted the responsibility for making
announcements himself, however displeasing they might be,
and to groans from the audience he explained that although
Miss Sutherland had a very bad cold, she would sing because
no understudy was available. Having craved their indulgence
Sutherland embarked on the task of coaxing her ailing voice
through a long and difficult performance. It improved as the
evening wore on, but her indisposition had a dampening effect on
her colleagues; in the pit Serafin, with a rather too sympathetic
baton, allowed the tempo to drag, and many people were seen to
leave before the final curtain.

As a show-piece for Sutherland, the opera was a dismal failure. Mercifully the critics reserved judgement for later performances, realizing that the role was well within her capability, but
they were unable to resist commenting that without an outstanding soprano on top form the opera was hardly worth performing
at all. Yet appreciation for the genre was growing almost in spite
of the critics, many of whom made no secret of the fact that they
preferred Wagner to Bellini, referring to the former with awed
reverence and dismissing the latter for the triviality of the
story and the banality of the music. Such a view was a cross
Sutherland and Bonynge would learn to bear.

Sutherland's debuts in San Francisco, Chicago, New York and
Milan were now firmly in her diary and her American debut with
the Dallas Civic Opera as Alcina and Donna Anna followed
closely on her final performance of *La sonnambula* in London.
She had half expected a cultural hick town which might not be
ready for Zeffirelli's highly individual production of an unfamiliar
Handel opera. But since its creation in 1957 the Dallas Civic
Opera had earned a reputation for artistic achievement and starry
casts under the Musical Director, Nicola Rescigno. *Alcina*,
borrowed from the Fenice and performed in the vast State Fair
Music Hall, continued this trend. The critics marvelled at the
purity of Sutherland's technique and total command of her vocal
resources, describing a voice of exquisite beauty, cool pianissimo
and translucent top notes; and there was nothing unsophisticated
about the appreciation of an audience as warm and enthusiastic as
any Sutherland had experienced.

Allowing for rest and rehearsal they were able to accept just a fraction of the lavish hospitality only Americans can offer. She was presented with an illuminated scroll making her an honorary citizen of Dallas, and they visited Lily Pons, ablaze with emeralds even at teatime. Sutherland was enchanted. They left Dallas loaded with gifts showered upon them for Adam.

On her return she sang Amina again at Covent Garden, and Noël Goodwin, who had refrained from comment with regard to the unfortunate first night other than to say it should have been cancelled, was concerned on this occasion by the way Sutherland 'broke up some of the phrases apparently for dramatic effect, instead of concentrating on shaping the pure line of melody'. This point echoes what Philip Hope-Wallace had written in *Opera Magazine* of a performance of *Lucia* in July 1959: 'I hope she will not strain too much after expressiveness at the expense of sheer limpid singing which is the essence of *Lucia*.' This is interesting, for in years to come Sutherland was to be criticized frequently for never sacrificing the vocal line for the sake of expression, and compared unfavourably with Callas, who constantly did.

In December 1960 she gave her first solo concert at the Albert Hall, but notwithstanding the effortless brilliance of much of her singing in four great arias, Andrew Porter was conscious of the same difficulty with regard to shaping a relatively simple cantilena:

> This is not carping. There is no-one like Miss Sutherland today; she is stupendous, superb; and for that matter the old critics always had some little reservations about their favourites. Yet one feels convinced that if Miss Sutherland could listen attentively to Galli-Curci, Tetrazzini and Melba (artists whom in some respects she already surpasses) she could be greater still. And so I for one won't be entirely happy until she gets it.

> *Financial Times*, 13 December 1960

Desmond Shawe-Taylor had given similar advice in a lengthy dissertation rather reminiscent of a school report at the time of her debut in *La traviata*, but Sutherland felt that she learnt far more from an awareness of her own faults, of which Bonynge, if anything, was hypercritical. To try to learn the technique of singing by listening to the recordings of others was a highly risky business. One would be inclined to copy not only the virtues, but also, albeit unconsciously, the faults and mannerisms as well. To listen to old recordings for a proper understanding of certain performing traditions was a different matter. She had cut her teeth on those of Galli-Curci, Tetrazzini and Melba, while

Bonynge in his tireless research into neglected music had accumu-
lated a vast collection of ornamentations and embellishments
going back much further to Malibran, Pasta and Grisi. He had
acquired an original score of *I puritani* with the variations Bellini
had written for his beloved Malibran, complete with bravura
finale, and it was a great thrill to discover that this final cabaletta
fitted Sutherland like a glove.

Vocal compatibility, however, was the exception rather than
the rule, for such variations illustrated to an amazing degree the
peculiarly personal nature of their composition. Studying them
Sutherland often found that they were not comfortable for her
either emotionally or vocally. Together therefore they rearranged
and adapted some of these passages in such a way as to make
them more suitable for her voice.

Elvira was now a role as familiar to her as Lucia, and it was as
Elvira that she made her debut at the Teatro Liceo in Barcelona
on 30 December, but she arrived with a cold and by the opening
night the cold had become bronchitis. When she complained of
the difficulty she was having breathing, her dresser, Assun, produced a little replica of the Madonna of Montserrat, put in front
of it a rose from one of the bouquets that filled the dressing room,
and assured Sutherland that if she were to kiss it all would be
well. Willing to try anything, Sutherland kissed the statue and
unbelieveably had no further trouble with her breathing. The
next day she took a huge bunch of flowers to the real Madonna,
and Assun gave her the replica to keep. Sutherland was not by
nature superstitious, but she became unusually attached to the
ritual of the Madonna. Henceforward the statuette and a red rose
invariably stood before her on the dressing table.

She was such a success in Barcelona that the final performance
was turned into a gala in her honour; she sang the whole of *I
puritani*, and, knee-deep in flowers, '*Ah, non giunge*' by way of
an encore in true prima donna fashion. From there she went to
Sicily, where Bellini was born, to sing Elvira in Palermo and treat
her audience to Malibran's final cabaletta. It was probably being
heard for the first time in public, for Malibran had died exactly a
year after Bellini at the tragically early age of 28 without singing
Elvira. The audience went wild with delight:

> It was a happy addition, giving new symmetry to the finale,
> and proving also to be a very fine piece of music. Miss
> Sutherland sang it with panache and the opera ended in a
> blaze of glory.

William Weaver, *Opera Magazine*, February 1961

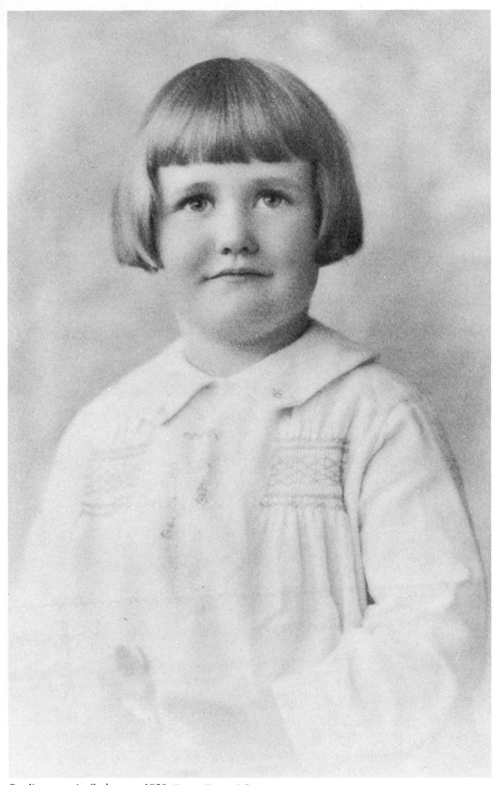

Studio portrait, Sydney, c.1930. Decca Record Company

TOP LEFT *Winner of the Mobil Quest in 1950. Joan receives congratulations from runners-up David Allen and William Smith.*

TOP RIGHT *A student performance of Euripides' play* Iphigenia in Tauris *at The Royal College of Music, 1951, with Joan as one of the Greek Chorus.*

BELOW Norma *at Covent Garden, 1952, with Joan as Clotilde and Maria Callas making her London debut as Norma.* Roy Round

TOP LEFT *The proud mother: Joan with Adam, February 1956.*

TOP RIGHT *In 1956 Joan was the first English soprano to sing the Countess in* Le nozze di Figaro *at Glyndebourne.* Guy Gravett

BELOW *Working at home with Richard, c. 1959.*

Sutherland sings the title role of Lucia di Lammermoor *at Covent Garden for the first time, February 1959.* The Photo Source

ABOVE *Rehearsing* Lucia *with Zeffirelli, Covent Garden, 1959.* Express Newspapers

BELOW *Sutherland takes a curtain call after her Italian debut in* Alcina *at La Fenice in 1960, and is hailed as* La Stupenda. The Photo Source

TOP LEFT *With Guiseppe Modesti in* I puritani *at Glyndebourne, 1960.* Guy Gravett

TOP RIGHT *With Gianni Raimondi in* Lucia di Lammermoor *at La Scala, 1964.* La Scala

BELOW Beatrice di Tenda *with Dino Dondi as Filippo, La Scala, 1961.* La Scala

ABOVE *Zeffirelli's production of* I puritani *at Covent Garden, 1964.* Houston Rogers, Theatre Museum, London

BELOW *A new production of* Lucia di Lammermoor *opens the season at the Metropolitan in October 1964.* Louis Mélançon, New York

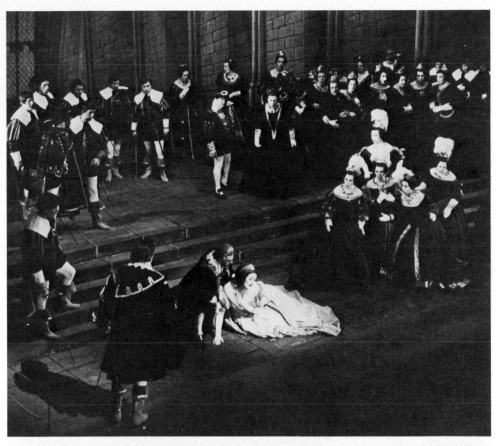

ABOVE LEFT *A triumphant homecoming. The last performance of* La sonnambula, *Melbourne, 1965.* The Photo Source

ABOVE RIGHT La fille du régiment *with Pavarotti at Covent Garden, 1966.* Anthony Crickmay

RIGHT Norma *with Marilyn Horne at Covent Garden, 1967.* Reg Wilson

Onward then to sing Lucia in Venice, the scene of her stupendous triumph in *Alcina,* and at the beginning of February 1961 she embarked on a recital tour of the United States with Bonynge as her accompanist, which meant missing Adam's fifth birthday. Over the years she was to miss a great many of them and she is amazed that he grew up without bearing a grudge. Anxious to see as much of him as possible they had tried the experiment of taking him everywhere with them, but he was becoming spoilt and it did him no good to be constantly told what clever parents he had. Now he had a young Swiss nanny, Ruthli Brendle, who was to become a permanent member of the Bonynge household and far stricter with Adam than Sutherland would ever be.

When Ailsa returned to Australia Mrs Sutherland and Auntie Blos, now also in England, took over her flat in Ladbroke Grove, but it had not proved a very salubrious area for two elderly ladies living alone. They now all lived under the same roof in Cornwall Gardens, Kensington, and for Adam, who may have lacked the companionship of other children in pre-school days, there was no lack of emotional security. While Sutherland missed him dreadfully, she left him in the knowledge that he enjoyed the care and attention of Ruthli, a loving grandmother and an adoring great-aunt.

It was while rehearsing for a concert performance of *Beatrice di Tenda* in New York Town Hall that Sutherland heard that her mother had died in London. The news was doubly shattering because Mrs Sutherland had not been ill. In fact the previous evening she had dined with Phyllis and Dorothy, who still lived in Pembridge Crescent, and had been full of her plans to go to Milan for Sutherland's debut at La Scala in April. It was suggested the concert should be cancelled and a flight arranged for her to fly home for the funeral. Shocked and helpless with all the miles separating them she telephoned Auntie Blos, who urged her to continue with the concert as her mother would have wished. So rather than disappoint all the people who had bought tickets for this eagerly awaited New York debut, she went out and sang. It had been a distressing decision to make, but choked with emotion and occasionally with tears in her eyes, Sutherland gave a remarkable performance of an opera never before heard in America. Afterwards, it seemed all the city's operatic intelligentsia crowded backstage to congratulate her. Only Noël Coward, aware of the unusual circumstances in which she sang, restrained his enthusiasm, later explaining in his own inimitable way: 'I enjoyed it so much, I refrained from coming round to your dressing room to tell you so.'

She had negotiated the florid passages of Bellini's opera with stunning ease and unfailing precision, and Harold Schonberg, the music critic of the *New York Times*, referred to her as 'a great singer ... supreme singer':

It is a beautifully coloured voice, one that ascends effortlessly to the E in alt and most likely beyond. Where most sopranos have trouble with B flats and Cs, Miss Sutherland is at her most secure above the staff. And withal she preserved the colour, warmth and style. In concerted numbers her voice soars above the ensemble without ever becoming hard or jagged. She is a supreme technician ... She phrases like an artist, and she never tries to take centre stage in the ensemble numbers. She had numerous ways of changing the colour of her voice, in accordance with the dramatic and stylistic needs of the moment, and she does not hesitate to do so ... in somewhat altering the coloratura she follows precedent.

Harold Schonberg, *New York Times*, 22 February 1961

There had been such a demand for tickets that two further performances were arranged in the much larger more prestigious Carnegie Hall. The concerts were also memorable for bringing Sutherland and Marilyn Horne together for the first time. The role of Agnese was a big break for Horne who had dubbed the singing voice of Dorothy Dandridge in the film *Carmen Jones* and served a rigorous operatic apprenticeship in Germany. Coached by her husband, Henry Lewis, she had readily taken up the bel canto challenge, soon to embrace the genre with wholehearted commitment.

Beatrice di Tenda was also to provide Sutherland with the vehicle for her debut at the shrine of Italian opera, La Scala, where Bellini's penultimate opera had not been heard for more than a century. The subject was originally Dumas' *Christina di Stockholm*, and the libretto by Romani was well underway when Bellini, inspired by a ballet called *Beatrice di Tenda*, abandoned Christina. This change of heart caused a permanent rift between Bellini and Romani who was now under some pressure to complete the libretto in time for the première. Not surprisingly it was delayed for a month and the first performance at the Fenice in 1833, with Pasta in the title role, received only a lukewarm reception. *Beatrice* never became really popular and by the mid-1840s had fallen from performance altogether, not to be seen again for almost a century. The most recent revival had been in Palermo under the baton of Vittorio Gui, who was to conduct at La Scala for Sutherland's debut.

There was, however, a note of discord, for Bonynge and Gui had not been able to reach an agreement about the version of the score to be used. The essence of the problem was the final cabaletta for Beatrice as she goes to her death. Bellini had scored this bravura finale for Pasta, although he later toyed with the idea of replacing it with a soprano-tenor duet of which he had drafted the outline. It was this amended version, with his own orchestration, that Gui had used in Palermo and with which he now hoped Sutherland would comply. Bonynge, however, did not feel that the duet was sufficiently Bellinian in style, and besides, in Sutherland's view the cabaletta, '*Ah, la morte a cui m'apresso*', was dramatically and musically essential to her characterization of Beatrice. To cut this would completely alter her conception of the wronged and outraged woman going defiantly to her death.

It was a difficulty incapable of compromise so Gui was replaced by Antonino Votto, and *Beatrice* by a rather conventional static production of *Lucia di Lammermoor*. The sets, not a patch on Covent Garden's, were old and shabby, Sutherland's costume was cleaned because the Italians had no stomach for Arturo's blood, and since the spotlight operator was unable to keep her in his beam as she darted around the stage in the mad scene it soon became apparent that she would have to sing it standing still. Sutherland had been warned that La Scala audiences, reputedly some of the most critical in the world, had a tendency to 'sit on their hands' and were more than capable of whistling off the stage a singer who failed to come up to expectations. At the dress rehearsal there was no wild enthusiasm from the scanty audience of singers, among them, Renato Scotto. However, Sutherland did not find the apparent coolness unduly depressing for other signs were encouraging. The orchestra applauded after the mad scene — a rare occurrence — and the Director not only arranged for her to sing Beatrice the following month with Antonino Votto, and the cabaletta intact, but had already approached her about singing again next season.

On the first night the audience did everything but sit on their hands. They cheered and applauded the first aria and thereafter took every opportunity to demonstrate their enthusiasm. At the end of the performance pink carnations torn from the garlands decorating the auditorium showered onto the stage as she took numerous curtain calls. The critic of *L'Avanti* lost count of the number — there were in fact 30 — during a 15-minute ovation, and in a restaurant where she dined later that night everyone rose to cheer her as she came in. Noël Goodwin's conviction that she could become as great as Callas was becoming a reality:

Here is a style of singing artistry which few singers learn to master today. She has deepened her study of the role of Lucia and her voice soars with tremendous ease and fluency, but with greater colour and depth of personality now ... Miss Sutherland would be the last to suggest that she is in the same class as Callas when it comes to dramatic acting, but she is certainly above her in sheer beauty of voice.

Noël Goodwin, *Daily Express*, 15 May 1961

Il Giorno described her as 'a great singer ... an ideal Lucia'. She had triumphed in Milan, even to the extent of winning over the Callas and Tebaldi partisans, who, rumour had it, threatened to break up the performance.

Within days of the final *Lucia*, rehearsals began for the new production of *Beatrice*, but the luckless opera was again postponed when the Queen paid an official visit to La Scala. In the limited time available she was entertained by an *ad hoc* performance of the sextet from *Lucia* against a back-drop of *I puritani*, those for *Lucia* being too old to do honour to the occasion, and the curtain at last went up on *Beatrice di Tenda* on 10 May. Once again Andrew Porter was eloquent in praise of Sutherland and appreciative of the opera:

I have never before heard her sing out so fully, so clearly, so generously. Her tendency to fidget with minutiae within a phrase, to the extent of spoiling the line of the whole, had disappeared. It was as if the great house had inspired her to a grander manner than ever before. It was effortlessly brilliant and surpassingly beautiful ... A vein of pure, clear melodic inspiration that I found irresistible, and beside this a power of dramatic ensemble explored in the finale of *Norma* and here further developed. For this reason the adventures of the unhappy Duchess cannot be dismissed — as by most of my colleagues they seem to have been — as trivialities. The music is too beautiful.

Financial Times, 16 May 1961

Sutherland's entourage in the meantime had expanded to include Anne Roughley. Affectionately known as Weenie, she was the younger sister of Richard's mother, and he first approached her with the idea of coming to work with them as Sutherland's personal secretary at the end of 1960. Only after some months of indecision did she agree to give it a trial run. Weenie had served with the Royal Australian Navy during the war, intercepting radio messages from Japanese submarines. After the war she became a fully qualified nursing sister, but recently, after a severe bout of Asian flu compounded the damage done by infantile diphtheria, she had been unable to continue her nursing career. Her new job had no precisely defined terms of reference, and it was soon clear that it would be no rest cure. Among her assets were a lively personality, a dry sense of humour, and ability to type — essential with the volume of mail that followed them everywhere — and a nonchalant versatility with regard to what she was driving and on which side of the road she was driving it. She acquired as she went along an aptitude for sifting the wheat from the chaff, both on the end of the telephone and at the stage door. She was afraid of no-one and stood in awe of no-one.

Weenie had not met Sutherland before and from what she had heard did not expect to find that she had the temperament of the archetypal prima donna. It came therefore as something of a shock when three weeks after her arrival she witnessed a spectacular Sutherland 'walk-out' in Venice.

Sutherland's overwhelming success in Italy had prompted the management of the Fenice to invite her to appear in a special gala performance of *La sonnambula*. The performance was scheduled only a few days after her final *Beatrice* in Milan on 21 May, and Sutherland had only been persuaded to accept by the assurance that the production would be firmly focused upon her. This meant that she would be able to sing Amina exactly as she was accustomed to singing it with Serafin. Unfortunately, when she arrived for the first rehearsal, the Director, Dr Floris Ammannatti, was not there to see his assurances honoured. The conductor for this gala performance was Nello Santi who had not come critically unscathed out of Sutherland's first performances of *La traviata*, and who had also been adversely criticized for his indifferent conducting of her first recital record. It soon became obvious that his conducting of *La sonnambula* was every bit as eccentric, and he made no bones of the fact that he considered Bellini's music 'old-fashioned'. When Sutherland asked if he would please conduct at the tempo to which she was used he refused to defer to her in any way. Santi had already had an altercation with the chorus prompting a mass exodus, and in spite of Sutherland's pleading, his obstinate and autocratic attitude effectively ruled out all attempts at a compromise.

Serafin observed that tempo was a matter for mutual agreement between singer and conductor — 'Whatever can be managed best', but while Sutherland tried desperately to come to terms with Santi's excessively slow tempo it interferred with her breathing and upset her phrasing. When Santi eventually suggested that she did not want to rehearse but only wanted the money, Sutherland could take no more. With 24 hours before curtain-up she walked out, her patience and good nature stretched to the limit, unmoved by threats to sue for 'moral and material damages'.

Sutherland returned to London on the first available flight from Milan, realizing as she fought her way through the bevy of reporters to the front door of Cornwall Gardens that although it was only a storm in a teacup, the press, only too anxious to depict her as another capricious prima donna, would stir it into something much more sensational, for such is the stuff of which a news story is made. The 'walk-out' was international news. She was offered time on radio and television to explain her case, but it was no-one's business but hers and she refused. Precious little had stopped the show going on since she started on the professional road in 1952: not colds, sore throats nor sinusitis; not abscessed ears, swollen legs nor back pain; not even her mother's death. If people were not prepared to make allowances for this one occasion, it was too bad. Thus, unsupported by the interviews she declined to give, assorted versions of the facts appeared in the popular press. Dr Ammannatti expressed his regret that the incident 'deprived La Fenice theatre of a singer for whom the Venetian public had affection and whom our theatre esteems', and expressed the hope that 'the controversy with Miss Sutherland could be solved in a friendly and honourable mannner to our mutual satisfaction and the advantage of opera'. Honour was satisfied by a medical certificate indicating blood clots in the antrums caused by a fall in the bath in Milan when she had knocked her head and bruised her eye. Her doctor advised several days rest and a little later a magnificent leather make-up case arrived from Dr Ammannatti with a letter inviting her to sing at the Fenice the following season. Santi shrugged it all off as a case of nerves and overwork on Sutherland's part.

The incident caused Sutherland much distress. Though she might privately acknowledge that this was the kind of behaviour often associated with a prima donna, it was not behaviour which came easily to her. She had not forgotten that the Fenice introduced her to Italy in the production of *Alcina*, earning her the soubriquet *La Stupenda*, but in spite of every effort on both sides, schedules conflicted and she was never to sing at the Fenice again.

Back on home territory, singing *Lucia* at Covent Garden, conducted by John Pritchard, an old and trusted friend, Sutherland anticipated no problems. But she could not have foreseen the prolonged applause following the sextet at the second of three performances which moved Pritchard to turn back the pages and play it again! An apt tribute perhaps to Nellie Melba to whose centenary this performance was dedicated, but it was an incident not without precedent, for Pritchard had also encored the last verse of the '*Mira o Norma*' duet with Callas and Stignani in 1957. There followed an extended interval while Sutherland recovered her vocal resources for the mad scene, and the next day it was publicly announced she had been awarded the CBE in the Queen's Birthday Honours List.

There followed a return visit to Paris for more *Lucias* and after the first of them Sutherland discovered to her dismay that she and Bonynge had committed each other to separate supper engagements: one with Elsa Maxwell and the other with Geraldine Souvaine, the presenter of the Texaco sponsored broadcasts from the Metropolitan Opera House. To offend either was out of the question, and it was not possible to join forces since Maxwell and Souvaine were not on the most amiable terms. Instead, Sutherland, Weenie and Russell Braddon had supper with Elsa Maxwell and later they joined Bonynge for a second supper with Geraldine Souvaine at a Paris nightclub. A far cry from the days when she disdained the use of a taxi in favour of the tube, and to indulge in a modest meal in a modest restaurant was 'splashing out a bit'. This was an example of the kind of social extravagance that could have become part and parcel of her life, but she had no wish to experience more than a fleeting acquaintance with the *beau monde* that Elsa Maxwell epitomized.

They left Paris at the end of June 1961 to spend time in a villa they had leased in Switzerland which had a magnificent view across Lake Maggiore. This was the first time such a break had presented itself since the middle of 1959 when her operation obliged her to rest, and it was not to be often repeated in the years to follow. As a base it was particularly convenient, situated close to the Italian border and an easily commutable distance from Milan and other European opera houses. It also made it possible for Sutherland to spend less time in the damp climate of England which was so harmful to her sinuses and benefit from cleaner, fresher air and more sunshine.

The villa rapidly filled with all the guests who had been casually invited to come and stay, and Ruthli, engaged to look after the infant Adam, complained about the amount of cooking to be done. Sutherland, in her domestic element, pottered around re-arranging furniture and hanging pictures, of which there were now a vast number since Richard's passion for collecting had become an obsession. Her sewing-machine hummed as she stitched curtains and bedspreads designed by a budding Swiss couturier, Heinz Weber Riva. Artistically draped in yards of silk, Sutherland sat for the first of the many portraits to be painted of her, and also for her dentist, Henry Pitt-Roche, a talented sculptor, in his spare time. She played with Adam as she contemplated his future education, and she worked with Richard on *Rigoletto* and *Lucia* which she was shortly to record in Rome.

After her success in *Lucia* when Walter Legge had promised her an exclusive recording contract with EMI, she had recorded Donna Anna in *Don Giovanni*, but with Callas in the same stable with a similar repertoire, EMI had second thoughts about a long-term contract with Sutherland. She was by now familiar with many of Decca's personnel and the engineers were coming to grips with the problems of capturing the full beauty of her voice, having recorded several recitals of operatic arias. When Decca at last recognized her potential and signed her up on an exclusive basis there was no reluctance on Sutherland's part.

En route to Rome they stayed in Franco Zeffirelli's holiday home which was without water, and arrived at his apartment in Rome where there was neither gas nor electricity. At the recording studio in the Academia Nazionale di Santa Cecilia the heat was oppressive and the sessions heavy-going. Sutherland was feeling unwell, but she would not cancel the recordings, and to show she bore no ill-will insisted on having dinner with Dr Ammannatti. She managed several takes of '*Caro nome*' before being confined to bed with a temperature of 101 degrees Fahrenheit; she did not take kindly to a blanket bath and what the doctor prescribed made Weenie wonder if he knew where the tonsils were.

Four days later she was back behind the microphones with a lot of ground to make up and anxious to do her big scene with Cornel MacNeil early in the session while she was still fresh. But MacNeil, who had had all the time in the world to do his heavy bits while Sutherland had been indisposed, wanted to do it in the evening. Fearful of another confrontation Sutherland suggested that they split the difference — half in the afternoon, half in the evening, but her sense of humour failed her when he flippantly remarked that they had fought their way through fairly well. Sutherland was beginning to learn that not all prima donnas were women.

The sessions for *Lucia* followed immediately. Sutherland was far from rested and her sinuses were 'gluggy', but with Pritchard conducting, Renato Cioni (who had sung the Duke in *Rigoletto*) more at ease as Edgardo, and Robert Merrill as Enrico regaling them with funny stories, the atmosphere was altogether more relaxed. Sutherland managed a perfect first take of the mad scene, and afterwards one member of the orchestra was so carried away that he jumped to his feet and shouted '*Brava*' before the red light went out. 'That was wonderful,' called Decca's Recording Director, Christopher Raeburn, over the public address system — which almost invariably meant another take. So predictable had it become that on one occasion his disembodied 'That was wonderful', was finished by someone in the gallery: 'I'll just come out.' He more than earned his credit in some record booklets for non-singing roles under the pseudonym Omar Godknow. As an appendix to *Lucia*, Sutherland also recorded the recitative and aria '*Ancor non giunse ... perchè non ho del vento*', with which Fanny Persiani had replaced Lucia's opening aria.

Back in London, Sutherland paid her routine visit to Ivor Griffiths and then went straight to Kingsway Hall to begin recording *Messiah* with Sir Adrian Boult. It was not Sutherland's first commercial confrontation with the work: soon after her success as Lucia, RCA had attempted to get a recording off the ground with Sutherland singing the soprano part and conducted by Sir Thomas Beecham, who claimed never to have heard of her. Their interpretations of the music were poles apart and before long Beecham decided he could not abide Sutherland at any price. Sutherland did not resist and was replaced by Jennifer Vyvyan. Even under Sir Adrian Boult, however, Sutherland's stylistic approach, especially with regard to the florid decoration, was not in keeping with that of her fellow soloists. Later Boult observed that perhaps 'Mad Scenes from Messiah' would have been a more apt title.

It was some years before Sutherland and Bonynge could tackle the work in their own way. Shorn of the enormous orchestral and choral forces usually associated with this popular oratorio, Bonynge's carefully researched version took on a lighter dimension more characteristic of performances in Handel's day. Already this chamber version was becoming a viable and acceptable alternative.

Hardly had the tapes stopped turning before Sutherland set off for Edinburgh in September for her second Festival season there. She had a crowded schedule, including the opening of a garden fête, several recordings for the BBC, a concert and five performances of *Lucia di Lammermoor*, for which there had been a great clamour for tickets. They stayed in a rented house in Edinburgh, and since they were not far from the Lammermoor Hills, Sutherland, escorted by the Chief Constable, Willie Merrilees, who had taken her under his wing, took a sentimental journey to Baldoon, where Janet Dalrymple, believed to be the prototype Lucia, had died just a month after marrying David Dunbar in 1669.

She proved a great success at the garden fête at a hospital for the physically handicapped, but her ears were troubling her again and the opening performance of *Lucia* was far from being one of her best. Of the second performance Harold Rosenthal noted in *Opera Magazine*: 'Those who were hearing her for the first time could not have been anything but pleased, for Miss Sutherland even below her top level is so much better than most singers at their best.'

As the concert in the Usher Hall approached, however, Sutherland was unusually apprehensive; she was feeling very much under par, and the little Madonna was receiving special attention. Even Weenie, passing the cathedral and bearing in mind that Sutherland's ancestors were Scots, went in and sent up a prayer. It must have paid dividends for Rosenthal thought she had never sung more beautifully.

Sutherland was enjoying the company of the Chief Constable, who had been a spy-catcher during the war. He took great pleasure in handing out photographs of himself in various disguises, along with buttons from the Earl of Dalkeith's coat. She wondered if, like the shroud, there were enough buttons to circle the globe, but he called her 'lassie' and drives in the police car were infinitely more comfortable than Richard's latest acquisition — a Jaguar coupé which played havoc with Sutherland's back. Merrilees had also given them tickets for the Tattoo, which had been sold out for months; a bit of light relief, however, for which she was to pay dearly, for the night was cold. She recorded a Celebrity Recital with Gerald Moore for BBC Television and arias from *La traviata* and *Alcina* for a special Festival transmission. The results were magnificent, which was something of a miracle for she had abscesses in both ears, causing her to cancel her last two performances of *Lucia*. Weenie fended off the press and as soon as Sutherland was able to travel the Chief Constable came to the rescue with a police car to take her to the airport and right across the tarmac to the waiting plane.

A week later, pumped full of penicillin, she set off for America to pick up from Anna Moffo in a single performance of *Lucia* at War Memorial Opera House, San Francisco. The audience gave her a warm reception, although Bonynge had been less than polite with regard to the conducting of Francesco Molinari-Pradelli, and had been heard hissing '*Porco, Porco*' from the stage box. Molinari-Pradelli had also been engaged to conduct for her debut at the Metropolitan, so it was as well that the incompatibility was apparent at this stage while there was still time to engage another conductor with whom they could establish a more satisfactory working relationship.

For the next seven weeks Sutherland and Bonynge zigzagged across America on a 12,000 mile tour, giving recitals and concerts and further performances of *Lucia* in Chicago, Dallas, San Diego and Los Angeles. Their recitals were enthusiastically welcomed in places where it was not practical to mount a full-scale opera or assemble an orchestra for a concert. Their repertoire was popular, although it was the operatic arias, preferably with coloratura, and songs such as '*Parla*' and 'Lo hear the gentle lark' — in fact the higher, faster and brighter the better — which roused audiences to a frenzy. On one occasion, however, the audience had registered polite disappointment at the lack of vocal fireworks in the printed programme, and to compensate Sutherland had sung the whole of the mad scene from *Lucia*.

Sutherland and Bonynge were developing a considerable presence on the platform together and it added greatly to her peace of mind to have him beside her, so finely tuned to her idiosyncrasies that he was able to bail her out of almost any difficulty.

At a concert in New York she was cheered to the echo by a capacity audience for her stunning performance of three Handel arias. To an equally enthusiastic audience she made her debut in *Lucia* at the Chicago Lyric Opera with Carlo Bergonzi as Edgardo, but on this occasion the excitement of the audience was not matched by the critics, and the press notices were disappointing:

> ... the most creamily sung *Lucia di Lammermoor* the company has yet offered the Donizetti fans ... Joan Sutherland's Lucy, while stylized and over-studied to the point of emotional remoteness was a musical achievement not to be denied.
> Don Hanahan, *Chicago Daily News*, 16 October 1961

> Miss Sutherland was Miss Sutherland. No actress, no singer to grip the imagination, fire the heart or excite the ultimate tribute. But again, after a sluggish first act, a mad scene with some good singing, including that liquid trill.
> Claudia Cassidy, *Chicago Tribune*, 19 October 1961

Claudia Cassidy, however, had become a thorn in the side of many artists appearing in Chicago, for she rarely had a good word to say about anyone.

Having already been the proud promoters of her American

debut in 1960, Dallas now presented Sutherland as Lucia with Renato Cioni as Edgardo, and 20-year-old Placido Domingo as the unloved husband, Arturo. The following year he sang Edgardo to Lily Pons' last Lucia in Fort Worth.

In Dallas she proved once more that she was the technical phenomenon of the day, but to Terry McEwen, their long-time friend and recording manager, Sutherland's singing seemed more than a little below par. With some concern he wondered if this was a continuing trend or merely a passing phase, but Bonynge's firm assurance that it was the side effects of the antibiotics and a disturbed physiological rhythm put his mind at rest.

With his uncanny instinct for the human voice Bonynge had guided her career this far with an unerring sense of judgement, and he was convinced that, like her mother, she would still be singing like an angel when she was 70. Yet it was becoming increasingly clear that she was over-committing herself. There had been occasions when Richard made her refuse the most attractive offers, telling her that she was not yet ready for them. She had worried about missed opportunities, protesting that the offers would not be repeated, and he had urged her to bide her time and learn her roles properly: 'They will ask you to sing in every opera house in the world.'

Now international status had brought invitations flooding in for years ahead, and, anxious to consolidate her reputation and prove it was not based on *Lucia* alone, she had accepted a particularly gruelling schedule already extending well into 1964. She had now, in November 1961, reached that all-important milestone in her career: her debut at the Metropolitan Opera House in New York, although for some time the debut had hung in the balance because of the labour dispute that dominated the Metropolitan in the summer of 1961. The management were in conflict with the Musicians' Union and in August Rudolf Bing had cancelled the 1961/62 season, releasing artists from their contracts. This enabled them to undertake engagements elsewhere, and by the middle of the month many of them had done so. Fortunately Sutherland was not among them, for with the intervention of the Secretary of Labor, Arthur Goldberg, a pay award was negotiated which satisfied the unions and saved the season.

A brief respite from her heavy programme might have been welcomed, but to have denied Sutherland her debut at this time might also have cheated her of the only opportunity to sing at the 'old' Metropolitan, already on borrowed time since the projected opening of the new building in the Lincoln Centre had been set for the summer of 1963. Architecturally tarnished but with its glorious tradition still gleaming brightly, to Sutherland the old house was the very essence of the Met. A sense of operatic history far outweighed its shabbiness and to have made her debut in a modern counterpart would not have been the same at all. Melba and Marjorie Lawrence had trodden the famous boards and it was no mean achievement to follow in their respected footsteps.

Lucia di Lammermoor was not a novelty to the Metropolitan. Hardly a season had passed without it since 1884 with no shortage of good Lucias, and there were some reservations about the need for another. Moreover union strife had done nothing to mitigate the financial situation, dependent on private benefactors, and there was no possibility of offering the new star a new production. There was undoubtedly a strong case to be made for replacing the production, for it was one of the oldest still in service at the Met, though not as old as Covent Garden's *La bohème* (since replaced), built for Melba and still in use in 1961. All the Met's Lucias from Lily Pons to Maria Callas had staggered in their madness down the almost perpendicular staircase soon to confront Sutherland.

She was apprehensive as she arrived in New York with only a week to prepare for the performance. Huge publicity had preceded her and although she had had great success on the concert platform with *Beatrice di Tenda*, sopranos come and go in that sophisticated city and New Yorkers were eager to have her reputation proved on the operatic stage. A Metropolitan audience could put the final seal of approval on a singer's career, with regular 'live' broadcasts ensuring a vast audience right across America. To succeed at the Met was of vital importance to an aspiring international singer. As rehearsals began, stars of the Metropolitan came to watch, with memories of past and great Lucias. But Sutherland, singing with a vitality and assurance which defied comparison, and refraining from only the very top notes, began to exert her own special charm.

The performance of 26 November 1961 was a benefit for the Metropolitan Opera Guild's Benevolent Fund. A glittering audience filled the House, though only a minority of thoroughgoing operamanes, many of whom had queued all day for standing room or returned tickets, knew what to expect. They generated an enthusiasm that was contagious and by the time the curtain went up the atmosphere was alive with excitement and anticipation. The excitement was unleashed in a volley of applause as Sutherland made her entrance, breaking her concentration. Confidence personified in rehearsal, it was only later she admitted that she could not recall a time when she had been more nervous. Nervous enough to cause the slight but noticeable lack of rhythm and the insecurity of pitch in her opening aria, but her voice warmed with every bar to its familiar limpid purity and she finished the cabaletta in sparkling form on a perfect high D. She had more than compensated for a nervous beginning and the audience were quick to demonstrate their approval. Encouraged by their response, Sutherland went from strength to strength, her voice soaring effortlessly above the sextet, by which time there was little doubt that she would fulfil the promise of her advance publicity. By the end of the third act, capping the mad scene with a full, strong, perfectly placed high E flat, the New York audience had taken her as warmly and completely to their hearts as those of London, Paris and Milan. They went wild, clapping, cheering and throwing their programmes in the air in a thoroughly uninhibited manner. The ovation went on and on, and the orchestra joined in. To silence the din and conclude the opera, the houselights were dimmed — but to no avail. In a great wave from the stalls, through the diamond horseshoe up to the gallery, the audience rose to its feet, refusing to let Sutherland go.

Outside the theatre she was mobbed by a crowd stretching across Broadway, and only with the greatest difficulty was she able to reach her car, a Rolls Royce arranged by Terry McEwen, and eventually driven away. At the party Geraldine Souvaine had promised her, the hostess', 'Hello, pleased to meet you', soon changed to, 'Who the hell are you?' as gatecrashers surged in. Congratulations flowed as freely as champagne, while at the hotel telegrams poured in and an extra room had to be found for the flowers.

The performance was also a considerable personal success for Silvio Varviso, the young Swiss conductor who replaced Molinari-Pradelli, but for the moment he was more in need of consolation than congratulations for during the mad scene a button had burst from his starched vest. Out popped the vest with every upward movement of his arm and the orchestra was vastly amused by his efforts to tuck it in again. 'Could it have happened in the provinces?' he wailed. 'No, it had to be the Met — and at my debut.'

In the early hours of the morning the newspapers were brought in. She had challenged the Lucias of Tetrazzini, Sembrich, Pons and Callas, and her success was resounding: 'A phenomenal singer'; 'a spectacular debut ... by popular acclaim she is the new queen of song'; 'A great coloratura soprano'; 'A

supreme moment for her and for the Met'. No other musical
event of 1961 had stirred so much interest; it was the most
profitable Benefit in the Guild's history and the Metropolitan
production fund was US $35,000 better off. Those who noticed
her shaky start were readily disposed to attribute it to the strain of
her debut. They described a voice of extreme beauty, the ele-
gance of her phrasing and the evident sincerity of her performance. The limitations of her characterization were acknowledged,
but Harold Schonberg affirmed that there was no-one around
with her 'combination of technique, vocal security, clarity and
finesse . . . with this kind of voice though, acting is supererogatory'.
He described the mad scene as 'flawless . . . her cadenza with the
flute as exciting a piece of singing as the lyric stage can show
today'. The *New York Journal* observed 'It is doubtful that any
other soprano has sung this famous scene so forcefully, so purely,
so easily, in more than a generation.' She 'came, she sang, she
conquered', wrote Irving Kolodin in *Saturday Review*, '. . . well
done and welcome, Miss Sutherland, may your prime be a long
and productive one'. And in *Opera Magazine* her first Metropolitan
Lucias were described as 'a fabulous series of performances'.

Her conquest of New York continued in Carnegie Hall, on a
stage decked with flowers from the Australian Society of New
York, when she appeared in her second concert for the American
Opera Society as Amina in *La sonnambula*. She was not happy,
however, for she had spent the day in bed nursing a cold, and
not only did she forget the words to '*Ah, non giunge*', but
the music as well. Nevertheless the critics put pen to paper for
the second time in 10 days to eulogize her performance and
Sutherland was relieved to read nothing but praise for her frantic
extemporizations:

> Like singers of the olden days, she interpolated her own
> cadenzas. The *raison d'être* of an aria such as '*Ah, non
> giunge*' is its extroverted bravura. When Miss Sutherland
> came to the second verse she started to soar all over the
> place, adding trills and turns and a dizzy variety of flawlessly
> performed pyrotechnics.
>
> Harold Schonberg, *New York Times*, 6 December 1961

The following day snow grounded all planes and Sutherland
took a train to Washington for a recital. Accompanied by
Richard, she delighted her audience at the Constitution Hall with
a programme which included, for a change, the mad scenes from
Hamlet and *I puritani*. The recital was followed by a reception at
the Australian Embassy where they were to spend the night as
guests of Sir Howard and Lady Beale. Sir Howard had first heard

Sutherland sing in Dallas, and she promised him then she would give a recital in Washington. Now he proposed a toast: 'An idea may be abroad that Australia produces nothing but kangaroos, rabbits and very bad ambassadors. In the field of music at least, tonight's performance has proved that we produce great artists too. I give you Joan Sutherland — *Prima Donna Assoluta*.'

6

Miss Sutherland to Rest

Sutherland had achieved unequivocal acclaim in the four major citadels of the opera world but the unrelenting pressure to attain that goal was beginning to take its toll. Strain and tiredness lowered her resistance to colds which had hovered threateningly over almost all her big moments, and although characteristically inclined to make light of any discomfort, pains in her back which had been troubling her for some time were now severe. She gave a recital in New York, but when the final performance of *Lucia* was subject to the same aberrations as the earlier *La sonnambula*, the danger signals could no longer be ignored. Jet travel had made the impossible possible, and Sutherland, who appeared to be fast perfecting the art of the impossible, was physically and mentally exhausted.

They postponed performances in Naples and returned to London where she was ordered to rest. She did so, but only for a week which was all she could spare before rehearsals at Covent Garden where she was to sing the Queen of the Night in a new production of *Die Zauberflöte*, for which three-guinea tickets were changing hands at 25 guineas. It was a role, however, in which she did not live up to expectations. Her voice was too soft-grained, lacking the cutting edge necessary to give authority to the music of the malevolent queen. The agility and precision of her singing were impeccable, but her performance lacked brilliance and much was made of the downward transposition of one of her arias by those who failed to appreciate that it was authentic Mozart. While she was comfortable and secure up to high E, she was 'pushing it a bit' to reach high F.

Conditions at home had not been conducive to a good performance, since fire had broken out at Cornwall Gardens while Sutherland was resting. Auntie Blos, whose eyes had never been the same since she mistakenly used corn-cure instead of eye-drops, lit a match to find her shoes under the bed. Fighting the fire until the fire brigade arrived filled Sutherland's lungs with smoke and seared her throat.

They had a few days in hand before flying to Palermo for three performances of *Lucia* when they discovered that the chorus and stage hands at the Massimo were on strike. Threats to pay off the artists and close the theatre notwithstanding, the leader of the claque called for his money and was grudgingly paid the going rate of 20,000 lire. After days of negotiation and indecision the curtain went up on a single performance, though they were paid for the three performances scheduled. Cornel MacNeil, who sang Enrico, came close to losing his fee — paid in cash — when he stowed his bag in the back of his hired car: the car was broken into, but to his immense relief the only thing missing was his wig-box! MacNeil definitely improved on further acquaintance, but there was no sign of a refund from the *chef de claque*.

Bonynge in the meantime was up to his ears in music preparing for his conducting debut at the Teatro Eliseo in Rome, which was not quite the impromptu affair indicated by some reports of the event. His ambition to become a conductor, thwarted by the Royal College of Music, had never faltered; his rapport with Sutherland and his frustration on the occasions — not infrequent — when she had been at odds with the conductor of the moment, merely increased his determination. The fracas at the Fenice had been the last straw, and when the problem arose with Molinari-Pradelli, Ann Colbert, their American agent, brought the idea into the open. There was never any prospect of his conducting for Sutherland's Metropolitan debut, but Decca had already set the wheels in motion for him to conduct a recording of *Alcina*.

He found that confronting a professional orchestra for the first time was a nerve-racking experience — in retrospect even reckless — for he had not made a study of conducting beyond a few pointers from Henry Lewis and observing others. He did, however, have the advantage of complete familiarity with the programme, and the Italian orchestra, willing to give him the benefit of the doubt, were patient and cooperative. Although one newspaper described him as a 'café–conductor', others were more appreciative, but it was not until March 1963 that he conducted opera for the first time with *Faust* in Vancouver.

More *Lucias* in Barcelona were followed by a return to La Scala in the production of *La sonnambula* Visconti created for Callas. As Amina, Sutherland chalked up another resounding triumph in Milan. Later in the month, however, walking on stage in Antwerp for a charity concert with the Belgian Radio Orchestra she slipped on the polished floor. She saved herself from falling, but in doing so badly jarred her back. The concert was to be repeated in Amsterdam, but after an agonizing train journey and a sleepless night it seemed unlikely that she would be able to give it. Showing more concern for her than for the concert, the agents called in a doctor who gave her injections. But it afforded only passing relief and during rehearsal, taking a deep breath to reach a high note, the pain caused was so severe that Sutherland collapsed and was led away in tears. Despite protests she went through with the concert. A doctor laced her into a maternity binder, she did not make the usual entrances and exits between items, and she adjusted her breathing and took only little breaths. When the concert was over nothing had been more honestly deserved than the tremendous ovation she received. She flew to London, mostly standing in the aisle because it was more comfortable to stand than to sit, and her doctor diagnosed an acute arthritic condition of the discs at the base of the spine. He prescribed the wearing of a steel corset and bluntly told her that she should work less and rest more.

Stoically she accepted the corset, but with rehearsals for three productions, 15 performances and an opera to record in the space of five weeks, there was little time for rest. They deferred a couple of recitals in Cumberland but no real consideration was given to cancelling anything else — with one exception. In January, when they began to take stock of the year's schedule serious thought had been given to the prospect of cancelling a nine-week concert tour of Australia planned for June; now this was inevitable. But her immediate obligation was to fulfil her engagements for which people had already bought tickets. So work on a production of *Alcina* went ahead — a great disappointment to Sutherland who hankered for a new Zeffirelli production of *La traviata*. But at least Alcina was not a physically energetic role, neither did it require her to kneel or prostrate herself upon the stage, which seemed to be her lot in almost everything else she did.

Londoners were no strangers to the conventions of *opera seria*, thanks to the work of the Handel Opera Society, and they had their own ideas of what to expect. On the whole this was not Zeffirelli's baroque confection from the Fenice. The result was a wide divergence of opinion as to its merits and a feeling that Zeffirelli's approach diminished the drama and detracted from the music. Noël Goodwin, however, thought that if there was a place on the operatic stage for Handel, this was exactly the way to do it, and Arthur Jacobs wrote: 'Zeffirelli is a born man of the theatre: although he has jettisoned Handel's drama his own entertainment is well worth seeing'.

Unquestionably recognized as a superb Handelian stylist, Sutherland recreated her St Pancras success with singing more brilliant, more accurate and more shapely than ever.

Alcina was closely followed by another revival of the much-maligned Fedorovitch staging of *La traviata*, which Sutherland had only just managed to get her teeth into at the end of the first series. This time she approached it with rather more confidence and gave a performance which raised fresh hope that here at last was another soprano capable of being a great all-round Violetta. The role requires a soprano who can cope with the bravura of the first act; a lyrical sweetness of tone and exceptional legato for the second and third and great dramatic power for the second scene of Act II. Sutherland on this occasion came near to possessing them all.

After such a success news of the cancellation of her Australian tour was received with much astonishment; doubly so since it burst through the press embargo, pre-empting the official announcement by the Australian Broadcasting Commission who were to have sponsored it. The story broke with all the trappings of sensational headlines: 'SUTHERLAND TO RETIRE' or 'SUTHERLAND CRIPPLED'. But more discreetly, and with greater accuracy, *The Times* headed its column: 'Miss Sutherland to Rest'. The *Sydney Sun* ran a two-inch front page headline: 'CRIPPLED', and the *Sydney Morning Herald* a leading article which read:

> Her tour of Australia was to have been more than an out-standing musical event. She was coming home in triumph as one of the greatest coloratura singers of our time.

It went on to say that the cancellation had also denied Australians the opportunity to 'indulge themselves in homage to a returning conqueror, who, for a change, would not have been a champion athlete'.

The final decision had been a great personal blow to Sutherland, for it would have been her first trip home since 1951. But it was obvious that she needed time to rest and for treatment on her back, without which the threat of becoming a permanent invalid was very real indeed. Photographers and journalists picketed the steps of Cornwall Gardens hoping for an interview, and later when she left for a recording session with Weenie gallantly trying to shield her from the intrusive flash bulbs they followed her to the car. *En route* to Walthamstow Town Hall placards were prominent bearing the legend: 'Opera Singer to Retire'. But Sutherland had no intention of doing any such thing. She had staved off a crisis once before; she had the guts and determination to do so again.

Sutherland was recording and performing at the same time

(*Alcina* and *La traviatia* respectively) — not something she was to make a habit of — and on one memorable evening half the cast were ailing. Sutherland had a cold and put her back out again when she sneezed. She went first to the doctor and then to Covent Garden, beating another wave of reporters by a whisker. Andre Turp sang Alfredo with a sore throat, Louis Quilico had kicked a piece of scenery and broken his toe, Alberto Erede had neuritis in his conducting elbow and the prompter had laryngitis! After the performance, disinclined to face the crowd that hugged the stage door, Sutherland escaped to a waiting car through the Mart Street exit. Only one woman was in the street to see her leave; she looked and nodded and went on her way with a conspiratorial grin.

Among those thrown into a panic about talk of retirement had been Victor Hockhauser, who was faced with an Albert Hall sold out for a Sutherland concert, but although every breath brought a stab of pain she gave her audience a night to remember:

. . . the singing of Miss Joan Sutherland was of the kind that makes one feel privileged to be living in the 1960s to experience it. In the first place it was the tone that ravished the ear; there was not a trace of grain to impair the lustrous purity of her voice, nor any incisive edge the price to pay for her clean firm line. Beautifully moulded melody, bejewelled by fioriture as accurate as they are delicate, streamed forth with apparent effortless breath control. Perhaps, most important of all in everything she undertook, there was unabounded expressive eloquence.

The Times, 2 April 1962

As an encore she sang a totally uninhibited '*Sempre libera*', supported by Bryan Balkwill on the podium, throwing all caution to the winds and joining in with Alfredo's offstage lines. It was a fitting end to a difficult London season.

There was still no immediate prospect of prolonged rest, however, for she had another series of *La sonnambula* at La Scala and two performances of *Beatrice di Tenda* in Naples in May held over from the beginning of the year. Not until these were safely behind her was she able to give her undivided attention to another new role, that of Marguerite de Valois — the last she would undertake until December. For the first production of *Les Huguenots* — or rather *Gli Ugonotti*, as it was to be sung in Italian — at La Scala for 70 years, the Italian opera house had hoped to engage Callas to sing the role of Valentine, an idea which got no further than the planning stage because Callas was going through her Onassis period and singing only occasionally. Thus the work was mounted with Sutherland as the Queen, Simionato as Valentine and Fiorenza Cossotto as Urbain. In the event, Callas sang *Medea* (her final performances at La Scala) which ran concurrently with *Gli Ugonotti*.

Meyerbeer had already written several moderately successful Italian operas before going to Paris where, chameleon-like, he adjusted his style to suit the French taste for five-act extravaganzas. He was once accused of bartering his soul for a 'mess of admiration', but he knew what the market required and had at his fingertips just the right formula for success. Taking full advantage of the high degree of technical expertise the Opéra could offer, *Les Huguenots* enjoyed enormous popularity from its première in 1836 until the end of the century. It had a star-studded history at the Metropolitan, the home of the tradition of '*la nuit de sept étoiles*' upon which so much of the opera's success depends, and at Covent Garden it was scarcely out of the repertoire for almost 50 years. When Wagner gained the ascendancy, however, it was clear that a taste for both was incompatible and Meyerbeer's fall from favour was more final than that of many ninteenth-century composers.

The role of Marguerite de Valois reputedly calls for the greatest soprano in the world. Not in itself a large role, what there is is spectacular and Sutherland sang it in a spectacular fashion. She was also the first singer known to follow the original stage directions and make her entrance at the end of the third act on a horse; this was an equestrian feat made more difficult by the heavy stage costume and obligatory steel corset.

Callas and Tebaldi attended the dress rehearsal, managing to do so without coming face to face, and afterwards, separately, congratulated Sutherland on her performance. Tebaldi, terrified of horses, was full of admiration for Sutherland's nerve, although she later came to terms with her fear and rode a horse as Minnie in *La fanciulla del West* to please Rudolf Bing. A special mounting block had been provided for Sutherland, but on one occasion this was nowhere to be found and the groom held wide his arms: 'Signora, I will catch you'. Contemplating him from a great height, Sutherland was doubtful and wisely chose to stay put until the block was firmly in position.

Milan newspapers enthusiastically praised Sutherland's performance (for example the *Corriere della Sera* pronounced that she 'stole the show'), but in Australia, still nursing a grudge about the cancellation of the tour, the *Sydney Morning Herald* reported: 'Heroine Sutherland sings opera on horseback', while a London newspaper described how she mastered a temperamental horse which reared several times: 'But Miss Sutherland remained in control and did not miss a note'. That the horse was temperamental is a myth one should hasten to dispel, for she was astride the horse, an ageing grey, for a scant five minutes, and it took all Sutherland's strength to keep his nose off the floor. *The Times*, though, in its assessment of her performance was more concerned with her singing than with the horse: 'Sutherland makes the highly ornamental music allotted to her glitter like jewels in a crown as they catch the light and send radiant beams in all directions.'

Together with Ganzarolli, Tozzi and Ghiaurov, it was a cast to conjure visions of earlier 'nights of the seven stars'. In fact Rudolf Bing, who was in the audience, thought it a cast one might hope to equal, but never surpass.

Sutherland, for her part, had had quite enough of horses. When she made her debut with the Opera Guild of Greater Miami she discovered that the director, Dr Arturo di Filippi, had a thing about animals, so it was no surprise when eight horses galloped across the stage in the first scene of *Lucia*. Sutherland, however, soon disillusioned him of the fanciful notion that she could make her entrance on horseback, leap off and simultaneously launch into her opening recitative. But a breathtaking extract of stable hung over the dressing rooms, even penetrating Sutherland's sense of smell which she swears has been impaired since that very necessary dental surgery.

Having salvaged from the following month some precious time at the villa she then sailed for New York in July, and much to her dismay faced accusations that her Australian tour had been cancelled to enable her to fulfil more prestigious engagements elsewhere. The cynicism came as no surprise to Sutherland for it had already been suggested that perhaps her back might improve if her fee were raised. She called a press conference and explained yet again the condition of her back: how difficult it was to sit for any length of time without acute distress, and therefore how impossible it had been to fly to Australia, and how she could never have sustained the arduous tour arranged by the ABC and the long hours of travelling involved. 'I am very upset I had to disappoint my own country,' she told them. 'I am Australian, and proud of it.' She was also plied with questions about the opening of the Sydney Opera House in 1964, since, for months in pursuit of copy, the press had tried to prise from her some kind of statement. It was true that she had been approached to appear at the opening, but so far no formal contract had been undertaken. There was nothing sinister in this, for it was likely that the Management Committee's reluctance to sign contracts — with anyone — was due to the growing realization that the Opera House would not be ready in 1964.

Sutherland had already received a taste of the kind of publicity expected of a prima donna in her skirmish with the Fenice, but recognizing that life in the limelight must always be exposed to public comment did not make it any easier to tolerate. But she did not dwell on it, for she had several concerts to give and 20,000 tickets had been sold for the first of these in the vast open-air Lewishohn Stadium. After a day's postponement for bad weather Sutherland sang arias from *La traviata* and the mad scene from *Lucia* to roars of approval from the largest audience of the season. But a disappointed crowd of hundreds stormed the stage when she declined an encore because, not expecting such enthusiasm, they had not prepared one. She gave similar concerts in Chicago and the Hollywood Bowl before returning to Europe the way they had come, by ocean liner.

As a kind of compensation for the Australian tour the idea of a television spectacular had been conceived: the most expensive and ambitious programme ever to be made for Australian audiences. It was to last an hour and take 15 hours to record, a tremendous gamble for Peter Bernados, the producer, who worked for months on the planning and coordination. He had been repeatedly warned that the project was impossible in the time available, but he brought it off without a hitch and the final result was a triumph for all concerned. For Sutherland, encased alternately in a black and a white corset, according to the needs of her costume, it had been a test of endurance, and her dedication commanded the highest respect from all those with whom she worked.

At the end of November, when she was due at La Scala to begin rehearsals for *Semiramide*, Auntie Blos had a stroke, and Sutherland refused to leave her until she regained consciousness. When she died without doing so, Sutherland arranged the funeral and eventually arrived in Milan far from note- and word-perfect to find the rehearsal atmosphere predictably tense.

Rossini's *Semiramide*, based on Voltaire's *Semiramis*, had remained virtually unperformed this century and was known only for its overture. It is virtuoso bel canto opera at its most grand. It took Rossini rather longer to compose than was his custom, but rather less than the 40 days stipulated in his contract. It was one of two operas he agreed to produce for the Fenice, and the first of these, *Maometto*, later to be revised as *Le siège de Corinthe*, had been a failure when it was first presented in Naples two years earlier. It was understood that Rossini would revise *Maometto* for the Fenice, but he was distracted from the project by other work, and *Maometto* was given in Venice in its original form, much to the disgust of the Venetian audience fobbed off with a Neapolitan reject. It did not bode well for the new and as yet unwritten opera which was now awaited with some hostility.

Semiramide, however, was so good that it overcame the hostility, and although the audience was slow to warm to the piece at the first performance in 1823 it was ultimately given a tremendous ovation and became a popular opera regularly performed throughout Europe. But like many operas of the genre it was performed less and less as singers leaned towards the verismo school and were no longer able to produce the kind of vocalization required for the difficult music.

When Sutherland arrived in Milan, she thought she knew the music, but, consultations notwithstanding, her score differed in several respects from that of the conductor, Gabriele Santini. Simionato, who was to sing the travesti role of Arsace, sympathetically agreed that because the words were so old-fashioned she was having trouble learning them too. But she was able to adlib in Italian, while Sutherland had to improvise a language all her own which fooled no-one. Santini was irascible and would frequently fly in a rage and jump up and down on the podium; if anyone missed a cue he joined in at the top of his voice, drowning the prompter and throwing everyone into a state of confusion. He was also heard loudly complaining as Sutherland stood with her back to him: 'What kind of production is this? All I can see is the English behind!' It was criticism of the producer, Margherita Wallmann, rather than of Sutherland, but slowly she turned, not in the least put out, and corrected him with the words: 'Australiano, maestro, and it's not *my* fault'.

It proved necessary to postpone the first night for two days, not an uncommon occurrence in Italy, but *Semiramide* did not go down as well as expected with the first night audience who tended to sit on their hands. In this singers' opera *par excellence* only Sutherland was totally in command of the music, which is fiendishly difficult and requires a coloratura technique from the soprano and from the mezzo-soprano, baritone and bass:

> *Semiramide* without Sutherland would have been impossible. In her presentation of Semiramis, Joan Sutherland takes the most decisive step forward since her Lucia. She is superlative...she dominates the stage. This is now a glamorous,

commanding Sutherland with a strong, fuller middle voice. She sings freely, astoundingly, unselfconsciously. She brings a great role to life, for she has both the technique for it and the artistic force to use roulades for eloquence. Beyond that there is the thrilling realization that far from resting on Lucia she is developing powers, conquering relative weaknesses, and the technique is so secure that there is every reason to anticipate a long series of increasing triumphs.

Andrew Porter, *Financial Times*, January 1963

While criticizing her diction in recitative, *Opera News* reported: 'Joan Sutherland confirms that she has no rivals today in coloratura technique.' And Franco Abbiati summed it up in one word: 'Unchallengeable'.

1962 had been a year of firsts and lasts. Never again was Sutherland to appear in *Die Zauberflöte*, she had given her last staged performance of *Beatrice di Tenda*, and she had added three complete operas and a unique recital album to the record catalogue. With *Semiramide* she launched a new role, eminently suitable, and one which she was to make very much her own. She had become the most sought-after British singer since Dame Eva Turner and Dame Nellie Melba and in the field of bel canto she was indeed proving herself unchallengeable.

7

The Architect of My Career

Unchallengeable or not, there was no time to coast along and take it all for granted. Not infrequently did Sutherland read about her precipitate rise to stardom as though it had been an effortless stroke of luck, whereas in fact it had taken 15 years to become an overnight success. The grinding hard work would have to continue for that success to be maintained, and she already knew it was far more difficult to maintain a standard than to set it.

Hers was not so much a career, more a way of life, and there was hardly a moment when she was not conscious of the next performance. She had the comfort of her partnership with Richard, and although the sacrifices were many the only one of any real significance to Sutherland was the need to spend so much time apart from her son, now being educated at the French *Lycée* in London.

Sutherland's father had a maxim: 'If you want to find time for everything, never let time find you doing nothing', and as she set sail for America at the beginning of 1963 a brief look at the diary assured her that apart from a short respite aboard the *Queen Mary*, there would be no time for anything beyond the call of duty for the next three months. So she made the most of the opportunity to relax, embarking on a piece of needlepoint with a decidedly ambitious design, and from which in one form or another she was to become as inseparable as Kirsten Flagstad and her knitting. The voyage was also greatly enhanced by the presence of Noël Coward, in spite of his insistence that he preferred Italian ships because 'there was none of that nonsense about women and children first'.

The final performance of *Semiramide* in Milan had been on 5 January. By the end of the month Sutherland had appeared in Kennedy's Inaugural Anniversary Concert in Washington, given a benefit with Stokowski in Philadelphia and recorded a television show with Dinah Shore and Ella Fitzgerald and a chat show with musical illustrations with Birgit Nilsson. Arriving late from Washington when snow held up all transport, Sutherland received the sharp edge of the Swedish soprano's tongue, and throughout the ensuing recording she referred to 'Birgit, dear', through gritted teeth.

Having been a frequent guest on the *Ed Sullivan Show* and appeared many times on *Bell Telephone Hour*, Sutherland was by now no stranger to the television cameras, although her attitude towards them was still one of sheer terror. Even though she could reach a much wider audience via television than would ever be possible from the stage, it was not a medium with which she was totally at ease. A zoom lens catching the full effort of a high note was not a pretty sight and she was as aware as the technicians that her mobile face so readily registered her grimaces of self-criticism, even with the most glorious sounds issuing from her throat.

At the beginning of February, she recorded another *Bell Telephone Hour* and gave concerts in New York, Boston and Chicago, by which time she was also rehearsing for *La sonnambula* at the Metropolitan and feeling understandably frayed at the edges. Sutherland's expertise in the field of bel canto had inspired the Met to mount this new production of an opera that had not been staged since Lily Pons sang Amina in 1935. It was a benefit performance, arguably with one of the hardest audiences to please. But although the enthusiasm did not match that of her first *Lucia* it was nonetheless a highly successful occasion with Sutherland singing Amina with great authenticity of style, interpolated cadenzas and a complete battery of perfectly placed top notes.

By international standards, *La sonnambula* was a low cost production and Sutherland was critical of the sets, which she found uncomfortable to work in, and of the costumes, which did not suit her. Rudolf Bing walked the mill-race to demonstrate its safety, but Sutherland was more concerned about the window from which she had to emerge onto it: so small that she appeared to be coming from it on hands and knees. While Rolf Gerard, the designer, wailed about his perspective, the roof was raised, but there was no simple remedy for the costumes. Bing once modelled a costume designed for Tebaldi in an attempt to convince her how good it looked, but no-one could persuade Sutherland she looked good in her *Sonnambula* costumes. Whatever may appear to have happened to the offstage temperament of this highly acclaimed prima donna, however, her ability to thrill and excite an audience was not in dispute. Generally the production was well received by the press, although for some critics even Sutherland's virtuosity could not raise the gentle, sentimental *La sonnambula* above the level of boredom. For them it was another chance to swipe at the 'triviality' of bel canto and one reviewer had the temerity to suggest that Sutherland's voice was not intrinsically a beautiful one.

Nicolai Gedda had been singing Elvino, but on the morning of the fourth performance Bing telephoned to say that he was sick and would be replaced by Dino Formichini. Sutherland accepted the extra rehearsal as an occupational hazard, but when by the third consecutive performance he was still indisposed, and covered on this occasion by John Alexander, Sutherland was unable to resist blaming Bing for Gedda's indisposition by giving him the tenor role in *Boris Godunov* at the same time. She had a vested interest in Gedda's well-being, as he was soon to sing with her in *I puritani*, but Bing could have countered her criticism by pointing out that she too was courting disaster by doing too much.

Bonynge was in Vancouver where he was making his operatic conducting debut, and in between times Sutherland was giving concerts in and around New York and as far afield as San Francisco and Los Angeles, with Silvio Varviso conducting. The American Opera Society was doing its best to corner the market in Sutherland debuts and now they provided Bonynge with the opportunity to make his New York debut conducting *I puritani* at Carnegie Hall. The concert was a huge success — for Sutherland, for Gedda, now thankfully recovered, and for Bonynge:

> For sheer bravura singing and unbelievable perfection, Joan Sutherland's performnce as Elvira was the highlight of the season. She has never been so free, so radiant, so transcendent; and when Nicolai Gedda soared to a high D in their duet in the last act and Miss Sutherland disappeared into the tonal stratosphere, the audience could hardly be blamed for becoming hysterical. Nor was it all fireworks. She sang *'Qui la voce'* very simply and touchingly created a living character.
>
> Robert Sabin, *Opera Magazine*, April 1963

It had been an unusually hectic season and they were pleased to return to London, even though setting foot on English soil was becoming an increasingly expensive business. Since her £10-a-week contract with Covent Garden in the early 50s, Sutherland's income had been steadily rising, and she had been earning in several different countries, which in itself made her affairs complicated and offered a challenge to her accountants. Although the Bonynges were spending a small proportion of their time in England, technically they still lived there and were therefore subject to British taxation. But the tax-haven was for the future;

in the meantime they solved an immediate problem of over-crowding by buying a large house in Cornwall Gardens for £23,000, hardly a snip in 1963. It had 14 rooms, one of which was large enough to accommodate two grand pianos, but since it had been divided into flats it was in need of considerable renovation before it could be occupied. For the next few months Sutherland's stage appearances were few, which gave her the opportunity to oversee work on the house, an interest shared by Russell Braddon who was buying their old flat at number 11, as well as to catch up on her personal life and enjoy a well-earned rest.

But life in the Bonynge household was never peaceful. Itinerant friends were always dropping in and Ruthli, who had been hardly able to boil an egg when she first came to look after Adam, was now quite adept at doing wonders with five loaves and two fishes. Sutherland's concept of rest is of a fairly active nature, for she is unable to sit still for long. An inveterate potterer, she finds housework relaxing. She has a passion for hardware shops and enjoys shopping both for herself and for other people. She once relieved Norman Ayrton of the headache of Christmas shopping, whisking him around a New York department store and accomplishing the lot in next to no time with something appropriate for everyone on his list. With a strong sense of Scottish thrift she has a shrewd eye for a bargain, hates waste and has a practical flair for making things do. Given a tablecloth, too long by far for any table they possessed, she cut off the excess and carefully stitched the offcut into eight dinner napkins. Essentially, rest at that time meant a break from being looked at and listened to, fêted and admired, and for more concentrated treatment on her back which was kept under control by a regular masseuse in London, Switzerland and New York — each with their own idiosyncrasies. In New York, Jenny persuaded Sutherland to take an evil looking mixture, beneficial to her kidneys, but as a result she had fled from her curtain-calls with consequences more violent than Montezuma's revenge.

Few careers require such total dedication as an operatic one, and it is not the glamorous life propaganda would have one believe. It is a life of ritual and routine, discipline and self-denial, hotels, airports, sweat and tears — and the pedestal is small. But rewards are great: the exhilaration that comes from a performance as perfect as human fallibility can make it, the unreserved appreciation of an audience, the shower of flowers, the shouts of 'Bravo!'. The pedestal is also somewhat precarious. 'La regina è morta, viva la regina!' came from the pen of an Italian journalist after Sutherland's debut at La Scala. A reference to Callas and a cruel reminder of just how tenuous one's grip on success might be. So although Sutherland rested in her own way, she still worked each day on new roles such as Norma, and Cleopatra in Handel's *Giulio Cesare*, and polished up those she was to record, for the summer of 1963 was a productive one in the recording studio, her records selling as fast as they could be pressed. In Geneva she recorded Micaela, one of her early roles, to Regina Resnik's Carmen; in London a recital album, her first in collaboration with Marilyn Horne, titled *The Age of Bel Canto*; in Florence a complete recording of *I puritani* and later excerpts from *Giulio Cesare*. With the exception of *Carmen* all were conducted by Bonynge, and the *Giulio Cesare* was a follow up to three performances for the Handel Opera Society, now in its eighth year, at Sadler's Wells Theatre, the last of which was a broadcast Gala in aid of the Sunshine Homes.

Giulio Cesare, one of Handel's most inspired and dramatic scores, predated *Alcina* and followed the same formalized structure of *opera seria*, with expressive recitative carrying forward the convoluted plot, and the da capo aria conveying a wide range of emotion. The two leading roles of Giulio Cesare and Sesto, originally written for castrati, had been translated to a mezzo-soprano Cesare and soprano Sesto, sung respectively by Margreta Elkins and Sylvia Stahlman. Norman Ayrton was the director faced with the difficult task of giving dramatic point to the da capo conventions and filling in endless bars of music before and after each aria. The opera was warmly received by the audience of Handel enthusiasts but the critics were unimpressed by the production and considered Sutherland's performance uninspired.

In spite of several joint recordings, however, Bonynge's public partnership with Sutherland had not extended beyond the concert and recital platform, a situation she was keen to rectify. There was nothing mystic about her talent, although she accepted the Svengali–Trilby analogy lightly and acknowledged him as the architect of her career: 'Half my success is due to him; why can't we share it in performance as well as behind the scenes?' It is doubtful that without his help she would have remained a secretary who sang a little on the side, since her ambition rose of its own accord beyond the routine office job for which she had trained, but it is certain that her career would not have developed along the same lines and would not have been of such a high profile. His understanding of her voice was total and she no longer saw any reason to chase all over the world to sing with conductors with whom she was not on the same wavelength.

When they returned to America in September 1963 this wish to share her success in performance with Bonynge was to be fulfilled. Several performances of *La sonnambula* were in hand in San Francisco and Los Angeles, where according to the *San Francisco Chronicle* Sutherland gave the finest coloratura performance in local history, and after taking the almost inevitable swipe at the score, described Bonynge's reading of it as 'spirited and intelligent'. However, it was *Norma* in Vancouver that represented the real milestone of 1963.

It had only been a question of time before Sutherland essayed this key role in the bel canto repertoire, but when Rudolf Bing suggested that she might like to sing it in the season following her Met debut, Sutherland felt she was not yet ready for it. The Met still cherished memories of Ponselle, Cigna, Milanov and Callas, and it seemed neither the time nor the place to undertake a debut of such magnitude. Norma is one of the great heroines of nineteenth-century romantic opera and one of the most taxing soprano roles. The singer who tackles it must have complete command of recitative and fioriture, sensitivity to Bellini's distinctive melodic line, the vocal technique of an acrobat and the physical and psychological stamina of a marathon runner. Lilli Lehmann found Wagner child's play in comparison, and Norma infinitely more demanding than all three Brünnhildes. The prospect of singing it for the first time was daunting, even outside the operatic mainstream, and it had preoccupied Sutherland for months.

Bellini was not a prolific composer in the mould of his contemporary, Donizetti; 'with my style, I have to vomit blood', he said, and he was at the height of his creative powers when he composed *Norma*, the ninth of his 11 operas and the one to command the most lasting respect. Romani provided the libretto from a contemporary play of the same name by Alexandre Soumet, an austere classical drama in distinct contrast to the pastoral romanticism of *La sonnambula*, his most recent work. Neither did it conform to the operatic conventions of the time. Romani and Bellini resisted the temptation to set the finale after Soumet's play with a mad scene for Norma and the inevitable cabaletta, providing instead one of the most impressive scenes in all opera, combining intense lyrical beauty with gripping drama in the inexorable climax of Norma's immolation. Bellini wrote *Norma* for Giuditta Pasta at La Scala where she was making a rather belated debut in 1831. At the première she had great difficulty with '*Casta diva*' which Bellini had already transposed down a tone from G to F to accomodate her, and having rehearsed strenuously right up to the last minute she and the rest of the cast were not in good voice. A large part of the score was not well received by the audience and Bellini was bitterly disappointed at a coolness amounting almost to hostility.

Bellini's melodic genius, however, was the envy of Verdi and he was much admired by Wagner for the way in which his music was so closely bound up with words. With the cast more rested, audience appreciation grew with successive performances, and *Norma* was greeted with wild enthusiasm for the rest of the season. Donizetti, who thought the initial judgement too hasty, wrote: 'Everyone is conquered by his sovereign genius.'

The Vancouver Opera Association had not existed when Sutherland made her debut in the city in 1958. With three short seasons to its credit it was still very much in its infancy, and it was a matter of considerable prestige for such a young company to secure a major debut of an international star. Irving Guttman was the Artistic Director, and Bonynge was to conduct all the performances of *Norma* and also a Benefit Concert. He had taken a decisive hand in selecting the rest of the cast and there was no doubt in his mind that Marilyn Horne, a mezzo-soprano with a technique to match Sutherland's, would be the ideal Adalgisa, and John Alexander was a stylish tenor she could look up to. It was already apparent that a vocal chemistry existed between Sutherland and Horne, as unique as it was inexplicable. The concert performance of *Beatrice di Tenda* had not provided an opportunity for their voices to blend in duet; *The Age of Bel Canto* — a conspectus of bel canto singing — had not yet been released, so this was the first occasion on which the perfect blending of two phenomenal voices could be demonstrated in public. The 'Druid duo' as Marilyn Horne dubbed it, had been launched.

The production was a great success, but with performances following too closely upon each other it was an uncomfortable time for Sutherland. Her anxieties, usually so well controlled out of consideration for her colleagues, were obvious to those who knew her well, and she was assailed by unpleasant attacks of nausea. Succeeding performances brought increased confidence, but she was well aware that in these initial attempts she had not fully realized the potential of by far the most challenging role since her first *Lucia*, and the one most open to comparison with other interpreters. On this occasion, however, the critics were unanimous in their praise for Sutherland and Bonynge in what had been a testing debut for them both:

Many of the performance's loveliest moments came when

Miss Sutherland sang opposite Marilyn Horne. I have never heard two voices that blended as beautifully as these. The liquid clear soprano mingled with Horne's big sumptuously-rich mezzo to such effect that the duet '*Mira o Norma*' can be singled out as one of the evening's high points.

William Littler, *Vancouver Sun*, 18 October 1963

In November the enormous Shrine Auditorium in Los Angeles was sold out to an enthusiastic audience for two performances of *La sonnambula* which Bonynge conducted. In Philadelphia they gave a one-off performance of *La traviata* at the Academy of Music, the oldest auditorium used for its original purpose in the United States. It was Sutherland's first operatic appearance in the city and probably the best locally-produced opera Philadelphia had experienced in decades. A gala atmosphere prevailed with a dressy audience giving her a tremendous ovation. Sutherland was in firm, clear voice and *Opera News* described a brilliant and glittering first act; a confrontation with Germont that was warmly felt; a dramatic gambling sequence and a poignant death scene. Bonynge's rapport with Sutherland showed no hint of indulgence except in the ornate cadenza in '*Ah, fors'è lui*' and the embellished '*Sempre libera*' — both entirely appropriate. Sutherland had welcomed this opportunity to make her American debut as Violetta, since interspersed with performances of *La sonnambula* she was to sing it again at the Metropolitan the following month.

Her solution to the vexed question of the *Sonnambula* costumes, which she loathed, was to provide her own, and much to Bing's dismay she rejected those for Violetta as well. Also designed by Gerard they included a pair of pantaloons. 'It amounts to a matter of taste, Miss Sutherland!' 'Yes, Mr Bing, yours or mine!'

With *La traviata*, however, she achieved a notable success, all the more remarkable since in a series of seven performances she appeared with five different Alfredos, and the only positive way for her to find out whom she was playing opposite was to send Weenie for a programme. The Met heard a Violetta recalling the days of Muzio and Bori. 'An upper range not so gloriously expounded in decades. Her E flat was just possibly the best ever heard in the house in *La traviata*', wrote Louis Biancolli in the *New York World Telegram*. In glorious voice she encompassed the role in all its moods, creating a believable Violetta which Schonberg defined as a 'most sensitive, appealing and warmly-sung conception'.

The performances at the Met reached into the New Year,

which began on an optimistic note when Sutherland was accorded the rare privilege of her own Gala Performance — a benefit for the West Side Institutional Synagogue. But a concert in Cleveland, Ohio was ill-timed, for with competition from Artur Rubinstein in another auditorium, the hall was only half-full. On the other hand two performances of the notoriously difficult *Semiramide* were staged with great success in Los Angeles, and in Carnegie Hall for the American Opera Society Sutherland's duets with Marilyn Horne in the same opera predictably brought the house down:

> It was expected that Miss Sutherland would follow the bel canto tradition in making her difficult role still more difficult, adding cadenzas and changing some of the vocal writing. But it was not expected, except by those with some secret information, that Miss Horne would follow Miss Sutherland right down the line. This she did and when the two were on stage the results were electrifying... This was thoroughbred singing of a kind that has all but vanished.

Harold Schonberg, *New York Times*, 19 February 1964

The fact that they were able to deliver the cadenza at all was a source of amazement to them both, for it was an invention of Bonynge's hastily written out before their first performance together in Los Angeles. Sutherland referred to his cadenzas as 'fly specks', impossible to read, but they tried an impromptu rehearsal in the dressing room and, unable to adjust to the right key, gave it up as bad job. At the last minute they decided to give it a go and the result was a supreme example of the tingling telepathy that epitomizes their unique vocal and artistic collaboration.

Another one-night stand, this time of *I puritani*, was given a rousing reception in Boston, where it was regarded as a particular triumph for Bonynge, conducting a fully-staged performance of the work for the first time and drawing from the orchestra the finest sounds heard in the Opera Group's six seasons.

This was a useful dry-run for their next engagement: Bonynge's conducting debut at Covent Garden, where the Zeffirelli production had been borrowed from Palermo. It was now two years since Sutherland had appeared at Covent Garden and she was given a feverishly excitable welcome from an adoring audience for a performance which Philip Hope-Wallace found 'dazzling, touching and above all beautifully toned'. Her portrayal of the bird-brained Elvira had gained in confidence since her Glyndebourne debut and according to some she was being heard to best advantage since her 1959 *Lucias*.

The big *scena* of madness in the second act with the refrain of '*Qui la voce sua soave*', a lovely elegiac melody, brought out her most affecting, colourful tone. With her husband Richard Bonynge in charge of the orchestra, Miss Sutherland was able to take the aria exactly as she wished, taking plenty of time over it (as I bet Grisi did originally) with a pretty strong use of rubato but a good forward impulse all the same. The ensuing cabaletta '*Vien diletto*' in its second appearance was ornamented in a manner which could properly be called stunning: decorations, trills and ornaments were darted into the hopping tune with a bravura to take the breath away (though not, amazingly, the diva's). In this kind of bravura singing Miss Sutherland has no peer and if it is not Tetrazzini rediviva, it is something you still would know is due to become a legend.

Philip Hope-Wallace, *Guardian*, 21 March 1964

Others, however, could still not stomach the work at any price and Peter Heyworth in the *Observer* was not alone when he considered that Sutherland was wasted on such a 'fatuous farrago'. Rosenthal recalled her beautiful Pamina, Desdemona, and Agathe and went as far as to hope that now Sutherland had proved beyond doubt she could sing music of this kind as no-one else could, she might consider returning to Mozart, Verdi and Weber. Far from calling it a day, though, what better than for her and Bonynge to devote themselves to the revival of operas which had been so long neglected for want of singers to sing them. Elaborate roulades, arpeggios and cadenzas introduced an element of risk into the proceedings — a kind of vocal highwire act — which added a whole new dimension to a performance.

Criticism of Bonynge's conducting on this occasion centred upon his hurried tempos, his indulgence towards the singers, especially towards Sutherland, and his inability to establish a true rapport between the stage and the pit. 'That Mr Bonynge knows his Bellini and loves him, is not in doubt,' wrote Rosenthal, 'but he has not yet had enough experience to be able to impose his will on all the forces at his command.' There would always be a wide divergence of opinion with regard to his conducting ability. As Sutherland's conductor he was horribly exposed and he had begun his conducting career with little or no technique and no possibility of acquiring it in some out-of-the-way place where no-one had heard of him. He was obviously a talented accompanist and voice coach with an ability to draw from a singer qualities of which they were not aware. Marilyn Horne credits him with convincing her that she was a coloratura mezzo-soprano, and he was already championing the talents of Luciano Pavarotti, but it was an ability which was particularly highly developed with regard to Sutherland. When he is conducting he knows her well enough to assess how much he can push her when she is in strong voice to do a little better, and when he has to be careful in order for her to shine. Sutherland's faith in him is absolute and she shares his passion for the music he has proved she could excel in. His knowledge of music is far more comprehensive than Sutherland's and he was earning himself a reputation as a scholar of Italian ottocento opera. Thanks to Sutherland's technical skill the repertoire was gaining momentum; the potential was limitless and his appetite for research insatiable.

Lucia di Lammermoor, however, was still very much in demand, and with more than 60 performances and countless mad scenes to her credit, Sutherland showed no signs of tiring of it. Thus, accepting her obligations more readily than other eminent singers, she joined the rather gruelling Metropolitan tour to give Boston, Cleveland, Atlanta, Minneapolis and Detroit their first taste of it.

Bing again offered Sutherland *Norma* to open the 1964/65 season, and it was a great disappointment to him and of some nuisance value when she decided, 'rather late in the day', according to him, that she was not yet ready for it. In fact she had no hesitation in accepting — on the understanding that Bonynge would conduct and Marilyn Horne would sing Adalgisa. Bing was later to write 'Marilyn Horne is a mezzo any international house can be proud to present', but he was not prepared to accept such pre-conditions of engagement. Bonynge was now conducting an increasing number of her performances, but Bing had not yet succumbed to the idea. So Sutherland opened the Met's last season on Thirty-ninth Street with a new production of *Lucia* conducted by Silvio Varviso, and when they left at the end of 1964 with no engagements for 1965, opera-watchers jumped to the conclusion that since Bing would not engage Bonynge, Sutherland would not sing, a conclusion hastily denied by Bing and Ann Colbert.

They were becoming a formidable partnership, not always pleasing to opera house managements who were, on occasion, to find them somewhat uncompromising. But Bing was capable of compromise if it suited him, and he was eventually to concede, as he put it rather unkindly in his memoirs: 'If you want the meat you have to have the bones.' Bonynge was scheduled to make his debut at the Met in 1966, by which time he would have added greatly to his experience, for in the interim he was to conduct for every one of Sutherland's performances, many of them in America. In Houston the orchestra played impeccably for him, while Sutherland sang arias from *Le nozze di Figaro*, reached top F in '*Bel raggio*', gave the wordless Gliere *Concerto for Coloratura* its United States première, and crowned the concert with a magnificent mad scene from *Lucia*. 'History will record the night', reported the *Houston Chronicle*. 'A concert so amazing none who were there could forget it!' The only regret was that the hall was a third empty — due perhaps to the sub-zero temperatures outside. When Sutherland repeated the concert two days later, the house was full but the top F missing.

1965 opened with a concert performance of *Alcina* in Carnegie Hall, where the American Opera Society had again taken the initiative in presenting an unknown work to New York audiences. But in spite of a performance described by Irving Kolodin as vocally and musically 'breathtaking, magnificent, even stupendous', it fell short of matching the total success of the equally unfamiliar *Beatrice di Tenda*, and Bonynge's conducting was deemed not to have lived up to the 1962 recording.

The Houston programme was repeated with great success in Cincinnati, New Orleans and Bloomington and they arrived in Boston in a snowstorm to begin rehearsals for Sarah Caldwell's unpredictable production of *Semiramide* in which Marilyn Horne sang Arsace in spite of being six months pregnant. To detract from her lump she wore a beard in the tradition of Alboni and endeavoured not to present too much profile to the audience, although a pregnant bearded Arsace was almost too much for Sutherland's sense of the ridiculous. Physical incredibility apart, separately and in duet they shone vocally and drew an enthusiastic response from audience and critics alike.

Since the cancellation of the Australian tour, thoughts of reconstituting something of a similar kind had never been far from Sutherland's mind. She and Bonynge had always looked upon it as a postponement until her back responded to treatment sufficiently for her to travel. But when Bonynge began to think seriously about plans to return home, it was not in terms of a concert tour, but a full-scale opera company. Preparation began as far back as the beginning of 1963, recruiting the international singers who were to make up the company. It had been a long and careful process and it was understandable that Sutherland and Bonynge had worked with many of them before — at Covent Garden in the early 50s and in various opera houses around the world in recent years. One of the first to find his name on the list of soloists was Luciano Pavarotti. Joan Ingpen, at one time Sutherland's agent, then casting director at Covent Garden, heard him singing with the Dublin Grand Opera Company and engaged him to cover for Giuseppe di Stefano in *La bohème*. Mrs Ingpen thought he might appeal to Sutherland, for he was taller than her, had a charismatic personality and a first-rate natural voice with the potential to sing her repertoire. He subsequently made a promising debut at Covent Garden as Rodolfo in almost all the performances of *La bohème* when di Stefano cancelled. The management liked him and immediately engaged him for further performances including *La sonnambula* with Sutherland in 1965. When she left for Miami to make her debut with the Opera Guild there in February 1965 Sutherland had not yet sung with Pavarotti. Her Edgardo for these performances should have been Renato Cioni, but Cioni had withdrawn in order to sing Cavaradossi to Callas' *Tosca* in Paris, leaving them at very short notice without a tenor. Bonynge immediately suggested Pavarotti to take his place, although Arturo di Filippi, the Director of the Guild, was very name conscious and shared the anxiety of most opera managers with regard to the second-hand recommendation of unknown hopefuls. But when a tenor is needed in a hurry, the field of choice is not great and Pavarotti was available.

He had been steadily making a name for himself in Europe; he had sung again at Covent Garden, several times at the Vienna Staatsoper and also at La Scala under Karajan. He had not however, sung in the United States and jumped at the chance to get his foot in the door. The *Miami Herald* reported that the audience went wild with enthusiasm for Sutherland and that Pavarotti won all hearts as Edgardo, and, proud to have introduced a new young tenor, di Filippi gave him a financial bonus. Edgardo was not a role which was new to Pavarotti: he had already sung it in Amsterdam, and *Lucia di Lammermoor* was now regarded as a fairly standard part of the repertoire. His acting, however, was still very much at the 'sing it to the gallery' stage, and he was just beginning to develop sufficient confidence in his vocal security to give more attention to his acting. But it was in Australia that he was finally cured of his tendency to sing downstage-centre — often with his foot on the prompt-box — when the curtain came down stranding him on the wrong side.

Sutherland's last operatic appearance in America for 18 months was in Philadelphia where she made her debut as Marguerite in *Faust*. It was an important debut — the first role she had undertaken in French, and being a great favourite of

Melba, the only new role she was to sing in Australia. She received a standing ovation and a dozen curtain calls in the Academy of Music and an equally enthusiastic reception for her second performance in Hartford, Connecticut.

The first performance of the 1965 revival of *Lucia* at Covent Garden was another unqualified success for Sutherland — in spite of the remains of a sore throat which inhibited rehearsals and made her wary of high notes. For Bonynge, however, it was a different story. Sutherland had a special affection for the Opera House, which she regarded as her 'artistic home', and was shocked at the end of the performance by the ugly sound of booing unmistakably directed at Bonynge. Sutherland enthusiasts, anxious perhaps to stir the pot, put it down to a handful of Callas fans taking time off from the queue for the June *Tosca*. While the press had tried unsuccessfully to create a rivalry between Callas and Sutherland, a very real conflict existed between their respective admirers, exacerbated now by the fact that Callas was obviously at the end of her career. Even in the early 50s there was strong partisan feeling among Callas devotees towards the supporters of other singers, and it soon became clear in some quarters that it was considered impossible to admire both singers simultaneously. They may have shared a similar repertoire, but in all other respects they were poles apart.

Bernard Levin rationalized the booing as the work of a small group who seemed to resent Bonynge for cashing in on his wife's success, and who were determined to boo him whatever the quality of his musical direction. Frank Granville Barker, himself critical of Bonynge's performance — which in spite of much shapely playing, lacked rhythmic pulse and excitement, thought such behaviour indefensible: 'If conducting of such standard were always to be given the bird, there would be precious few peaceful evenings at the Garden.'

Bonynge was treated to a similar demonstration after performances of *La sonnambula*, when critical comment ranged from 'conducted reliably' to 'gave a little help'. But he was unconcerned. Neither was he bothered by those who said he was only conducting because his wife was famous. He was aware that he still had a great deal to learn, but without genuine ability he would not have made much progress, and he was about to face the toughest test of his new career. The London season was over, and the Australian tour upon them with a rush: the project planned with such infinite care, the impossible dream now to be faced in reality.

8
Home, Sweet Home

The Sutherland–Williamson International Grand Opera Company brought to fruition the aspirations of a great many people. Since the beginning of the century when he had joined his three brothers in the concert business, Sir Frank Tait had been actively involved in theatre management. Amalgamating with J.C. Williamson in 1920, they pulled off two major coups with the Melba–Williamson Grand Opera seasons of 1924 and 1928, and went on to create a firm with a near monopoly in theatre management in Australia and New Zealand. They had been presenting opera on and off for half a century, and it was Sir Frank's greatest wish to bring Sutherland back to Australia as the prima donna of an international company.

For Sutherland it represented a long overdue return home, and since negotiations had begun in earnest she had looked forward to it with a mixture of joy and apprehension. When she left Australia in 1951 more interest had been shown in foreign artists than in home-grown talent, yet, paradoxically, they resented Australians leaving home to make a name for themselves elsewhere. She had departed anonymously as a Sydney secretary — what would the reaction be to *La Stupenda*? The tour was more ambitious than anything contemplated in the past, with seven completely new productions and the finest galaxy of operatic talent ever to have visited the southern hemisphere. The same operation in Melba's day would have reduced any entrepreneur to bankruptcy, and Williamson's last foray into an operatic enterprise resulted in a deficit of £55,000. Sir Frank was not therefore ignorant of the risk he was taking on behalf of The Firm, but he was not a man to allow his theatrical instincts to be clouded by a constant preoccupation with the balance-sheet.

Prior to Sutherland's departure for England, the responsibility for opera in Australia rested largely with impresarios prepared to back visiting opera companies. The Second World War put a stop to this international activity for a while, and, forced to turn to its native resources — of which, albeit underestimated, there was no shortage, two independent companies developed in Sydney and Melbourne. Eventually they joined forces for a highly successful season which became the first positive step towards the formation of a permanent company. Variously called the Australian Opera and the Elizabethan Trust Opera, the company continued with much encouragement and support to give a main season in the state capitals and a country tour with reduced ensemble and piano accompaniment, after which the entire company was disbanded until the next season. Opera on such a part-time basis, however, offered no job security and did not inspire the total commitment from singers and technicians necessary for it to develop and thrive. It was not until 1963, by virtue of a commercial liaison with Garnet H. Carrol, that the Trust was able to support a permanent company.

Unable in 1924 to recruit an all-Australian chorus, Melba had brought one from Italy, opening the floodgates to claims that anything Melba's 'dago' singers could do, Australians could do better. Bonynge had auditioned members of the chorus in Australia in 1964, some of whom had sung principal roles with the Elizabethan Trust Opera, and he was to find it one of the best choruses he had worked with. Since the Sutherland company could not avail itself of the state-based Symphony Orchestras he had also recruited a complete orchestra from scratch, but the Trust formed the backbone of the team of stage technicians. Bonynge also had sole responsibility for selecting the international singers who were to make up the company and the sopranos who were to sing when Sutherland was not scheduled to appear.

Bonynge's taste was also sharply reflected in the choice of repertoire, although, remembering the success of Melba's tours with such hard-core favourites as *La bohème*, *Tosca* and *Madama Butterfly*, Sir Frank had been anxious that Bonynge's choice seemed somewhat esoteric. But his enthusiasm for bringing the bel canto revival to Australia was overwhelming; it was a novelty to most young opera-goers, and since Sutherland was the focal point of the enterprise it was natural the operas chosen should be those in which she excelled. Ultimately the ones chosen were *La traviata*, which at that time was Sutherland's favourite opera; *Faust*, her newest role and a tribute to Melba; *Lucia di Lammermoor*, for obvious reasons; *La sonnambula*, because of all the roles in her repertoire, Amina was Bonynge's favourite; *Semiramide*, a great bravura role only Sutherland could sing; *Eugene Onegin* and *L'elisir d'amore* to broaden the picture. Only the first two were really familiar to Australian audiences and Sutherland would not appear in either of the last two.

Optimism and enthusiasm ran high, for the international season was bringing a slice of operatic Europe to Australia, offering experience otherwise only gained by going to London or Paris. The chorus began work in May and by the beginning of June opera officials were deputed to meet every plane as members of the company arrived on each flight. Pavarotti swept straight off the plane and into rehearsal, leaving his wife Adua in a state of utter bewilderment since she had never before been outside Italy, never travelled by plane, and spoke no English.

When Sutherland arrived in Sydney on 17 June 1965 *en route* for Melbourne the media were out in force. The plane, however, was late, and what should have been an hour between flights dwindled to a few minutes as she was rushed through customs between the international and domestic terminals. Looking every inch the diva in a new chinchilla coat, her red hair dressed in the bouffant style that prompted Noël Coward to remark: 'Joan darling, you're looking magnificently like the MGM lion today', she strode through the transit lounge shaking hands as she went, collecting flowers from a delegation of girls from her old school and fielding questions on all sides. In Melbourne she fled across the tarmac to take cover from some of the coldest weather the city had known, and under blazing arc-lights faced a battery of cameras and microphones and steered her way self-consciously through a press conference. She described her return home as the happiest moment of her life, appeared not to notice that no-one actually welcomed her back, and was only mildly irritated to be asked about retirement and why the prospect of singing in Australia gave her the jitters.

With reporters and photographers still in her wake she arrived for her first rehearsal in a large room in the Williamson workshop adjacent to Her Majesty's Theatre, through which a draught blew to rival a southerly buster. No-one knew it, but Sutherland was nervous and apprehensive about meeting the rest of the company, and was relieved to find her friend of Music Club days, Elizabeth Allen, there to help her over the first obstacle of introductions. What the company saw was a large unpretentious lady in comfortable shoes and a warm coat, disarming any tendency to treat her with deference. She impressed everyone from the chorus to the scene-shifters with her naturalness and sincerity, her ready smile and infectious sense of humour. Moffat Oxenbould, one of the stage managers, recalled her extraordinary professionalism: 'Never late for rehearsal, always willing to repeat if a problem arose and within days of her arrival she was everybody's friend and idol.' Her equable nature and fortitude were a con-

stant source of admiration to Norman Ayrton who was to direct
five of the seven operas, and he never hesitated to use her as an
example to the rest of the company should anyone show signs of
slacking. After a performance of *Semiramide* which had not
finished until well after midnight, Sutherland was on stage as
required next morning to rehearse *La sonnambula*. As others
drifted in wearily complaining of the rigours of the night before,
Ayrton gestured towards Sutherland: 'If she can do it, so can
you.'

Ayrton ran a tight ship. He was a stickler for lists and meticu-
lous organization which had stood him in good stead as Principal
of the London Academy of Music and Dramatic Art. Now his
multi-coloured rehearsal schedule was the pivot of all activity. It
was an almost impossible exercise in logistics, and they were
pressed for time and incredibly cramped for space. The small
production team, however, made it easier to dovetail rehearsals
and switch from one production to another as the need arose or
time permitted. As each new production reached its première, or
there was a change of cast, rehearsals during the day were followed by performances at night. It was a punishing schedule for
all concerned, especially so for Sutherland who was singing
almost every other night, and although on opening night she
breezed into the dressing room with the cheerful 'One down, 41
to go', she did not underestimate the responsibility facing her.
Her reputation and reliability were the lynchpin of the tour, her
prime concern to make all her performances good enough to
justify all the fuss made about them.

The gala first night of *Lucia di Lammermoor* in Melbourne
on 10 July could stand comparison with anything the Met could
turn on in its glitter of diamonds and dazzle of shirt-fronts.
Melbourne had seen nothing like it since Melba's last tour. Dress-
makers worked overtime, dress-hire firms exhausted their stock
of evening dress, medals were polished and safe-deposits emptied
of jewellery. In the street, in spite of sub-zero temperatures,
there was an audience to see the audience arrive, and in the foyer
the crush was so intense that liveried footmen were unable to roll
out the red carpet for the Administrator of the Commonwealth
and the Viceroy's party, who entered the auditorium to a roll of
drums.

If Melbourne had been a shade sceptical about Sutherland's
remarkable reputation when the curtain went up, it was all swept
aside by the first act, after which she received the first of many
ovations. At the end of the opera there were hopeful shouts of
'Encore', and the audience clapped and cheered. Music critics

struggled to find superlatives with which to embroider their copy and one described the success as 'as close to ultimate as we are likely to see'. Bonynge was praised for his reading of the score and his firm direction of an inexperienced orchestra, and the traditional production came as a welcome relief after the gimmicks of some recent local performances by producers with avant-garde ideas. The principal soloists more than lived up to their international billing, and it was a rare experience for Australian audiences to hear the sound of such powerful and well-matched voices blending in a full ensemble.

Eugene Onegin and *L'elisir d'amore* alternated with *Lucia* in the first week, with Pavarotti and Elizabeth Harwood scoring a great hit in the comic Donizetti, and Pavarotti was Sutherland's partner in *La traviata* when she made her second debut of the tour as Violetta. In the *Australian*, Kenneth Hince was moved to write that he had never heard a pair of voices like these on the Australian stage and was tempted to wonder if he might ever hear such perfectly matched excellence again: 'Perhaps we may, but it will be one chance in tens of thousands', and John Cargher had no difficulty in predicting that Pavarotti would join the operatic greats of the century. With Sutherland at the height of her career and Pavarotti at the beginning of his, *La traviata* was deemed to be the most artistically complete performance so far premièred.

The tour was providing Pavarotti with a valuable opportunity to test his vocal stamina against a gruelling schedule. He was amazed at the resilience of Sutherland's voice and how she managed to turn out such a consistently high standard of performance night after night. The secret, he was sure, lay in her phenomenal breath control. She showed him exercises to develop the muscles necessary for good vocal support, and at every opportunity he would wrap his hands around her rib cage to feel in practice what it was well-nigh impossible to expound in theory.

Beyond that, Sutherland has the ability to pace herself in performance, never expending too much vocal capital, keeping enough in reserve for the big moments and the usually spectacular finale — almost always finishing even the most gruelling performance in amazingly strong voice. To assess how much voice is needed to see her through a performance is at the heart of her attitude to rehearsal, where she invariably sings in full voice, only sparing the highest notes — pointing upwards to indicate her intentions. It is not uncommon for singers to simply 'mark' their roles, but in Sutherland's view it does not do to undersing if one's technique is a reliable one. Having established her tactics she does not then waste her voice in energetic vocalizing in the dressing room before a performance, and finds it exhausting listening to other singers who do. To her mind they use half their capital before setting foot on stage. At this point the need to conserve the voice is paramount. 'What you've got you need to save up', and Sutherland cites Jussi Björling's often quoted philosophy with regard to warming up: 'If I'm well I don't need to. If I'm not, it doesn't do any good.'

Another key factor in Sutherland's consistency of performance is the self-discipline necessary to keep social excesses at bay, for the one thing guaranteed to bring about failure is insufficient rest. Burning the candle at both ends is not conducive to vocal or physical well-being. It is her general rule never to go out on the evening before a performance and to rest on the day itself, pottering around the house, not talking too much and looking through her words.

In Australia, with performances on alternate nights this self-imposed restriction offered little scope for sightseeing, and what she was able to see of Melbourne largely amounted to the inside of their rented house in Toorak, the inside of Her Majesty's Theatre and what she was able to see from the car as she travelled between the two. She had to protect her essential rest from society hostesses and civic bodies falling over themselves in their eagerness to hold receptions, dinners and soirées in her honour. They had not all been so eager, however, to extend this hospitality to others, which irritated Sutherland who unselfishly secured them invitations which they were often none too keen to accept. While greatly flattered and well aware of her obligations in this respect, as invitations had flooded in months in advance some hard and tactful pruning was necessary. To fend off certain people sometimes required rudeness. Neither was she tempted by the jolly social diversions in which other members of the company indulged. Her greatest obligation was to her audience, and she never faced them without knowing she had done everything within her power to ensure she gave her best.

If Bonynge had any doubts about his choice of repertoire it was in respect of *Semiramide*, for which he had to fight the hardest with Sir Frank Tait. Yet in spite of Roger Covell's description of it as 'the authentic mothballed curiosity of the season', it took audiences in Melbourne and later in Sydney by storm (it was not performed in Adelaide or Brisbane). After a matinée performance the demand for curtain-calls was so great that it was impossible to strike the sets and the curtain was half an hour late going up for the evening performance of *Eugene Onegin*. With Sutherland aided and abetted in her vocal gymnastics by Monica

Sinclair as Arsace, she gave the most staggering show of singing heard in decades, according to Kenneth Hince:

> She put her voice through acrobatics which could hardly be imagined let alone thought possible. Passages of rapid detached notes poured from her with the ease of thought. The theatre was flooded with incredible grace notes, with trills in every part of her register. For the first time an entire generation was introduced to a world of bravura singing that disappeared almost a century ago.
>
> *Australian*, 2 August 1985

The season in Melbourne closed with *La sonnambula*, with Sutherland's performance of Amina ranging from 'miraculous' to 'merely superb' and Pavarotti a 'sensational' Elvino, and the curtain fell to the most astonishing ovation that Sutherland had received anywhere. Sir Frank and Lady Tait, who had hardly missed a performance, cheered and threw streamers along with the rest of the audience, and when a piano was pushed onto the stage, Sir Frank was heard to comment that Sutherland sang 'Home Sweet Home', better than Melba had ever done.

He must also have felt a certain sense of relief that after the first leg of the tour the company had broken even, which had not seemed possible after the first two weeks. Notwithstanding the artistic merit of the productions so far premièred, while Sutherland performances were virtually sold out, audiences had dwindled to an ominous few hundred on 'other' nights. Apart from a small minority of opera lovers, it was apparent that a social cachet was attached to attendance on a night when Sutherland was singing, and rather than admit to not having tickets, many took off up the coast to Surfer's Paradise. It merely confirmed what many feared: while Australia could soak up all the 'star' performances it was offered, there was no real demand for a repertory opera on a permanent basis. With bookings reflecting a similar trend in other cities it was evident that the season could be heading for financial disaster. Perhaps Sir Frank's misgivings about the choice of repertoire were correct; perhaps the seat prices were too high — there was no shortage of criticism in this respect. Yet performances of *La traviata* with Pavarotti and Joy Mammen were not sold out, and that could reasonably be called a potboiler. For a Sutherland Gala night — the first performance of each opera in Melbourne and Sydney — the top price was ten guineas, and it was seven guineas on subsequent nights. But Williamson's had returned thousands of pounds worth of bookings to people who would have paid anything to hear Sutherland, but not half the price for anyone else.

An opera company cannot thrive on three nights a week and unless the response could be stimulated in Sydney it did not augur well for the future of the new opera house at present under construction. It was hardly surprising that Sutherland kept referring to it as 'the effigy' and Ayrton saw it as a potential white elephant. However, after an extensive publicity drive bookings picked up as the season progressed. Other artists received recognition in their own right and Pavarotti developed a following all of his own.

There were fans galore to see them off in Melbourne and the next night they opened in Adelaide with *Lucia* to a lukewarm reception in comparison to the near hysteria of Melbourne. The strain of the impossible schedule was beginning to tell and Sutherland felt no obligation to stay for the final curtain — until Weenie reminded her that the stage-door keeper had especially asked for his basket of flowers to be presented on stage. Without hesitation, on went the bloody nightgown and she took her place with the other principals to what the Adelaide press referred to as 'a tumultuous ovation' from a 'rapturous capacity audience'. Adelaide, however, which gives its all to its biennial Festival, had found the Grand Opera Season a little overpowering.

There was, and still is, a fierce cultural rivalry between Melbourne and Sydney, and a well-known adage in Australian show business that a show which opens in Sydney dies in Melbourne. It was purely for reasons of logistics that the 'show' had opened in Melbourne, since all Williamson's workshops were there, but Sydney never forgave Melbourne for having the privilege of opening the season, and it was fully expected that the opening night in Melbourne would pale into insignificance beside what Sydney society had to offer. But notwithstanding glittering jewels from both sides of the footlights there was rather a sense of anti-climax, a direct result perhaps of two days of press coverage of the kind Sutherland could have done without. The tour could not have been given more prominence had it been a royal progress, and since their arrival in Australia pressure from the media had been relentless. Not content, however, with exceptional vocalism and artistic achievement, they wanted personal sensation as well. Sutherland did not actively seek publicity nor positively shy away from it, but their insatiable appetite for the human angle was a source of great annoyance and distress. It was only with hindsight that she recognized her *naïveté* in expecting the press to respect her privacy; as an international celebrity her every action and comment was newsworthy and she was fair game to the media.

An already fomenting relationship with the press came to a head in Sydney. Exhausted after 10 weeks of non-stop rehearsal and performance Sutherland and Bonynge hoped for a quiet arrival and a hasty retreat to their rented apartment in Point Piper. As the plane taxied to a standstill they were horrified to find an army of reporters and photographers and radio and television crews with microphones and cameras poised. They were in no mood to be photographed or questioned and anyway a press conference had been arranged for the following day. They struggled to reach the airport building, their irritation obvious, and in the scrum Bonynge overheard a particularly offensive remark, lashed out and sent an expensive camera flying. The acrimony they left behind did not bode well for the press conference at a Sydney restaurant where the proprietor had prepared a fish dish in Sutherland's honour. He was quite unprepared for the continuing saga of the previous night, with Bonynge telling the assembled journalists what he thought of their antics at the airport, and the highly charged atmosphere erupting with catcalls. Bonynge responded by calling them a herd of orang-utans, provoking another eloquent exchange and eventually he and Sutherland walked out, to return only after much persuasion from the proprietor who had taken a lot of time and trouble over his sauce.

Things were little better at a civic reception a few days later. 'I'd rather be on stage than face an audience like this', Sutherland snapped when it was plain that the pressmen almost out-numbered the guests. During her short prepared speech she was obliged to stop mid-phrase to complain that she could not hear herself speak above the noise of the cameras, and by the time she was through she was so strung up that she was overheard saying to Norman Ayrton that she would never come back to Sydney. The next day she was due to speak at a lunch arranged by the New South Wales National Council for Women: 'We would like to give you honour at an informal luncheon,' the President had said, 'as if it were being held in one of our own homes.' But when Weenie discovered that all four television channels were to be represented she advised Sutherland to plead sickness and cancel rather than walk out. Had she known that the function was to be televised she would not have accepted, and Weenie said as much to the public relations officer, Mrs Emerald Tapley Timms, who was in a state of near panic as she urged the cameramen to be as unobtrusive as possible: 'Give me your cooperation boys. I'm almost a candidate for Broughton Hall' (a psychiatric hospital). Sutherland did attend, however, and the occasion passed without a hitch. She talked of her schooldays at St Catherine's; her dreams of singing at Covent Garden when no-one took her seriously; her return to Australia and the hope that someday, before she was too old, she might come back to sing in the opera house. She shook hundreds of hands, signed numerous autographs, and when she had had enough of the blinding banks of cameras and lights she said so.

Sutherland was not accustomed to public speaking, and at that time had no liking for it. It was an unwelcome aspect of her public life and those who chose to misunderstand merely saw her as another temperamental prima donna. If her public relations were lousy, as one American journalist complained — well, she wasn't in the business of PR. Under the exceptionally taxing circumstances of the tour all she wanted was to be allowed to get on with the job, which amounted to accomplishing the rest of the tour without any artistic egg on her face.

Operatically the Sutherland–Williamson tour was a tremendous success, and Bonynge's choice of repertoire thoroughly vindicated. It had been Sutherland's severest test to date; a test of endurance and self-discipline in which her reputation was proved beyond doubt to be based on more than just hearsay or the engineering wizards of the recording studio. Melba's tour of 1911 had been so successful financially that she could hardly wait to repeat the experience. The Sutherland–Williamson company had taken intimidating risks, not in the hope of large profits but because they believed in something; there were fewer losses than had at first seemed likely, but they were in no hurry to undertake such a venture again, and they no longer had Frank Tait's gambling instinct to spur them on. While the company was in Adelaide, on the second leg of the tour, he had died at the age of 81; sad news, not only for the company but for the Australian theatre as a whole, for he had given a lifetime of dedicated service to the arts.

In a sense the Sutherland–Williamson Grand International Opera Company was an anachronistic throwback to Melba's day; Frank Tait's last magnificent gesture to the theatre in which he had devoted his life. But he died with the knowledge that the tour had been a great artistic success and with the satisfaction of a dream fulfilled.

9

Light Relief

A holiday on the Barrier Reef had been talked about, but Sutherland had no inclination to linger in Australia, leaving the day after the last performance in Brisbane — with less fuss than when they arrived — for two weeks on Tahiti.

She had no engagements for the rest of 1965 other than to record Beethoven's Choral Symphony — the first of many re-recordings — in Vienna with Hans Schmidt Isserstedt. Christmas was spent at Les Avants in Switzerland, the first at home since 1962, and immediately afterwards recording began in London of *Semiramide* and *Beatrice di Tenda*. Both were conducted by Bonynge and in *Semiramide* Sutherland was partnered by Marilyn Horne, and, as Orombello in *Beatrice*, Pavarotti was recording his first complete opera. It is hard to believe that Decca did not jump at the chance to put Pavarotti under contract — or Marilyn Horne, come to that — but James McCracken and Mario del Monaco recorded for them and they saw no urgent need of Pavarotti as well. Having conducted most of Sutherland's recordings since 1962, Bonynge carried considerable clout at Decca, and it was sustained pressure from him and Sutherland that secured Pavarotti's contract.

Not everyone, however, had capitulated to Bonynge as a conductor, and the BBC only agreed to him conducting a gala performance programme because Sutherland would not sing without him, but they compensated for refusing him a screen credit by paying him twice the normal fee. Everyone in his entourage was happy with this arrangement for Bonynge was an inveterate spender, and the tax inspectors were forever breathing down their necks.

Bonynge had not made his conducting breakthrough at La Scala either, and when Sutherland set off for Milan at the beginning of April 1966 it was to sing Donna Anna under the baton of Lorin Maazel. The latter had been a boy wonder and Musical Director of the Deutsche Oper at 35. But battle lines were once again drawn up for he did not like appoggiature, and Sutherland had by this time sung Donna Anna on numerous occasions, always with appoggiature. Maazel, however, was very much the new boy at La Scala, and when he complained that he was unable to work with Sutherland it was made quite clear that it would be easier to replace him than to replace her. Sutherland found this all rather tedious, and had she not had the company of such congenial colleagues the situation would have been quite intolerable. Maazel, his feathers well and truly ruffled, muttered, 'of course, *she* knew Mozart personally', which Sutherland found amusing, but he addressed them all by their surnames and on opening night committed the cardinal sin of neglecting to visit the principals in their dressing rooms before the performance.

Sutherland had already made up her mind that she would not sing at La Scala again unless Bonynge was her conductor, and since this was never to be Donna Anna was her swan song in Milan. When asked in an interview with *Il Giorno* what she thought of Milan audiences, Sutherland lead with the chin: 'They're the only audiences in the world who need a claque to indicate when to applaud,' she told them. The claque was an abomination, and she resented every lire of the 30,000 she had dutifully paid.

Sutherland's next major role was in *La fille du régiment* which she was to sing for the first time at a Royal Gala performance at Covent Garden at the beginning of June. Sir David Webster, keen to introduce more Mozart, had suggested *Die Entführung aus dem Serail* to Sutherland, but neither she nor Bonynge were particularly interested, and they floated the idea of Donizetti's comic opera instead. There was a soft spot in Webster's heart for Sutherland — soft enough to accede to her wishes at least on this occasion, and *La fille* went into the forward planning. It was a marvellous vehicle for Sutherland; an ideal outlet for her endearing sense of fun. She was approaching a significant birthday and it was just what she needed to lift the 40s blues. But it was to be sung in French, making it only her second appearance in a French role, with dialogue as well, and light-hearted or not it still had to be learnt the hard way. Other difficulties paled into insignificance beside those she experienced learning a new role. She rarely had trouble with the music, but the words were another thing altogether. In the early days she had often been obliged to forego a planned visit to the theatre, with Bonynge leaving her, sometimes in tears of despair, to struggle with the libretto of yet another role. Her poor memory was the scourge of her life and it became no more retentive with familiarity or the passage of time.

La fille du régiment was written for the Opéra Comique at a time when Donizetti's operas were especially popular in Paris. So much so that in some quarters he was regarded as an Italian interloper. As a result the première in February 1840 was an unhappy affair, not entirely because of the unsatisfactory cast, but because a hostile and chauvinistic element in the audience were bent on discrediting Donizetti. Hector Berlioz, struggling for recognition in Paris and resentful of Donizetti's reputation, wrote a critique petulantly complaining: 'one can no longer speak of the opera houses of Paris, but only of the opera houses of M. Donizetti'. Berlioz accused him of rehashing a score heard previously in Italy — a heinous crime which Donizetti strenuously denied. With an opera that was charming and unsophisticated, and which provided a splendid vehicle for bravura singing from the soprano and tenor, Donizetti had demonstrated his total command of the *opéra comique* tradition.

Berlioz and a disappointing première notwithstanding, *La fille* went on to enjoy considerable success in Paris, with a record number of performances at the Opéra Comique alone. Donizetti had also prepared an Italian version for La Scala, in which the traditional spoken dialogue was replaced by recitative, but something of its charm was lost in translation, and the opera was only moderately successful in Italy. In England, where an abundance of hummable tunes and the appeal of a notable prima donna were the prerequisites of success, it fared much better. *La fille* certainly abounded in catchy tunes, and with Jenny Lind, Henriette Sontag and Marietta Piccolomini giving their various interpretations of the *vivandière*, Marie, the opera was a resounding hit in London.

Henry Chorley, the nineteenth-century critic, described it as light, familiar and catching, in fact 'everything the pedants find easy to condemn'. But at Covent Garden in 1966 it was not the lighthearted *naïveté* of the piece which disturbed them so much as the overall tone of the production itself. While praising the musical merits of the performance, which with Sutherland and Pavarotti were substantial, the director, Sandro Sequi, was criticized on all fronts for exceeding the bounds of good taste with his crudely exaggerated stage business. Tempted by Sutherland's comic flair, he had been seduced into allowing her to play the comedy too broad. Though some may shudder at the very idea, it was an opera that positively encouraged audience participation, especially in the boisterous Rataplan, and on one occasion someone found the temptation irresistible: '*Qui vient?*', calls Sulpice hearing Marie's offstage roulades: 'Joan!', came the reply from the gallery. But the work held no appeal for Noël Goodwin:

Nothing quite so feeble in character, so bereft of any stage style, and so lacking in any real musical worth has been seen and heard here for many years. The production by Sandro Sequi veered erratically from sentimental romance to slapstick farce.

Daily Express, 7 June 1966

On the other hand the music critic of *The Times* was reminded how Donizetti keeps the slender plot going so that both acts seem utterly worthwhile, and he recognized a different Sutherland, an essentially lighthearted prima donna, longing to escape from the tragic heroines that were her stock in trade:

> ... the gay, good humoured, unsophisticated tomboy ... she enjoys herself immensely ... and her enjoyment is infectious. But the role is then to be sung and the strength of this production was the vivacity and accuracy, the nuance and modulation of timbre of Miss Sutherland's singing in the gay numbers, and the unforced artistry she brought to the pathetic solos — '*Il faut partir*' and '*Par le rang*' particularly. But nothing that she did was more admirable than the weight and balance of the delicious trio in the second act when Maria and Sulpice are reunited with Tonio.

The Times, 9 June 1966

Conductor Carlo Felice Cillario recalls noticing the staff of Glyndebourne strutting out before the end: 'In England we don't like such a style of comedy,' they said, leaving him a little ashamed of his 'vulgar' taste; a taste shared by the majority of the audience and the Queen Mother, still enthusiastically applauding well into the numerous curtain-calls.

Sutherland and Bonynge abhorred the charge of élitism so often levelled at opera and rejected the idea that their role was anything other than that of entertainers. The critics would carp, and there would always be the so-called purists shocked to discover that Covent Garden did not confine itself to 'serious' art, but for Sutherland *La fille* had been a welcome release. It was not, however, to find a regular place in the repertoire of the Royal Opera House. It was given again the following season to much the same critical flak and enthusiasm from the audience, and was later sold to the Metropolitan where it was received with greater generosity of spirit. New York audiences and critics, did not, it seems, regard their opera house as a hallowed precinct which would be sullied by the humorous and slight.

By September, Sutherland was back into mad scenes in a big way with performances of *I puritani* in San Francisco and *Lucia* in

Philadelphia. Her return to the Met for the 1966/67 season included Donna Anna under Karl Böhm and *Lucia* which Bonynge was to conduct in his debut at the Met — the new Met in Lincoln Center, which Sutherland described with more truth than tact as 'a cheap cinema'. With a typical Australian directness she is apt to say what she thinks — and then think, sometimes with disastrous results. A colleague inevitably shorter than she made a pass at her. 'Don't be silly', she said, patting him on the head. Later, to make amends, she sent him a painting of birds for his birthday, only to discover too late that he hated birds.

The old Met had caused a lot of sadness with its passing, for with it went the nostalgia of old traditions, and memories which could not be easily recaptured in the modernity of the new building with its retractable snowflake chandeliers and Chagall murals. But Sutherland was pleased to be back after a season's absence and the audience welcomed her with enthusiasm. The critics found her interpretation of Lucia greatly developed, with no loss of vocal quality, and the mad scene better than ever. The *Wall Street Journal* thought she had surpassed all previous performances at the Met: 'There was an electric quality about her, proceeding as much from her personality as from her voice, that lit sparks everywhere.' Bonynge was highly praised for his interpretation of the bel canto tradition and for his instinctive sympathy for the voice, appreciated more here than at Covent Garden, and it was apparent to Schonberg how well Sutherland and Bonynge worked together: '... understanding each other's ideas about tempo and phrasing — cooperating with split second precision ...'.

It was success all the way. *Don Giovanni*, hastily prepared and reaching the first performance without benefit of orchestral rehearsal, was deemed one of the best seen at the Met for many years. Sutherland got on well with Karl Böhm, the veteran Austrian conductor and a dedicated Mozartian whose judgement she respected. She valued praise and reassurance from those she trusted and he showered her with unsolicited compliments.

Bing had by now resigned himself to Sutherland wearing her own costumes, but for *Don Giovanni* she surprised him and wore those designed for the production. Since, however, the previous Donna Anna had been Leontyne Price, some readjustment was necessary; anyway Sutherland always kept a piece of black velvet handy so she could alter her costume to cope with the effects of the waffles and syrup she found so hard to resist. Many a time Weenie had devoured more of a cake than was decently polite to keep it away from Sutherland, for if there was a weakness in her self-discipline it was a passion for bread and cakes — especially the home-made variety — and for other sweet things. A dish of bavarois had been delivered to Cornwall Gardens by some friends with a hotel in Cumberland for Sutherland to taste in the hope that she would allow them to name it after her. Her approval was total!

With a different cast and Bonynge conducting, Sutherland repeated Donna Anna for the Boston Opera Group, where Sarah Caldwell, thriving on tight corners, only came up with a Don Giovanni at the last moment, and there were concerts and recitals which entailed a good deal of travelling. She went from New York to Philadelphia and thence to Newark; to Boston and back to New York — twice; from Toronto to Montreal via Boston and Bloomington; back to New York via Chicago and then to Vancouver via Seattle. Waking up, even at home, required minutes to orientate herself, and she never risked stumbling to the bathroom half-asleep. She would be forgiven for not knowing whether she was in the Massey Hall or the Academy of Music, and which clothes had been left in which dry-cleaners in which city, but in spite of the inevitable winter delays caused by fog and snow she took it all in her stride, although the atmosphere of pressurized aircraft dried her throat, disturbed her ears, aggravated her sinuses and did not help her shake off a persistent cold.

Her first appearance as Lucia in Vancouver for the Vancouver Opera Association was something of an event, unique in the history of the VOA, and all performances were sold out well in advance of the first night. So when she arrived in Vancouver and immediately took to her bed there were a number of people with their fingers on the panic button.

The production, lavish in comparison to the routine affairs of previous seasons, had been made possible by the joint resources of the VOA and Festival Canada. Sutherland recovered sufficiently to participate in two rehearsals, though moderating her high notes. On the opening night, cold apart, superlatives were heaped on Sutherland's performance, which left no doubts in the minds of the audience as to how and why *Lucia* had catapulted her to stardom. It was a memorable operatic experience and an event of some consequence in the evolution of the Vancouver Opera Association.

She was not entirely free of her cold when they drove to Seattle, where she was to make her debut with the Seattle Opera Association. Neither was she completely *au fait* with the role of Lakmé, her third consecutive debut in the French repertoire. *Lakmé* had been made famous in America by Lily Pons, a light coloratura soprano, but Bonynge thought it would benefit from a rather hcavier voice. He considered it an ideal role for Sutherland, although she had no illusions of herself as an Indian temple dancer.

Delibes is more readily associated with the familiar ballets *Coppélia* and *Sylvia*, but he wrote many light works for the Théâtre Lyrique and three for the Opéra Comique of which *Lakmé* is by far the best known. Like his contemporary Massenet, he supplied a demand, writing an opera that conformed to the operatic fashion current in Paris: an exotic tale of romance and mysticism set in the India of the British Raj. *Lakmé* was an enormous success at its première in 1833 with Marie van Zandt in the title role. In fact so successful that it even survived later performances when she was hissed off the stage believed to be the worse for drink! Later, Melba became one of the composer's favourite interpreters. She studied with Delibes who was so impressed with her that he did not share the concern of the Directors of the Monnai in Brussels about her execrable French: 'It's all the same to me whether she sings in French, German, English or Chinese, as long as she sings!' So he may not have been too disturbed by Sutherland's French, which Bonynge insisted she spoke with a Marseillaise accent.

Lakmé continued to form part of the basic French repertoire until well into the twentieth century, after which it did not retain its hold with the same tenacity as *Faust* or *Carmen*, only occasionally being revived outside France when a singer appeared who could do justice to the title role. Bonynge was sure that it could charm a modern audience, quite apart from the obvious spectacle of the immortal Bell Song, which is not a gratuitous piece of soprano exhibitionism but every bit as significant in its dramatic context as the Duke's '*La donna è mobile*' in the last act of *Rigoletto*. The critics proved him right:

> Most coloratura sopranos have voices that give the impression of being rather brittle; like delicate silver reeds that might splinter in the gale of a high E. Not Miss Sutherland. Her voice is like a pliant golden cord: full, rich, beautiful throughout her extraordinary range. The vocal instrument is something to gasp over and so is the artistry with which she uses it. This was apparent throughout the performance last night, but it was never more obvious than in her first act duet . . . Miss Sutherland's . . . obvious intent was to blend and balance her voice with Miss Tourangeau's in order to serve the music and not her own ego.

Wayne Johnson, *Seattle Times*, 11 April 1967

A brief stop-over in London enabled Sutherland to indulge in a lightning shopping spree for household goods, then it was on to Vienna for the May festival. In spite of signing a guest contract with the Staatsoper she had not appeared in Vienna since 1959, and now she was to make her debut as Euridice in Haydn's *Orfeo ed Euridice*.

Haydn composed a number of operas, mostly by command as court entertainment, but they never assumed the merit of his better-known chamber music and symphonies and rarely became popular beyond the place of origin. *Orfeo ed Euridice*, however, was commissioned for the Kings Theatre, London in 1791, but due to internal theatrical intrigues it was never performed during the composer's lifetime. Indeed it was premièred as recently as 1951 at the Florence Festival with Maria Callas and Tyge Tygeson in the title roles. *Orfeo* conforms to the classic style of *opera seria* with a conventional arrangement of arias, duets and choruses, but unlike Handel who painted vivid musical characterizations, Haydn does not succeed in bringing his characters to life either through the music or the libretto.

The role of Euridice lies in the middle and lower registers of the soprano voice and as such is not a completely satisfactory one for Sutherland. The only real opportunity for vocal display is the Genio's aria '*Al tua seno fortunato*', and since this is the kind of show-piece expected of her, she created the precedent of singing this as well. It pleased her admirers, if not the academics, but gave rise to the odd situation of Sutherland, having died as Euridice, reappearing loosely disguised as the Genio to lead Orfeo down to Hell, and returning as Euridice in the closing scene to be mutely reunited with Orfeo in death. Ironically, this aria, filched from the Genio, caused Sutherland a good deal of trouble as she struggled with its vocal complexities. Yet despite threats to throw herself off the tallest building should she fail to come to terms with it by the next performance, perfect delivery of the piece seemed constantly to elude her. Since it was unfamiliar, unrecorded opera, however, it was unlikely that anyone other than she or Bonynge was aware of her lapses.

Nevertheless it was the stuff of which festivals are made, and it went down well in Vienna, where American tourists who had obtained tickets for the Staatsoper were heard to complain when they discovered that Sutherland was singing at the Theater an der Wien.

> Rudolf Hartmann's Vienna production is as romantic, con-
> centrated and as mobile as it can be within the limits of *opera
> seria*, and with Sutherland and Gedda both in absolutely

superb voice on the opening night, a triumph for the singers, producer and Richard Bonynge was assured ... the show stopped more than once for ovations lasting five minutes. One wondered whether Haydn ever visualized this kind of production or this kind of singing, but for most people the unique Sutherland tone, with its stunning top notes and sudden tragic inflections was the sort of thing that makes a festival experience.

Kenneth Loveland, *Music and Musicians*, August 1967

After the festival it was a relief to get back to Covent Garden and more familiar territory with *La fille du régiment*, but it was only an interlude, for in August Sutherland sang Euridice in Edinburgh to a variable reception:

Her Euridice was regal and gracious, and she was in splendid voice which thrilled the big audience ... the orchestra performed excellently. For this and the evening's success great credit goes to the energetic and perceptive Bonynge.

Duncan Heggie, *Edinburgh Evening News*, 28 August 1967

Joan Sutherland really only came into her own on one occasion — when she sang the florid aria Haydn wrote for the Genio. Here we had a fine display of scales, roulades and ornamental figurations executed with great ease and accuracy, if not with any great spirit. Eurydice's music, lyrical and lying in the middle and lower part of the soprano voice was not suited to her, and although the arioso in the death scene was scrupulously studied, it was impossible not to feel that she was out of her true element.

Martin Cooper, *Daily Telegraph*, 28 August 1967

Euridice was not a role she was to develop a great affinity for, although the aria '*Al tua seno fortunato*' found a place in her concert repertoire, where she was able to sing with the added security of the score.

In the autumn of 1967 Sutherland recorded Verdi's *Requiem* with Georg Solti and the Vienna Philharmonic. A performance of Bonynge's version of *Messiah* with a small chorus and orchestra was well received at the Festival Hall with Sutherland at her 'silver gleaming best', and at the end of November she made her Covent Garden debut as *Norma*. It was now four years since she last sang it in Vancouver, and it had not been seen at the Royal Opera House since Callas sang it there in 1957. The new production by Pier Luigi Pizzi, directed by Sandro Sequi and with Marilyn Horne as the other half of the 'Druid duo', was awaited with high hopes and much expectation.

Bonynge hinted to Rudolf Bing that Sutherland's portrayal would be different, and being different it was inevitably critically controversial. Neither of them saw Norma as a Medea-like character, nor an Amazonian fury with a paranoid lust for revenge, but rather as the victim of an irreconcilable personal conflict in which an overwhelming sense of patriotic duty triumphs over a craving for retribution. The essence of Sutherland's Norma is the quality of womanliness, with no suggestion of the tigress, and Sandro Sequi was absolutely in accord with this approach. To him Sutherland represented the ideal Norma: 'She has the delicacy, purity and line of the true Bellini style. She is lyrical, intimate, subtle and tender.' Sutherland has a greater capacity for projecting the emotions of love, sympathy and despair than for hate, anger and animal passion, and on this account Sequi chose to emphasize the warmth of her personality and concentrate on the private side of Norma's schizophrenic existence. The stress was therefore on the vocal rather than the dramatic aspects of the role and the result was unqualified praise for her vocalization; but almost all the critics agreed, after passing reference to the perennial problem of blurred vowels and weak consonants, that it was a characterization that lacked dramatic compulsion. Frank Granville Barker described it as 'the perfect soporific', and Zeffirelli thought Sutherland and Montserrat Caballé were like 'singing armchairs'.

There is in the operatic sphere scope for more than one interpretation of Norma, but it was a Callas role *par excellence*, and few could resist the temptation to compare the two and generally find Sutherland wanting. If Sutherland had not such a high regard for Callas it would have been both depressing and tiresome to be constantly compared — to be reminded of her own weaknesses as critics habitually concentrated on Callas' dramatic impact while glossing over her vocal deficiencies. Charles Osborne once observed how heartily tired he was of being told that since Callas was such a great actress he must pretend not to notice how badly she often sang. Sutherland's response to her critics was to point out: 'You can listen to what everyone says, but the fact remains you have to get out there and do the thing yourself', but she never subscribed to the view that beauty of timbre and smoothness of line should be subordinated to the drama and the vocal line mangled in a lather of histrionics.

The eighteenth-century singing teacher Pier Tosi wrote: 'I do not know if a perfect singer can at the same time be a perfect actor, for if the mind is at once divided by two different purposes he will incline more to the one than the other. What a joy it would be to possess both to a perfect degree.' Sutherland would say 'Amen' to that, but she felt there were too many interdependent elements involved for a singer to be carried away by a role in the way a straight actor can be. She once said:

> If you get emotionally involved to the extent of letting the emotions take over, you'll not get to the end of the opera — and you are restricted by the fact there are only so many beats in a bar.

With regard to her diction, she thought that there had been a tendency to iron out the words in pursuit of a beautiful sound, but her critics did not seem to take into account the tessitura of much of the music she sings — so far out of the spoken register that it is almost impossible to enunciate: 'The words cannot always be distinct. If they were one couldn't sing the notes. If I didn't round the tone as much as I do, I'd never get up there, I'd just be screeching.' No-one had ever accused her of that, but she had worked on her diction and 'spot the consonant' jokes were wearing a bit thin.

Sequi's production of *Norma* was unobtrusive; the settings were elegant and austere with only a suggestion of Stonehenge in the final scene. Symbolically all the men were dressed as priests and all the women as nuns, although Sutherland's first act costume was not only singularly unbecoming with its wimple and veil, but in blatant contradiction to the libretto. It delighted the singing fans although Noël Goodwin described it as a 'needlessly pallid specimen of music theatre', while the correspondent of *The Sunday Times* wrote: 'More than once the thought struck me that if we happened to drop into such a *Norma* in any opera house of today we should count ourselves lucky.'

This opinion was not shared by the anti-Bonynge claque, now almost a permanent feature of Sutherland performances at Covent Garden, bombarding him with hissing and booing all the more disgraceful since it was widely understood that the culprits had gone along with the specific intention of barracking him regardless of the quality of his conducting. It was an irresponsible demonstration and there was no denying Sutherland's displeasure. The safety curtain was lowered, much to the disappointment of enthusiastic Sutherland supporters chanting 'We want Joan', and afterwards pleading a dinner engagement she left the Opera House uncharacteristically refusing to sign programmes.

1968 also saw the advent of the London Opera Society under the Directorship of Michael Scott. Along similar lines to the American Opera Society, its laudable objective was to present operas of great musical interest largely neglected by opera companies, and to introduce many fine artists not hitherto heard in London. Self-financing and non-profit making, it was greeted with mingled enthusiasm and doubt. It was launched at the Albert Hall with Meyerbeer's *Les Huguenots*, the summit of grand French opera. This was a prime candidate for concert treatment, for the story of romance and political intrigue culminating in the St Bartholomew's Day Massacre is the stuff of which epics are made. But, dependent for its success on stellar casts and spectacular scenic effects, most opera houses are understandably wary of taking it on. Artistically the performance was a huge success. *Opera Magazine* described it as 'music-making of an ultra-professional standard . . . No-one could have caught the spirit of the work better than Joan Sutherland, brilliantly and apparently effortlessly flashing through Marguerite's music.' Michael Scott was commended for his adventurous initiative and Bonynge praised for his musical direction, although the necessary editing did not meet with unanimous approval.

The financial result, however, was disappointing, and it looked as though the LOS had overreached itself. The performance was far from sold out, a fact not easily disguised in an auditorium the size of the Albert Hall. Several factors contributed to this poor attendance, not least of which was an element of overexposure on Sutherland's part, for she had completed a hefty season in London. The advertising had also been painfully inadequate and the high seat prices outweighed the curiosity value of an opera in which Sutherland did not dominate all five acts.

Future plans, which were no less ambitious, included *Lucrezia Borgia* and *Nabucco* with Montserrat Caballé and Elena Suliotis making their respective London debuts; Sutherland and Horne in *Semiramide*; and Renata Tebaldi, absent from London for some years, in *Adriana Lecouvreur*. To pre-empt the risk of further failure those subsequent seasons were sold on a subscription basis and the venue changed to the smaller Theatre Royal Drury Lane (with the exception of *Lucrezia Borgia* which was performed at the Royal Festival Hall) and every performance played to a capacity house.

However, even on this scale opera is a costly business, and although most of the original schedule came to fruition and in its brief and exciting history enjoyed great artistic success, it eventually floundered with thousands of opera lovers holding tickets for the much coveted *Adriana Lecouvreur* in 1970. *Semiramide* was fortunately not among the casualties and in February 1969 there was no shortage of enthusiasm when Sutherland and Horne joined forces once more in some of the most technically demanding music ever written. They polished off Rossini's extravagant solo numbers and duets in an exhibition of superlatively accomplished singing that made one wish that as a postscript to Rossini's centenary year the performance could have been extended to a fully staged production.

It had, however, formed part of the 1968 Florence Festival, of which great things were expected as part of the rebirth of the city devastated by floods when the Arno burst its banks in 1967. On paper the plans for the festival had looked good: Elena Suliotis, hailed as the 'new Callas', with Tito Gobbi and Jon Vickers in a performance of *Otello* directed by Visconti and conducted by Edward Downes; Renata Scotto and Boris Christoff in Meyerbeer's *Roberto il diavolo*; Scottish Opera presenting *Albert Herring*, and *Semiramide* with Sutherland and Bonynge.

Before the festival was underway, however, Suliotis, Gobbi and Visconti had pulled out of *Otello*, leaving Downes with a conducting debut that could be nothing but disappointing. *Roberto il diavolo* was poorly attended, a sadly misconceived production described by one critic as a fine example of how not to present an unfamiliar early-nineteenth-century opera, and it soon became apparent that all was far from well with *Semiramide*. Wladimiro Ganzarolli, who had sung the difficult role of Assur at La Scala, was finding it no easier the second time around. As the opening night approached he grew more and more anxious, and to make matters worse the *chef de claque* had not called for his money. To Ganzarolli, known to be a nervous singer, this could only mean one thing — he was going to be booed. The strain proved too much, and at the last minute he was replaced by Renato Cappechi who went on stage still clutching the score.

For the role of Arsace the Festival management had engaged Monica Sinclair instead of the Italian singer they preferred. If they rejected Sinclair they might be in danger of losing Sutherland and Bonynge as well, so they turned a blind eye to the union ruling stipulating no more than two non-Italian artists in any given series of performances. Although Sinclair had sung Arsace with great success during the Australian tour she was no longer comfortable in the role, and the Bonynges' loyalty to a friend misfired. She did her best with it, but her best was nowhere near good enough to silence comparison with Simionato and it provoked derisive booing from the gallery. Sutherland fumed and at the final curtain when Bonynge joined the production team of Sandro Sequi and Pier Luigi Samaritani on the stage to a renewed barrage of booing and hissing she made no attempt to hide her annoyance. As at Covent Garden after the new production of *Norma*, curtain-calls were perfunctory and disapproval was expressed by the lowering of the safety curtain.

The atmosphere in the theatre had not been favourable to a good performance. Patrons in the gallery had brought along noisy children who munched sandwiches; they talked through the recitatives, booed the arias and applauded the cabalettas; behind the scenes the chorus kept up a noisy chatter. Matters improved only marginally at successive performances and the audience had often been too quick to demonstrate their appreciation of Sutherland, which only served to throw into higher relief their appalling hostility towards Sinclair. At the second performance she edited some of the wilder notes, and when the applause began at the end of the duet Sutherland took her hand and held it aloft, defying the gallery to boo. There were shouts of '*Brava, Sutherland*', but no booing.

The strength of partisan feeling in Italy caused great misery to many singers, and Ganzarolli, who did not pluck up the courage to return until the final performance, was by no means the first to be intimidated in this way. Jon Vickers, not a man easily fazed, was once afraid to sing there and always treated Italy with kid gloves. The 1968 Maggio Musicale had a strong bias towards British and Commonwealth artists, which may have inspired a certain amount of resentment in this the spiritual home of opera, and Sinclair was convinced she represented one non-Italian too many. It may have been significant that she had refused to pay the claque, although that is not insurance against a poor performance as one tenor discovered when the claque leader returned his money and booed all subsequent performances. For Sutherland, however, bringing faultless timbre, precise tessitura and absolute assurance to one of her finest roles, it was a personal triumph. But another Italian opera house had fallen from grace in her eyes, and it was to be many years before she was to risk it again.

Sutherland had now been on the international circuit for almost a decade. Consolidating her reputation with a dozen new roles, she had opened up the whole field of bel canto, demonstrating a style of singing thought to have vanished beyond recall, and succeeding, she considered, by always being able to 'deliver the goods'. An over-simplification of an obvious truism, for she had, of course, been able to deliver the goods in a rather special way. Sutherland has a vocal range from low G to E in altissimo — F, if pushed; clarity and purity of tone above G and A in the treble

TOP *Sutherland as Cleopatra in the Hamburg Staatsoper's 1969 production of* Giulio Cesare *with Lucia Popp and Ursula Boese*. Hamburg State Opera

BELOW *The final scene from* Rodelinda *at the Holland Festival, 1973.*

TOP LEFT *As Antonia in* Les contes d'Hoffmann *with Domingo at the Metropolitan in 1973.* Louis Mélançon, New York

TOP RIGHT Esclarmonde *in San Francisco, 1974, with Aragall as the knight Roland.* Carolyn Mason Jones, San Francisco

BELOW La traviata *at Covent Garden in 1975 with Heather Begg as Flora, Alfredo Kraus as Alfredo and Louis Quilico as Germont Père.* Stuart Robinson

TOP *With Pavarotti in a new production of* I puritani *at the Metropolitan, 1976.* J. Heffernan, New York

BELOW *In 1977 Covent Garden celebrated Sutherland's silver jubilee with* Maria Stuarda. *Tourangeau was Elizabeth I.* Anthony Crickmay

LEFT *Jogging in a one-horse gig with Ron Stevens as Danilo, in* The Merry Widow, *Sydney, 1978.* The Australian Opera, photo William Moseley

BELOW *An enthusiastic reception for a recital in Seoul, South Korea, 1978.*

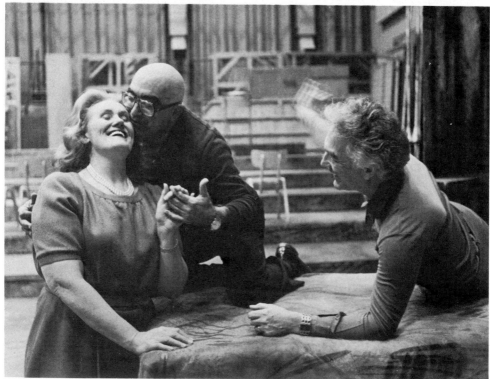

ABOVE *A carpet of daffodils after a performance of* Lucrezia Borgia *at Covent Garden, 1980.* BBC Hulton Picture Library

BELOW *Rehearsing* Esclarmonde *at Covent Garden, 1983 with Lotfi Mansouri and Bonynge.* Reg Wilson

ABOVE *Sutherland's last new role: Ophélie in Thomas'* Hamlet, *Toronto, 1985.* Canadian Opera Company, Gary Beechey

LEFT Anna Bolena *with Jerry Hadley as Percy, Houston, 1986.*

Defying the years: Lucia at Covent Garden, 1985. Clive Barda

stave which few singers can match and with what Walter Legge calls that 'immediately recognizable personal timbre', which often marks the difference between the great and the merely good. Beyond this she possesses a quality not invariably associated with coloratura sopranos: while others have a tendency to thin out and become shrill and hard above the stave, Sutherland has a mellifluous warmth of tone more characteristic of dramatic sopranos which makes her unique among coloraturas. Her technique in the coloratura department is such that she can deliver rapid arpeggios quite out of the ordinary, and florid passages of exceptional clarity and agility, and she has a beautifully even trill — a rapid articulation of two distinct notes, rather than a glorified wobble which in some cases has to pass for one. She has the confidence and technique to depart from the printed note with style and taste, and her ability to take a long phrase with the purity and subtlety of an instrumentalist she applies to magnificent effect to Bellini's long-lined melody.

They had been warned in the early days that her voice would not last, but with the passage of time it had become warmer and richer, losing nothing of its accuracy and refinement in coloratura; it had also gained in power and dramatic compulsion and the lower register seemed darker and stronger. There was certainly no need to pay too much heed to the Jeremiahs and with their careers set fair, Sutherland and Bonynge decided to sell their magnificent London home and take up permanent residence in Switzerland. They had already given up the lease on the villa near Locarno and bought a chalet at Les Avants, next door to Noël Coward and only an hour's drive from Geneva. Packing up at Cornwall Gardens had coincided with recording *Les Huguenots* at Kingsway Hall, tasks of marathon proportions completed at roughly the same time. The move had been accomplished by the middle of April, although much of the building and renovation work in progress at their new home had been hampered by the premature arrival of the Bonynges and their entourage together with four containers of furniture and effects.

There were other things for Sutherland to worry about in the shape of Norma and Violetta, which she had not looked at for a year and, with performances in South America only weeks away, there was work to be done. With no possibility of peace at home and with Coward's establishment accessible through a hole in the hedge, she and Bonynge were able to escape from the chaos and the dust and borrow a piano. On the stairs, eavesdropping on the rehearsal, would sit Coward, Coley and the gardener, and one can only suppose there was less ranting than usual for Coward always said how delightful it was to have such 'naice neighbours'.

Pleased to leave the chaos behind, they set off for Argentina, a country they had not visited before, to sing at the Teatro Colon, a theatre with a history of international renown. The Colon's vast and richly luxurious auditorium could seat 2,500 with ease and crammed to capacity over 1,000 more. The acoustics were perfect and the backstage facilities the envy of many famous houses. The opera season was supported by a mainly youthful audience, considered discriminating but intolerant of the second rate; as generous with their brickbats as their bouquets, Sutherland and Bonynge were to receive a sample of both.

Signing the contract had seemed a good idea at the time, but revolutions are almost two-a-penny in Latin America, and the present director of the opera house had taken office with the latest change of political regime, and had had nothing to do with engaging Sutherland, Bonynge, nor Renato Cioni, who was to sing Alfredo, two years earlier. The first night reception was a stormy one and it was not, under the circumstances, surprising that the music critic of the *Buenos Aires Herald* noticed signs of nervous tension throughout the performance. At the stage door, however, a crowd had gathered, ashamed and embarrassed by the noisy antics of a minority of their compatriots. Programmes and record sleeves were autographed and Weenie was kept busy with hundreds of requests for photographs. For a gala performance on the day before Liberation Day there had been such a demand for tickets that the rarely used 'mourning' boxes were opened up, and there was only a handful of empty seats on the eve of a one-day general strike when everything else in the city had begun to grind to a halt. For the gala the final interval had been extended so the National Anthem could be played exactly on the stroke of midnight.

After *La traviata* in Buenos Aires they took off for a few days for a fascinating trip to Macchu Picchu and Lake Titicaca, and then began rehearsals for *Norma*. In performance many critics felt that Fiorenza Cossotto, who was singing Adalgisa, tried to out-sing Sutherland, thereby upsetting the balance of the duets, although Sutherland was hardly aware of what seemed obvious to everyone else. Anything remotely resembling gamesmanship generally flowed over her, though there was one occasion when she had been so irritated by Raina Kabaivanska's attempts to upstage her in *Beatrice di Tenda* that when, as Agnese, she fainted at Beatrice's feet and the hem of her costume trailed across Kabaivanska's face, the temptation to leave it there had been quite irresistible.

The production of *Norma* at the Metropolitan in March 1970 was one of only two new productions to survive the union disputes which cut the 1969/70 season by half. Bonynge conducted and Marilyn Horne, singing Adalgisa, was making her Metropolitan debut. *Norma* could no longer be regarded as a new role for Sutherland, but it was still by far the most challenging: 'For me Norma is the most wonderful role I sing. She has very human feelings; it would be a crime to think one could repeatedly sing *Norma* without finding anything new.' Her schedule for the year was top-heavy with *Normas* and she thought that singing the role so often during that time strengthened her voice, so her perform- ances were not hampered by vocal shortcomings. With Marilyn Horne as comfortable with the bel canto tradition as Sutherland they stirred each other to great things, and their singing of '*Mira o Norma*', firmly in the mould of Ponselle and Telva, according to Schonberg, was worthy of the stupendous ovation it received.

On the dramatic front, however, Sutherland never completely came to grips with the full gamut of emotions sufficiently to satisfy those not won over by her voice alone, and never was critical opinion so widely divided as on this occasion. On the one hand, Schonberg in the *New York Times* 'couldn't have cared less' about Sutherland's well catalogued failings:

> Miss Sutherland still has the most glowing, the richest, the most sensuous sounding voice of any soprano before the public, and she is one of the most exciting technicians . . . she sang with more tension than she has done in the past, build- ing to meaningful climaxes, phrasing with style, using inter- polated cadenzas in such a way that they had expressive qualities without interfering with the flow of the line.

While *Opera Magazine*, on the other hand, had nothing good to say either about the production or the casting, describing it as a 'travesty of Bellini's masterpiece — for its general attitudes and aims in production, conducting, singing and stage deportment, it was one of the worst performances of a great opera I have ever suffered through'. Clearly not a sentiment shared by an audience who cheered it to the echo at every opportunity.

Irving Kolodin was delighted to have Sutherland back in New York after an absence far too long:

> Such a career as hers, however long, is always too short, and to have a year or two spent entirely elsewhere is a deprivation New Yorkers can ill afford. She returns with vocal splendour undiminished, with her all but inhuman accuracy wholly at her bidding and the fastidious kind of musicianship — her trademark — more subtly employed

than before ... for the casual opera goer this 'version' of *Norma* will appeal for the virtuosity of the two principals and the compatibility of the '*Mira o Norma*' duet in particular. Thanks to Miss Sutherland's more than ordinarily low range and Miss Horne's more than ordinarily bright high register, they sometimes create the illusion of the same voice singing two different lines ... Admirable as it was in its own re- strained way Richard Bonynge's conducting was all too dis- posed to favour the vocal patina at a cost to the dramatic structure of which it is a prominent part, but only a part.

Saturday Review, 21 March 1970

And the sting in the tail was once again the spectre of Callas, as Kolodin concluded: 'Beautifully sung, it was almost devoid of effective direction, meaningful action, verbal eloquence, or shafts of dramatic lightning, thus dating to about 250 BC.'

But none of this detracted from the occasion of two important debuts. Always the first to applaud someone else's talent spon- taneously, Sutherland left Horne alone to face the barrage of applause which told her unequivocally how successful her debut had been. Awash with inexpressible emotions it occurred to Horne: 'What a freaky, fantastic thing it is that two people were actually destined to come together like this', but her wish that the Metropolitan might give them another opportunity to show what they could do together, perhaps in *Semiramide*, was to go unfulfilled.

After the Metropolitan Tour of *Norma*, Sutherland and Horne returned to London for a revival at Covent Garden. It was a production which improved on further acquaintance. Stephen Walsh in the *Observer* was not alone in finding that 'the merits of Sandro Sequi's well ordered production and Pier Luigi Pizzi's sets now seem more apparent than on first viewing'. It was received rapturously by the audience, but critical opinion was much the same as before. Although *Norma* is her favourite role, Sutherland is well aware of its complexities and pitfalls — she has even described it as a 'cow of a role' — and she desperately wanted to get it right on all levels. 'I don't know if you thought the *Norma* had improved', she asked a friend. 'I feel it has, and I can play with it more now, although it is a terribly taxing role for anyone and cannot be taken "easily" in many places. She just never stops.'

This round of *Normas* were among the last performances of Sir David Webster's administration of the Royal Opera House. 'The Quiet Showman' was bowing out after 26 years with a Royal Gala tribute of marathon proportions in the presence of Queen

Elizabeth the Queen Mother and a house full of loyal supporters. There was only one alteration to the scheduled programme: it had included Sutherland singing 'Casta diva', and this was replaced by the mad scene from Lucia di Lammermoor. Webster had seen Sutherland graduate from Clotilde to Norma but she just could not face singing another 'Casta diva'. 'Somehow the Lucia seemed so much more appropriate on such an occasion. It really was due to David that my whole career was given the chance to emerge.'

She was pleased to have a summer break in Les Avants, and then it was back to New York for more Normas and six spaced-out performances of La traviata with the Met's usual variety of Alfredos. The Gerard–Guthrie production had died with the old Met, its place taken by a new one mounted for the opening season of Lincoln Center directed by Alfred Lunt, and Sutherland's Alfredos were among the aristocrats of tenors — Giacomo Aragall, Pavarotti, Carlo Bergonzi, Alfredo Kraus and Domingo; at the Met the star system was alive and well.

Sutherland will remember 1970 as being a year of Normas, for from March onwards she had sung little else apart from four performances of Les contes d'Hoffmann for Seattle Opera. Although she had sung the roles of Olympia, Giulietta and Antonia with great success individually at Covent Garden in the 50s, this would be the first time she had undertaken all three roles as well as that of Stella which was customarily a walk-on part. Representing personifications of Hoffmann's ideal love, it makes dramatic sense for them to be portrayed by the same soprano, which was what Offenbach had in mind but which was not generally the case in performance. Sutherland did not, however, regard a performance of Hoffmann as any more vocally demanding than Lucia and certainly not half as taxing as Norma. She was particularly at home with the French lyric repertoire, and as comfortable with the mezzoish sultriness of Giulietta and the sustained lyricism of Antonia as the coloratura display of Olympia. The strain lay more in the four elaborate changes of costume and make-up — right down to the skin each time, a problem she shared with the men who sang the multiple bass and tenor roles.

Les contes d'Hoffmann was Offenbach's swan-song. He had outrun the popularity of the operettas which earned him the title 'the Mozart of the Champs-Elysées', and desperately wanted to write a serious work on a grander scale for the Opéra Comique. His subject was taken from a play by Jules Barbier and Michel Carré which was in turn based on the short stories of E.T.A.

Hoffmann, an early-nineteenth-century romantic writer. Offenbach, however, was a sick man and the musical inspiration did not
flow as readily from his pen for *Hoffmann* as for the lighter bread-
and-butter works he was still obliged to turn out. He worked at a
feverish pace, sensing that his time was limited: 'Make haste and
produce my opera. I have not much time left', he wrote to the
director of the Opéra Comique. 'My only wish is to see the first
night.' But his wish was not to be granted and he died before he
had completed the orchestration. The score was finished by
Ernest Guiraud with the aid of Offenbach's notes and the first
performance at the Opéra Comique, just four months after the
composer's death, was the triumph which he had dreamed of.

However, Guiraud and the director of the Opéra Comique
had taken many liberties with the structure of the score in the
process of getting it onto the stage, and Offenbach's proposed
dialogue was set as recitative to bring the work into line with
grand opera. This made the work excessively long, so the
Giulietta scene was taken out and the Barcarolle, far too good to
cut completely, transferred to the Antonia scene. A quartet in the
Epilogue was rejected only to reappear as a septet in the Giulietta
scene which, altered almost beyond recognition, was resurrected
for later performances in Vienna. The piano score for the
Antonia scene has since come to light, but most of the original
material is believed to have been lost when the Opéra Comique
burned down shortly after the première of *Hoffmann*. Not surprisingly, the more usual published editions have come to bear
little relationship to Offenbach's original score. For years music-
ologists have been researching into a definitive version and
Bonynge, a passionate devotee of Offenbach, had endeavoured
to reconstruct the opera, restoring dramatic shape and continuity
which were more in keeping, in his view, with Offenbach's original
intentions.

Bonynge was in no doubt that Offenbach intended dialogue.
'He didn't suddenly change his entire style to grand opera,' he
explains, 'but wrote a grander *opéra comique* in which the
musical numbers stand out like jewels amidst the dialogue.' He
therefore scrapped the recitative by Guiraud *et al*, and with
reference to the original libretto and the Barbier–Carré play
restored the dialogue. He also discarded all the music which was
obviously Guiraud's, rearranged the Giulietta scene and used the
Barcarolle as a prelude to it — it has no logical place in the
drama, but is too good to cut completely — and returned the
quartet to the Epilogue where it provides Stella with a singing
role to give the work a more substantial climax.

Norman Triegle, the American bass, raised the only significant objection to Bonynge's version, causing a major hiccup as
the opera went into production. Engaged to sing the multiple role
of the evil genius, he was disturbed to find the version used was
not the one he was accustomed to, maintaining that Bonynge's
version, apart from requiring him to learn passages of spoken
French, so drastically altered his role that the part bore no
relationship to that for which he had been contracted. A rep-
resentative of Seattle Opera assured Triegle that if he would say
what he needed to be coaxed back into the production, then it
would be done. But the differences were irreconcilable and
Triegle was replaced by another American bass, Joshua Hecht.

The Seattle *Hoffmann* could not have been given a warmer
nor more enthusiastic reception, and critical comment was generally favourable. Schonberg in the *New York Times* described it as
an 'unusual and utterly absorbing performance — an ingenious
production by Allen Charles Klein, one that set the proper mood
in a most stylish manner, and a production that was smartly
directed by Bliss Hebert'. The only reservation was with reference to the dialogue, but there always would be reservations
about the virtues of performing opera in the original language to
an English-speaking audience, and the argument becomes more
forceful when extended to dialogue.

A couple of *Traviatas* and a few *Normas* at the Metropolitan
preceded Christmas at Les Avants and then it was on to Hamburg
for another series of much acclaimed *Giulio Cesares* at the
Staatsoper. A new production of *Lucia* followed, directed by
Peter Beauvais, and for the first time since her debut, Sutherland
was encouraged to take stock of her portrayal. Beauvais was a
television producer who tended to see everything in relation to
the small screen, which Sutherland found unnerving, even to the
point of wanting to go home. After more than a hundred performances and with a great sense of loyalty to Zeffirelli, she
thought she could never change her conception of *Lucia*. She
persevered, however, and Beauvais' refreshing approach brought
a new intensity to her interpretation. He even introduced a long-
shot as a prelude to the mad scene, with Lucia seen through an
open door sitting beside Arturo's body, covered in blood as a
reminder that Scott's Lucy had stabbed him repeatedly. The
Italians would not have approved.

It was these performances, discovering that she had so much
more to offer the part, that prompted the second recording of
Lucia just 10 years after the first.

In Hamburg, Edgardo was sung by Placido Domingo — her twenty-first Edgardo, and they were performances to be treasured for Domingo was now a top-flight international singer, very expensive and very much in demand, and it was not a partnership many opera houses could afford. Domingo rates these *Lucias* among the greatest performing experiences of his life. Sutherland's technique astounded him, as it had Pavarotti, and he was as impressed as everyone else by her unspoilt simplicity and her and Bonynge's kindness. The admiration was mutual.

Another of Sutherland's partnerships was about to run its course — at least for the time being — for much the same reason. Marilyn Horne had carved her own individual niche in the bel canto revival and was now very much in demand in her own right. The Chicago Lyric Opera had managed to get them together for the 1971 season in *Semiramide*, but it would be more than 10 years before they were seen together again on the operatic stage. *Semiramide* was unashamedly a prime example of 'museum opera', but considered worthy of gala treatment to open the seventeenth season of the Chicago Lyric Opera. The combination of Sutherland and Horne, especially after their tremendous success in *Norma* at the Metropolitan, was a powerful box-office attraction and people flocked from far and wide to catch up on this Rossini rarity which had not been staged in America since Melba appeared in it in 1895.

It did not disappoint. Sutherland and Horne stunned the audience individually and with their sublime duets in the Sequi–Samaritani production borrowed from the Teatro Comunale in Florence. It was essentially a musical experience, described by the *Chicago Daily News* as an 'operatic entertainment of the simplest most basic kind', and the sense of occasion was boosted by 600 bottles of Californian champagne served to the capacity audience. Afterwards the festivities extended to the Hilton Hotel for the Opera Ball where trumpeters dressed in operatic costume accompanied the march of the opera stars with a fanfare. For Sutherland the job did not end when the curtain came down but continued in the dressing room and at the stage door where invariably a crowd gathered with record sleeves and programmes to be autographed. She greatly appreciated the devotion of her fans, but there were occasions when a big society function was just too much. While 500 people took their seats, Sutherland stood and waited. She joined the march of the opera stars and then politely made her excuses and left, to raised eyebrows and shaking heads. Hungry, tired, and emotionally wound up, it was a question of self-preservation and she was at the end of her tether.

10
A Trio of Debuts

After Chicago Sutherland could look clearly ahead to her first new role since Euridice in 1967, that of Donizetti's Maria Stuarda.

War Memorial Opera House, the home of the San Francisco Opera, is second only to the Metropolitan in the American operatic league table. Under the General Director Kurt Herbert Adler, it is noted for its initiative in securing the United States debuts of many artists who later become the darlings of the Met, and also for presenting many American firsts. Among these was *Maria Stuarda*. Perhaps because of her Scottish antecedents, Sutherland had an open admiration for Mary Queen of Scots and an instinctive sympathy for her plight as the innocent victim of Elizabeth I's machinations. It was a welcome departure from the lovesick teenagers that occupied so much of her attention, and one of her most personally satisfying and successful portrayals.

Maria Stuarda was based on Schiller's play *Maria Stuart*, and since Romani was known to have several plans in hand for Donizetti it was assumed that they included the libretto for this latest composition. Alas, Romani, having experienced obstruction from the censors with *Lucrezia Borgia* the previous year, feared more of the same and was not willing to oblige. Donizetti turned therefore to the hack librettist Giuseppe Bardari and, as Romani had anticipated, its birth was turbulent and frustrated at every turn by the Neapolitan censors. The problems were manifold. There was strong evidence that the King of Naples had taken exception to the work on the grounds that the tragic nature of the story did not lend itself to the gala occasion it was meant to celebrate. On the other hand he might have been deferring to the sensibilities of his Queen, who attended the dress rehearsal and was so shocked at the scene of Mary's confession that she had to be taken from her box in a state of collapse.

Whatever the cause, the opera was banned and Donizetti constrained to find an alternative subject to accommodate his score. Pietro Salatino provided another libretto, and with some new music and a little judicious reworking of the original, Donizetti submitted the revised version to the censors as *Buondelmonte*, and as such it was given its first performance at the San Carlo, Naples in October 1834. It was another year before its first airing in its original form at La Scala, and under circumstances no less fraught. The prima donna engaged to sing the role of Elizabeth decided it was unworthy of her and walked out; Donizetti was preoccupied with the death of his father, and Maria Malibran, who was to create the role of Mary, had fallen sick. Even Donizetti described her as voiceless on the opening night, and the audience was not sympathetic. It was far from being one of his most popular works and he despaired of it. But worse was still to come. After the sixth performance and with Malibran restored to vocal health the Milanese censors stepped in, objecting to the scene in which the two Queens abuse each other, demanding the deletion of the word *bastarda*, and forbidding Mary to kneel before Talbot in the confession scene. Malibran, however, refused to concede to alterations that diluted the dramatic impact of the role and the opera was banned for the second time in its troubled history.

It was not until 1865, after Donizetti's death, that *Maria Stuarda* was performed at the San Carlo, the theatre for which it was composed, by which time it had undergone the usual amendments and transpositions to accommodate various singers. After a century of neglect, therefore, it was difficult to assemble an authentic score and that used in San Francisco was based on the Malibran edition of 1835 and painstaking research by *Opera Rara*, a group of enthusiasts who specialize in the revival of nineteenth-century operas.

More than a vehicle for virtuoso singing, it exploded the myth that bel canto opera is dramatically static, and was a triumph for San Francisco Opera. Whatever it might have been in the hands of Romani, Bardari's libretto provides a compact dramatic entity which loses nothing in the liberties it takes with English history. The apocryphal meeting of the two Queens, a brilliant theatrical device in Schiller's play, provides the opera with one of its most telling moments. The score is not lacking in technically demanding virtuoso music, but apart from the fiendishly difficult coloratura and a final scene which builds to a relentless climax, the role of Maria makes demands on the middle voice. Bonynge maintained that Sutherland's middle voice was still fresh and big with added strength and warmth because she had not pushed on it too much when she was young, and she was more than able to cope with Maria's music which might, in fact, have been tailor-made for her.

The 1971/72 season was Sir Rudolf Bing's last as Managing Director of the Metropolitan, and the comic hit of the season was *La fille du régiment* with Sutherland and Pavarotti. But Bing's term of office ended as it had begun with Verdi's *Don Carlo*, and the icing on the cake was a Benevolent Fund Gala in his honour with Sutherland and Pavarotti and a host of artists who had played a prominent part in the Bing years. Bing, in command to the last and ever mindful of the tendency galas have to overrun, issued a memo urging those taking part not to prolong their curtain-calls or be seduced into giving encores, but it was still one o'clock in the morning before the final curtain fell on the end of an era.

A coda to the season and a tribute to Bing's fondness for Verdi, who had received high priority in the repertory, was a three-week Verdi Festival. Featuring seven of the Met's Verdi productions and a roster of star singers, it provided Sutherland with the only opportunity of her international career to sing Gilda — the role she had auditioned, in English, way back in 1958. Sharing the performance with Luciano Pavarotti singing his first Duke at the Metropolitan, and Sherrill Milnes his first Met Rigoletto, she received reviews couched in the same glowing terms as those for her earlier performances:

> She sang a sensitive Gilda — intense rather than girlish, using her famous trill and wide range, not as a vehicle for virtuosity, but as a legitimate means to enhance the music. She looked well and acted simply and convincingly, and all but melted the proscenium when she had a long cantilena to deliver.
>
> Harold Schonberg, *New York Times*, 12 June 1972

It was an occasion when great singers with great voices thoroughly at the service of the music demonstrated that grand opera in its fullest sense is still very much appreciated. Bonynge, conducting *Rigoletto* for the first time, turned in one of his most polished performances with 'artful, beautifully coordinated conducting' that Schonberg had hitherto thought outside his province.

Sutherland opened the fiftieth season of the San Francisco Opera with a lunchtime concert in Union Square. To the thousands jammed into the plaza she was introduced by the Mayor as 'the voice of the century', and office and construction workers leaned from windows and hung from rooftops to catch sound and sight of it. She was presented with the key to the city and a commemorative book on behalf of the Governor of California, Ronald Reagan. She reciprocated with copies of *Les contes d'Hoffmann*, her latest recording, and the Mayor suggested it would be well for the Governor to sit down quietly and listen to it!

A beautiful, polished production of *Norma* opened the season proper, and Sutherland applied purity of phrasing, colour of voice and perfect command of breath to the long-lined melody at the heart of Bellini. 'Rarely had she performed with greater ease, command and vocal finesse', wrote Robert Commanday in the *San Francisco Chronicle*. She still, however, failed to satisfy in the dramatic aspects of the role, until the third act 'when her portrayal rose magnificently in the arias and ensembles preceding Norma's purification and self-immolation'.

At the end of the year she took on another of Donizetti's mature heroines when the Vancouver Opera Association mounted a production of *Lucrezia Borgia*. It was virtually its North American première, for it had been given only one performance at the Metropolitan in the first decade of the century, and had not been seen since.

Mercadante had been commissioned by La Scala to set the libretto of *Lucrezia Borgia* for the soprano Henriette Meric-Lalande, but the macabre subject did not appeal to him and he had set his heart on *Sappho*. Meric-Lalande, however, would not accept *Sappho*, having set her heart on *Lucrezia*. It therefore fell to Donizetti to compose the opera, and it was as well he worked best under pressure, for there were less than three months before the scheduled première. The libretto was based on Victor Hugo's play *Lucrèce Borgia* which was enjoying considerable success in Paris, and Romani had it well underway for Mercadante, although, like the latter, he was uneasy about the rather unsavoury nature of the subject. He had already glossed over the fact that in Hugo's play Gennaro is presented as the son of an incestuous relationship between Lucrezia and her brother, but this delicate piece of editing was not enough to prevent a Milanese family of Borgias taking offence and focusing the attention of the censors upon it. Donizetti's main problem, however, lay in the fact the play did not lend itself easily to operatic treatment. There was an unusually large number of principals and the character of Lucrezia as an anti-heroine defied the romantic conventions and precluded the traditional love duet. Nagged by his conscience, and with a degree of historical integrity not normally associated with librettists, he had doubts, confirmed today, as to the accuracy of Lucrezia's infamous reputation. Also, Meric-Lalande demanded a coloratura show-piece finale, which was not an unusual request as it adhered to the accepted bel canto formula, but the opera was to end with the death of

Gennaro, and Donizetti and Romani had steered away from such a stereotyped finale as being dramatically inappropriate. But with Meric-Lalande insisting on the final note, time was running out and the only thing to do was to provide her with her bravura finale.

Lucrezia Borgia was given its first performance at La Scala in December 1833, with Meric-Lalande past her vocal prime, the rest of the cast not in best voice and the sets and costumes below par by La Scala standards; the evening was not a conspicuous success. However, the opera gained in popularity and completed its first season before the censor's axe fell, and it only reappeared in Italy disguised by a change of title and setting. When it eventually escaped from censorship in the 1850s it enjoyed greater popularity than *Lucia di Lammermoor*, especially at Covent Garden, but by the end of the century it went the way of most operas of the genre, falling out of favour in the wake of Strauss, Puccini and Wagner, and has rarely been performed since.

Bonynge had already conducted a concert performance with Montserrat Caballé in London and he set about his first staged production with infectious enthusiasm, researching a fairly definitive version of the score and retaining the final *scena*. Lucrezia Borgia is not a role for a light coloratura soprano. It requires a large dramatic voice with the same coloratura technique as that required for Lucia; at once lyrical and impassioned, it exploits the depths of the soprano range to a greater degree than Maria Stuarda, only rising to the vocal stratosphere in the fioriture of the bravura finale. Such a finale, despite Donizetti's protestations in this instance, was *de rigueur* in the nineteenth century and no less so in the twentieth. Without it an audience of Sutherland enthusiasts would have felt cheated. One can also strongly assert that it does serve a dramatic purpose as an entirely legitimate expression of Lucrezia's anguish and remorse at the death of her son.

The agility and lightness of Sutherland's voice coupled to the maturity of timbre made it an ideal role at this time in her career, and in Vancouver she demonstrated her supreme command of bel canto to perfection. The Vancouver audiences were eager to hear Sutherland again after an absence of five years, and they were equally keen after seasons of bread-and-butter opera to hear an unknown work that cynics were content to dismiss as a museum piece best left on the archive shelves.

In contrast to the sombre *Lucrezia Borgia*, Sutherland entered 1973 in high spirits with *La fille du régiment* with Pavarotti at the Metropolitan, where audiences were still unselfconsciously lapping up Donizetti's comic opera. March and April were professionally inactive, but in May she returned to London to sing *Lucia* with Pavarotti singing his first Edgardo in London. The lighting was a little too irritatingly stygian, but Zeffirelli's production was still going strong. Approaching her one hundred and fiftieth performance, Sutherland was in splendid voice and her Lucia had lost none of its amazing quality or freshness over the years. Her mad scene was still an unequalled tour de force. The auditorium echoed to ecstatic stamping and cheering; she was pelted with flowers and streamers and left the stage laden with bouquets. There was always a new audience for Sutherland's Lucia and whatever other role she might decide to abandon, it was impossible to think Lucia would be among them. Fears that these might be her last in London had created an overwhelming demand for tickets, and when booking opened the queue, which had begun to form several days earlier, wrapped itself round the Opera House.

After so many years as international celebrities Sutherland and Bonynge were in a strong position to influence what she sang. Years of bit parts and uncongenial roles at Covent Garden had been followed by the hectic pressures of establishing a firm grip on the world circuit. Now she was able to enjoy the luxury of choosing what she sang, where she sang it, and, increasingly, with whom she sang. Few of her new roles filled her with such enthusiasm as that of Rosalinde in *Die Fledermaus*.

At 24 Johann Strauss inherited his father's orchestra and the waltz craze, which he continued to gratify with ever more elegant and sophisticated waltzes, perfecting a genre of indestructible charm and vitality. The waltz was at the heart of *Die Fledermaus*, the first wholly successful attempt to provide a Viennese parallel to Offenbach's highly acclaimed operettas in Paris.

With such a long-standing tradition of operetta and musical comedy in Australia, it was natural for Sutherland and Bonynge to have a special affection for them. Sutherland had been brought up on Gladys Moncreiff, with fond memories of *Rio Rita* and *The Maid of the Mountains*, and during the war years operatic starvation had only been relieved by performances of Gilbert and Sullivan. Sutherland had recorded a two-disc album of musical comedy items from Offenbach through Oscar Strauss and Leo Fall to Sigmund Romberg which she dedicated to 'Our Glad', and which was enormously popular. It should have come as no surprise to anyone who had seen *La fille du régiment* that she would take to Rosalinde like a duck to water, treading a stylistic path between Vienna and Broadway to emerge a winner on all points. She had even taken great pains to learn the Csárdás in Hungarian and was mortified to read a reviewer's comment: 'Her well-known vowel mannerisms sounded delightfully, unintelligibly Hungarian'. Bonynge conducted, and the English translation, with which more than a few liberties had been taken, was directed by Lotfi Mansouri who shared their enthusiasm for operetta.

After *Die Fledermaus* Sutherland went on to Chicago, where *La fille* was on loan from the Met, to stun the Lyric Opera with her sense of comedy, although the critic of the *Chicago Tribune* saw fit to pick it to bits. On this occasion her Tonio was Alfredo Kraus, not altogether at home with the comedy, but very much on top of his high Cs.

Thence back to New York, to the Metropolitan for the Hebert-Klein *Les contes d'Hoffmann* borrowed from Seattle and adapted to the Met's vast stage. Under new management and oppressed with financial difficulties which necessitated the cancellation of several planned projects, the Met was going through a period of artistic doldrums. While extolling the virtues of shared or borrowed productions, what had seemed imaginative and attractive in Seattle appeared to Peter Davis in the *The Times* as somewhat provincial and unworthy of the Metropolitan. The singing however 'attained a level of excellence rarely encountered in the house these days'. It could have been nothing less with Sutherland and Domingo in fine voice and, according to Schonberg, 'when he and Miss Sutherland blended in their duets the house was filled with the kind of controlled forward-projected sound rare in this day and age'.

Bonynge's version of the score was regarded as a marked improvement on the more usual editions, and Schonberg, who had been less than happy with his conducting of the same opera in Seattle, now conceded that he conducted with 'taste and refinement ... but the important thing is he continues to develop as a technician'. He had lost nothing of his deep consideration and understanding of the needs of the singers and when Sutherland succumbed to an attack of gastric flu and cancelled a performance — her first in 12 seasons in New York — he smoothed the path to substantial personal success for her stand-in, Colette Boky.

Bonynge had survived hostile criticism — some of it of an intensely personal nature — to establish a career in his own right, and he was developing as a recording artist quite independently. He was and still is a recognized authority on bel canto with such an extensive personal archive of rare and neglected music that museums turn to him for reference. His passionate belief that in the opera house, the position of the singer is paramount is almost a personal creed. Understanding the physical processes of singing far better than most conductors, he believes that his role is to get the best out of the singer. As a conductor of belcanto, where the voice is the thing, he has special endowments, and singers have enormous confidence in him, secure in the knowledge that he is on their side. He helps and supports them, allowing them to set their own pace, which may vary from performance to performance, and in times of conflict will subordinate the music to the singing. He is especially sensitive to breathing problems and on one occasion was heard to yell abuse at a conductor for not allowing a singer time to breathe: 'I don't care what's written in the score, they must be allowed time to breathe if they need it.' That Bonynge had become a figure regarded with some respect in the musical world was a source of much pleasure and satisfaction to Sutherland, even if it meant that he had rather less time to spend with her. He still conducted for her performances, lay the groundwork for new roles and kept a watching brief on the old, but private rehearsals were becoming less intensive, and they enlisted the help of Sylvia Holford as accompanist and *répétiteur*.

Sylvia Holford, a professional pianist and cellist, had come to them in an hour of need as Bonynge's assistant for the last two of the children's series *Who's Afraid of Opera?* for CBS. Asked to prepare *Rigoletto*, no-one had thought to tell her it had been cut to 30 minutes, so she arrived somewhat over-prepared. But as Bonynge pursued his own career, Sylvia took over whenever necessary as Sutherland's *répétiteur*. Sutherland no longer vocalized every day; rest was often best between performances two or three days apart, and vocal workouts consisted mainly of learning new roles and concentrating on the parts of her current repertoire likely to give her trouble. Having discussed in some detail what was required with Bonynge, Sylvia worked with Sutherland to put it into effect.

After the Metropolitan tour of *Les contes d'Hoffmann*, Sutherland and Bonynge made a leisurely journey via Mexico City, Tahiti and Noumea to Australia, where they were to appear in the newly opened Opera House and put their seal of approval on the miracle of architecture and acoustics glinting in the sunlight on Bennelong Point. Its turbulent development had made it one of the most controversial projects in the world, but when Sutherland had visited it in 1965 with gantries dominating the superstructure and no obvious signs of how the interior would turn out, she had not been alone in expressing certain doubts.

It was in 1956 that Jörn Utzon, a Danish architect of great vision but little actual experience, submitted the winning entry in an international competition to design 'a proposed national opera house'. An unfortunate choice of words since the building was intended to be a performing arts complex whose prime function was not that of an opera house, but to provide a permanent home for the Sydney Symphony Orchestra. Two halls had been envisaged: the largest would be for orchestral concerts, large-scale opera, ballet and dance, choral works and pageants; the smaller one for drama productions, intimate opera, chamber music, concerts, recitals and lectures. The terms of reference clearly stated that these priorities should not be changed or compromised in any way. Preliminary work was begun in May 1958 before it was known whether it was possible to translate Utzon's futuristic design into reality. The geometric complexity of the roof 'shells' posed problems to tax the ingenuity of the most experienced structural engineers, problems which were to take years of experiment and computer calculation before the building could take on its uniquely recognizable shape. The scheduled opening date came and went, and with a change of State Government in 1966 there was growing alarm over the slow progress being made as construction costs escalated.

Friction developed between Utzon and the government officials involved with the project, the architect resigned and the responsibility for the completion of the building fell to a panel of Australian architects whose first task was to re-examine the plans for the interior. Utzon's designs had included specifications for four auditoria, the largest of which was to have been a dual-purpose concert hall and opera theatre — to him a feasible proposition. The panel, however, came to the conclusion — mistakenly, in the light of future events — that a concert hall suitable for the performance of opera was acoustically impossible. To strive for such duality would result in an auditorium that would not be wholly satisfactory for orchestral music or opera. The fact that the 1966 opera season had been short and poorly attended might also have lent weight to the argument that a large opera theatre was not an economic proposition. Consequently the major hall was stripped of its proscenium arch, the stage concreted over and some highly sophisticated scene-shifting equipment dumped in its crates by the Parramatta River.

In its final state, the complex, under four acres of ceramic tiling and one and a half acres of laminated glass, consisted of a magnificent concert hall with fine acoustics and a seating capacity of 2,800, an opera theatre with seating for 1,400, a drama theatre and a cinema. In the meantime a look at the development of the Australian Opera shows that although short and poorly attended the 1966 season was artistically better than anything prior to the Sutherland–Williamson tour the previous year. As a result the New South Wales Government granted the AO a subsidy with a view to establishing a permanent company. Also in 1967 the Elizabethan Trust Orchestra was formed for the sole support of the opera and ballet companies which had hitherto relied on the state-based ABC Symphony Orchestras, with the attendant burden of constant rehearsal. It is ironic, therefore, that as opera in Australia was taking a significant up-turn it was relegated to a theatre too small in its seating capacity and stage facilities for opera on a large scale.

As a performing arts centre, however, nothing can detract from the facilities the Sydney Opera House offers, nor the originality of the architecture which dominates one of the most beautiful harbours in the world and must surely rank as one of the modern wonders of it.

Sutherland had been fully convinced that she would be too old to sing in the Opera House by the time it was finished, and try though she might she had not been able to juggle her schedule to include the official opening by The Queen. But nine months later, in time to celebrate the first 21 years of the Australian Opera, Sutherland and Bonynge were returning as guests of an established company already learning to make the best of the Opera House and all its shortcomings. The production was *Les contes d'Hoffmann*, her best yet, directed by Tito Capobianco and designed by José Varona, in Bonynge's edition of the score, which was now well run-in.

Questions had been asked in the Legislative Council when the contract was under negotiation, seeking assurances that the supporting cast would be predominantly Australian. This was not possible in Melba's day, hence her company of Italian singers, but now the fact that the company could provide such a cast was the result of a long and arduous struggle to build a permanent ensemble with a base in Sydney. With the exception of Huguette Tourangeau, a French-Canadian, the Australian Opera provided a strong supporting cast which gave an impeccable performance.

The decision to perform the opera in French, however, caused some consternation in the company for it meant that they had to learn it again in English for subsequent performances in Adelaide. But it was standard practice for international singers to stipulate the language they would sing in. Having sung her Hoffmann roles in French for so long, Sutherland had no wish to change on this occasion, and what was wrong with singing it in French in Adelaide?

Les contes d'Hoffmann opened the new season with a gala performance that even eclipsed in its sense of occasion the memorable first night of the Sutherland–Williamson tour. The audience was there to pay tribute to Sutherland rather than Offenbach and they received generous measure, for *Hoffmann* afforded a broad view of Sutherland's talents, and the production was lavish and spectacular by the highest international standards. It is a difficult opera to stage, a story of mystery and imagination and a bizarre journey into the poet's dreams, and Varona and Capobianco played the Gothic nightmare quality for all it was worth. Being only the second live broadcast from the Opera House (the first was the opening performance of *War and Peace*), a commentator helped the action on its way. As Sutherland appeared a voice, hushed and reverent, murmured: 'Sutherland's appearance', and a few moments later: 'She sings'. And sing she did to the unanimous praise of the critics:

> In the Act I Doll Song she demonstrated something very like sporting prowess. The tempo was fast, the variations and cadenzas were dazzling, and there were impeccably proportioned echo effects, diamond-cut staccato passages and fearless excursions in the D flat–E flat area of the soprano range. She spared herself nothing in counterfeiting the mechanical arm and body movements of Olympia, nor in singing from a reclining position as Giulietta. She is no great actress but there was a real difference between each of her interpretations, not least in the warmth of Antonia and the hauteur of Stella. Miss Sutherland brought the audience to its highest pitch of excitement in the surging phrases of her Act III trio (superbly paced by the conductor). Here she was the complete dramatic soprano.

Roger Covell, *Sydney Morning Herald*, 17 July 1974

In 1965 the formation of the company, the building and rehearsing of seven new operas in such a short space of time, and a heavy touring schedule had put an incredible strain on all concerned, and Sutherland had found the responsibility for much of the success of the tour an awesome burden. Her emotions about this second homecoming were ambivalent. Although looking forward to the vastly exciting prospect of working in the new Opera House, *en route* to Australia she wrote to a friend of 'the Sydney ordeal — it's not easy to go home'. In spite of her apprehensions she felt thoroughly at home with the company and it came as no surprise to them to find her punctilious and conscientious about attending rehearsals or to spot her queueing for coffee in the canteen. After years at the top she was as natural and unspoilt as ever and still 'our Joan' at heart.

The trip was a most satisfying and rewarding experience for those on both sides of the footlights. Two Recitals in the Concert Hall — her first in Australia since 1951 — were also an enormous success. Like the Royal Albert Hall, which she loves, she found the acoustics congenial and pronounced it one of the finest halls in the world in which to sing. To some it was something of a miracle that Sutherland was still in her prime, and while the press continually harked on retirement, there was a great sense of urgency to see and hear as much as possible of Sutherland before this actually came about. So when it was announced from the stage after the final performance of *Hoffmann* by the General Manager, John Winther, that Sutherland and Bonynge had agreed to become life members of the Australian Opera, which presumably meant they would be seen on a more regular basis, the news was greeted with much jubilation. No-one at that time could see the ramifications of this in the restless evolution of opera house politics, but for the moment it was the ultimate seal of approval.

There was now a clear indication in the record catalogues that Bonynge's enthusiasm for the French repertoire was not confined to Offenbach. He had already recorded, apart from *Hoffmann*, *Lakmé* and *Les Huguenots*, an album of French arias with Sutherland, and another of ballet music and entr'acts from French operas. His latest preoccupation was with Jules Massenet. The discovery of some Massenet letters in a London junk shop had stimulated his long and exhaustive research into the life and work of Massenet, and the result was a comprehensive collection of his scores and a great affection for his music. There was a degree of inevitability about Bonynge's affinity for Massenet, since he shared the composer's deep love and understanding of the workings of the human voice. Bonynge was especially attracted to the romantic opera *Esclarmonde*, the composition of which had been greatly inspired by the voice of one singer in particular — the American soprano Sibyl Sanderson. Unlike many nineteenth-century composers who could turn out an opera on demand at break-neck speed, Massenet never delivered a work 'without keeping it beside me for months, even years'. He had already been working on *Esclarmonde* for some time before he met Sibyl Sanderson, the singer who was to have such a profound influence on it. As well as an ear for a beautiful voice,

Massenet had an eye for a pretty face, and Sanderson was an exceptionally beautiful woman with a voice of great purity and agility with a seamless legato range of three octaves including a true G in altissimo. To Massenet she was the perfect incarnation of the enchanted Esclarmonde; he became completely obsessed by her, and her influence on the final score of *Esclarmonde* went far deeper than the formidable vocal line which reflected exactly her capabilities — including the high G. So closely was she involved in the composition that Massenet dedicated the opera to her and insisted she added her name to his at the bottom of the score.

Esclarmonde was premièred at the Opéra Comique in May 1889. It was not a grand opera in the tradition of Meyerbeer, but a lyric drama based on a medieval French legend to a libretto by Alfred Blau and Louis de Gramont. In the richness of the symphonic orchestration and the use of leitmotiv it owed much to the influence of Wagner, for whom Massenet had an unconcealed admiration. Nevertheless the melodic recitatives leading to lyrical arias and ensembles remained typically French and essentially Massenet. It was an exotic and lavish production with nothing spared in the attention to detail, all minutely supervised by the composer. It was a visual and aural extravaganza of magical invocations, sensuous love and heroic deeds, much enjoyed by the audience, but coolly received by the critics who resented the Wagnerian flavour and missed the eighteenth-century charm of *Manon*.

Yet it was a tremendous personal success for Sibyl Sanderson who went on to sing the role more than a hundred times. After her death Massenet actively discouraged performances of the work; after his own death it was occasionally revived, but by the mid-1940s it was gathering dust on the archive shelves.

Esclarmonde was an ideal role for Sutherland. Massenet's sensuously melodic score, with flights of coloratura, lyrical arias and passages of dramatic declamation suited her voice to perfection. But Bonynge had contemplated the score for a number of years, driving Sutherland nearly crazy with his constantly reiterated: 'This is absolutely marvellous — listen to this — imagine singing that', before he was absolutely convinced it was worthy of a modern revival. It was Kurt Herbert Adler, Director of San Francisco Opera, bolstered by an adventurous sponsor in the person of Mrs Rudolf Light, who had the courage to indulge this conviction. Lotfi Mansouri, another Massenet enthusiast, directed and Beni Montressor designed it. Having directed *Don Quichotte*, *Manon* and *Thaïs*, Mansouri was already aware of the peculiarly theatrical nature of Massenet's compositions. He left nothing to chance; every dramatic inflection, every breath was clearly indicated in the score, and the stage directions were no less specific. 'I was scared stiff when I first looked at the score', confessed Mansouri as he considered the problems of presenting a phantasmagoria of virgins and a heroine who has to fly! He was not tempted to modernize the opera or play down the fairy-tale quality of it, but emphasized the romantic nature of the work. Beni Montressor did not share the same enthusiasm, but found it sufficiently Wagnerian to inspire him. With painted scrims and gold-encrusted gauzes he created a magical world of enchanted isles and Byzantine splendour, and heightened the effect with subtle lighting and coloured vapour. It was a breathtakingly beautiful production.

In spite of his all-consuming enthusiasm, Sutherland had not been at all sure that Bonynge was right to revive *Esclarmonde*, and she found it one of her most difficult roles to learn. Also, as her forty-eighth birthday approached, she thought she was getting a bit long in the tooth for these romantic ingenues. *Lucia* was the exception, but she had sung her last Gilda two years earlier and she had long since decided she could no longer romp on as Amina. At War Memorial Opera House, though, the audience were more than willing to suspend belief and revel in an evening of fine bravura singing, endless melody and visual fantasy. It was refreshing to find that romantic escapism, uncomplicated by the obscure symbolism so beloved of the critics, still had a welcome place on the operatic stage, and Sutherland was over-joyed that Bonynge was acknowledged with praise in his own right instead of as 'the diva's also-ran':

> Bonynge conducts with sweep, drive and passionate commit-ment ... Miss Sutherland started out tentatively in the first act, but soon coped magnificently with the extraordinary demands of the music — in turn lyrical, dramatic and colora-tura. She brought melting lyricism, thunder, enchanting staccati and a few hair-raising high notes to the challenge.
> Martin Bernheimer, *Los Angeles Times*, 11 November 1974

> In the title role, Joan Sutherland not only sang the pyrotech-nics brilliantly (the Invocation in Act I with a high D at the end of each verse was masterful), yet managed the sensuous music of the duets with that creamy middle voice which she alone among coloratura sopranos commands.
> Stephanie von Buchau, *Pacific Sun*, 13 November 1974

Esclarmonde is an opera depending almost entirely for its

success upon vocal talent of a specialized kind, and Bonynge's confidence in the work had been thoroughly vindicated on this occasion. Schyler Chapin, who succeeded Rudolf Bing as General Manager of the Met, also appreciated its box-office appeal and two years later the Met borrowed the same production.

Herbert Breslin's expansive publicity declared Sutherland as 'the supreme soprano of the century. She may be the greatest soprano of any century, but we have no way of judging. We do know she is the only person in the world who can sing *Esclarmonde*.' Sutherland lived up to expectations, although at the first performance there was a noticeable beat on some sustained notes and the occasional attack was a little below par, but according to Harold Schonberg:

Sutherland's rich, warm and vibrant voice had never been heard to better advantage ... the big soaring line is there, the golden sound remains unparalleled, and there was some radiant singing. Miss Sutherland's instrument is still unique.

This was one of Bonynge's memorable performances. He led *Esclarmonde* with style and spirit and with a firm rhythmic base not always encountered in his work in the past. Mr Bonynge was very careful to work with the singers holding the orchestra to a level which the voices could easily penetrate. Yet he did not neglect the scoring and the orchestra sounded firm, sonorous and, most important, sensuous. It was a most satisfactory evening and it could well spark a look at some other virtually forgotten Massenet operas.

New York Times, 20 November 1976

It was of no consequence to the audience who packed into the Met for ten sold-out performances, that Sutherland by this time had turned 50. She was philosophical about it: 'Not everyone gets to celebrate their fiftieth birthday playing a 19-year-old nymphomaniac', and she was thrilled that it had been so well received in New York.

11

Do You Think I'd Sing Any Better If They Made Me a Dame?

Sutherland hankered in vain after a new production of *La traviata* at Covent Garden, but in January 1975 she sang Violetta in the predominantly black-and-white 1967 Visconti production, and the belle époque costumes suited her to perfection. Violetta had become, with Norma, one of her favourite roles, and it was always a challenge, but, alas, like Norma, one in which she was never to completely satisfy the critics. Nevertheless she produced a golden stream of secure sound and gave a convincing and poignant portrayal of Violetta, and Bonynge conducted some of his most successful performances at Covent Garden to date.

The 1975/76 season saw a bonanza of performances with Sutherland and Pavarotti in America, which proved to be the last operatic performances they gave together. They had maintained a consistent partnership since 1965, but Pavarotti was rapidly becoming one of the highest-paid tenors in the world, and as a double act they were too expensive for their schedules to converge except in the recording studio or on the concert platform in immensely hyped-up gala simulcasts (simultaneous television and radio broadcasts). The bonanza began with *Il trovatore* in San Francisco.

As a girl, Sutherland had sung Manrico to her mother's Azucena in the duet *'I nostri monti'*, a great favourite at home, and 20 years ago she had sung the Act IV duet with Frederick Sharpe in a BBC broadcast. To sing Leonora had long been an ambition of hers, the more realistic of two she once owned to. The other was to sing the tenor aria from the last act of *Lucia*, and the closest she came to that was at a party, accompanied by Richard, with Silvio Varviso conducting with a bread-stick.

In Verdi's operatic output, *Trovatore* falls between *Rigoletto* and *La traviata*, when his reputation was such that any opera he composed was guaranteed an audience, with opera houses competing for the distinction of presenting the première. Verdi was fascinated by Spain and greatly attracted to Antonio Garcia Gutierrez's play *El Trovador*, especially for its portrayal of filial and maternal love and for the character of Azucena for whom he had great sympathy. The draft libretto, however, which was supplied by Cammarano, gave Verdi the impression that the librettist was not happy with the subject, and rather than produce an opera which did not fully capture the boldness and originality of the play which so appealed to him, Verdi set it aside and turned his attention to a commission for the Fenice — *La traviata*. But Cammarano persevered and Verdi's confidence in the work grew, so that when the former died suddenly, Verdi was sufficiently inspired to allow Cammarano's protégé Emanuele Bardare to complete the work from his notes.

Il trovatore was given its first performance at the Teatro Apollo in Rome in January 1853, and the enthusiasm of an audience eager for Verdi's latest work was not dampened by having to wade through a foyer flooded with water from the Tiber, and the opera was a sensational success. As with *Rigoletto* and *La traviata*, it went against the conventional grain, but the dark, brooding melodrama with more than a hint of horror had a vicarious fascination for a mid-nineteenth-century audience. Within a year over 30 productions had been mounted in Italy alone and within a decade it became a frequently performed opera throughout Western Europe. With such a wealth of luscious music it has survived to the present day despite constant attempts at parody, accusations of vulgarity and the propagation of the myth that the plot is incomprehensible and difficult to follow. If there is a flaw in Verdi's masterpiece it lies in a score which makes such strenuous demands on the singers. Charles Osborne, however, describes it as the 'veritable apotheosis of bel canto opera', and Bonynge, conducting the work for the first time, viewed it as such rather than holding the more customary opinion that it is merely the forerunner to Verdi's mature works.

According to Caruso, *Il trovatore* is so packed with drama that all it requires for a successful performance is the four greatest singers in the world, well nigh impossible advice for any opera manager in the current economic climate. However, with Sutherland and Pavarotti joined by Obratsova and Wixell, Herbert Adler had brought together, in the words of the *New York Times*, 'an international dream cast', and the degree of excitement which always attends a debut performance ensured that neither love nor money could buy a ticket within days of booking opening.

Sutherland faces all opening nights with a degree of apprehension, but the mental and physical strain attendant on a first performance in a major new role was compounded on this occasion by a tooth abscess. The pain and the strain showed briefly in

an initial unevenness, but she went on to give a strong performance, meeting the demands of the music with vocal beauty and
agility and passages of discreet coloratura. In restoring cabalettas
usually avoided by other singers, she brought a new dimension
and symmetry to Leonora's music. Alexander Fried in the *San
Francisco Examiner* thought she attained in her portrayal of
Leonora a more expressive grip than was often the case in more
stylized coloratura roles.

Pavarotti ran vocally true to form including the wondrous high
Cs in '*Di quella pira*', not written by Verdi but which audiences
have come to expect. There were those who found the performance lacking in fire and passion, but what it failed to provide in
this area it made up with great singing, and did not disappoint an
audience out to be excited by Verdi's familiar score.

The critics said much the same of the partnership in *Lucia di
Lammermoor* in Chicago the following month: amazement and
awe at the vocal virtuosity, overshadowed by a lack of warmth in
the dramatic interpretation. Acerbic reviews from the Chicago
critics were not unusual, yet the audience amply demonstrated
with their cheers of approval that Sutherland could astonish those
who had been listening to her for 17 seasons as she did those
hearing her for the first time. She kept saying she was getting too
old for some of her most taxing roles, but after such a reception
she 'suddenly didn't feel so old'. The critics may have nit-picked,
but audiences clamoured for more. Richard Dyer, the music critic
of the *Boston Globe* described her voice at this time:

> The voice retains the clarity of its youth, and its springing
> upward flight to the exultant high E flat. But now it brings
> into play the chiaroscuro, the mingling of light and shade,
> the warmer colours that come only with the disciplined
> development and physical maturity.

Bonynge thought that while retaining its youthfulness it was not
white and artificially girlish: the voice had fattened and was
warmer and more beautiful than it was at the beginning. It was in
good shape for Elvira in the Met's new production of *I puritani*
and she and Pavarotti were raring to go.

Sutherland had last sung in *I puritani* in San Francisco in 1966 and
for years she had pleaded with Rudolf Bing to revive it for her at
the Met where it had only been performed a handful of times and
not at all since 1918. Her pleas, however, had fallen on deaf ears
and when the New York City Opera launched a new production
with Beverly Sills in 1973 the possibility of a change of heart
had seemed remote. She was mortified therefore when Schyler

Chapin, who succeeded Bing in 1972, offered Sills a new production of *I puritani* for her Metropolitan debut in 1975. Although an internationally acclaimed soprano and the darling of the New York City Opera, Sills had never appeared at the Met, since her repertoire was substantially the same as Sutherland's and Caballé's, and Bing thought the latter two were better at it. Chapin had absolutely no idea how much potential there was in this situation for a first-class row, until it was hinted that if Sills were to sing Elvira, Sutherland might think twice before signing any further contracts with the Met. Fortunately it did not come to that and Sills graciously agreed to make her debut in Rossini's *Le siège de Corinthe* instead.

In 1976, therefore, Sutherland appeared in a new production of *I puritani* which endeavoured to recapture the contemporary ambience of the 1835 original — what the Italians call *riezumiazione*, and of which Covent Garden's *Lucia* was a fine example. Ming Cho Lee's elegant and tasteful décor with scenes bearing a marked resemblance to the hand-painted lithographs of the era were, however, too muted for Andrew Porter's taste, and John Higgins in *The Times* thought the vocal performances worthy of better staging. Other critics were unequivocal:

> Joan Sutherland, now at the summit of her splendid powers, sang with a greater directness and verbal clarity than I have heard from her and as a consequence *'Qui la voce'* was more beautiful and touching than in the past. But the special glory of her performance is the way in which she commands the ensembles; there is hardly anything in opera today as thrilling as the sound of that lustrous voice ringing out with ease and authority over the combined forces of orchestra, chorus and soloists.
>
> Dale Harris, *Guardian*, April 1976

In *Opera News* Robert Jacobson acknowledged Bonynge's influence on the performance: 'Richard Bonynge brought his expertise in this period, leading with more vitality than ever before, but never afraid to indulge his singers or his orchestra in Bellini's rich melodic outpouring.' Lord Harewood thought Sutherland's entrance in the polacca *'Son vergin vezzosa'*, carrying her wedding veil, was a moment of pure magic; some of the most splendid singing he had ever heard from her. With Sutherland, Pavarotti, Milnes and Morris representing the closest one could get to a twentieth-century reincarnation of Grisi, Lablache, Rubini and Tamburini, and the sumptuous costumes of Peter Hall, to the eyes and ears of most people *I puritani* was an unequivocal success.

In 1974 Bonynge had opened another chapter in his career to become Musical Director of the Vancouver Opera Association, and Sutherland was looking forward to a break from the 'heavies' with her debut as *The Merry Widow* in April 1976, her first appearance in Vancouver since he had taken office. 'It's for my equilibrium', she explained, 'I die so often.'

Vancouver audiences had previously been thrilled by her *Lucia* and honoured to have secured her world debuts in *Norma* and *Lucrezia Borgia*. Expecting more of the same calibre, when a new production of *The Merry Widow* was announced the principal reaction was one of disappointment. The introduction of an operetta into the repertoire of an opera house was not without precedent, and even Bing in his first season at the Met launched a new production of *Die Fledermaus* in an attempt to capture a wider audience.

At its première in 1905, *The Merry Widow* revived the declining fortunes of the operetta industry, inspiring an enthusiasm for the genre not equalled since Strauss and Offenbach had been on everyone's lips. Lehár's previous work, however, had not been a success, and the Director of the Theater an der Wien did not hold out much hope for *The Widow*. It was produced on a shoe-string with a hotch-potch of sets and costumes from other productions as a stop-gap until another show could be rehearsed. But contrary to expectations it was a huge success; Lehár became a household word and *The Merry Widow* achieved the distinction of being one of the few operettas acceptable in the repertory of many international opera houses.

In Vancouver, with so much of Sutherland's more usual repertoire unexploited it was considered a waste of her talent, a contention she was apt to dismiss as unutterable musical snobbery. But matters were not helped by a recently reported interview in which Sutherland suggested that Vancouver — and Sydney, where Bonynge was also Musical Director — would be good places for trying things out. It was a maladroit remark made in the context of much meatier operatic fare, but which smacked of Melba's 'Sing 'em muck'. Instead, therefore, of providing a platform for a unique Sutherland debut the Vancouver Opera Association saw themselves as a proving ground for a role Sutherland wanted to get out of her system and took it as a slight. On the other hand there was obviously high curiosity value in a great prima donna letting her hair down, and on the evidence of six sold-out performances, Sutherland in *The Widow* was better than no Sutherland at all.

The Vancouver production leaned more towards musical

comedy than operetta, following the pattern of the first London performance with Lily Elsie at Daly's Theatre. With music from other Lehár scores arranged for the purpose by Douglas Gamley, Bonynge interpolated an overture and a ballet and a gratuitous finale for Sutherland in the form of 'Love Live Forever' from *Paganini*. Of course, the purists complained. An operetta such as this requires an artistically light touch; it must effervesce rather than boil over. While it may benefit from a great voice, they said, it does not necessarily suffer through lack of it. While awarding her 'A' for effort, the general feeling was that as Anna Glavari, Sutherland was miscast.

Bonynge had succeeded Edward Downes as Musical Director of the Australian Opera in 1976, and *Lakmé*, one of ten new productions for the year, was the first he undertook in that capacity. His first season, however, took place against a background of financial crisis which threatened the very existence of the company. As a national company the Australian Opera was 20 years old and celebrating three years in its new home, but a recent cut in government subsidy, a deficit of nearly one million dollars and a proposal to cut the orchestra by 12 members threw the management into a frenzied appeal for more commercial sponsorship. In an attempt to make the most of Sutherland's box-office appeal and recoup some of the losses, tickets for *Lakmé* were sold at a premium, as also were several performances with Kiri te Kanawa making her debut with the AO. *Lakmé* therefore represented an expensive night at the opera. Brian Hoad thought it quite probably the most expensive entertainment ever staged in Australia, and the ABC disparagingly doubted that the Australian Opera could produce anything worth that much! A commodity, however, is worth whatever the customer is prepared to pay, and all 11 performances were sold out well in advance and could have been over and over again.

'World class' and 'international standard', whatever the ABC might think, were phrases frequently applied to the AO, where productions could stand comparison with the best other major opera houses could offer, but such accolades do not come cheaply. The media were afflicted with an almost obsessive preoccupation with the cost of producing opera in general, and the cost of engaging Sutherland in particular was to be the subject of an ongoing saga.

The first performance of *Lakmé* was a gala occasion, part of a first-night subscription series which was something of an innovation, with souvenir costume prints and chocolates handed out by flunkies in eighteenth-century livery. Backstage, however, the atmosphere was far from festive, as the orchestra held a meeting to protest at the uncertainty of their future which delayed the raising of the curtain by 40 minutes. The audience were getting restive by the time John Winther appeared to read out a prepared statement.

Sutherland was eventually welcomed back with cheers, streamers and flowers after a performance of considerable emotional power, yet by the standard she herself has set she was not in her best form. Roger Covell in the *Sydney Morning Herald* thought she sounded a little tired vocally, and Brian Hoad noticed 'an edginess about her entire performance . . . some persistent roughness of tone in the middle register'.

But she had not been oblivious to the tensions backstage as she tried to relax with her needlepoint while the Union held up the show, neither did the reinstatement of the prompt-box, not a familiar sight in Sydney, do much to mitigate her usual attack of first-night nerves. Sutherland's poor memory was by now well known, in fact it was publicly declared when a woman interrupted a concert in Washington to ask why she always sang with a book in front of her, and was told quite bluntly: 'I have a lousy memory, that's why!' She had last performed *Lakmé* with a very conscientious prompter who, when asked why he prompted so loudly, cheerfully replied: '*She* likes to hear every word' — but not so the back row of the auditorium! These performances were a long way behind her now, but she had come back to it so freshly that she could have sworn she had never sung the part before. The prompt-box was her security blanket and her response to a stereotyped memo from Kurt Herbert Adler saying: 'Please note there will be no prompter at War Memorial Opera House for the 1966/67 season', had been equally short and to the point: 'Please note, I'll not be singing without a prompter.'

Lakmé, an excellent example of French operatic literature, took its place in an AO repertoire not overendowed with French works. It was not intended simply as a vehicle for Sutherland, but as an ideal ensemble piece with a title role which could be admirably filled by other sopranos in the company. For all its charm, however, it did not allow Sutherland's famous vocal pyrotechnics full rein and Sydney opera-goers hungered for *Lucia* or *Norma*. It was, however, several seasons before their hunger was satisfied.

The first season of the Australian Opera to come under the direct influence of Richard Bonynge as Musical Director was launched with *Lucrezia Borgia*, one of ten operas in a nicely balanced season. It was the first bel canto opera to be taken into the repertoire of the AO and the reception was variable, polarizing into a pro- and anti-bel canto lobby. To some it was a typical example of museum opera, tedious and lacking in musical colour, while others welcomed it as a highly theatrical piece abounding in good tunes. It is an undisputed vehicle for a dramatic coloratura soprano, but Donizetti's ensemble writing provides opportunities for several principal singers thereby making it a rewarding opera for a company that prides itself on the quality of its ensemble.

Sutherland credited the director, on this occasion George Ogilvie, with having helped her to develop the role greatly since she had last sung it. There were those, however, who thought that he had accepted Sutherland's apparent limitations too readily and that he could have done more to help her develop the character more strongly as Victor Hugo conceived it: moral deformity purified by motherhood. Sutherland always acknowledges the need for firm direction. She needs someone who does not stand in awe of her, a director who not only makes her do things but is also not afraid to tell her if something she has done was not good enough. But as Brian Hoad pointed out, baddies are not really her line: 'The very idea that she could be repellent is unthinkable,' he wrote in the *Bulletin*, '. . . Much of her magic on stage is that she remains consistently her own rather lovable self.' Sutherland had experienced some difficulty reconciling the wicked character of Lucrezia with the more lyrical passages of Donizetti's music, and especially difficult was the emotional transition from the cantilena of the Prologue to the dramatic confrontation with Don Alfonso in Act I. She had been more than happy to cling to the recently confirmed belief that Lucrezia was not an evil instigator but a puppet in the hands of a powerful manipulator, and she had played the role with the emphasis on obsessive motherhood rather than malevolent monster.

The financial problems of the Australian Opera were by no means a thing of the past, but they had succeeded for the present in averting the worst effects. The new production of *Lucrezia Borgia* had been made possible by sponsorship from Qantas Airways, but the need for economies had entailed cutting back the sets from those originally proposed. However, Kristian Fredrikson, a young Australian designer still relatively new to the operatic scene, created stage pictures suggestive of Renaissance decadence. His costumes were an exercise in elaborate splendour, if on this occasion a trifle over-ornate for Sutherland. 'A triumph of upholstery' was how someone described it, but designers seemed to think that because she was big, she could carry everything they ever wanted to put on a costume, and a costume weighing in the region of 20 kilos was not unusual.

Bonynge had been convinced that with singers to sing what in practice can be a difficult opera to cast, *Lucrezia Borgia* was capable of giving great enjoyment. The Australian Opera had a top-rank mezzo-soprano in Margreta Elkins for the travesti role of Maffio Orsini, and a superb baritone in Robert Allman, making the first act with Sutherland one of the most dramatically powerful in the whole opera. The weak link was the tenor Ron Stevens, testing the water of bel canto for the first time after a marathon run of Don Josés and finding himself out of his depth as Gennaro. The seven principal supporting roles had been filled with accomplishment from the ranks of the Australian Opera.

She (Miss Sutherland) was sufficiently on top of the challenge to make the music sound appropriate to the drama and to remind a devotedly attentive house of the old tradition of coloratura as an expressive device. In one respect it was easier for her: for this final outburst of vocal splendour she had only to match her own abnormally high and abnormally consistent standards of performance and the ever-watchful, ever-flexible conducting of Richard Bonynge.

The single and electrifying contrast occurred when Robert Allman as the head of the Este family and Lucrezia's husband confronted her with a voice as sturdy and resolute ... This was a conflict of titans, and it proceeded, as it must do in opera, through the thrust of the sung word even more than through gesture and movement.

Roger Covell, *Sydney Morning Herald*, 6 June 1977

Following *Lucrezia Borgia*, Sutherland took a brief departure from her usual repertoire into verismo with Puccini's *Suor Angelica*, a role perfectly matched to her voice and temperament and one which proved to be one of her most moving and dramatically satisfying:

It is a role which demands a carefully paced progression from subtly underplayed ensemble work, through the dramatic fireworks of the duet, into the final scene of dazzling solo ecstasy ... Sutherland handles all the demands magnificently ... The interplay with her sister nuns is ensemble work at its most sensitive. The explosive meeting with her aunt is played out with all the new-found power of her lower registers. And in the closing scene, the more familiar Sutherland soars heavenwards as only she can.

Brian Hoad, *Bulletin*, 30 July 1977

Sentimental and melodramatic, *Suor Angelica* is often regarded as the weakest of Puccini's one-act operas, a view not shared by Sutherland or Bonynge, who have it high on their list of Puccini

favourites. Sutherland, sparing nothing in her physical representation of the opera's essential ingredients — hope, anguish and
despair — gave a performance which, combined with elegant
sets, sensitive production and what Roger Covell described as
the 'shining ingredient' of Bonynge's conducting, added up to a
total theatrical experience which was one of the AO's greatest
successes.

The distance of the Australian Opera from other major opera
houses made a constant traffic of artists inconvenient and expensive. Making a virtue of necessity the company had developed a
fine ensemble which included many artists who had returned
home having made a name for themselves elsewhere. The result
was an excellent company whose special strength lay in the high
quality and consistency of its productions. Bonynge's responsibility as Artistic Director of the Vancouver Opera Association
was to raise the company to the same high standard and revitalize
the repertoire with productions of quality and interest. He saw
excellent prospects for training a resident company of Canadian
artists and he wanted to get away from the VOA's policy of
planning three or four operas over an eight-month period towards
two seasons a year — short at first, but expanding as resources
permitted — presenting opera on a repertory basis. His target
was to set the VOA on the path to becoming an operatic centre
on a par with San Francisco and Chicago.

The autumn season of 1977 was the first to present three
operas concurrently in the space of one month: *La fille du
régiment*, *Don Giovanni* and Massenet's romantic French opera
Le roi de Lahore. Sutherland was to sing both Donna Anna and
Sita. *Le roi de Lahore*, based on a Hindu fable, was first performed in 1877 at the Paris Opéra. Massenet already had a
considerable reputation as an orchestral composer but with *Le
roi de Lahore*, his third opera, he sealed his success as a theatrical composer. Even in this early work he demonstrates the great
sensitivity to the human voice which characterizes all his operas,
and, full of youthful enthusiasm, he poured a wealth of inventive-
ness into the score.

Massenet looked upon his work as a labour of love, devoting
years to a single composition — not at all like Donizetti who once
turned out four operas in the space of one year. Unlike Verdi
who constantly moaned that he could see no escape from it,
Massenet was essentially a man of the theatre, presiding over
every detail of the preparation with the same almost obsessive
care that he gave to his music. The production, visually and

vocally, exploited all the resources of the vast Opéra, and with all the musical and dramatic effects a Parisian audience could possibly want, *Le roi de Lahore* was an instant and overwhelming success. Within five years it had been acclaimed in Europe and South America, and Massenet, an inveterate traveller, continued to oversee many of the productions and to adjust and polish the score until it met with his entire satisfaction.

Although unheard of for more than 50 years, Bonynge had been keen to revive *Le roi de Lahore* in the wake of the success of *Esclarmonde*. The idea that once one has heard *Manon* one has heard all there is of Massenet was anathema to him — comparable to saying that when one has heard *Das Rheingold* one has heard all Wagner has to offer. An overall definitive style is not unique to Massenet. Ignoring the sceptics, Bonynge was sure that *Le roi de Lahore* and *Esclarmonde* would be able to take their place in the present-day repertoire with *Manon*, *Werther* and *Thaïs*, which were no longer regarded as out of the ordinary.

Le roi de Lahore opened the 1977 Vancouver season with a production that lived up to its advertising: 'Exotic! Lavish! Rich! Beautiful! Romantic!'. Sandro Sequi directed with appropriate feel for the period and Fiorella Mariani, a disciple of Zeffirelli, achieved sumptuous effects with exotically painted scrims in a similar way to those employed by Beni Montressor for *Esclarmonde*. Bonynge was highly praised for his musical direction and his command of the newly formed Vancouver Opera Orchestra, and above all for his initiative in reviving an opera which in the eyes of the critics did not fall into the let sleeping dogs lie category:

> Joan Sutherland's voice had been getting darker and richer over the past few years. While she has hardly given up the bel canto coloratura repertory that first brought her fame, she has not been investigating many new works from this area of late and seems to be moving more and more into heavier spinto territory. Sita in *Le roi de Lahore* is another step in this direction. The music contains no coloratura at all, an even less showier vehicle than her last Massenet undertaking, *Esclarmonde*. What the role does require is pliant legato phrasing; firm, warm tone, and perfectly knit registers, all qualities that Miss Sutherland has in abundance. One interpolated high D, strong, brilliant and thrillingly in focus, also proved that she has lost none of her power in stratospheric regions. Although hardly a flashy attention-getter, Sita offers Miss Sutherland some splendid opportunities to display the more subtle aspects of her vocalism

and the character's gentle, slightly dreamy nature suits her temperament nicely, as well.

Peter G. Davis, *New York Times*, 6 November 1977

The season had been regarded as a breakthrough in Vancouver, approaching the kind of programming and production of Bonynge's long-term vision. But Bonynge's pioneering spirit had frightened the Board of Directors to death. When an interviewer, casually commenting on the challenge of depicting a Hindu paradise, wondered what a Hindu heaven looked like, Bonynge's reply that it depended how much money there was to spend on it was a measure of the tension behind the scenes. The Board seemed to like the prestige of breaking new ground but were afraid of the attendant risks. The three-opera season had hardly represented an extravagant spending spree. *La fille du régiment* was the original Covent Garden production and was now on loan from the Met; *Don Giovanni* was by courtesy of the National Arts Centre, Ottawa, and *Le roi de Lahore*, part of an exchange programme with Seattle Opera, had cost a modest — in operatic terms — Can. $75,000. The problem lay in the concept of a repertory season. In spite of travel organizers promoting operatic package tours and holiday weekends to attract a wider audience throughout British Columbia, the population was too thin on the ground to fill an auditorium the size of the Queen Elizabeth Theatre for a concentrated season. That Vancouver opera-lovers made up in enthusiasm what they lacked in numbers was no consolation at the box-office, and an announcement of a deficit put paid to Bonynge's forward planning.

The Vancouver Opera Association was facing many of the same problems as the young Australian Opera in pre-Opera House days, with no permanent singers or musicians and each new season assembled from scratch. Bonynge's resident artists programme had been abandoned for lack of funds, but he had succeeded in establishing an orchestra. He had pressed for public sponsorship and launched an energetic fund-raising campaign to supplement ticket sales which accounted for only 50 per cent of the income. His relationship with the Executive Director, Barry Thompson, had however become an uneasy one. After one particularly violent disagreement over casting proposals when he refused to sign the work permits for foreign artists chosen by Bonynge in preference to Canadian nationals, his position as Artistic Director had become untenable. When his contract came up for review Bonynge did not take up the option. This was a great disappointment to Bonynge, who had taken up the challenge of the Vancouver Opera with enthusiasm and determination, and succeeded in his short term as Artistic Director in putting Vancouver on the operatic map. With her performance as Donna Anna in the opera in which she made her debut in Vancouver nearly 20 years earlier, Sutherland's career in the city had come full circle.

1977 was the year of Sutherland's Silver Jubilee in London as well as of Her Majesty the Queen's. It was 25 years since Sutherland had first walked onto the stage at Covent Garden, during which time she had appeared in 17 seasons, singing 30 roles in 23 different operas. But there were no wild celebrations, no gala performances in the more formal sense, just a heart-warming welcome from her legions of admirers eager to show that she was still greatly loved and missed after several seasons absence.

It was not celebrated by a new production either, but, borrowing the English National Opera's 1973 production of *Maria Stuarda*, Sutherland was given the opportunity to sing one of her favourite roles in the first performance of Donizetti's opera at the Royal Opera House. Desmond Heeley's simple, dignified production was both economical and effective; John Copley was on hand to take charge of it and Sutherland felt confident under his direction. She had now sung the requisite number of performances for the 'lips to be greased', and the role was now fine-tuned, her conception of Maria restrained and touching:

> Sutherland owes her global fame by no means only to an ability to sing higher and faster than anyone else; what made this a rare experience was above all the beauty and evenness of her cantilena, the ease with which she dominated the house ... it included more so than earlier in her career a capacity to identify with the part ...
>
> Peter Stadlen, *Daily Telegraph*, 16 December 1977

In no way had 25 years diminished the agility with which she could throw off the top notes; her high D flats were ringing and precise, there was no trace of the pronounced beat that marred some of her performances the year before and there was ample evidence her voice remained an incomparable instrument — still one of the vocal miracles of our time. In no way had 25 years diminished her ability to please an audience either, and she was cheered to the echo night after night. After the final performance John Tooley came before the curtain to deliver a short speech of appreciation for her years of service to the Opera House, but he was slow to pick up his cue, a third of the audience had already left and he was heckled with shouts of: 'About time too', and 'How about a DBE?'

There was an assumption at Covent Garden that Sutherland appeared so rarely because John Tooley and Colin Davis, the Musical Director, were not over-sympathetic towards her preferred repertoire. The audience were not perhaps convinced by her assurances that this was not the case; in reality it was the Inland Revenue which prevented her from wearing out her welcome.

The DBE, of course, was not in John Tooley's gift, though doubtless he had made representations along with many others in the appropriate quarter. Sutherland had been deeply touched when Russell Braddon had warned her of his lobbying in this respect, and her response typical: 'Do you think I'd sing any better if they made me a Dame?' Probably not, but Sidney Edwards expressed the feelings of many when he declared it was nothing less than a disgrace that such an honour had not yet been awarded. But Bonynge's award of a CBE in the Jubilee Honours was a source of much pleasure and pride to Sutherland. It signified recognition of his contribution to the arts which she thought had hitherto been grossly underestimated.

For all her colossal success in *Maria Stuarda*, the necessity of being laced into heavy costumes and sustaining a three-hour performance had not filled Sutherland with the usual enthusiasm. Not naturally itinerant, home was never where the suitcases were. She loathed the hassle of travelling and longed to stay put, preferably at Les Avants where she could spend more time in the garden she loved, and where she planted the bulbs but seldom saw the flowers. Bonynge had urged her on towards the first night and the warmth and affection of the audiences had done the rest. She closed her speech in response to John Tooley with some reassuring words: 'As you all seem to enjoy it so much, I shall stumble on for a few more years.'

Sutherland began 1978 in Sydney where it was the holiday season and just the right time to let her hair down in *The Merry Widow*. The press thought so too, and were more generous in their appreciation of the production and to Sutherland's performance in it than their Canadian counterparts. But the venture was not without its critics. The Australian Opera had long recognized that operetta had a legitimate place in the repertoire and had taken both *The Merry Widow* and Gilbert and Sullivan works firmly to its bosom. The central debate, as in Vancouver, was whether or not it was right for a prima donna of Sutherland's standing to 'prostitute' her art to the common taste. Once again persistently sold-out houses were testimony to its popularity. It obviously appealed to those people frightened away by the trappings of grand opera, and enabled Sutherland to reach a much wider audience. In Australia especially, where there is a proprietorial regard for her, and where opera is heavily subsidized from public funds and often accused of being élitist, this is an important consideration.

The problems, however, of mounting opera in the Concert Hall were manifold: there was no proscenium, no curtain and no wing-space; the sets were built on scaffolding which did not permit significant changes of set, and because they had to remain *in situ* for the run of an opera it meant that the hall could not be used for anything else during that time. However, since an experimental *Aida* had proved such a success, performances there had become a regular feature of the summer season.

Designers had risen to the challenge with great ingenuity and Kristian Fredrikson built the sets around a sweeping mobile staircase, and his elegant art-nouveau décor brought gasps of delight from the audience. Lotfi Mansouri, who also directed in Vancouver, found the Concert Hall a stimulating place in which to work, and far more exciting than the intimate Opera Theatre might have been for a more conventional production.

They also experienced problems with the spoken dialogue, for although the Concert Hall acoustics tend to flatter the singing voice, dialogue had to be delivered at a very measured pace to come across clearly. Strangely, given her past horror of the spoken word, of all the cast Sutherland came to grips with the problem most readily and for once in her life was praised for the clarity of her diction:

> Sutherland is not, of course, the usual image of the Widow, who some believe should be young and beautiful ... Hers is the robust country bumpkin from the Pontevedrian country-side who innocently caught the eye of the local banker and so found fame and fortune. Her extensive dialogue is delivered with as much stilted care as any Eliza Doolittle, her waltzing is a little stiff and she handles her feathered fans like Mrs Mop. Yet her sense of fun is irresistibly contagious, her warmth is palpable, her romantic affectations naïvely touching and sincere, and she sings like the legendary Pontevedrian nightingale. Theoretically this all might seem to add up to an incongruous performance, but in practice, here, as elsewhere, it is just this incongruity, that mixture of the banal and the sublime, the gawky girl and the grand dame which lies at the heart of Sutherland's theatrical magic.

> Brian Hoad, *Bulletin*, January 1978

Although Sutherland had already performed several roles with the Australian Opera that she had not sung widely elsewhere, and one, *Suor Angelica*, exclusively in Sydney, there was a craving to hear her in some of the roles that she could sing better than anyone else. 'Her voice is still warm and fresh and magnificent,' wrote Maria Prerauer, 'but for how long? They want to hear her in the big roles, where there is no-one to beat her. Now they want to hear her sing, not waltz all night.' They did not have to wait long. *The Merry Widow* interlude was followed by Donna Anna at the Metropolitan, and in July she was back in Australia again to sing *Norma*. It was four years now since she had last sung it, and those with suspicious minds were wondering if perhaps she might be past it. But in the event all doubts were cast aside as Sutherland showed Sydney what bel canto was all about to give some of her most critically successful performances of her toughest role, and whipping up one of the wildest receptions ever witnessed in the Opera House:

> To declare that what Sutherland does is remarkable at this stage of her career is a totally inadequate compliment. It would be remarkable at any stage of a leading soprano's career. I think of such things as the exact placing of the decorations in her celebrated opening aria, '*Casta diva*', or the high D plucked with apparent effortlessness out of the air at the end of one of her duets with Adalgisa; even more of the sheer stamina she displays in this heroic role; the unfailing flow of lustrous and substantial tone she delivers throughout an evening of the most challenging vocal demands. It is true that she does not engage in as many dizzy adventures as she once may have done in the theatre, or as she still may on record. But the effect of this is not to diminish the part but to make us appreciate all the more the grace and line and supple energy of the music she sings.
>
> Roger Covell, *Sydney Morning Herald*, 7 July 1978

Sutherland and Margreta Elkins provided singing in their duets together that would long remain in the memory and Brian Hoad referred to it as 'an evening of a lifetime ... the sort of magical performance rarely found in a lifetime of opera-going'.

The production, however, by Sandro Sequi and Fiorella Mariani, with its odd mix of pre-Raphaelite women and warriors in horned helmets, was variously described as irrelevant and inept. 'The set is simply awful,' declared John Carmody, 'and what the producer does with it hardly better.' But all was gloriously compensated by the strength of the singing; the ears were satisfied if not the eyes.

The first performance of *Norma* was followed by a gala supper in the Opera House to launch a fresh appeal for funds, for although rescued from an earlier crisis by commercial and private sponsorship matched by a government grant, the Australian Opera was again in financial difficulties. Among the guests were the Governor-General, the Prime Minister and captains of industry and commerce. Since the Government had made it quite clear that no more help could be expected from them, the annual deficit had become a permanent feature only sustainable by continued support from the private sector.

The need to balance the books, however, was not the only problem facing them at this time. With a turnover of three General Managers in less than 10 years and, incidentally, the same number of Musical Directors, the company had acquired a poor reputation in administration, and now faced the prospect of losing a fourth. Peter Hemmings, the former General Manager of Scottish Opera, had taken over from John Winther in 1977 under the impression that he would have overall control of the company, and his sloppily negotiated contract failed to indicate that this would not be so. It soon became apparent that between Hemmings and Bonynge there was no great meeting of minds with regard to artistic and musical policy, and Bonynge felt that Hemmings was concerning himself with matters of casting and musical direction beyond his brief. Bonynge had sought clarification of the position from the Board of Directors, who passed the buck to a sub-committee which came up with a compromise: 'The Musical Director to have primary responsibility for the choice of repertoire and casting and the General Manager to have ultimate responsibility for the planning of the work of the company'. This recommendation, accepted by the Board, did not clarify the position at all for Hemmings, who thought such a *modus vivendi* unworkable. It seemed to him that the Board were committed to keeping Sutherland and Bonynge in Australia at almost any cost, and if that view coloured all their decisions it was obvious that he no longer had general control of the company.

The financial and administrative affairs of the Australian Opera had for some time attracted unfavourable press comment. It was a large budget organization dispensing a hefty government subsidy and the press were ostentatiously concerned that every cent should be minutely accounted for and every action justified. The so-called Bonynge–Hemmings Affair was taken up by the media with great vigour, and the relationship of Sutherland and Bonynge to the Australian Opera became the subject of much speculation. The constant refrain was Bonynge's influence on the repertoire and the fees paid to Sutherland. The latter, it was alleged, commanded fees on a guest artist basis while the number of performances she gave rose to that normally associated with a permanent member of the company. There was a suggestion that she was appearing too often, at the expense of other international guest artists. Was she a multi-million dollar asset or an extravagant drain on resources? The Australian Opera had eagerly welcomed the couple into the company after their return in 1974. With Bonynge's appointment as Musical Director the emphasis of their performing schedule had shifted from Europe and America to Australia, where Bonynge was now obliged to spend five months of the year. They had a deep commitment to the AO and in terms of professionalism and inspiration they were an enormous asset, and this was reflected in the loyalty and appreciation of their fellow artists. 'Their value to the Australian Opera is inestimable,' wrote one commentator in the first flush of enthusiasm. Yet even before the first night of *Hoffmann* in 1974 the press were drawing attention to the fees Sutherland was 'believed' to be commanding. In this respect Bonynge was unequivocal: 'I think Joan deserves every cent she is paid. If you're not worth it you won't get it.' At the peak of a profession in which tomorrow is not guaranteed, Sutherland was earning but a fraction of the fees paid to other top entertainers, who had often not had to work so long and so hard to get there. But as the deficit yawned wider the question was not whether she deserved them so much as whether the AO could afford them.

With the opening of the Opera House, the Australian Opera had been enjoying a period of unprecedented growth and popularity, and as season followed season Sutherland's ability to put bottoms on seats had become eminently estimable. She was undoubtedly good box-office, and the key to the opera boom which made it possible to extend the 1979 season to 16 operas, forming as fascinating a repertoire as any opera house would be proud to offer.

The criticism of Bonynge focused upon the repertoire, which reflected his personal taste and by definition had an overt bias towards those operas best suited to Sutherland. Yet these works constituted only a small part of the total output, and there is nothing unusual in the repertoire of an opera house being shaped by the incumbent Musical Director. Bonynge recognized the impossibility of pleasing all the people all the time, but his objective was to present as varied a package as possible within the parameters of the AO's resources with something for everyone. He was not satisfied by constantly performing the standard works, although they necessarily formed the backbone of the repertoire, and he thought audiences shared that view. At some future date another Musical Director would exert his influence, but in the meantime it would have been a failure of some magnitude not to take the fullest advantage of what Sutherland and Bonynge had to offer.

To obviate the difficulties a 'repertoire committee' was set up with power of veto over any decisions taken in this respect. For the time being the Board had succeeded in taking the heat out of the situation and Hemmings was reconciled to taking the current option on his contract into 1980.

Malign press speculation, however, had not been confined to problems of funding, repertoire and personality clashes behind the scenes. It was taken a mischievous step further with suggestions that Sutherland and Bonynge might renege on next season's performances in Melbourne — for which they had only a verbal agreement — if the Board failed to resolve the situation in their favour. That they could be considered capable of such a dishonourable act was deeply offensive.

Bonynge stayed on in Sydney to conduct Kiri te Kanawa's first Violetta, and Sutherland, not surprisingly, retreated to the haven of Les Avants. At the end of November, together again, they recorded *Suor Angelica* and collections of Mozart and Wagner arias, and while Sydney continued to debate whether or not she was too much of a good thing, Sutherland and Bonynge gave a triumphant concert at Covent Garden, the proceeds of which went to the Australian Musical Foundation — a newly formed organization to help struggling young Australian musicians in London.

In December they set off to tour *Norma* in Holland with the Netherlands Opera, and she was singing *Norma* in Utrecht on New Year's Day when it was officially announced she had been created a Dame Commander of the Order of the British Empire in the New Year Honours List. Sutherland was already on her way to America as the congratulations poured in, although the excitement was rapidly eclipsed in the media by the news that she had been 'sacked by the Metropolitan Opera'. It was a dramatic word for an undramatic incident which stemmed from the fact that Sutherland at 52 had wisely decided that a role she had been engaged to sing as early as mid-1977 was no longer within her capacity.

The role in question was Constanze in Mozart's *Die Entführung aus dem Serail* for the 1979/80 season. It was a role she had never sung before and she had accepted the opportunity gladly; at the same time performances of *The Merry Widow* and *Semiramide* were negotiated for 1982. When she began to study the role, however, she did not find it comfortable for her voice. She had no trouble with the high notes, but she was unable to sustain the exceptionally high tessitura without putting a strain on her voice. She had succeeded in maintaining her place at the top of the operatic tree by dint of self-discipline and always knowing precisely what she could and could not do, and she was not about to put that at risk now. Earlier in her career she could have carried it off with ease, but now it was too late. 'I should have done it 15 years ago. Constanze doesn't go above high D, but it lies much higher than Lucia,' Sutherland explained. 'I could have made all the notes, but my voice is heavier now and I would have had to do some harmful forcing. I decided I did not want to stand on the stage of the Metropolitan with my reputation and feel uncomfortable; so finally, respectfully, I turned the part down.' It was the closest she ever came to singing a debut role at the Met. It was not a spectacular, last-minute walk-out she had inflicted on them. It was 13 months before the première and although it was a disappointment Sutherland's withdrawal was apparently accepted with understanding and without rancour. The sparks only began to fly when Sutherland learned that *The Merry Widow* had been cancelled.

While denying that this was tit-for-tat, it nevertheless seemed an ungrateful gesture on the part of an international opera house where Sutherland had enjoyed enormous success for 17 seasons. Although such a package deal is not uncommon in the field of long-term operatic planning, Sutherland and representatives of the Met rejected the suggestion that it was regarded in this light. It appeared that the Metropolitan had not particularly wanted to do *The Merry Widow* in the first place. New York City Opera had a production of it, and it was therefore not high on the Met's list of priorities. Or perhaps, since they felt a version which might have been marvellous with Sutherland would not be adaptable to other sopranos, it was a question of style. It was Sutherland's Merry Widow they did not want, not *The Merry Widow* in itself. Her tomboy vivandière, Marie in *La fille du régiment*, had been, and would again be acceptable, her Anna Glavari a different thing entirely.

It saddened Sutherland that the Met did not share her enthusiasm for a role so dear to her heart, and the idea that Bonynge's version of it was not sophisticated enough for the Metropolitan audience she dismissed with a single unrepeatable expletive. She did, however, have the last word, for it was not long before there was some confusion with regard to the dates scheduled for *Semiramide*, and that too fell by the wayside.

With the Met strongly asserting that they would not be dictated to by singers, Sutherland joined the ever-growing band of artists who at some time in their career had fallen out with that august institution. When Rudolf Bing fired Maria Callas in 1958 it was seven years before she could be coaxed back, but by then her voice had lost much of its power and brilliance. Reconciliation took less time in Sutherland's case, but the shadows of her career were lengthening, and she was the first to admit there was no way of knowing what her voice might be capable of in several years time: 'If I can't sing when the time comes, they'll have to forgive me.'

While all this furore was going on amidst concern for Sutherland's vocal decline, and even wilder predictions that it could be her last performance in New York, she gave a concert with Pavarotti in Avery Fisher Hall. Their first concert together, it was one of the most talked about events in New York's musical year and widely hyped as the 'Concert of the Century'.

For Sutherland, under the circumstances it was one of her more 'horrendous experiences'. Broadcast and televised live across America in an arc-lit auditorium in which she could clearly pick out colleagues from the Met and, as far as she could tell, every opera manager in and out of town, she faced the biggest audition imaginable. Stricken with panic, she sang a garbled version of a duet from *La traviata* and she and Pavarotti came off stage so shaken that they threatened not to go out again unless the lights were turned down. Nevertheless with a soprano who has the most 'beautiful trill in the world', and a tenor 'who made love to his audience' the concert was a phenomenal success, and as the rafters rang with cheering and applause and flowers showered onto the stage, radio and television audiences in their millions must have pondered on the loss to the Metropolitan. To any who doubted, it was forcefully driven home that Sutherland was not called *La Stupenda* for nothing. 'There is not a pair of singers alive who could match this combination of style and prodigal outpouring of voice ... this is what Italian opera is all about: a maximum of voice coupled to musical taste ...', enthused Harold Schonberg in the *New York Times*. He also referred to reports that the Metropolitan could do very well without such operatic superstars, and added: 'if this is a true statement, the man who said it must be out of his ever-loving mind'. Robert Jacobson described the event as:

... one of the vocal events of the decade ... the soprano

remains a miracle, having doggedly kept to the repertory that suits her best, while the tenor's ventures into Puccini seemingly have not tarnished his power in Donizetti. Here were two legendary figures living up to their reputations, giving the American television audience a taste of magnificence ... the two conveyed at close range, the very exhaltation, the catatonia, the chanciness, the very communicating powers of singing.

Opera News, 17 January 1979

It was as the Merry Widow that Sutherland returned to Sydney immediately after this sensational concert, and she returned on a vocal high. Yet despite the euphoria of her DBE, in which Australians took a very natural pride, there were still no shortage of dissenting voices. In the interim a warehouse fire had destroyed the entire productions of some 30 operas, among them *The Merry Widow* and *Lakmé*, and to a howl of protest *The Merry Widow* had been rebuilt. A brilliant performance could not lessen the resentment of those who believed that it had occupied workshop time allocated to *Das Rheingold*, and had thus put back the long-hoped-for plans to embark on the Ring Cycle. Nor could it deflect the criticism that to cast Sutherland as the Widow was like taking a sledge-hammer to crack a nut. In its second season, though, it continued to bring a great deal of pleasure and fun to the thousands who flocked to see it, not only in Sydney, but in Adelaide and Melbourne later in the year.

The turmoil within the Board of the Australian Opera with regard to administration and lines of authority had not abated and factions were developing behind the scenes. The Board were also aware that Hemmings had been promoting his own ideas unilaterally and incurring unsanctioned expense in the process. Among them were plans for the company to visit the Edinburgh Festival and to get the Ring Cycle underway. Bonynge's vehement opposition to mounting *The Ring* had earned him a reputation as a Wagner-hater which was quite unjustified. He had been in accord with Hemmings to present *Die Meistersinger*, although home-made sets would have made sounder economic sense than to borrow the production from Scottish Opera. His objections to *The Ring* were of a pragmatic nature related to the dearth of Wagnerian singers and the limitations of the Opera Theatre.

In response, however, to the clamour from other states for a larger slice of the government-subsidized operatic cake and to shake off the AO's image as the Sydney Opera Company, Hemmings had initiated an interstate tour as part of the 1979 programme. Sutherland's participation in this was an integral part of the exercise, and for performances of *La traviata* in Melbourne there had been a vast increase in tickets sold on subscription. Violetta was one of five different roles Sutherland would perform in four state capitals, and Melbourne, where she had not sung for 14 years, enjoyed the very real satisfaction of hearing her in a role not so far sung in Sydney.

The enthusiastic reception from the 3,000-strong audience in the Palais Theatre evoked memories of the noisy ovations of the Sutherland–Williamson tour, and Peter Burch in the *Australian* described Sutherland as 'superb for her second coming' in a performance which was 'persuasive and deeply considered'. David Gyger, reviewing the Melbourne season for *Theatre Australia* thought that Sutherland's credibility as a singing actress and vocal artist was increasing by leaps and bounds, and that it constituted ample compensation for the occasional sign of strain at the top or loss of agility.

In Brisbane Sutherland sang *Norma*, and many thought she had never sounded better. 'Perhaps some of the sheer volume and bravura of the 60s has gone, but there was a glorious sense of mastery in the voice,' reported the *Australian*, '. . . the attack on the high notes with not a trace of reaching for them is simply staggering.'

At the end of April, Sutherland returned to Europe for a group of recitals and a concert performance of *Lucia di Lammermoor* in Stockholm. Then back to Sydney for her debut performance of the year as Electra in the Victorian State Opera's *Idomeneo*, which became the earliest opera in the AO repertoire.

Probably the least well known of Mozart's operas, *Idomeneo* had only recently gained favour in the world's major opera houses. As a means of introducing *opera seria* to Australia it was an ideal work, for although firmly in the *opera seria* mould Mozart had rejected some of the more stereotyped conventions of the genre in favour of a more flexible approach. It was his first real operatic success; the fulfilment of a commission from the Elector of Bavaria for a work to be performed in the exquisite Cuvillies Residenztheater, Munich in 1781. Giambattista Varesco, Court Chaplain at Salzburg, provided the libretto from a suitably heroic text, but the fashion for *opera seria* had already run its course, and Mozart was hampered by Varesco's strict adherence to its more rigid manifestations. Only half the music was completed by the time Mozart arrived in Munich, and the rest he tailored to the particular talents of the singers at his disposal, one of which was the castrato Vincenzo del Prato. Improvisation was still commonplace, but in *Idomeneo* Mozart wrote out the embellishments and did not encourage the singers to devise their own. Overcoming the difficulties with his librettist, Mozart breathed new life into an obsolescent musical form. An idealization of *opera seria, Idomeneo* at the same time blazed the trail for the great masterpieces in which Mozart was to develop the dramatic possibilities of opera to perfection.

Given singers who can cope with the technical complexities of the bravura writing, *Idomeneo* more than merits a revival. Mozart had revised the work many times with the need to adapt to different singers, and in the absence of a castrato for the first performance in Vienna he had rewritten the role of Idamante for a tenor. There were therefore enough authentic Mozart variations to cater to the individual singers available to the Australian Opera. Bonynge's editing had been minimal, confined mostly to pruning the recitatives which would otherwise have resulted in a performance too long for modern tastes.

Sutherland as the anti-heroine Electra was an unexpected piece of casting, for the lyric-soprano role of Ilia had seemed a more natural choice. But Bonynge had been persuasive. Her dramatic coloratura voice provided a pleasing contrast in the ensemble to Leona Mitchell's lyric-soprano Ilia and Margreta Elkins in the tenor role of Idamante, and Electra proved to be a singularly successful role for Sutherland:

> It is one of her active roles. Electra does not waste time on gentle regrets. She spits fury when thwarted. As always such a dramatic challenge brings out the athletic best in Sutherland. Her rapid notes whizz past in perfect formation, yet with a size and quality that are truly heroic. Her Act III aria *'D'Oreste d'Ajace'* ... is designed in this performance as the culmination of Act III and in effect, the whole opera. Sutherland's big passionate performance fulfils this design.
>
> Roger Covell, *Sydney Morning Herald*, 5 July 1979

Ron Stevens, however, after a month of illness was less successful in the fiercely demanding title role, and was replaced by Serge Baigildin half-way through the second performance. Then Baigildin also succumbed to flu and the scheduled *Idomeneo* was replaced by a memorable performance of *La traviata* with Sutherland singing her first AO Violetta.

Bonynge had hotly contested Hemming's choice of Ron Dowd, the veteran Australian tenor who had previously sung the role in Melbourne, in preference to the younger Stevens, and the critical hatchets were out again with accusations of poor programming, miscasting and extravagance. For Hemmings the 'repertoire committee' had been an inadequate solution and his departure from the company was precipitated by discussions he undertook with the Victorian State Government with regard to the future of opera in Melbourne, which the Board viewed as a direct conflict of interests. When it became public that his contract would not be renewed beyond 1980 the affairs of the AO hit the headlines again with a renewed attack on Sutherland and Bonynge. Sinister suggestions of a conspiracy on their part to dominate the Australian Opera were patently ridiculous as were rumours that Sutherland had left a sealed envelope with her solicitors to be opened if she were obliged to leave in a hurry.

They had fallen in love with the city of their birth and bought an apartment overlooking the harbour, wanting nothing more than to share in the development of the Australian Opera and continue to work with the company in peace and harmony. However, after performances of *Don Giovanni* in Melbourne Sutherland did leave Australia in a hurry to snatch a few more precious days in Les Avants before recording sessions began in London for *Le roi de Lahore*.

The highlight of Sutherland's autumn season was a return to America for another 'Concert of the Century' in Avery Fisher Hall, this time with Marilyn Horne, their first appearance together since *Semiramide* in 1971. Busy and conflicting schedules had kept them apart, and the mutual knowledge that Horne wanted more from her career than to enter the history books as 'Sutherland's mezzo'. Amidst all the advertising ballyhoo they did pause to wonder if the vocal chemistry would still be there after such a long separation, but the unique compatibility was still in evidence, and in a wide variety of solos and duets there was never a hint of 'anything you can sing, I can sing better'. Of the cabaletta to the duet *'Mira o Norma'*, Harold Schonberg wrote: 'the singers worked together like thoroughbreds, breathing the same, tossing perfectly matched phrases at each other, snapping off the coloratura with infinite ease'. He described Sutherland's overpowering prodigality of voice in *'Ah fors'è lui'*: 'Violettas are probably not supposed to have this kind of sound, but Miss Sutherland was not going to throttle down, and this was one of the largest scale performances one is likely to hear in our time'. *'Vilja'* poured forth in beautifully sumptuous sound, and just to listen to the florid passages of the duet from *Semiramide*, wrote Speight Jenkins in the *New York Post*, 'was a lesson for anybody interested in the art of singing'.

The next day Sutherland and Bonynge celebrated their Silver Wedding — quite a record as theatrical marriages go, and Ailsa made the cake she had promised in 1954.

12
Transposition

Almost 21 years to the day since she made her debut, the Australian Opera mounted a new production of *Lucia di Lammermoor* to celebrate the occasion. It was the most lavish production of the 1980 season and publicity reached an all-time high. But while a new generation of opera-lovers were agog to see her in the role she had made spectacularly her own, some thought it too late for a revival of *Lucia*. The excitement mounting in Sydney in anticipation of these performances was compared by John Copley to the Callas fever that gripped Covent Garden for *Tosca* in the 60s. For the dress rehearsal hardly an empty seat could be found, and Sutherland gave a full performance, high notes included. Yet as she approached the high E flat at the end of the mad scene you could have heard a pin drop as the audience waited expectantly to see if she would make it. Effortlessly she sailed to the end of the cadenza, announced 'Not today', and collapsed backwards onto the stage to a gale of laughter and tumultuous applause.

On opening night she brought the audience to its feet in a prolonged standing ovation with a performance that deflated her detractors and put her fans on cloud nine. John Carmody described it as 'spellbinding'; Frank Harris as 'stunning . . . a night to remember'.

Every thread of the production was of a supremely high standard, from Michael Stennett's romantically beautiful costumes to the breathtaking ingenuity of Henry Bardon's sets, which transformed the lofty heights of the Concert Hall into a life-size Castle of Ravenswood. Under the brushes of a make-up artist Sutherland shed half her 53 years, and John Copley, an artistic pillar of the Australian Opera with a string of fine productions behind him, welded all the theatrical forces together to magnificent effect. Sutherland thought that the ideas behind it were similar to the Zeffirelli original, but Copley had worked with her before on *Lucia* and thought that little remained of Zeffirelli in Sutherland's own performance. Bonynge also thought that her interpretation had changed from that of a young girl to a more haunting introspective woman, and that she was singing it better than ever. For her part, Sutherland compared singing *Lucia* to wearing a pair of comfortable old shoes.

Another role she was singing better than ever was Lucrezia Borgia, and three weeks later she was given an ecstatic welcome in it at Covent Garden in another Copley production. In a skilful cost-cutting exercise he and John Pascoe had assembled a sumptuous production with thousands of pounds worth of existing scenery from almost every Covent Garden production he had directed, and Stennett again evolved some magnificent costumes.

Lucrezia Borgia had been popular at Covent Garden well into the 1880s with casts reading like a nineteenth-century operatic *Who's Who*, and on this occasion the Opera House fielded one which could hardly be bettered. Apart from providing Sutherland with a great role, the opera had impressed Copley as being an especially theatrical work when he had seen it in Sydney, and he was quite unselfconscious about the stylized bel canto traditions inherent in it. There were quibbles from the critics about dramatic values and spurious references to Grisi and Tietjens, but Sutherland was in remarkably agile voice, right up to the high E flat of the final cabaletta, investing the controversial finale with such high drama as to squash forever the notion that it is dramatically inappropriate.

Although Sutherland never had enough time at home to put it to the test, when she speculated on retirement — which she did every time she packed for another long-haul flight — Bonynge always told her that she would be bored. But at times such as this, ankle-deep in daffodils before the final curtain in one of her favourite opera houses, she suspected he was right. The reaction of an audience was a powerful motivating force, and, deeply touched by the warmth of the reception, she hoped she might manage to turn out a few more winners before, as she put it, 'I finally bite the dust'. She and Bonynge were confident that Verdi's *I masnadieri*, with which the Australian Opera were celebrating the tenth anniversary of its devolution from the Elizabethan Trust Opera, would be another such winner.

Verdi composed *I masnadieri* for Her Majesty's Theatre, London in 1847, the first of only a handful of his operas to be premièred outside Italy, and as such a social and musical event with every ingredient for success. Firstly, there was intense artistic rivalry between the Royal Italian Opera at Covent Garden and Benjamin Lumley at Her Majesty's, and in pursuit of dominance Lumley had achieved a unique coup in engaging a great Italian composer to write an opera specifically for his theatre. Secondly, the production was focused on Jenny Lind, whom Verdi had seen when she made her debut in Bellini's *Norma*. Her personality had appealed to him, although he had not liked her penchant for showing off her technique in fioriture. Lind, however, was a cult figure in London, and although the fashion for excessive ornamentation was *passé* in Italy, Verdi was obliged to indulge this passion and she wrote her own cadenzas for her main arias. Thirdly, the theatre enjoyed the patronage of Queen Victoria, a great admirer of Jenny Lind, and the presence of the Queen and Prince Consort turned the first performance into a Royal Gala. And last, but by no means least, Verdi supervised the rehearsals and was to conduct the opera himself.

Before the opera began Verdi was given a lengthy ovation, and time and time again he was called before the final curtain and pelted with flowers to cries of '*Eviva, Verdi! Bietifol!*' Apart from Henry Chorley, who had no time for Verdi anyway and who thought it the worst opera ever to have been presented at Her Majesty's, the critics were enthusiastic, although Verdi had reservations about its success. After several performances in London and a sensational success in Paris it lost its hold on the public, and it was berated in Italy where it offered no competition for *Macbeth*.

Verdi had worked simultaneously on both operas. In *Macbeth* he had escaped from the operatic conventions of the day and achieved a deeper dramatic and psychological involvement in his characterization. With *I masnadieri* this eluded him, largely due to the pedestrian nature of Mafei's libretto which failed to sustain the impact of Schiller's play *Die Raüber* on which it was based.

With Sutherland, Donald Smith, Robert Allman and Clifford Grant forming an all-Australian team of principals in their element in early Verdi, the gala performance at the Sydney Opera House was described by David Gyger as a night of 'vocal ecstasy'. The superb singing and musical direction far outweighed the inconsistencies of a plot convoluted even by operatic standards, and gave rise to a justifiable display of national pride.

A few performances later, however, Robert Allman was stricken with a virus and so began a run of misfortune that turned a casting director's dream into a nightmare. Allman was replaced by Eric Badcock, the winner of the 1978 Sutherland Scholarship, but he was out of his depth in the role of Francesco at this time and was ungenerously booed. At a subsequent performance Paul Ferris had taken over from Donald Smith who found himself in vocal difficulties minutes after curtain-up, and the next performance was cancelled when he too was indisposed. Allman returned to complete the series, but Ferris sang Carlo for the remaining performances. The long-awaited partnership of Sutherland and Smith, two of Australia's best loved artists, had been short-lived, for soon afterwards Donald Smith announced his retirement from the operatic stage.

To underwrite the risk and provide a second cast of the same calibre as the first would make the performance of any opera a practical and economic impossibility, but without a first-rate cast in what was essentially a singers' opera it was feared that there was little future for *I masnadieri*. Not everyone thought it a good example of early Verdi, and those critical of the programming policy of the Australian Opera saw it as another Sutherland–Bonynge indulgence and a waste of the resources which could have been more usefully applied to a new production of the more worthy *Il trovatore* or *Rigoletto* or *Ernani* or *Luisa Miller* — or almost anything!

With the abrupt departure of Peter Hemmings at the end of 1979, a change had taken place in the hierarchy of the Australian Opera. Ken Tribe, a Sydney solicitor, had been installed as interim General Manager and the Australia Council, which administers government subsidy to the arts, initiated an Inquiry. Ostensibly to examine the most effective way of promoting opera and music theatre in Australia, it was widely perceived to have been inspired by the Board's handling of what had come to be known as 'the Hemmings affair'. The 1980 winter season therefore took place against the background of a line-by-line media analysis of the Inquiry's recently published report — or, at least, those parts of it relating to the Australian Opera. The report reassessed the development of opera (and music theatre) in Australia and examined the distribution of federal and state subsidy. It was critical of the leadership of the company and accused it of financial incompetence, although there was praise for its artistic achievement and wholehearted endorsement of the AO's status as the 'national' company. Among its recommendations, however, was a phasing out of the prohibitively expensive interstate touring programme and expansion of the repertoire to include more operetta and musical comedy. The Inquiry found no evidence of an unacceptable bias in the repertoire but urged a more positive approach to contemporary and indigenous works. It did, however, express concern that too much reliance was being placed on Sutherland as the main attraction and that not enough consideration was being given to the post-Sutherland era.

With the sacrifice of interstate grant that would necessarily follow a reduction in touring, an expansion of the repertoire would place an added burden on the New South Wales Government which was not overly sympathetic to the arts. In 1979 they had given Aus. $610,000 in subsidy with one hand, and taken back Aus. $770,000 in rent for the Opera House with the other. Perhaps it was significant that the AO's deficit for the same year was in the region of Aus. $700,000, but far from following the Inquiry's recommendations for increased state funding, the existing subsidy was frozen for the next three years. Things were going to get worse before they got better — if ever they were to get better.

Sutherland and Bonynge had been criticized for gathering around them a coterie of singers, designers and directors and loyally promoting them — not always with overwhelming success — and some people felt that managers accepted a package at the expense of local artists who could do the job as well, if not better. The Sutherland–Bonynge Circus was not therefore regarded with affection, least of all by those outside it, but when confronted with the notion Sutherland explains: 'We've been in the business a long time — we have a lot of friends.' This system was a matter of convenience and an effort to avoid taking risks with the unknown, rather than a form of artistic nepotism; they wanted a team who shared a love and understanding of their particular *métier* and could turn out a reliable performance whilst being agreeable and fun. They had discovered which opera houses they preferred and which singers, designers and directors they were comfortable and confident with. One trusted colleague with whom Sutherland had enjoyed some of her greatest successes was the director Tito Capobianco, then General Manager of San Diego Opera. Capobianco had a reputation for giving the city more than it expected, and the afternoon of Sunday 5 October 1980 was the occasion of a unique event in the Civic Theatre: a performance of *Die Fledermaus* with Sutherland as Rosalinde and Beverly Sills singing Adele in her last operatic performance.

Throughout their careers Sutherland and Sills had matched fioriture with fioriture in a parallel repertoire but there was no rivalry between them. They had previously met only briefly, and their dispute over who should sing *I puritani* at the Met had been a third party affair with nothing personal in it. Capobianco, an enthusiastic admirer of both divas, had teased them with the idea of *Die Fledermaus* for years, neither of them taking him very seriously. But with patience and the deceit of telling each the other had agreed, the idea became reality. He even persuaded them to alternate in their roles in a series of performances, but in the event

Sills had obligations to the New York City Opera, of which she was the Director, which made the extra rehearsals impossible.

Sutherland's Rosalinde was viewed in a much more sympathetic light than her Anna Glavari, and the production was an unashamed show-case for two prima donnas who liked to be frivolous occasionally. Infectious enjoyment flowed both ways across the footlights, and with the added delight of Sherrill Milnes singing the Drinking Song from *Hamlet* at Orlofsky's party, it was a spectacular conclusion to Beverly Sills' vivacious career.

For Sutherland the year concluded with more highly acclaimed *Lucias* in Melbourne and Adelaide, and the ABC had the good sense to broadcast it. She and Bonynge then made a quick dash home for Christmas and the New Year where they swotted up Desdemona for a new production of Verdi's *Otello* for the Australian Opera at the end of January. This did not represent a change of tack — which some had recommended years ago — only a brief sabbatical from the 'cackling'. It also meant a change of conductor, and in a rare break with tradition Sutherland sang Desdemona with Carlo Felice Cillario, a former Musical Director of the Australian Opera. Like everyone with whom she worked, he was impressed by her cool nerves, her good nature and the wonderful sense of fun she communicated, but he was surprised at her need for reassurance. 'I'm such a disaster,' she told him, 'and you never correct me.'

Earlier in her career she had shown great promise as Desdemona, but she had only sung a handful of performances — not enough to develop the potential of the role fully. But Brian Hoad thought she had left her comeback a little too late, for she could no longer project the youthful innocence necessary for a wholly convincing portrayal, Nor was she in her best voice on the opening night, giving a lacklustre performance except for the Willow Song and *Ave Maria* in the final scene. On the other hand, Maria Prerauer thought she was in 'glorious soaring voice' in an opera more worthy of her than the 'silly potboilers' she usually sang. At later performances, however, she was in consistently better voice, her phrasing characteristically effortless. With the Australian Opera's extravagance almost received thought, the *Financial Review* referred to the staging as 'unnecessarily lavish', while in Brian Hoad's opinion it was an 'old-fashioned, economy-style production'. It had been mounted in the Concert Hall rather than the Opera Theatre in order to maximize Sutherland's box-office appeal, and although some thought the production as a whole lacked drama, Maria Prerauer considered it one of the AO's finest and a new high for the director George Ogilvie.

There was nothing remotely lacklustre about Sutherland's contribution to a concert in New York, with Pavarotti and Horne offering vocal competition in the best sense. Sutherland's supreme technical resources still astonished with the smooth integration of registers and undiminished power at the top of the range. She sang some of her familiar duets and solos and broke new ground with the trio from *Ernani*, with the bass part of Silva transposed to accommodate Marilyn Horne in by far the most off-beat of her travesti roles and ended with the more conventional trio from *Il trovatore*. The concert, 'an old-fashioned glorification of the human voice', in the words of Peter G. Davis in the *New York Times*, was repeated a few days later and simulcast in the *Live from Lincoln Centre* series. Sandwiched between the two had been a Presidential Concert in Washington, but with the broadcast in mind, Sutherland and Horne decided they had overcommitted themselves and gave it a miss. Sutherland and Pavarotti then moved on to Pittsburgh for another joint concert, a social event accompanied by the usual hype — in fact the organization of a reception and supper had kept the secretary of the Pittsburgh Symphony on her toes for more than a year.

On her way to sing *Norma* for her debut with the Canadian Opera Company in Toronto Sutherland sang a brilliant Violetta in Memphis, and was welcomed with great warmth and hospitality at Rock Hill, North Carolina, in a concert to mark the twentieth anniversary of her American recital debut.

In Toronto her Norma was the operatic event of the year, and although one reviewer thought that she demonstrated astonishing vocal health, others were aware of less precision in recitative and a lack of clarity in the coloratura passages. She began tentatively, suggesting a need to conserve vocal resources, but as the evening progressed, William Littler in the *Toronto Star* observed: '. . . it was as if her voice was taking a series of transfusions. She kept sounding better and better'.

She was actually fighting a troublesome virus which she had not shaken off by the time she arrived in Melbourne to sing Desdemona, but she was on form for *La traviata* in Sydney, with even more sympathy for Violetta after six weeks of poor health.

The second of Sutherland's vintage revivals for the Australian Opera was a new production of *Les Huguenots*, in what Roger Covell described as the 'most interestingly diverse repertory in the history of the Australian Opera'. It was probably also the biggest gamble of Bonynge's Musical Directorship, and the doom-merchants were quick to forecast disaster, for the presentation of Meyerbeer's work makes great demands physically and financially on the resources of any opera company. In Australia, however, *Les Huguenots* had been a mainstay of the nineteenth-century repertoire, so popular that one intrepid touring company had even given performances in a Queensland saloon bar on a stage improvised from billiard tables. Bonynge thought it merited revival, although it needed to be cast from strength and few short-cuts could be taken with the scenic effects Meyerbeer had conceived on a Cecil B. de Mille scale. It is an opera one either loves with a passion or regards as a tired old warhorse, but with a spectacular fusion of music and action there is much to admire in it, and as an ensemble work it was an ideal vehicle for the Australian Opera. With the exception of Sutherland and Marilyn Zschau as Valentine, the AO was able to muster a splendid cast from the resident company — a remarkable fact, and a practical necessity in view of the Equity maximum of only six overseas guest artists in any one season.

In her short but vocally strenuous role of Marguerite de Valois, Sutherland was 'vocally immaculate' and 'splendidly imperious', and Ken Heely in *Theatre Australia* thought she had never sung with 'more majesty, confidence, power and bravura'. She had no truck with horses this time, but Bonynge had still not convinced her that her Act II aria, *'O beau pays'*, in spite of familiarity, was not every bit as difficult as she perceived it. Bonynge's conducting and the overall standard of the singing made it a far more auspicious revival than the pessimists predicted. The costumes were magnificent, but in line with the current financial plight of the AO the spectacle fell short of Cecil B. de Mille. However, the production offset criticism that the AO's programming policy was not designed to demonstrate the excellent ensemble quality of the company.

In San Francisco a month later audiences revelled in Sutherland's performance in *The Merry Widow,* but Lotfi Mansouri's new dialogue had apparently taken a turn for the worse and one or two reviews were worthy of inclusion in Diana Rigg's anthology *No Turn Unstoned.* Naturally it was these that found their way into the Sydney press, but Sutherland enjoyed the part so much that she jumped at the chance to sing it, and although she had now chalked up twice as many *Merry Widows* as *Maria Stuardas*, she was still a long way from hanging up her dancing shoes and divesting herself of Anna Glavari, despite her critics.

In sharp contrast she spanned the New Year at Covent Garden in Visconti's now somewhat diluted 1964 production of *Il trovatore*, and her Leonora was awaited with much interest. Sutherland was well equipped for the role, as comfortable with the cantabile of *'Tacea la notte'* as with the bravura of *'Di tale amor'* and the inventive brilliance of the interpolated cadenzas. She had been working hard on floating her top voice, so essential to Leonora's music, turning a new ease in high pianissimo to magnificent effect, and her phenomenal trill was stunningly demonstrated in *'D'amor sull'ali rosee'*. Above all, she seemed to feel the music instinctively and her eloquent contribution to the final ensemble radiated the authentic Sutherland style.

As the new General Manager of the Australian Opera it did not take Patrick Vietch long to appreciate the depths of the financial crisis which afflicted it, and it was difficult to reconcile the high standards expected of a 'flagship' company with increasing financial constraints. Although income from private sources had risen dramatically in the past four years he feared that the momentum could not be maintained in order to bring the finances around fast enough to prevent retrenchment of activities and personnel.

With cuts in interstate subsidy, a touring commitment to Adelaide and Melbourne was constantly under threat. There were other ways, however, of making the performances of the Australian Opera accessible to as many people as possible and Bonynge had for a long time been floating the idea of open-air concerts in Sydney, convinced that they could become as much a regular feature of the AO's season as the Met's performances in Central Park. In January 1982 Sutherland appeared in the first of these concerts in the Domain — a performance of *La traviata* — and Sydney was invited to 'Witness a Legend, Free'. Even in Sydney, though, the weather cannot be guaranteed, and the scheduled date was rained off. But two days later a crowd of 15,000 gathered under a threatening sky, armed with pac-a-macs and ground-sheets, and the rain conveniently confined itself to the interval. Good as the performance was within the limits of the sound system, the atmosphere was the thing. It was an 'outreach' project, more evangelistic than profitable, which had achieved its purpose in attracting a huge crowd, many of whom had never set foot in an opera house. It was the first of many such concerts.

To sing to an enthusiastic audience of thousands in the great outdoors was an exhilarating experience for Sutherland, but the real joy of the New Year was her son's wedding in Sydney.

Adam had no inclination to follow his parents in the music world and there had been no parental pressure for him to do so. As a child he had shown more interest in football and skiing with a wily technique for avoiding piano practice. As he grew up his recreational interest in music leaned more towards jazz than classical music, but he was fluent in four languages with a love of hotels not shared by his globetrotting parents. He had joined the jet set on an occasional basis at the age of five and first visited Australia aged nine; once he had finished at his international Swiss boarding school not far from Les Avants he trained in hotel management and worked his way through the ranks. He had now been working at the Sydney Hilton for two years, and it was there that he met his English fiancée, Helen. Sutherland and Bonynge were now able to see more of him than they ever had as a child; at one time they had missed eight consecutive birthdays, and were mildly surprised that he seemed to enjoy the company of what he referred to as his 'aged Ps'.

The wedding took place at a church in Kings Cross, Sydney, and the weather was more cooperative than it had been for the concert. At Rocca Bella, the Bonynges' Whale Beach house where the reception was held, the light breeze stirring the frangipani on the pool was not strong enough to blow the marquee into the sea as Sutherland had feared.

1982 was a year of stunningly successful performances in some of Sutherland's favourite roles, and her performance of *Lucrezia Borgia* in the Australian Opera's revival of the 1977 production was one of her finest, and acknowledged as such even by her severest critics. As fire had destroyed the original sets the production was revamped in the Concert Hall, where Sutherland's voice and Fredrickson's costumes were displayed to better advantage than in the smaller Opera Theatre.

After a recital in Perth, Sutherland and Bonynge returned to Europe to commute from Les Avants to recitals in Venice and Genoa. She sang a much acclaimed concert performance of *Lucrezia Borgia* in Stockholm and then on to Holland at bulb time to trundle *Lucia* around the cities, a show that was very much her own in spite of the best cast the Netherlands Opera could provide.

In June they were back in Australia to launch another new innovation: the live simulcast, which was the only feasible way of bringing the output of the national company within the reach of such a sprawling population. It had taken six months of hard talking to persuade the ABC to cooperate and a new production of *Die Fledermaus* with Sutherland as Rosalinde was chosen for an experimental transmission, the success of which far exceeded the most optimistic forecasts. Sutherland was deluged with letters of appreciation from people for whom a trip to the Opera House was impossible; the AO received 45,000 requests for souvenir programmes and the viewing figures peaked at 2.5 million. Sydney was reconciled to Sutherland's need to let her hair down now and again and she waltzed triumphantly onto the stage demonstrating a stylish comic flair, and her impersonation of the Hungarian Countess, complete with Zsa Zsa Gabor accent, brought the house down.

Now that techniques were less intrusive Sutherland was more relaxed before the cameras, confident that the technicians would do alright by her and not thrust a camera down her throat as she reached for a high note. Television exerted its own influence on opera and she recognized it as a medium she had to put up with, quite apart from the obvious attraction of reaching an audience of millions rather than thousands.

In September the 'Druid Duo' were back in business in San Francisco for a memorable series of *Normas* in Terry McEwen's first season as General Director of War Memorial Opera House. With no concessions to the advancing years, and their vocal chemistry still intact, Horne at 48 was an astounding Adalgisa and Sutherland at 56 an awesome Norma. The latter gave a sensitive and compelling performance which, vocally and dramatically, towered above that of a decade before. Sutherland stopped the show with *'Casta diva'*, and together they brought the house to its feet with the celebrated duets. 'Incomparable is the word for Sutherland', wrote Robert Commanday in the *San Francisco Chronicle*. Sutherland's reaction to the reception was more basic: 'Not bad for a couple of old broads!'

Sutherland celebrated her thirtieth anniversary at Covent Garden in a Development Fund Gala with reminders of some of her past successes and in good enough voice to banish thoughts of retirement. If she seemed a little preoccupied during John Tooley's speech at a reception afterwards it was because she had just heard the news she had been longing for – Adam's wife, Helen, was expecting a baby, and Sutherland was overjoyed.

Considering she was in such excellent voice it was hard to understand how word got round New York, where she was due to sing *Lucia*, that she was expected to pull out at the last minute. An impertinent suggestion in view of her impeccable record of reliability. Wind of the rumour sent Sutherland into overdrive with a performance described in the *Wall Street Journal* as 'stupefying'. 'Welcome back,' cried a voice from the balcony after her first aria, a sentiment shared by the rest of the audience who found her long absence from the Met incomprehensible, for by the very laws of nature time must be running out for Sutherland. Yet she sounded remarkably like the Joan Sutherland of 20 years

ago. She could still fill every corner of the Met with volumes
of rich, vibrant, securely focused tone; still execute flights of
coloratura with ease and precision; still dominate the sextet in a
manner more than a match for the most glowing memories of a
younger Sutherland, and still launch a soaring E flat and hold it
for an incredible eight bars. The critics were ecstatic and the
audiences cheered and stamped in a quite uninhibited way. Donal
Henahan summed it up in the *New York Times:*

> We were hearing a soprano, who, though late in her career,
> had mastered her craft so completely and taken such good
> care of her instrument that she could still carry off one of the
> most demanding roles and bring an audience to its feet.

Both she and Bonynge are convinced that her vocal longevity
owes everything to a sound technique acquired with long and
disciplined training, and also a great deal to the careful way she
has managed her career. She comes from a background where the
work ethic was strong; her mother had passed on her own discipline of the 'vocalise' and instilled in her the importance of good
breath control to give the voice proper support. And by adopting
Mrs Sutherland's mezzo-soprano repertoire she had not strained
in the early days after high notes that she could not reach. Later,
with Bonynge beside her not afraid to say 'no' to importuning
managers, she had doggedly stuck to the repertoire that suited
her best. Neither has she dashed from continent to continent
fulfilling concurrent engagements, but formalized her career in
terms of travelling, rehearsal and performance to allow for sufficient rest. She has taken one or two risks in her anxiety to be
home for Christmas whenever possible, but she considers jet
travel the scourge of the opera singer, ruinous to the voice physically and psychologically.

Self-discipline and emotional stability have also played a part
and her placid nature, credited with having a calming effect on
other singers, has protected her from many of the stresses and
strains of a highly competitive profession. Melba used to say,
'When you are climbing up, you just do your best. When you are
the diva, you have to be the best always', a premise Sutherland is
conscious of, but not neurotic about. First-night nerves are one
thing, but she has worked with singers who get themselves in such
a lather of nerves that she wonders how they manage to get on the
stage at all. There is no need to be nervous if one is prepared, but
not all singers are blessed with such a reliable technique.

An unquenchable sense of humour and the capacity to defuse
a potentially volatile situation are also a great bonus. She once sat
at a recording session quietly doing her needlepoint while the

tenor of the moment was exercising his temperament, observing as she took her place beside him, 'I thought I was the prima donna round here'. There is little doubt in Sutherland's mind who the real prima donnas are in the broader sense, and she is renowned for keeping her head when all around are losing theirs. It was Sutherland, for instance who took control when a hire-car dropped them at the Albert Hall and drove off with all the music in the boot! And when she lost her petticoat — not for the first time — in the last act of *Otello* in Sydney, her Emilia, Heather Begg, discreetly picked it up — but Sutherland was concerned that her black underwear would be visible through her nightdress. She often wondered if the audience thought it odd that Desdemona had climbed into bed in her dressing gown.

She does not deny a great desire to scream and shout sometimes, but basically she regards tantrums as unproductive and exhausting. Bonynge admits that she can get mad at him sometimes, but she has never been known to criticize another singer or take advantage of being a star, though she has proved herself capable of taking a resolute stand if artistic standards are being compromised.

There was no sign of any slacking in Sutherland's workload, and her schedule for 1983 was one of her most varied, ranging from operetta to French lyric through baroque, lyric Verdi, verismo, rarified bel canto and *opéra comique,* a repertoire to tax the recall of better memories than Sutherland's. It began with *Die Fledermaus* in the Sydney Domain where there were larger crowds than the previous year, followed by a concert with Pavarotti and a television audience of millions throughout Australia and New Zealand. For Pavarotti, the arch publicist of himself and his art, it was the first visit to Australia as an international star. He wooed the media actively, but the box-office hysteria and journalistic hype was hard to live up to, and while Pavarotti was deemed by the critics to have 'played it safe', Sutherland took all the risks in the world with some of her most brilliant music and was in exceptionally spectacular voice.

Pavarotti had fulfilled a long-standing promise to Sutherland and Bonynge to come to Australia, and the concert was a major event for the tenth anniversary year of the opening of the Sydney Opera House, Also, on a benefit gala basis it lopped Aus. $300,000 off the AO's deficit, the largest amount ever raised in Australia for an indoor concert.

Sutherland was also singing in the first revival of the Australian Opera's 1981 production of *Alcina* — their first Handel opera —

and one which added, according to Brian Hoad, 'a rare and beautiful jewel to its crown of achievement'. With full enjoyment depending very much on an understanding of the conventions of the period, Handel is not opera for the uninitiated. *Idomeneo* had been a step in the right direction, but it was quite a stylistic leap from there to *Alcina*. Robert Helpmann's decision to give the production the full baroque treatment had been inspired by a visit to Stockholm's Drottningholm Court Theatre, the only surviving baroque theatre with the original, innovative stage machinery in working order. He was captivated by the magical transformations achieved there, and the great barley-sugar waves were among the effects reproduced in Sydney. Pascoe designed some glitteringly authentic costumes which reputedly left not a sequin in Sydney, and rather than 'camp it up', as some had feared, Helpmann directed with taste, style and respect for the conventions. The result was a feast of enjoyment on every level — musical, visual and dramatic. The Australian Opera was fortunate in having singers with a knowledge and understanding of the style, and the vocal accomplishments to put it into practice, and Bonynge had appropriately decorated the vocal and orchestral line.

Sutherland had not sung Alcina since 1965, and the role made strenuous demands on stamina and memory. She had always been afraid of getting lost in the endless filigree of Alcina's arias, and at this stage in her career she felt it was more or less inevitable that she would. A spot of transposition did not escape the notice of the critics, who were apparently unaware that she was still singing the role in the same tonality as she had in 1957. However, she demonstrated a voice which had lost little of its range, power and flexibility, and that she could still sing the role with such panache 25 years after her debut in it was a source of wonder to many.

Genoa, the city in which Sutherland had sung her first *Lucia* in Italy, was the scene of her final performance as Violetta in *La traviata*, a role she had never before sung in that country. With labour problems and shortage of money, however, opera in Italy was going through a bad patch and the increasingly disruptive behaviour of the audiences becoming something of a scandal; only days before Pavarotti had been practically booed off the stage in the final scene of *Lucia di Lammermoor* at La Scala.

This was an unpromising background to the engagement of Lamburto Furlan as Alfredo, for although he was Italian he was known to have pursued his career mainly in Australia, and his engagement was seen locally as another instance of Sutherland and Bonynge promoting a protégé. The reality of the situation was very different. Having been unsuccessful in obtaining any of the tenors on their preferred list, the management of the Teatro Margherita had turned to an agent in Rome who had Furlan on their books. They referred to Bonynge with regard to his suitability, and Bonynge, who had worked with him before, knew him to be a nervy singer but one who showed promise, and neither he nor Sutherland had any objection to working with him. However, a nervous start provoked an outburst of hissing and whistling which continued through much of the first act. The middle two acts passed without disturbance but after one false note in the last act, the jeering began again and Bonynge had had enough.

Overwhelmed with disgust at such despicable treatment of Furlan, he laid down his baton and left the pit. Sutherland, who had been finding it well nigh impossible to sustain any atmosphere above the racket, was only too pleased to follow his example. She rose from her sofa and, taking Furlan with her, left the stage. Reassurances from opera house personnel that the hostility was not directed at her was beside the point. Wild horses would not have dragged them back, and they swept from the theatre leaving chaos in the wings and near riot in the auditorium. Before long, however, the performance was underway again with another conductor and Sutherland's understudy, but when Furlan appeared again there was a plaintive wail from the audience: 'It's still the same tenor.'

Sutherland and Bonynge were convinced that it had been a prearranged demonstration against the management, which many believed had been appointed on the basis of political affiliation — a growing trend in Italy — and in which they had no wish to become involved. It had given them both great satisfaction to walk off, but their legal advisors were warned to expect a suit for breach of contract, although in the event the matter was not pursued. It was soon water under the bridge as far as Sutherland was concerned, but the fiasco in Genoa could not fail to be regarded as one of her more sensational farewells.

As she cast off Violetta, Sutherland was about to take on another new role, that of Francesco Cilea's *Adriana Lecouvreur*. Cilea is one of several composers remembered for a single work; his output was limited and *Adriana* his only lasting success. Performed for the first time at the Teatro Lirico, Milan in 1902, it was helped to success by Caruso as Maurizio and Angelina Pandolfini recreating the role of the celebrated eighteenth-century French actress Adrienne Lecouvreur, already enshrined in theatrical history by Sarah Bernhardt.

Adriana is from the verismo school, thus Sutherland's role was outside her normal repertoire; a big challenge dramatically with great swings of emotion, it was not one cynics readily associated with her, though it offered plenty of opportunity to spin a long, sumptuous vocal line. It was an opera championed in the past by several ranking prima donnas and was enjoying a renaissance, and Bonynge thought it a greatly underestimated work.

The man responsible for this production was Tito Capobianco in his final season as General Manager of the San Diego Opera, and, guided by Capobianco, Sutherland's portrayal of Adriana had considerable dramatic impact. Her vocal tone was as beautiful as ever, but applied with more weight and dramatic force, and she handled the declamatory test-piece — the speech from *Phèdre* — with subtlety and finesse. Once she had come to grips with the conversational nature of the work, it was a role very much to her liking and one which lay well for her voice at this stage in her career.

Another role she was happy to undertake at this time was Leonora in *Il trovatore*, as much for the pleasure of getting her voice around Verdi's luscious music as for the fact that the full burden of the performance was equally divided among the principals and did not fall on her shoulders with quite the same weight as *Lucia* or *Norma*.

Il trovatore had not been seen in Sydney since 1967 and it was warmly welcomed, although the production by Elijah Moshinsky, Sidney Nolan and Luciana Arrighi was predictably controversial. The costumes were updated from sixteenth-century Spain to Risorgimento Italy, and Nolan's abstract backdrops disturbed the traditionalists. Nevertheless it was regarded as a distinguished if somewhat idiosyncratic production. The Australian Opera had gathered together one of the strongest casts ever assembled for a Verdi opera in Sydney — at least, since the blighted *I masnadieri* — and although Kenneth Collins, making his debut with the AO, had replaced Francisco Ortiz at relatively short notice before the opening night, on this occasion everything went without a hitch. Lauris Elms was a magnificent Azucena, and according to Maria Prerauer, Sutherland's vocal quality was as 'ravishing and beguiling' as ever, and Roger Covell found her in splendid voice and more thoroughly warmed up from her first entrance. However, when she returned to Sydney it had not been Verdi's Leonora uppermost in her mind, but the excitement of seeing her month-old granddaughter Natasha for the first time.

Il trovatore was by far the most prestigious of the Australian Opera's 1983 productions, for the AO's deficit was fast becoming a burning issue, and it was no longer possible to mount a full quota of new productions. Under the circumstances it was still more difficult to justify the staging of works outside the standard repertoire. But as the purse-strings tightened elsewhere, operas of limited revivability had been successfully presented in semi-staged versions, and the AO produced *Semiramide* in this way. With the minimum of action and sets and costumes assembled mostly from stock, it cost a fraction of the new *Il trovatore*. *Semiramide* had been an enormous success during the Sutherland–Williamson tour, and indeed elsewhere with the right cast. The formidable title role, which Sutherland always sang with such relish, still lay well for her, and partnered by Lauris Elms as Arsace, the general view was that it was better done this way than not done at all.

The following month, just weeks before her fifty-seventh birthday, she felt a bit like a 'granny trying to be kittenish' in performances of *La fille du régiment* for the Met's centenary season. They were performances which nearly did not take place at all, for earlier she had caught her heel on a loose stair-carpet and crashed headlong through a double-glazed window. Covered in blood she had presented a horrific sight to those who came to her aid and had been lucky to escape with a few stitches in her neck. As though nothing had happened, 24 hours later she was coping easily with Marie's tricky coloratura, effortlessly shaping every legato line.

In comparison she was in less good voice when the curtain went up on *Esclarmonde* at Covent Garden before Christmas, and to Sutherland and Bonynge, since they cared deeply about the work, the critical response was a great disappointment. In the eyes of the critics it did not live up to the promise of Massenet's *Werther* or *Manon*, recent productions of which had been highly praised, and they could find little good to say about the production which had been borrowed from San Francisco. Rosenthal ventured to doubt the wisdom of presenting such a specialized piece simply to satisfy the whim of a particular singer, although Arthur Jacobs thought Sutherland of all people had earned the right to appear at Covent Garden on her own terms. It was the very rarity of the work and the fact that it was outside the repertoire normally associated with Sutherland at Covent Garden that created such interest, and it was one of those quirks of fate that external influences mitigated against the total success it could have been.

Sutherland approached the first night far from well, and she was nervous and edgy in consequence, a situation not helped by a 40-minute delay while the theatre was searched for a bomb. Then her entrance was marred as she wobbled precariously on a plinth that had not been bolted securely into place. When she was too unwell to sing the next performance, *Madama Butterfly* replaced *Esclarmonde*; apologies were made for the indisposition of the tenor at the beginning of the second performance, and in the middle of the third the audience were again evacuated into the freezing night while a search was made for another bomb.

Because Sutherland was unwell, the first performance of the series — and the one attended by the critics — was vocally uneven, but 'there was much that was beautiful', wrote Arthur Jacobs in *Opera Magazine*, 'much that was exciting, and the whole vibrated with an artist's commitment'. The high curiosity value of these performances made them treasured experiences for many opera-goers, for without Sutherland and Bonynge, *Esclarmonde* might never have seen the light of day.

Opera in the Sydney Domain was now in its third year and thunderous applause greeted NSW Premier Neville Wran's promise of a permanent concert bowl in the city. To be called the Dame Joan Sutherland Music Bowl, it was a great honour for her, if a bit of a mouthful for a nation which never uses two words where one will do. But the Domain concert now attracted crowds of a size unequalled since the political rallies of Jack Lang in the 30s with singers barely visible from the back and gusts of wind playing havoc with the sound system. But those close enough to the stage heard Sutherland sing a *Lucia* which made nonsense of reports from London that her vocal cords were 'worn' and 'frayed', and she was in opulent voice for *Adriana Lecouvreur* in the Opera Theatre. An undoubted vehicle for a grand diva, it was also an excellent piece for the company as a whole, with a marvellous role for a seconda donna and a confrontation scene to compare with that in *Maria Stuarda*. A huge success with the audience, it was frowned upon by many of the critics who regarded it as a minor opera given a priority it did not deserve over works of far greater substance and merit. In essence, a lavish and well-sung production could not conceal the musical weaknesses of a work not considered worthy of Sutherland — 'a gross waste of a national treasure' according to Peter Robinson in the *Financial Review*. However, it was radiantly sung by Sutherland in a touchingly vulnerable performance, and David Gyger in *Opera Australia* thought she fulfilled the dramatic requirements admirably and that her performance justified the revival.

After *Adriana* Sutherland went home for two months to enjoy the garden and learn *Anna Bolena* for a new production with the Canadian Opera Company. It was the brainchild of Lotfi

Mansouri, General Manager of the COC, in collaboration with the Lyric Opera, Chicago. Sutherland was the *raison d'être* of the production which would also be seen in Detriot, San Francisco, Chicago and Houston.

Donizetti composed the music for *Anna Bolena* at the usual break-neck speed at the home of Giuditta Pasta, who was to create the title role. It went into rehearsal scarcely two weeks before the première at the Teatro Carcano, Milan in 1830 with Donizetti suffering agonies of doubt in spite of an excellent cast which also included Filippo Galli as Henry VIII and Rubini as Percy. Italian composers and audiences alike were fascinated by English history, but with the usual free adaptation of historical fact Romani's libretto made good theatre and elevated Donizetti to the ranks of Italian composers already regarded with respect — among them Bellini — and brought him a measure of international recognition. 'It seemed the public had gone mad,' wrote Donizetti to his wife, 'everyone said they could not remember having been at such a triumph.' With Pasta, Galli and Rubini it maintained its popularity and it was the first of Donizetti's operas to be performed in Paris and London. Alas, for want of singers who could negotiate the music it fell into neglect for the best part of a century until it was revived in Bergamo in 1956. Shortly after La Scala mounted it for Callas, and it became the earliest of Donizetti's works to become familiar to twentieth-century audiences.

Desperately trying to call a halt to the extension of her repertoire, Sutherland had required a deal of persuasive talk from Bonynge and Mansouri to overcome her reluctance to undertake another demanding role at this stage in her career. It had already been deferred, not because it was a big sing, but because it was a big learn. She had found herself at one point faced not only with Anna Bolena, but relearning Alcina and coming to grips with Adriana Lecouvreur as well. Maintaining the enthusiasm for the actual singing was not difficult, but she had reached saturation point with Donizetti's music. *Anna Bolena* was shot through with shades of *Maria Stuarda*, *Lucrezia Borgia* and even Bellini's *I puritani*, and similar phrases in the same key with the same notes and almost the same musical cues filled her with a dread of taking the wrong turn and finding herself singing the wrong opera. In this respect she found the musical mnemonics Sylvia Holford had devised for keeping her on the right track a great help. The role of Anna Bolena, however, suited Sutherland temperamentally. She was more at home as the innocent victim than the scheming opportunist, and it was a character that she could readily respond to. It is a heavily emotional and dramatic role with a contiguity of low, middle and high music, and like most of her roles she had to go for broke in the final scene.

Will Crutchfield, reviewing the performance for the *New York Times* on 29 May, put the downward transposition into perspective:

> If she does this solely for the sake of the high notes she apparently feels she must add at the end . . . then it must be questioned whether the loss of brilliancy is worth it. But if it is this transposition that allows her continuance in roles that would otherwise be too tiring, then we can only be grateful.

For many singers half Sutherland's age transposition was commonplace even in a far less taxing repertoire. In Sutherland's case it was only a matter for raised eyebrows since throughout her career she was renowned for taking the higher option — even singing '*Casta diva*' in the original key of G, which had been too much for Pasta. She may no longer sing all the high notes — for her most recent Lucias she had transposed the first half of the mad scene down a tone to avoid the first of the scene's high E flats — but those she went for were ringing and accurate.

But there has always been more to Sutherland than stratospheric notes above the stave. According to Tom Sutcliffe in a tribute at the time of her Covent Garden Jubilee, what audiences pay to hear 'are the phenomenal strength and beauty of her voice. It is one of the most extraordinary instruments of our time, with agility, dramatic impact, pathos and exceptionally even fullness seamlessly knit together throughout its very wide range.' In most respects this is as true now as it was then, for incredibly her voice is unspoiled by time. A slight loss of vocal power is undeniable: the top is neither as high nor as easy as it once was, and she takes a little longer to warm up these days. But she has lost none of her ability to sustain a long legato line; the tone is as rich and creamy as ever, and she can still achieve feats of legerity of which many singers only dream.

Sutherland's success in *Anna Bolena* did not come as a surprise to Mansouri, who thought it was likely to become one of her finest roles, nor to the disappointed producer of the aborted CBC television recording, Norman Campbell. With her in-built apprehension of first nights and a potential audience of millions she decided at the eleventh hour not to allow the recording to take place. 'She need not have worried', said Campbell, 'she was magnificent', and the recording was rescheduled for a later performance.

One of Donizetti's earliest successes had provided Sutherland with a marvellous new vehicle at this late stage in her career. The

Canadian Opera Company's production, mounted with care and devotion, was good value in every sense. A strong supporting cast, most of whom were taller than Sutherland, were dwarfed by John Pascoe's huge, richly detailed sets. Stennett's costumes were of the sumptuous splendour expected of him, and Sutherland was now past master at coping with extravagant trailing hems. But the weight was something else, and Stennett promised her, 'the next lot will be like a bunch of feathers'. But she wanted no new mountains to climb, and was quite content to leave the rest of Donizetti's untapped heroines to someone else. It had taken her so long to learn it, Bonynge agreed, 'it had better be her last role'.

Meanwhile there were ominous rumblings in the Board Room of the Australian Opera, for the Australia Council, concerned about the percentage of the arts subsidy consumed by 'flagship' companies, was recommending a re-distribution over a more diverse area of musical activity. The AO saw this, quite correctly, as advance warning of a further cut in an already declining subsidy. Consistently successful in wooing audiences, and with a capacity to fund its own growth from increased box-office revenue and income from private sources, the company had recorded a profit for the past two years and was on the way to eliminating the deficit. What it needed was a buffer against inflation in the form of a stable index-linked subsidy, without which forward planning was a hit-and-miss affair. Although the Australia Council acknowledged that Australia needed at least one full-time opera company if standards were to be maintained, the possibility of abandoning year-round programming if the AO was unable to live within its means could not be ruled out. With pleas for extra funding falling on deaf ears, retrenchment had to be considered and as various future options were bandied about Bonynge became a victim of a managerial shake-up when he was replaced by Moffat Oxenbould as Artistic Administrator, answerable only to Patrick Vietch and the Board, still under the chairmanship of Charles Berg. It was a bold stroke for the Board to take for Bonynge had given more to the AO in terms of dedication and enthusiasm than was demanded by his half-yearly contract, and one they handled in a singularly insensitive way. Arriving in Sydney for the winter season Bonynge and Sutherland were met by Vietch and Berg, and hardly had they time to collect their jet-lagged wits before Bonynge was advised of his new position as Musical Director Emeritus. In an earlier crisis Vietch had flown to San Francisco to thrash out problems of rescheduling with

Bonynge, and they were hurt and angry that such a decision as this could be taken without prior warning. Sutherland was so upset that she felt like packing and flying home on the next plane.

When tempers cooled, however, Bonynge issued a statement that there was no-one he would rather see as Artistic Director than Moffatt Oxenbould who had given years of service to the company in one capacity or another since the early 60s. But the timing of such a coup could not have been worse, for the Australian Opera was about to celebrate the tenth anniversary of Sutherland's return to Australia with a revival of the 1974 production of *Les contes d'Hoffmann*. Obviously it was difficult to carry on as if nothing had happened; rehearsals were rather frigid and the first night was a somewhat tense affair, a little lacking in the warmth and generosity of spirit that had created so many unforgettable nights.

One of the criticisms constantly levelled at the Australian Opera was the notably light representation of twentieth-century works in the repertoire, thus giving audiences little incentive to regard opera as a living, evolving artform. The output of indigenous works was compared unfavourably with productions of Britten, Tippett and Walton at Covent Garden since the war, and many thought the AO must seek contemporary works to win a wider audience and justify a continued subsidy. Yet excursions into indigenous opera had met with limited success and some spectacular failures, for contemporary works with a relevance to everyday life, often with discordant, unvocal music, cannot be relied upon to fill theatres in the same way as the classics. Rudolf Bing was of the opinion that a better case could be made for the 'proposition that opera will never die unless the new works are performed'. In tandem with providing a platform for national talent, a heavily subsidized company also has a duty to provide entertainment for the greatest number of people. A third of the AO's productions since 1979 had in fact been twentieth-century works, ranging from Richard Strauss to Benjamin Britten, although all were too old to qualify for the contemporary repertoire the critics were urging. Even *The Carmelites* of Poulenc did not qualify, but it was enjoying a rash of new stagings and the AO's 1984 production was regarded as exemplary.

Once asked, having established her international career, if she would again sing contemporary opera, Sutherland had replied, 'Yes, with a gun at my head', but she had found Madame Lidoine one of her more congenial forays into twentieth-century music and was happy to contribute to a performance in an ensemble role rather than as leading light. By the nature of *The Carmelites*

– a series of dialogues and displays of over-exposed emotions – it translated well to the small screen, but even as one of the more user-friendly of modern works, both in the theatre and as a simulcast, it did not achieve the same mass popularity as *Die Fledermaus, Il trovatore* or *Adriana Lecouvreur*.

Bonynge's contract did not expire until 1986 and although much of his planning had already gone to the wall, neutralizing his position did nothing to deflect the deepening financial crisis and retrenchment was beginning to seem inevitable. Two of the most freely discussed options were to revert to the *stagione* system whereby artists are engaged for one production at a time, or scale down their activities and operate on a half-yearly basis. Either option would have a calamitous effect on the company, which had been built up with such dedication over the years. The roster of principals and full-time orchestra and chorus would have to be disbanded, and directors, designers and conductors lured to Australia since the opening of the Opera House would drift away again.

Sutherland felt that the Australian Opera, one of the few repertory companies retaining a full-time ensemble, and with standards of professionalism not always found in large international houses, was creating conditions in which singers could develop as she had in London. Members of the company could take on major roles one night and no-one refused to undertake a small part a few nights later. She and Bonynge were passionately concerned to see the AO preserved; the Opera House was a talking point around the world and failure to preserve the company would inflict incalculable damage on the whole cultural image of Australia. But while the Prime Minister, Bob Hawke, was praising the work of the company and describing it as 'one of our great institutions', the Australia Council was still refusing to increase or index-link the subsidy, and the New South Wales Government was refusing to refund a million Australian dollars mistakenly paid in pay-roll tax since 1978.

The Dame Joan Sutherland Music Bowl had not yet materialized, but an estimated 80,000 people saw *Les contes d'Hoffmann* in the Sydney Domain, although as a result of bad publicity and uncertainty about the future the summer season in the Opera House had been poorly attended. Even a new production of *Norma*, an infinite improvement on the 1978 version, had not succeeded in filling the Concert Hall, although Sutherland's performance was referred to as 'flawless' by Brian Hoad.

In Melbourne, however, tickets had been sold out in record time for a gala performance of *Les contes d'Hoffmann* which was to open the Australian Opera's first season in the new Victorian Arts Centre. But on top of the financial and administrative difficulties the AO was in the thick of a long-running dispute over travelling expenses exacerbated by Vietch's refusal to meet the unions in person. In Melbourne the situation reached a climax when one of the three unions involved refused to allow the curtain to go up. Charter flights had brought people from New Zealand and America especially for the performance, which had been announced as Sutherland's final apearance in the multiple *Hoffmann* roles. Sutherland had sat fully made-up in her dressing room as the unions thrashed it out, and when the performance was finally cancelled 45 minutes after the curtain was due to rise, distress, disappointment and anger was widespread. The ABC had to abandon the planned simulcast and it cost the Australian Opera over Aus. $100,000 in ticket revenue, a loss they could ill-afford on the verge of bankruptcy.

The booking for *Lucia di Lammermoor* at Covent Garden in the spring was also hugely oversubscribed, although many refused to believe that Sutherland, approaching 60, could sing a Lucia that was anything other than a pale shadow of past glory. But part-nered by Carlo Bergonzi, himself already past 60, the reigning Lucia showed no signs of abdicating that title. Sutherland humbled those who had come to see the bails fly with an amazingly fresh performance, no less powerful than of old, and still unbelievably possessing its famed agility and precision. An increased aware-ness of words and an ability to colour the voice with more subtlety were ample compensations for any loss of youthful brilliance, and few sopranos could float Donizetti's phrases into the auditorium as Sutherland could. Her mad scene was an exciting musical and dramatic experience which drew from the audience a spontane-ous and lengthy standing ovation.

Notwithstanding affectionate jibes about operatic Darby and Joan, Sutherland and Bergonzi had worn better than the now vintage Zeffirelli sets, and when the curtain stuck on opening night and they had to begin again, it occurred to her that 'We're not the only geriatrics here'. But in *Opera Magazine* Rosenthal referred to the performance as a 'great' one, and Robert Hender-son summed up his review in the *Daily Telegraph*: 'In an age when youth is everything, it is a comforting thought that maturity is best.'

Back in Sydney, however, for an effective, economy produc-tion of *I puritani* with sets and costumes borrowed heavily from *Lucia*, critical opinion was divided with regard to Sutherland's performance as Elvira. John Carmody, always one of her fiercest critics, was becoming increasngly querulous about her performances, yet Brian Hoad thought she was still supreme in the bel-canto field. She was still able to sail immaculately through Bellini's melodic line and still negotiate trills, runs and top notes with unswerving ease. There were the usual 'slow to warm up' comments, and a minor transposition did not escape notice, but with the co-operation of the costume and make-up departments she was still able to draw the character of Elvira with remarkable youthfulness.

Sutherland had needed a lot of persuasion from Lotfi Mansouri and from Bonynge to convince her that she could convey the same quality as Ophélie in Thomas' *Hamlet*. She had thought that her learning days were over, but she allowed them to talk her into it for the Canadian Opera Company. She had recorded it, they argued, so why not sing it on stage, and when she protested that she was a bit ripe for it, Bonynge reminded her that Ellen Terry had played the role of Ophelia at 60. Sutherland was a little short of her own sixtieth birthday, and although she had not yet seen her new grandson, Vanya, born in Sydney in September, she was a grandmother twice over, sometimes feeling it, and was conscious of the fact that she was twice as old as Lesley Richards who was to play Hamlet's mother. It was also an extraordinarily difficult role, but a short one, and she was already familiar with the bravura mad scene.

Hamlet had never been performed in Canada, and seldom in any country since the early part of the century, but after its première at the Paris Opéra in 1868 it quickly became part of the standard repertoire there and was more popular than *Faust* or *Aida*. Not an opera with the dramatic punch of *Macbeth*, the essence of *Hamlet's* tuneful and well-constructed score is French romanticism. The libretto by Jules Barbier and Michel Carré spreads across five acts and, with scant regard for Shakespeare, Hamlet survives to become King. For the first performance at Covent Garden Thomas amended this with Hamlet killing the King before committing suicide. In Toronto Bonynge merged the two, so that Hamlet, mortally wounded by Laertes at Ophélie's funeral, is goaded by the ghost into killing the King, and expires across Ophélie's body.

Mansouri once again surrounded Sutherland with a worthy cast — one of the reasons they liked working with him so much. 'A star and five puppet singers is not the way to do it,' explains Bonynge, 'though a lot of houses do.' Mansouri pays attention to detail and knows the words and music of the opera he is directing

which many do not. It was a rewarding role for Sutherland as she
warmed to the part of Ophélie; she had lost none of her ability to
send shivers down the spine and according to William Littler in
the *Toronto Star* she negotiated the mad scene 'with a combination of clarity and tonal beauty that remain the envy of her
colleagues'.

In his eight years as General Manager of the Canadian Opera
Company, Lotfi Mansouri had presented 34 new productions,
many of them works not seen in Canada before. He was prepared
to take risks and shared Bonynge's view that audiences wanted
more than *Butterflies, Bohèmes* and *Traviatas*. Productions which
were unique appealed to him because they made good calling
cards, as evidenced by his much travelled *Anna Bolena* which
had, as Mansouri predicted, become one of Sutherland's finest
roles. 'There is simply no-one before the public with this charisma
of tone and mastery of technique', wrote Richard Dyer in the
Boston Globe when she sang it in Chicago, and the music critic of
the *Tribune* described her as 'a musical phenomenon who brings
us that much closer to understanding the golden age of vocal art'.
Donal Henahan rated her stirring concert performance in Avery
Fisher Hall as one of the best in New York's musical year. In view
of what he considered 'a depressing lack of vocal talent on many
Metropolitan evenings', it was regarded as a crying shame that
the Met was not part of the COC's *Anna Bolena* consortium, and
in Boston and Washington critical acclaim went far beyond what
Sutherland might dismiss as 'being kind to an old lady'.

For nearly three decades she has travelled the world taking risks
with the big, florid roles, extending the boundaries of the repertoire, and in spite of the lack of sympathy of some of the critics,
she has succeeded in filling opera houses wherever, whenever
and whatever she sang. She may be more selective about the high
notes now, but the middle range is better than ever and she
can still captivate an audience with the sheer beauty, strength
and richness of her voice and the warmth and sincerity of her
personality.

Neither is she shying away from the challenges. At the beginning of 1986 people queued all night in Sydney for Sutherland's
last performances of *Lucia di Lammermoor* with the Australian
Opera, and many thought she surpassed the excellence of those
five years earlier. 'Her claim to all-round pre-eminence in this
the greatest role of her career,' wrote David Gyger in *Opera
Australia*, 'was not about to be relinquished.' In March her concert programme in New Zealand included '*Casta diva*', complete

with recitative and cabaletta, 'Qui la voce' from I puritani and Lucia's mad scene. She sang Norma in Barcelona, La fille du régiment in Pittsburgh and in June, Houston succumbed to the full power of Sutherland's vocal charisma in Anna Bolena. In July she sang in a new production of La fille in Sydney, although a perforated eardrum caused the cancellation of her American concerts with Pavarotti. However, after an enforced rest she returned to New York to celebrate her sixtieth birthday and the twenty-fifth anniversary of her Metropolitan debut in a revival of I puritani, and her first appearance was greeted with such a barrage of applause and cheering that she was eventually obliged to leave the stage and begin all over again. Her diary, full to the end of 1988, includes performances of Il trovatore at the Metropolitan, Adriana Lecouvreur in Toronto, Anna Bolena at Covent Garden and Lucia in Barcelona.

When Sutherland had first visited Ivor Griffiths in Wimpole Street he had told her that she had the strongest vocal cords he had ever seen, including those of Melba, and Melba's voice had remained fresh and pure right up to the last of her many farewells in 1926 — coincidentally the year in which Sutherland was born. More than 30 years later a consultant in San Francisco found her vocal cords in pristine condition still, and there were those who remembered the excellent estate of Mrs Sutherland's voice at the age of 72. Nevertheless she takes each day as it comes, conscious that she is perhaps vocally on borrowed time. But she still loves to sing and although she has Bonynge's assurance that he will tell her when it is time to call it a day, she feels that it will ultimately be the hassle of travelling that will signal the end of her career.

Sutherland's contribution to opera in the last half of the twentieth century is phenomenal. She would not recognize it, nor even acknowledge it, but she has transcended the normal confines of fame to become, in the words of the music critic Fritz Spiegl, 'an institution almost beyond praise or criticism however she performs'. She once said that she was born with a sightly unusual larynx and had been exploiting it ever since. And so she has. The plump, unprepossessing girl had realised all her dreams. That perceptive judge Neville Cardus had told her to stay in Australia and be a big fish in a small pool. It was well-meant advice, but spectacularly wrong; gifted with the voice of the century, she has shared it with millions.

CATALOGUE OF PERFORMANCES

The following symbols are used: *—debut performance; †—also broadcast on radio; ‡—also broadcast on television. Operas and recitals sung only for radio and television transmission have not been noted except in the case of live radio broadcasts of special interest. Composers are noted when not indicated in the text.

The following abbreviations are used: c.—conductor; p.—producer; d.—designer; P.—pianist. Where two designers are noted, the first indicates the set designer and the second the costume designer.

Programmes of recitals are given in the appendices beginning on page 237. Venues are only noted in the case of London, Milan, New York, Paris, Sydney and Vienna.

STUDENT PERFORMANCES
Christmas Oratorio c. Henry Krips; Sydney Town Hall: 12 Dec. 1946
Acis & Galatea Galatea; Eastwood Masonic Hall, Sydney: June 1947
Dido & Aeneas Dido; Lyceum Club, Sydney: Aug. 1947
Olivet to Calvary (Maunder); Sydney Town Hall: Apr. 1949
Elijah (Mendelssohn); Eastwood Masonic Hall, Sydney: Dec. 1949; Parramatta City Hall, Sydney: Mar. 1950
Samson Dalila & Israelite Woman; Sydney Town Hall: 15 Jul. 1950
Messiah Sydney Town Hall: Nov. 1950
Judith Judith; James Wilson (Holofernes), Ronald Dowd (Bagoas); c. Goossens; Sydney Conservatorium: 9, 12, 18, 22 June 1951
All at Sea (Geoffrey Shaw) Mrs Empson (Act II only); Parry Theatre, Royal College of Music, London: 12 May 1952
Il tabarro Giorgetta; Gordon Farrell/Kenneth Fawcett (Michele), Edward Byles (Luigi), Kenneth McKellar (Ballad Singer); c. Richard Austin, p. Carey, d. Peter Rice/Pauline Elliot; Parry Theatre, Royal College of Music, London: 16, 18 Jul.

1952
The Magic Flute First Lady*; Matters/Walters (Papageno), Lanigan (Tamino), Leigh (Pamina), te Wiata (Sarastro), Bak/Hollweg (Queen of Night), Howe, Watson (Ladies); c. Pritchard, p. West, d. Messel; Covent Garden: 28 Oct., 1 Nov., 6, 11 Dec.
Aida High Priestess*; Brouwenstijn (Aida), Shacklock (Amneris), Johnston (Radames), Williams/Walters (Amonasro); c. Barbirolli, p. West, d. Cruddas; Covent Garden: 3, 6, 14 Nov.
Recital (appendix 1); P. Gerald Moore; Wigmore Hall, London: 7 Nov.
Norma Clotilde*; Callas (Norma), Picchi (Pollione), Stignani (Adalgisa), Vaghi (Oroveso); c. Gui, p. Enriquez, d. Barlow; Covent Garden: 8, 10, 13, 18†, 20 Nov.
A Masked Ball Amelia*; Edgar Evans (Riccardo), Walters (Renato), Watson (Ulrica); c. Pritchard, p. Rennert, d. Barlow/Stone; Covent Garden: 29 Dec.

1953

The Magic Flute First Lady; Geraint Evans/Matters (Papageno), Lanigan/Pears (Tamino), Leigh (Pamina), Nowakowsky/te Wiata (Sarastro), Hollweg/Bak (Queen of Night), Howe, Watson (Ladies); c. Pritchard, p. West, d. Messel; Covent Garden: 16, 19 Jan.

Aida High Priestess; Brouwenstijn/Hammond (Aida), Shacklock (Amneris), Johnston (Radames), Walters/Edwards (Amonasro); c. Barbirolli, p. West, d. Cruddas; Covent Garden: 28 Jan., 5, 11 Feb.

Aida High Priestess; Zadek/Lafayette/Kinasiewicz (Aida), Shacklock (Amneris), Johnston/Marlowe (Radames), Edwards/Walters/Williams (Amonasro); c. Barbirolli/E. Young, p. West, d. Cruddas; Royal Opera House tour: Cardiff: 16 Feb.; Edinburgh: 23 Feb.; Glasgow: 2, 14 Mar.; Liverpool: 18 Mar.; Manchester: 28 Mar., 1 Apr.; Birmingham: 11, 15 Apr.

A Masked Ball Amelia; Edgar Evans/Johnston (Riccardo), Walters/Edwards (Renato), Coates (Ulrica); c. Tausky, p. Rennert, d. Barlow/Stone; Royal Opera House tour: Cardiff: 18, 27 Feb.; Glasgow: 11, 13 Mar.; Manchester: 30 Mar., 2 Apr.; Birmingham: 13 Apr.

The Marriage of Figaro Countess Almaviva*; Geraint Evans (Figaro), Walters (Count Almaviva) Leigh/Dunne (Susanna), Mills/Zareska/Pollak (Cherubino); c. J. Gibson, p. Latham, d. Gerard; Royal Opera House tour: Edinburgh: 24 Feb.; Manchester: 4 Apr.; Birmingham: 18 Apr.

Wagnerian Concert Brangäne; *Tristan und Isolde*: Act II; c. Barbirolli; Manchester: 9 Apr.

Elektra Overseer*; Schlüter (Elektra), Kupper/Kinasiewicz (Chrysothemis), Coates (Clytemnestra), Braun (Orestes); c. Kleiber, p. Hartmann, d. Lambert; Covent Garden: 13, 15, 23, 27 May

Aida High Priestess; Callas (Aida), Simionato (Amneris), Baum (Radames), Walters (Amonasro); c. Barbirolli, p. West, d. Cruddas; Covent Garden: 4, 6, 10† June

Norma Clotilde; Callas (Norma), Simionato (Adalgisa), Picchi Pollione) Nero (Oroveso); c. Pritchard, p. Enriquez, d. Barlow; Covent Garden: 15, 17, 20, 23 June

Aida High Priestess; Zadek (Aida), Shacklock (Amneris), Johnston (Radames), Walters (Amonasro); c. Barbirolli/E. Young, p. West, d. Cruddas; Royal Opera House tour: Bulawayo, Rhodesia: 30 Jul., 1, 5, 10, 14, 19, 25, 29 Aug.

Gloriana Lady Rich*; Lanigan (Essex), Cross/Shacklock (Elizabeth I), Dalberg (Raleigh), Matters (Cecil); Royal Opera House tour, Bulawayo: 11, 15, 20, 22, 24 Aug.

Die Walküre Helmwige*; Fisher (Sieglinde), Harshaw (Brünnhilde), Hotter (Wotan) Hook, Turner, Coates, Watson, M. Sinclair, Shacklock, Howitt (Valkyries); c. Stiedry, p. Schramm, d. Pemberton; Covent Garden: 19, 24, 26, 30 Oct.

Carmen Frasquita*; Rankin/Shacklock (Carmen), Johnston/Edgar Evans (Don José), Rothmüller (Escamillo), Yeend/Leigh/Morison

(Micaela); c. Pritchard/Downes, p. Asquith, d. Wakhevitch; Covent Garden: 2, 7, 10, 18, 26 Nov., 12, 28, 31 Dec.
Aida High Priestess; Brouwenstijn/Hammond (Aida), Shacklock/ Rankin/Watson (Amneris), Johnston (Radames), Rothmüller (Amonasro); c. Barbirolli/E. Young, p. West, d. Cruddas; Covent Garden: 2, 7, 11, 18, 26 Dec.

1954
Aida High Priestess/Aida*; Hammond/Sutherland (Aida), Shacklock (Amneris), Johnston/van der Zaalm (Radames), Rothmüller (Amonasro); c. E. Young, p. West, d. Cruddas; Covent Garden: 2, 22 Jan. (High Priestess), 4 Feb. (Aida)
Carmen Frasquita; Shacklock (Carmen), Edgar Evans/Johnston (Don José), Rothmüller (Escamillo), Morison/Stuart/Turner/Leigh (Micaela); c. Downes/Pritchard, p. Asquith, d. Wakhevitch; Covent Garden: 5, 12, 27 Jan., 9, 12 Feb.
Gloriana Lady Rich; Pears/Lanigan (Essex), Cross/Shacklock (Elizabeth I), Dalberg (Raleigh), Otakar Kraus (Cecil); c. Goodall, p. Coleman, d. Piper; Covent Garden: 29 Jan., 2, 16 Feb.; Royal Opera House tour: Cardiff: 11 Mar.; Manchester: 30 Mar.; Birmingham: 13 Apr.
Aida High Priestess; Hammond (Aida), Shacklock/Watson/Coates (Amneris), Johnston (Radames), Rothmüller (Amonasro); c. E. Young, p. West, d. Cruddas; Royal Opera House tour: Croydon: 24, 26 Feb.; Manchester: 3 Apr.; Birmingham: 17 Apr.
Die Walküre Helmwige; Fisher/H. Konetzni (Sieglinde), A. Konetzni (Brünnhilde), L. Hoffmann/Kamaan (Wotan), Raisbeck, Toros, Coates, Watson, M. Sinclair, Shacklock, Denise (Valkyries); c. Goodall, p. West, d. Pemberton; Royal Opera House tour: Croydon: 5, 9 Mar.; Manchester: 2 Apr.; Birmingham: 6 Apr.
Carmen Frasquita; Shacklock (Carmen), Edgar Evans/Rowland Jones/ Johnston (Don José), Rothmüller (Escamillo), Leigh (Micaela); c. Pritchard/Downes, p. Asquith, d. Wakhevitch; Royal Opera House tour: Cardiff: 8, 12 Mar.; Manchester: 1 Apr.; Birmingham: 5, 16 Apr.
Der Freischütz Agathe*; Edgar Evans/Johnston (Max), Otakar Kraus/ Dalberg (Kaspar), Leigh (Aennchen); c. Downes, p. West, d. Furse; Royal Opera House tour: Manchester: 23, 26 Mar.; Covent Garden: 13 May, 12, 16 Jul.
La buona figliuola (BBC broadcast) Lucinda*; Cuénod (Armindoro), A. Young (Conchiglia), Morison (Cecchina); c. Mackerras; 22, 25 Apr.
Elektra Overseer; Schlüter (Elektra), Rysanek (Chrysothemis), Coates (Clytemnestra), Otakar Kraus (Orestes); c. Kempe, p. Hartmann, d. Lambert; Covent Garden: 30 Apr., 4, 12 May
Der Ring des Nibelungen Woglinde*, Helmwige, Woodbird*; Otakar Kraus (Alberich), Frantz (Wotan), Raisbeck (Wellgunde), Thomas (Flosshilde), Fisher (Sieglinde), Harshaw (Brünnhilde), Raisbeck, Toros, Howe, Iacopi, Johnson, Shacklock, Denise (Valkyries),

Svenholm (Siegfried), Kuen (Mime); c. Stiedry, p. Hartmann, d. Hurry; Covent Garden: First Cycle: 27 May, 2, 8, 17 June; Second Cycle: 21†, 23†, 25†, 29† June

Concert *Exsultate Jubilate* (Mozart); c. Woolf; St Martin-in-the-Field, London: 26 June

Aida High Priestess; Hammond/Shuard (Aida), Shacklock/Rankin (Amneris), Johnston (Radames), Walters/Geraint Evans (Amonasro); c. E. Young, p. West, d. Cruddas; Covent Garden: 3, 7, 19, 23 Jul., 14, 20, 28 Dec.

Carmen Frasquita; Rankin/Shacklock/Howe (Carmen), Edgar Evans/ Johnston (Don José), Geraint Evans (Escamillo), Hale/Leigh/Morison (Micaela); c. Pritchard/Downes, p. Asquith, d. Wakhevitch; Covent Garden: 9, 21 Jul., 28, 30 Oct., 24, 30 Nov., 4, 7 Dec.

Promenade Concert Lisa's aria, Act I, *The Queen of Spades* (Tchaikovsky); c. B. Cameron; Royal Albert Hall, London: 2† Aug.

The Tales of Hoffmann Antonia*; Glynne (Crespel), Patzac/Edgar Evans (Hoffmann), Uhde/Otakar Kraus (Dr Miracle), M. Sinclair/ Coates (Mother's voice); c. Downes, p. Rennert, d. Wakhevitch; Covent Garden: 17, 20, 23 Nov., 1, 13 Dec.

Der Freischütz Agathe; Edgar Evans/Johnston (Max), Dalberg (Kaspar), Leigh (Aennchen); c. Downes, p. West, d. Furse; Covent Garden: 22, 30† Dec., 15, 25 Jan. 1955

1955

The Midsummer Marriage Jenifer*; Richard Lewis (Mark), Otakar Kraus (King Fisher), Leigh (Bella), Lanigan (Jack), Dominguez (Sosostris), Langdon, Coates (The Ancients); c. Pritchard, p. West, d. Hepworth; Covent Garden: 27†, 31 Jan., 8†, 11, 22 Feb.

The Tales of Hoffmann Antonia, Giulietta*; Edgar Evans (Hoffmann), Howitt (Nicklaus) Otakar Kraus (Dappertutto, Dr Miracle), Coates/M. Sinclair (Mother's voice), Glynne (Crespel), Sutherland/Hale (Giulietta), Morison/Sutherland (Antonia); c. Downes, p. Rennert, d. Wakhevitch; Royal Opera House tour: Glasgow: 28 Feb. (G), 5 Mar. (A/G), 7 Mar. (G); Edinburgh: 14 Mar. (G), 16 Mar. (A); Leeds: 21 Mar. (G); Manchester: 28 Mar. (G), 2 Apr. (A/G); Coventry: 11 Apr. (G), 13 Apr. (A)

Aida Aida; Shacklock/Coates (Amneris), Johnston (Radames), Geraint Evans/Walters (Amonasro); c. E. Young, p. West, d. Cruddas; Royal Opera House tour: Glasgow: 1 Mar.; Manchester: 5, 9 Apr.; Covent Garden: 23 Apr.

Missa Solemnis (Beethoven) (BBC broadcast); other soloists: Cavelti, Pears, Standen; c. Schwarz; 15, 16, 20 Apr.

Operatic Concert with other artists (further information unknown); Brierly Hill, West Midlands: 27 Apr.

Der Ring des Nibelungen Woglinde, Helmwige; Otakar Kraus (Alberich), Hotter/Schoeffler (Wotan), Hale (Wellgunde), Halliday (Flosshilde), Rysanek/Hilde Konetzni (Sieglinde), Harshaw (Brünnhilde), Shuard,

Hale, Coates, Iacopi, Berry, Shacklock, Howe (Valkyries), Svenholm (Siegfried); c. Kempe, p. Hartmann, d. Hurry; Covent Garden: First Cycle: 10, 14†, 27 May; Second Cycle: 8, 10, 17 June. NB: Sutherland did not appear in *Siegfried*.

The Tales of Hoffman Olympia*; Edgar Evans (Hoffmann), Veasey (Nicklaus) Otakar Kraus (Coppelius), Nilsson/Tree (Cochenille), Geraint Evans (Spalanzani); c. Downes, p. Rennert, d. Wakhevitch; Covent Garden: 16, 18, 22 June, 20, 22 Jul.

Aida High Priestess; Stella (Aida), Stignani (Amneris), Penno (Radames), Gobbi (Amonasro); c. Molinari-Pradelli/E. Young, p. West, d. Cruddas; Covent Garden: 11, 13, 16†, 18 Jul.

Promenade Concert *Te Deum* (Dvorak); c. Sargent; Royal Albert Hall, London: 8† Aug.

Euryanthe (Weber) (BBC broadcast) Euryanthe*; Vroons (Adolar), Böhme (Ludwig), Otakar Kraus (Lysiart), Schech (Eglantine); c. Stiedry; 30 Sep., 1 Oct.

Recital (appendix 2); P. Bonynge; Wigmore Hall, London: 7 Oct.

Celebrity Concert with other artists (further information unknown); P. Hardie; Manchester: 12 Oct.

Carmen Micaela*; Radev/Shacklock (Carmen), Johnston/Nilsson (Don José) Ronald Lewis (Escamillo); c. Downes, p. Asquith, d. Wakhevitch; Covent Garden: 20, 25, 31 Oct., 4, 14, 19, 24, 30 Nov., 27, 29 Dec.

Aida (concert performance) Aida; Nancy Thomas (Amneris), Byles (Radames); c. Walter B. Smith; Exeter: 30 Oct.

Golgotha (BBC broadcast); Marjorie Thomas, Midgley, Griffiths, Anthony; c. Sargent; Royal Festival Hall, London: 9 Nov.

1956

La clemenza di Tito (BBC broadcast) Vitellia*, Richard Lewis (Tito), M. Sinclair (Sextus), Vyvyan (Servilia), Pollak (Annius), Hemsley (Publius); c. Pritchard; 11, 12 Mar.

Verdi Requiem c. Fleming; Coventry: 24 Mar.

Messiah c. Mansel Thomas; Cardiff: 30 Mar.

The Tales of Hoffman Antonia; Robinson (Crespel), Richard Lewis (Hoffmann), Otakar Kraus (Dr Miracle), Shacklock (Mother's voice); c. Downes, p. Asquith, d. Wakhevitch; Covent Garden: 19, 21 Apr., 28 June, 9 Jul.

The Magic Flute First Lady; Geraint Evans/Walters (Papageno), Lanigan (Tamino), Morison (Pamina), Kelly (Sarastro), Graham/ Dobbs/Coertse (Queen of Night), Hale, Berry (Ladies); c. Kubelik/ J. Gibson, p. West, d. Messel; Covent Garden: 24, 27 Apr., 3, 8, 12 May, 18, 20, 30 June

Concert Mahler's Fourth Symphony; c. Kempe; Royal Festival Hall, London: 2 May

Concert of Sacred Music with Norma Proctor; Brecon, Wales: 6 May

Concert *Magnificat* (Monteverdi); other soloists: J. Sinclair, Schneiderhan,

Proctor, W. Brown, Pears; c. Walter Goehr; Royal Festival Hall, London: 13 May

Der Ring des Nibelungen Woglinde, Helmwige; Otakar Kraus (Alberich), Hotter/Pease (Wotan), Raisbeck (Wellgunde), M. Sinclair (Flosshilde), Fisher (Sieglinde), Harshaw (Brünnhilde), Shuard, Hale, Coates, Iacopi, Berry, Shacklock, Thomas (Valkyries), Windgassen (Siegfried); c. Kempe, p. Hartmann, d. Hurry; Covent Garden: First Cycle: 24, 28 May, 6 June; Second Cycle: 11, 12, 16 June. NB: Sutherland did not appear in *Siegfried*.

Le nozze di Figaro Countess Almaviva; Bruscantini (Figaro), Roux (Count Almaviva), Rizzieri (Susanna), Canne-Meijer (Cherubino); c. Gui/Silem/Pritchard, p. Ebert, d. Messel; Glyndebourne: 6, 10, 14†, 18, 20, 27 Jul.; Liverpool: 10, 12, 14, 22 Sep.

Die Zauberflöte First Lady; Geraint Evans (Papageno), Häfliger (Tamino), Lorengar (Pamina), Guthrie/Bernadic (Sarastro), Dobbs (Queen of Night), Canne-Meijer, M. Sinclair (Ladies); c. Gui, p. Ebert, d. Messel; Glyndebourne: 19†, 22, 25 Jul., 3, 7, 9, 11, 13 Aug.

Promenade Concert *Martern aller Arten (Die Entführung aus dem Serail)*; c. Boult; Royal Albert Hall, London: 3† Sep.

Concert Jesu Joy of Man's Desiring (Bach), Mass in C Minor (Mozart); c. Wyn Morris; Llanelly, Wales: 7 Oct.

Mass in C Minor (Mozart) c. Victor Fleming; Coventry: 27 Oct.

The Magic Flute Pamina*; Geraint Evans/Walters (Papageno), Pears/ Richard Lewis (Tamino), Dalberg/Kelly (Sarastro), Coertse/Graham (Queen of Night); c. J. Gibson/Kubelik, p. West, d. Messel; Covent Garden: 10, 13 Nov., 14, 18, 28 Dec.

1957

Die Meistersinger von Nürnberg Eva*; Witte (Walther), Pease (Sachs), Dalberg (Pogner), Geraint Evans (Beckmesser), Pears (David), Marjorie Thomas (Magdalene); c. Kubelik/Goodall, p. Witte, d. Wakhevitch; Covent Garden: 28, 31 Jan., 8, 11, 13 Feb.

Carmen Micaela; Muriel Smith (Carmen), Johnston (Don José), Allman (Escamillo); c. Matheson, p. Asquith, d. Wakhevitch; Covent Garden: 5 Feb.

The Midsummer Marriage Jenifer; Richard Lewis (Mark), Glynne (King Fisher), J. Sinclair (Bella), Lanigan (Jack), N. Thomas (Sosostris), Langdon, Coates (The Ancients); c. Pritchard, p. West, d. Hepworth; Covent Garden: 21†, 28 Feb.

The Magic Flute Pamina; Geraint Evans/Walters (Papageno), Lanigan/ R. Jones (Tamino), Dalberg/Kelly/Langdon/Rouleau (Sarastro), Graham (Queen of Night); c. J. Gibson/Kubelik, p. West, d. Messel; Royal Opera House tour: Cardiff: 8, 9, 12 Mar.; Manchester: 25, 29, 30 Mar.; Southampton: 8, 12, 13 Apr.

Alcina Alcina; Carvalho (Ruggiero), Scheepers (Morgana), M. Sinclair (Bradamante), Kentish (Oronte); c. Farncombe, p. Besch; Handel

Opera Society, St Pancras Town Hall, London: 19, 20 Mar.
Verdi Requiem c. George Weldon; Swansea: 4 May
Rigoletto Gilda*; Otakar Kraus (Rigoletto), Verrau/Midgley (Duke), Langdon/Rouleau (Sparafucile), Howitt (Maddalena); c. Downes, p. Bailey, d. Gellner; Covent Garden: 8, 14, 17, 20, 28 May, 1 June
The Magic Flute Pamina; Walters (Papageno), Lanigan (Tamino), Rouleau/Kelly/Langdon (Sarastro), Coertse/Graham (Queen of Night); c. James Gibson, p. West, d. Messel; Covent Garden: 25, 28 June, 6, 15, 17 Jul.
Der Schauspieldirektor Mme Hertz*; Lagger (Herr Frank), A. Young (Vogelsang), Labay (Mlle Silberklang), Griffiths (Herr Buff); c. Balkwill, p. Besch, d. Rice; Glyndebourne: 5, 7†, 12, 14, 16, 18, 20, 23 Jul.
Mitridate Eupatore (BBC broadcast) Laodice*; Boyce (Farnace), M. Sinclair (Tratonica), Byles (Nicomede), J. Cameron (Mitridate); c. Appia; 16 Aug.
Emilia di Liverpool (BBC broadcast) Emilia*; Cantelo (Bettina), McAlpine (Thomson), Alan (Asdrubale), Dowling (Claudio); c. Pritchard; 8 Sep.
Promenade Concert Quintet (*Die Meistersinger*) with Pease, Johnston, Nilsson, Howe; c. B. Cameron; Royal Albert Hall, London: 11† Sep.
Der Ring des Nibelungen Woglinde; Otakar Kraus (Alberich), Hotter (Wotan), Hale (Wellgunde), Marjorie Thomas (Flosshilde), Windgassen (Siegfried), Nilsson (Brünnhilde); c. Kempe, p. Potter, d. Hurry; Covent Garden: First Cycle: 25† Sep., 4 Oct.; Second Cycle: 7, 12 Oct. NB: Sutherland did not appear in *Die Walküre* nor *Siegfried*.
Götterdämmerung Woglinde; as above; Covent Garden: 14, 17 Oct.
The Tales of Hoffmann Antonia; Langdon/Robinson (Crespel), Johnston/Edgar Evans (Hoffmann), Otakar Kraus/Robinson (Dr Miracle), Elms (Mother's voice); c. Downes, p. Rennert, d. Wakhevitch; Covent Garden: 30 Oct., 5, 7, 13, 21 Nov., 2, 18 Dec.
Carmen Micaela; Resnik/Zareska (Carmen), Vickers/Johnston/Edgar Evans/Nilsson (Don José), Ronald Lewis/Dickie (Escamillo); c. Matheson/Kubelik, p. Asquith, d. Wakhevitch; Covent Garden: 31 Oct., 2, 8, 11, 15, 18, 20, 28 Nov., 10 Dec.
Otello Desdemona*; Vinay (Otello), Otakar Kraus (Iago), Lanigan (Cassio); c. Downes, p. Potter, d. Wakhevitch; Covent Garden: 21, 27, 30 Dec.

1958
The Carmelites Mme Lidoine*; Walters (Marquis de la Force), Lanigan (Chevalier de la Force), Morison/Dunne (Blanche), Fisher (Mother Marie); c. Kubelik/Matheson, p. Wallmann, d. Wakhevitch; Covent Garden: 16, 18, 21†, 24, 27 Jan.; Oxford: 10 Mar.; Manchester: 24 Mar.
Rigoletto Gilda; Shaw (Rigoletto), Lance/R. Thomas/Kirkopp (Duke), Langdon/Rouleau (Sparafucile), Berry (Maddalena); c. Downes, p.

Gellner, d. Bailey; Covent Garden: 5, 8, 10, 13, 18, 21 Feb., 5 Apr., 27 May; Oxford: 12, 25 Mar.; Manchester: 26, 29 Mar.

Concert aria *Vorrei spiegarvi, O Dio* (Rossini), aria *Primo amore piacer del ciel* (Beethoven); c. Blech; Royal Festival Hall, London: 19 Feb.

Carmen Micaela; Shacklock/Resnik (Carmen), Edgar Evans/Johnston (Don José), Ronald Lewis/Walters (Escamillo); c. Matheson, p. Asquith, d. Wakhevitch; Royal Opera House tour: Manchester: 20 Mar.; Covent Garden: 24 June, 7 Jul.

St Matthew Passion (Bach) other soloists: Proctor, A. Young, J. Cameron, Cuenod, Hemsley, J. Ward; c. Pritchard; Liverpool: 4 Apr.

Concert Mahler's Resurrection Symphony; c. Barbirolli; Manchester: 14, 15 May

Applausus Musicus (Handel) (BBC broadcast) Temperentia*; M. Thomas (Prudentia), R. Lewis (Justilia), Cameron (Theologia); c. Newstone; 24 May

Centenary Gala I dreamt I dwelt in marble halls (*The Bohemian Girl*: Balfe) duet with Lanigan; c. Pritchard; Covent Garden: 10 June

Don Giovanni Donna Anna*; London (Don Giovanni), Rubes (Leporello), Andrew (Donna Elvira), Alarie (Zerlina), Simoneau (Don Ottavio); c. Goldschmidt, p. Rennert, d. Maximowna; Vancouver: 26, 29, 31 Jul., 5, 7, 9 Aug.

Recital (appendix 3); P. Bonynge; Sevenoaks, Kent: 4 Oct.

Der Ring des Nibelungen Woglinde, Woodbird; Otakar Kraus (Alberich), Hotter (Wotan), Hale (Wellgunde), Marjorie Thomas (Flosshilde), Varnay (Brünnhilde), Windgassen (Siegfried), Klein (Mime); c. Kempe, p. Potter (reh. only), d. Hurry; Covent Garden: First Cycle: 19, 29 Sep., 3 Oct.; Second Cycle: 6, 9, 11 Oct. NB: Sutherland did not sing in *Die Walküre*.

Samson Israelite Woman*; Vickers/Lanigan (Samson), Lindermeier/ Carlyle (Dalila); c. Leppard, p. Graf, d. Messel; Leeds: 14, 15, 16, 17, 18 Oct. (eve. & mat.); Covent Garden: 15, 18 Nov., 12 Dec., 3† Jan. 1959

Recital P. Bonynge; *Tornami a vagheggiar (Alcina), Bist du bei mir* (Bach), Let the bright seraphim *(Samson), Parla* (Arditi), *Mattinata* (Leoncavallo), *Regnava nel silenzio (Lucia di Lammermoor)*; Horsham, Sussex: 25 Oct.

Te Deum (Bruckner) & *King David* (Honegger); c. Sargent; Leeds: 19 Nov.

Don Giovanni Donna Anna; Geraint Evans (Don Giovanni), Lawrence (Leporello), Bartlett (Elvira), Clark (Zerlina), Troy (Ottavio); c. Balkwill, p. Besche; Dublin: 24, 26, 28 Nov., 1 Dec.

Grand Opera Concert with other artists (further information unknown); Dublin: 29 Nov.

Messiah other soloists: Proctor, Pears, Alan; c. Pritchard; Liverpool: 20, 27 Dec., 2 Jan. 1959

1959

Lucia di Lammermoor Lucia*; Neate/Gibin (Edgardo), Geraint Evans/ Shaw (Enrico), Langdon/Rouleau (Raimondo); c. Serafin, p. Zeffirelli, d. Zeffirelli; Covent Garden: 17, 20, 23, 26†, 28 Feb.

Concert Beethoven's Ninth Symphony; c. Barbirolli; Manchester: 6, 7 May

Alcina (Radio Cologne broadcast) Alcina; Wunderlich (Ruggiero), Van Dyke (Morgana), Proctor (Bradamante), Monti (Oronte); c. Leitner; 15 May

Samson Israelite Woman; Vickers/Lanigan (Samson), Carlyle/Wells (Dalila); c. Leppard/J. Gibson, p. Graf, d. Messel; Covent Garden: 8, 12, 25 June

Recital (appendix 4); P. Bonynge; Australia House, London: 18 June

Rodelinda Rodelinda*; Elkins (Bertarido), Herincx (Garibaldo), Baker (Eduige); c. Farncombe, p. Besch, d. Pidcock; Handel Opera Society, Sadler's Wells Theatre, London: 24, 26† June

Lucia di Lammermoor Lucia; Alfredo Kraus (Edgardo), Shaw (Enrico), Langdon (Raimondo); c. Balkwill, p. Zeffirelli, d. Zeffirelli; Covent Garden: 10, 14, 16, 18 Jul.

Don Giovanni (concert performance) Donna Anna; Waechter (Don Giovanni), Taddei (Leporello), Schwarzkopf (Donna Elvira), Sciutti (Zerlina), Alva (Don Ottavio); c. Davis; Royal Festival Hall, London: 18†, 20 Oct.

Concert *Qui la voce (I puritani), Care selve (Atalanta), Tornami a vagheggiar (Alcina)*; c. Boult; Royal Festival Hall, London: 27 Oct.

Concert mad scene (*Lucia*); c. Harvey; Royal Festival Hall, London: 31 Oct.

Recital (appendix 4); P. Bonynge; Manchester: 3 Nov.

Concert with other artists (further information unknown); New Theatre, London: 8 Nov.

Concert Beethoven's Ninth Symphony; other soloists: Boese, Vickers, Frick; c. Klemperer; Royal Festival Hall, London: 28, 30 Nov.

Don Giovanni Donna Anna; Waechter (Don Giovanni), Berry (Leporello), Lipp (Donna Elvira), Gueden (Zerlina), Dermota (Don Ottavio); c. Hollreiser, p. Witt, d. Neher; Vienna Staatsoper: 3, 5 Dec.

Otello Desdemona; Guichandat (Otello), Protti (Iago), Zampieri (Cassio); c. Wallberg, p. Karajan, d. Reinking/Wakhevitch; Vienna Staatsoper: 17, 19 Dec.

Messiah other soloists: Proctor, Pears, Alan; c. Pritchard; Liverpool: 30 Dec., 2 Jan. 1960

1960

La traviata Violetta*; McAlpine/Lanigan (Alfredo), Walters/Quilico (Germont); c. Santi, d. Fedorovitch; Covent Garden: 8, 22, 27, 30 Jan., 4, 14 May

Concert Mahler's Fourth Symphony; c. Boult; Birmingham: 28 Jan.

Lucia di Lammermoor Lucia; Turp (Edgardo), Shaw/Geraint Evans (Enrico), Langdon/Rouleau (Raimondo); c. Balkwill, p. Zeffirelli, d.

Zeffirelli; Covent Garden: 5, 8, 10, 13 Feb., 9, 13, 16, 22 Dec.

Alcina Alcina; M. Sinclair (Ruggiero), Cecilia Fusco (Morgana), Dominguez (Bradamante), Clabassi (Melisso), Monti (Oronte); c. Rescigno, p. Zeffirelli, d. Zeffirelli; Venice: 19, 21, 23 Feb.

Lucia di Lammermoor Lucia; Gianni Raimondi (Edgardo), Panerai (Enrico), Maionica (Raimondo); c. Serafin, p. Zeffirelli, d. Zeffirelli; Palermo: 11, 13, 15, 20 Mar.

Lucia di Lammermoor Lucia; Gianni Raimondi (Edgardo), Dondi (Enrico), Zaccaria (Raimondo); c. Rescigno, p. Zeffirelli, d. Zeffirelli; Genoa: 31 Mar., 3, 5 Apr.

Lucia di Lammermoor Lucia; Vanzo (Edgardo), Massard (Enrico), Rouleau/Mars (Raimondo); c. Derveaux, p. Zeffirelli; Opéra, Paris: 25, 30 Apr., 7 May

I puritani Elvira*; Filacuridi (Arturo), Blanc (Riccardo), Modesti (Giorgio); c. Gui/Balkwill, p. Enriquez, d. Heeley; Glyndebourne: 24, 26, 28 May, 1, 3, 5, 9, 14, 18†, 24, 26 June; Edinburgh: 24, 26, 31 Aug., 3, 8†, 10 Sep.

Verdi Requiem other soloists: Cossotto, Ottilini, Vinco; Royal Festival Hall, London: 12 June; Edinburgh: 21† Aug.

Samson (concert performance) Israelite Woman; Lanigan (Samson); c. James Gibson; All Souls, Langham Place, London: 19 June

Don Giovanni Donna Anna; Blanc (Don Giovanni), Geraint Evans/ Bruscantini (Leporello), Ligabue (Donna Elvira), Freni (Zerlina), Richard Lewis (Don Ottavio); c. Pritchard/Gellhorn, p. Rennert, d. Maximowna; Glyndebourne: 1, 3, 5, 7, 9, 11, 16, 20, 22, 24†, 29 Jul., 3, 5 Aug.

Promenade Concert *Qui la voce (I puritani)*; c. B. Cameron; Royal Albert Hall, London: 1† Aug.

Recital P. Bonynge; *Son vergin vezzosa (I puritani), A, fors'è lui (La traviata)*, mad scene (*Lucia*); Worthing: 7 Aug.

Promenade Concert *Di cor mio, Tornami a vagheggiar (Alcina), Regnava nel silenzio...Quando rapita (Lucia)*; c. Sargent; Royal Albert Hall, London: 13† Aug.

Concert *Di cor mio, Tornami a vagheggiar (Alcina)*, mad scene (*Lucia*); c. Pritchard; Liverpool: 4 Oct.

La sonnambula Amina*; Lazzari (Elvino), Rouleau/Ward/Robinson (Rodolfo), J. Sinclair/Eddy (Lisa), Berry (Teresa); c. Serafin/Balkwill, p. Mediola, d. Sanjust; Covent Garden: 19, 21, 25†, 28, 31 Oct., 3, 7 Nov., 1, 3, 5 Dec.

Recital (appendix 4); P. Bonynge; St James's Palace, London: 27 Oct.

Alcina Alcina; Thebom (Ruggiero), Moynagh (Morgana), M. Sinclair (Bradamante), Zaccaria (Melisso), Alva (Oronte); c. Rescigno, p. Zeffirelli, d. Zeffirelli; Dallas: 16, 18 Nov.

Don Giovanni Donna Anna; Waechter (Don Giovanni), Taddei (Leporello), Schwarzkopf (Donna Elvira), Ratti (Zerlina), Alva (Don Ottavio); Dallas: 20, 23 Nov.

Recital (appendix 4); P. Bonynge; Keele, Staffs: 29 Nov.

Concert *Regnava nel silenzio... Quando rapita (Lucia), Ah, fors'è lui...*

sempre libera (La traviata), O luce di quest'anima (Linda di Chamounix), mad scene (*Hamlet*); c. Balkwill; Royal Albert Hall, London: 11 Dec.

I puritani Elvira; Jaja (Arturo), Ausensi (Riccardo), Gaetani (Giorgio); c. Rosada, p. Cardi; Barcelona: 30 Dec., 3, 6 Jan. 1961

1961

I puritani Elvira; Gianni Raimondi (Arturo), Zanasi (Riccardo), Mazzoli (Giorgio); c. Serafin, p. Zeffirelli, d. Zeffirelli; Palermo: 12, 15, 17 Jan.

Lucia di Lammermoor Lucia; Cioni (Edgardo), Savarese (Enrico), Antonini (Raimondo); c. La Rosa Parodi, p. Zeffirelli, d. Zeffirelli; Venice: 24, 26, 29 Jan.

Recital (appendix 4); P. Bonynge; Rock Hill, S. Carolina: 2 Feb.; Danbury, Connecticut: 5 Feb.; Mount Lebanon, Pittsburgh: 11 Feb.; Oklahoma: 13 Feb.; Englewood, NJ: 23 Feb.; Richmond, Virginia: 25 Feb.; Vancouver: 27 Feb.; Aurora, NY: 6 Mar.; Montreal: 9 Mar.; Toronto: 13† Mar.

Concert *Care selve (Atalanta), Nel cor più non mi sento (La molinara:* Paisiello), *Gran dio che regoli (Ines di Castro:* Bianchi), *Di cor mio, Tornami a vagheggiar (Alcina), Ritorna o cara (Rodelinda),* Let the bright seraphim (*Samson*); c. Callaway/Stanger; Dunbarton Oaks, Washington DC: 7 Feb.; Chicago: 3 Mar.

Concert sleepwalking scene (*La sonnambula*), mad scene (*Lucia*); c. Paul Kletzki; Dallas: 15 Feb.

Beatrice di Tenda (concert performance) Beatrice; Cassilly (Orombello), Horne (Agnese), Sordello (Filippo); c. Rescigno; American Opera Society: NY Town Hall: 21 Feb.; Carnegie Hall, NYC: 1, 11 Mar.

I puritani Elvira; Filacuridi (Arturo), Taddei (Riccardo), Modesti (Giorgio); c. Rescigno, p. Zeffirelli, d. Zeffirelli/Hall; Genoa: 22, 26, 29 Mar.

Lucia di Lammermoor Lucia; Gianni Raimondi (Edgardo), Bastianini/ Meliciani (Enrico), Modesti (Raimondi); c. Votto, p. Frigerio, d. Nicola Benois; La Scala, Milan: 14, 17, 20, 27 Apr., 3 May

Beatrice di Tenda Beatrice*; Campora (Orombello), Kabaivanska/ Varcelli (Agnese), Dondi (Filippo); c. Votto, p. Enriquez, d. Collonello; La Scala, Milan: 10†, 13, 17, 19, 21 May

Lucia di Lammermoor Lucia; Vanzo/Turp (Edgardo), Shaw/Dinoff/ Quilico (Enrico), Rouleau/Godfrey (Raimondo); c. Pritchard, p. Anderson (rehearsed only), d. Zeffirelli; Covent Garden: 6, 9, 12 June; Edinburgh: 25, 28† Aug., 1 Sep.

Lucia di Lammermoor Lucia; Vanzo (Edgardo), Massard (Enrico), Serkoyan (Raimondo); c. Dervaux; Opéra, Paris: 16, 19, 24 June

Concert *Di cor mio, Tornami a vagheggiar (Alcina)*; arias (*Beatrice*); c. Pritchard; Edinburgh: 4 Sep.

Lucia di Lammermoor Lucia; Cioni (Edgardo), Ruzdak/Heater (Enrico), Tozzi (Raimondo); c. Molinari-Pradelli, p. Yannopoulos, d.

Ming Cho Lee/Bauer-Ecsy; San Francisco: 23 Sep., 25 Oct.
Recital (appendix 4); P. Bonynge; Lawrence, Kansas: 25 Sep.; Omaha, Nebraska: 28 Sep.; Atlanta: 30 Sep.; Syracuse, NY: 2 Oct.; Hartford, Connecticut: 4 Oct.; Montclair, New Jersey: 20 Oct.; San Francisco: 7 Nov.; Dallas: 11 Nov.; New Brunswick, NJ: 20 Nov.; Princeton, NJ: 28 Nov.; Washington: 11 Dec.; Great Neck, NY: 13 Dec.
Concert *Ombre pallide, Mi restano le lagrime, Tornami a vagheggiar (Alcina)*; c. Waldman; Grace Raney Rogers Auditorium, NYC: 9 Oct.
Lucia di Lammermoor Lucia; Tucker/Bergonzi (Edgardo), Zanasi (Enrico), Wildermann (Raimondo); c. Votto, p. Zeffirelli, d. Zeffirelli; Chicago: 14, 16, 18 Oct.
Concert sleepwalking scene (*La sonnambula*), mad scene (*Lucia*), *Ah, fors'è lui (La traviata)*; c. Paray; Worcester, Massachusetts: 23 Oct.
Lucia di Lammermoor Lucia; Cioni (Edgardo), Ruzdak (Enrico), Clabassi/Engen (Raimondo); c. Molinari-Pradelli, p. Yannopoulos, d. Cho Lee/Bauer-Ecsy; San Francisco: 25 Oct.; Los Angeles: 29 Oct., 4 Nov.; San Diego: 2 Nov.
Lucia di Lammermoor Lucia; Cioni (Edgardo), Bastianini (Enrico), Zaccaria (Raimondo), Domingo (Arturo); c. Rescigno, p. Maestrini, d. Zeffirelli; Dallas: 16, 18 Nov.
Lucia di Lammermoor Lucia; Tucker/Peerce (Edgardo), Testi/Guarrera (Enrico), Moscona/Giaiotti (Raimondo); c. Varviso, p. Defrère, d. Rychtaric (1942); Metropolitan, NYC: 26 Nov., 2, 9†, 15, 21 Dec.
La sonnambula (concert performance) Amina; Cioni (Elvino), Flagello (Rodolfo), Allen (Teresa), di Tullio (Lisa); c. Rescigno; American Opera Society, Carnegie Hall, NYC: 5 Dec.; Philadelphia: 17 Dec.

1962
Die Zauberflöte Queen of Night*; Geraint Evans (Papageno), Richard Lewis (Tamino), Carlyle (Pamina), David Kelly (Sarastro); c. Klemperer, p. Klemperer, d. Eisler; Covent Garden: 4†, 6, 8 Jan.
Lucia di Lammermoor Lucia; Gianni Raimondi (Edgardo), MacNeil (Enrico), Vinco (Raimondo); c. Sanzogno, p. Zeffirelli, d. Zeffirelli; Palermo: 21 Jan.
Concert *Ah, Ruggiero crudel . . . Ombre pallide (Alcina), Qui la voce (I puritani)*, mad scene (*Hamlet*); c. Bonynge; Rome: 25 Jan.
Lucia di Lammermoor Lucia; Turp (Edgardo), Lamachia (Enrico), Cohen (Raimondo); c. Rivoli, p. Pablo Civil; Barcelona: 28 Jan., 1, 3 Feb.
La sonnambula Amina; Alfredo Kraus (Elvino), Vinco (Rodolfo); c. Votto, p. Visconti, d. Tosi; La Scala, Milan: 10, 13, 15, 18, 20 Feb., 12, 15, 18, 23 Apr.
Concert mad scene (*Lucia*), mad scene (*Hamlet*), *E strano. . . sempre libera (La traviata)*; c. Erede; Antwerp: 23† Feb.
Concert *Ombre pallide (Alcina)*, mad scene (*Lucia*), *Son vergin vezzosa (I puritani), Sempre libera (La traviata)*; c. Erede; Amsterdam: 25 Feb.
Alcina Alcina; Elkins (Ruggiero), Vaughan (Morgana), M. Sinclair

(Bradamante), Robinson (Melisso), Macdonald (Oronte); c. Balkwill, p. Zeffirelli, d. Zeffirelli; Covent Garden: 8, 10, 14, 17 Mar.

La traviata Violetta; Turp (Alfredo), Quilico (Germont); c. Erede/ Balkwill, p. Ayrton (reh. only), d. Fedorovitch; Covent Garden: 21, 24, 26, 29 Mar., 4, 7 Apr.

Concert *Cavatina (Beatrice), O beau pays (Les Huguenots),* mad scene *(Lucia), Addio del passato, Sempre libera (La traviata),* c. Balkwill; Royal Albert Hall, London: 1 Apr.

Beatrice di Tenda Beatrice; Cioni (Orombello), Elkins (Agnese), Zanasi (Filippo); c. Rescigno; Naples: 4, 6 May

Gli Ugonotti Marguerite de Valois*; Simionato (Valentine), Corelli (Raoul), Ganzarolli (de Nevers), Cossotto (Urbain), Ghiaurov/Vinco (Marcel), Tozzi (St Bris), c. Gavazzeni, p. Enriquez, d. Nicola Benois; La Scala, Milan: 28, 31 May, 2, 7†, 12 June

Concert *Ah, fors'è lui. . . sempre libera (La traviata),* mad scene *(Lucia);* c. Rosenstock; Lewishohn Stadium, NYC: 24 Jul.

Concert mad scene *(Lucia);* c. Clutyens; Chicago: 26 Jul.

Concert *Ah, fors'è lui. . . sempre libera (La traviata), Qui la voce (I puritani), O beau pays (Les Huguenots),* mad scene *(Hamlet);* c. Bonynge; Hollywood: 2 Aug.

Recital (appendix 4); P. Bonynge; Rosehill, Cumberland: 5, 7 Oct.

Semiramide Semiramide*; Simionato (Arsace), Ganzarolli (Assur), Mazzoli/Ferrin (Oroe); c. Santini, p. Wallmann; La Scala, Milan: 17, 19, 22, 26, 29 Dec., 1, 5 Jan. 1963

1963
President Kennedy Inaugural Anniversary Concert (further information unknown); Washington DC: 18 Jan.

Concert mad scene *(Lucia);* c. Stowkowsky; Philadelphia: 26 Jan.

Concert *V'adoro pupille (Giulio Cesare), Regnava nel silenzio (Lucia), Bel raggio (Semiramide), Qui la voce (I puritani);* c. Bonynge/Varviso; White Plains, NY: 6 Feb.; Newark, NJ: 10 Mar.

Concert *Piangero la sorte mio, V'adoro pupille (Giulio Cesare),* Let the bright seraphim *(Samson), Preghiera (Ines di Castro:* Bianchi), *Nel cor più non mi sento (La molinara:* Paisiello), The soldier tir'd *(Artaxerxes:* Arne); c. Bonynge; Englewood, NJ: 9 Feb.; Brooklyn College, NYC: 16 Mar.

La sonnambula Amina; Gedda/Formichini/Alexander (Elvino), Tozzi/ Hines/Flagello (Rodolfo), Chookasian (Teresa), Scovotti (Lisa); c. Varviso, p. Visconti/Butler, d. Gerard; Metropolitan, NYC: 21, 27 Feb., 4, 7, 14, 19, 23, 30† Mar., 2, 12 Apr.

Concert *V'adoro pupille (Giulio Cesare), Nel cor più non mi sento (La molinara:* Paisiello); Let the bright seraphim *(Samson);* The soldier tir'd *(Artaxerxes),* mad scene *(Hamlet);* c. Bonynge; Boston: 23 Feb.

Concert recit & aria *Ernani involami (Ernani), Bel raggio (Semiramide), Und ob die Wolke (Der Freischütz),* mad scene *(Hamlet);* c. Bernstein; Philharmonic Hall, Lincoln Centre, NYC: 26 Mar.

Concert Let the bright seraphim (*Samson*), The soldier tir'd (*Artaxerxes*), *Io non sono più l'Annetta* (*Crispino e la comare*: Ricci), *Bel raggio* (*Semiramide*), mad scene (*Hamlet*), c. Bonynge; Los Angeles: 5 Apr., San Francisco: 7 Apr.; Washington: 27 Apr.

I puritani (concert performance) Elvira; Gedda (Arturo), Blanc (Riccardo), Diaz (Giorgio); c. Bonynge; American Opera Society: Carnegie Hall, NYC: 16, 24 Apr.; Philadelphia: 18 Apr.

Recital (appendix 4) with Elkins; duet *Serbami ognor* (*Semiramide*); P. Bonynge; Croydon, Surrey: 10 June

Giulio Cesare Cleopatra*; Elkins (Giulio Cesare), Lawrenson (Ptolemy), Guy (Cornelia), Stahlman (Sextus); c. Farncombe, p. Ayrton, d. Warre; Sadler's Wells Theatre, London: 20, 22, 26† June

La sonnambula Amina; Cioni (Elvino), Cross (Rodolfo), Cole (Teresa), Meneguzzer (Lisa); c. Bonynge, p. Mansouri, d. Nagy; San Francisco: 14, 17, 22 Sep.; Los Angeles: 2, 4 Nov.

Norma Norma*; Horne (Adalgisa), Alexander (Pollione), Cross (Oroveso); c. Bonynge, p. Guttman, d. McLance/Mess; Vancouver: 17, 19, 22, 24, 26 Oct.

Concert with Cole, Cross, Alexander; duet *Serbami ognor* (*Semiramide*) with Cole, *Bel raggio* (*Semiramide*), quartet (*Rigoletto*), duet *Sulla tomba* (*Lucia*) with Alexander, mad scene (*Hamlet*); c. Bonynge; Vancouver: 29 Oct.

La traviata Violetta; Alexander (Alfredo), Bacquier (Germont); c. Bonynge, p. Guttman; Philadelphia: 12 Nov.

Concert Let the bright seraphim (*Samson*), The soldier tir'd (*Artaxerxes*), *Io non sono più l'Annetta* (*Crispino e la comare*: Ricci) *Bel raggio* (*Semiramide*), mad scene (*Lucia*); c. Bonynge; Toronto: 22 Nov.

La sonnambula Amina; Alexander (Elvino), Tozzi/Macurdy/Giaiotti (Rodolfo), Martin/Chookasian (Teresa), Scovotti (Lisa); c. Varviso, p. Butler (rehearsed only), d. Gerard; Metropolitan, NYC: 5, 10, 23 Dec., 8 Jan. 1964

1964

La traviata Violetta; Kónya/Labò/Gedda/Tucker/Morell (Alfredo), Sereni/Rudzak (Germont); c. Schick, p. Guthrie, d. Smith/Gerard; Metropolitan, NYC: 14, 28 Dec. 1963, 2, 11†, 17, 21, 24 Jan.

Opera Gala *La traviata* Act I: Violetta, Kónya (Alfredo); *Lucia* mad scene, in concert; *La sonnambula* Act III: Amina, Gedda (Elvino), Tozzi (Rodolfo), Scovotti (Lisa); c. Schick/Varviso/Varviso; Metropolitan, NYC: 5 Jan.

Concert Let the bright seraphim (*Samson*), The soldier tir'd (*Artaxerxes*), *Io non sono più l'Annetta* (*Crispino e la comare:* Ricci), *Bel raggio* (*Semiramide*), mad scene (*Hamlet*); Cleveland, Ohio: 14 Jan.

Semiramide Semiramide; Horne (Arsace), Cross (Assur), Rhul (Oroe); c. Bonynge; Los Angeles: 29, 31 Jan.

I puritani Elvira; Craig (Arturo), Cross (Riccardo), Malas (Giorgio); c.

Bonynge, p. Caldwell, d. Burlinghame/Voelpel; Boston: 12 Feb.

Semiramide (concert performance) Semiramide; Horne (Arsace), Cross (Assur), Malas (Oroe); c. Bonynge; American Opera Society, Carnegie Hall, NYC: 18, 20 Feb.

Concert Let the bright seraphim (*Samson*), The soldier tir'd (*Artaxerxes*), Bel raggio (*Semiramide*), Ah, non giunge (*La sonnambula*); c. Bonynge; Hartford, Connecticut: 22 Feb.

I puritani Elvira; Craig/Macdonald (Arturo), Bacquier (Riccardo), Rouleau (Giorgio); c. Bonynge, p. Zeffirelli, d. Zeffirelli; Covent Garden: 20, 23, 26, 30 Mar., 1, 4, 7, 10 Apr.

Lucia di Lammermoor Lucia; Morell/Tucker/Bergonzi (Edgardo), Colzani/Bardelli (Enrico), Wildermann/Ferrin (Raimondo); c. Varviso, p. Wallmann, d. Collonello; Metropolitan Opera House tour: Boston: 19 Apr.; Cleveland, Ohio: 23 Apr.; Atlanta: 16 May; Minneapolis: 23 May; Detroit: 26 May.

Concert *Ah, fors'è lui ... sempre libera (La traviata)*, mad scene (*Lucia*); c. Ormandy; Michigan: 30 Apr.

La sonnambula Amina; Alexander/Gedda (Elvino), Hines/Tozzi (Rodolfo), Chookasian/Kriese (Teresa), Scovotti (Lisa); c. Varviso, p. Visconti/Butler, d. Gerard; Metropolitan, NYC: 3, 9 May

Concert: Pestalozzi Village Let the bright seraphim (*Samson*), Regnava nel silenzio (*Lucia*), sleepwalking scene (*La sonnambula*), mad scene (*Hamlet*); c. Bonynge; Berne, Switzerland: 4 June

Lucia di Lammermoor Lucia; Gianni Raimondi (Edgardo), Cappucilli (Enrico), Ferrin (Raimondo); c. Sanzogno, p. Wallmann; La Scala, Milan: 12, 15, 18, 20, 23 June

Lucia di Lammermoor Lucia; Kónya/Labò/Alexander (Edgardo), Merrill/Sereni/Harlea/Colzani (Enrico), Giaiotti (Raimondo); c. Varviso, p. Wallmann, d. Collonello; Metropolitan, NYC: 12, 16, 24, 27 Oct., 14, 20 Nov., 5†, 14, 24 Dec.

La traviata Violetta; Ilosfalvy (Alfredo), Waechter (Germont); c. Bonynge, p. Mansouri; San Francisco: 1, 3, 5 Nov.; Los Angeles: 8, 10 Nov.

Opera Gala *La traviata* Act I: Violetta, Alexander (Alfredo); c. Schick; Metropolitan, NYC: 29 Nov.

Concert *Voi che sapete, Deh vieni, non tardar, Dove sono (Figaro), Bel raggio (Semiramide)*, Concerto for Coloratura (Gliere), mad scene (*Lucia*) 19 Dec. only; c. Bonynge; Montreal: 8 Dec.; Houston: 17, 19 Dec.

1965

Alcina (concert performance) Alcina; Elkins (Ruggiero), Hurley (Morgana), M. Sinclair (Bradamante), Malas (Melisso), Montal (Oronte); c. Bonynge; American Opera Society, Carnegie Hall, NYC: 3, 5 Jan.

Concert *Voi che sapete, Deh vieni non tardar, Dove sono (Figaro), Bel*

raggio (*Semiramide*); Concerto for Coloratura (Gliere), mad scene (*Lucia*); c. Bonynge; Cincinnati, Ohio: 9 Jan.; New Orleans: 19 Jan.; Bloomington, Indiana: 21 Mar.

Semiramide Semiramide; Horne (Arsace), Rouleau (Assur), Hoekman (Oroe); c. Bonynge, p. Caldwell, d. Senn/Pond/Voelpel; Boston: 5, 7 Feb.

Lucia di Lammermoor Lucia; Pavarotti (Edgardo), Sordello (Enrico), Cross (Raimondo); c. Bonynge, p. Stivenello, d. Wolf; Miami: 15, 20 Feb.; Miami Beach: 17 Feb.; Fort Lauderdale, Florida: 23 Feb.

Faust Marguerite*; Verrau (Faust), Cross (Mephistopheles), Opthof (Valentine), Elkins (Siebel); c. Bonynge, p. Guttmann, d. Rome/ Brooks van Horne; Philadelphia: 9 Mar.; Hartford, Connecticut: 16 Mar.

Lucia di Lammermoor Lucia; Turp/Macdonald (Edgardo), Bryn Jones (Enrico), Rouleau (Raimondo); c. Bonynge, p. Anderson (rehearsed only), d. Zeffirelli; Covent Garden: 3, 6, 8, 11, 17 May

La sonnambula Amina; Pavarotti (Elvino), Rouleau (Rodolfo), Elkins (Teresa), Woodland (Lisa); c. Bonynge, p. John Copley (rehearsed only), d. Sanjust; Covent Garden: 26, 29 May, 1, 4, 7, 10 June

SUTHERLAND–WILLIAMSON TOUR

Lucia di Lammermoor Lucia; Alexander/Pavarotti/Remedios (Edgardo), Opthof/Allman (Enrico), Grant/Rouleau/Cross (Raimondo); c. Bonynge, p. Ayrton, d. Dorati; Melbourne: 10, 12, 14, 17 Jul.; Adelaide: 16, 18 Aug.; Sydney: 31 Aug., 2 Sep., 2 Oct.; Brisbane: 11, 16 Oct.

La traviata Violetta; Pavarotti/Alexander/Remedios/Montal (Alfredo), Opthof/Allman (Germont); c. Bonynge/Krug, p. Ayrton, d. Dorati; Melbourne: 20, 22, 24, 26 Jul.; Adelaide: 25, 27 Aug.; Sydney: 16, 18, 20, 27 Sep., 6 Oct.; Brisbane: 13 Oct.

Semiramide Semiramide; M. Sinclair/Elms (Arsace), Rouleau/Malas/ Cross (Assur), Maconaghie (Oroe); c. Bonynge, p. Ayrton, d. Dorati; Melbourne: 29, 31 Jul., 7 Aug.; Sydney: 4, 6, 22, 29 Sep., 4 Oct.

La sonnambula Amina; Pavarotti/Ward (Elvino), Rouleau/Malas/Cross (Rodolfo), Cole/Elms (Teresa), Harwood/Yarick (Lisa); c. Bonynge, p. Scheepers, d. Dorati; Melbourne: 3, 5, 14 Aug.; Sydney: 11, 24 Sep., 9 Oct.

Faust Marguerite; Alexander (Faust), Cross/Rouleau (Mephistopheles), Opthof (Valentine), Elkins/Beaton (Siebel); c. Wiebel, p. Ayrton, d. Dorati; Melbourne: 10, 12 Aug.; Adelaide: 21, 23 Aug.; Sydney: 9, 13 Sep.

1966

Concert *Di cor mio, Tornami a vagheggiar (Alcina),* Concerto for Coloratura (Gliere), *Bel raggio (Semiramide)*, sleepwalking scene (*La sonnambula*); c. Bonynge; Royal Albert Hall, London: 20 Feb.; Antwerp: 18 Mar.

Lucia di Lammermoor Lucia; Antonioli (Edgardo), Colmagro (Enrico), Marchica (Raimondo); c. Bonynge, p. Collonello, d. Collonello/Casa d'Arte Fiori; Copenhagen: 25, 28 Feb., 3 Mar.

Don Giovanni Donna Anna; Ghiaurov (Don Giovanni), Ganzarolli (Leporello), Lorengar/Ligabue (Donna Elvira), Freni (Zerlina), Alva (Don Ottavio); c. Maazel, p. Squarzini, d. Allio; La Scala, Milan: 19, 21, 25, 30 Apr.

Concert *Di cor mio, Tornami a vagheggiar (Alcina)*, Concerto for Coloratura (Gliere), *Bel raggio (Semiramide)*, sleepwalking scene (*La sonnambula*); c. Bonynge; Champs Elysées Theatre, Paris: 28 Apr.

Concert *Di cor mio, Tornami a vagheggiar (Alcina), Ah, fors' è lui (La traviata)*, mad scene (*Lucia*); Stuttgart: 3 May; Hamburg: 6 May

La fille du régiment Marie*; Pavarotti/Ward (Tonio), Malas (Sulpice), M. Sinclair (Marquise); c. Bonynge, p. Sequi, d. Anni/Escoffier; Covent Garden: 2, 8, 11, 14, 17, 23, 27 June, 2 Jul.

Concert *Ombre pallide, Di cor mio (Alcina), Care selve (Atalanta)*, Soft complaining flute (Ode to St Cecilia's Day: Handel); c. Bonynge; Oxford: 30 June

I puritani Elvira; Alfredo Kraus (Arturo), Wolansky (Riccardo), Grant (Giorgio); c. Bonynge, p. Frusca, d. Sormani/Marcello d'Ellena; San Francisco: 20, 23, 29 Sep., 2, 8 Oct.; Sacramento, California: 5 Oct.

Concert *Non mi dir (Don Giovanni), Bel raggio (Semiramide), Ernani, involami (Ernani), Ah, fors'è lui (La traviata)*; c. Bonynge; San Antonio, Texas: 15 Oct.

Concert *Non mi dir (Don Giovanni), Non àn calma (Montezuma:* Graun*), Bel raggio (Semiramide)*, Bell Song *(Lakmé)*; c. Bonynge; Atlanta: 20 Oct.

Concert *Non mi dir (Don Giovanni), Non àn calma (Montezuma:* Graun*), Ernani, involami (Ernani)*, Bell Song (*Lakmé*); c. Bonynge; White Plains, NY: 26 Oct.; Washington: 17 Dec.

Lucia di Lammermoor Lucia; Molese (Edgardo), Colzani/Ausensi (Enrico), Sgarro (Raimondo); c. Bonynge, p. Guttmann, d. Brooks van Horne; Philadelphia: 1, 4 Nov.

Concert with Horne; Selection from: *Non àn calma (Montezuma:* Graun*)*, Bell Song (*Lakmé*), *Surta la notte (Ernani)*, duet *Sous le dôme épais (Lakmé)*, duet *O rimembranza, Mira o Norma (Norma)*; c. Bonynge; Los Angeles: 19, 21, 26 Nov.

Concert *Non mi dir (Don Giovanni), Non àn calma (Montezuma:* Graun*)*, mad scene *(Hamlet)*, Bell Song (*Lakmé*); c. Bonynge; Houston: 30 Nov.

Lucia di Lammermoor Lucia; Alexander/Tucker (Edgardo), Colzani (Enrico), Ghuiselev (Raimondo); c. Bonynge, p. Wallmann, d. Collonello; Metropolitan, NYC: 12, 21, 24, 28, 31† Dec.

1967

Don Giovanni Donna Anna; Siepi (Don Giovanni), Flagello (Leporello) Lorengar (Donna Elvira), Hurley (Zerlina), Alfredo Kraus/Gedda (Don Ottavio); c. Böhm, p. Graf, d. Berman; Metropolitan, NYC: 4, 9, 12, 17, 28† Jan.

Concert *Bel raggio (Semiramide)*, *Son vergin vezzosa (I puritani)*, *Io non sono più l'Annetta (Crispino e la comare:* Ricci), c. Kertesz; Philadelphia: 21 Jan.

Concert *Non mi dir (Don Giovanni)*, *Non àn calma (Montezuma:* Graun*)*, *Ernani, involami (Ernani)*, Bell Song (*Lakmé*); c. Bonynge; Toronto: 2 Feb.; Newark, NJ: 11 Feb.

Don Giovanni Donna Anna; Diaz (Don Giovanni), Gramm (Leporello), Elkins (Donna Elvira), Tourangeau (Zerlina), Driscoll (Don Ottavio); c. Bonynge, p. Caldwell, d. Smith/Simmons; Boston: 6, 8, 15 Feb.

Concert *Non mi dir (Don Giovanni)*, *Non àn calma (Montezuma:* Graun*)*, mad scene (*Hamlet*), Bell Song (*Lakmé)*; c. Bonynge; Bloomington, Indiana: 23 Feb.

Concert *Ah, fors'è lui (La traviata)*, mad scene (*Hamlet*); c. Peletier; Montreal: 28 Feb.

Lucia di Lammermoor Lucia; Alexander (Edgardo), Cossa (Enrico), West (Raimondo); c. Bonynge, p. Guttman, d. Rinfret/Mess; Vancouver: 11, 15, 22, 25, 29 Mar.

Lakmé Lakmé*; Poretta (Gerald), Tourangeau (Mallika), Hecht (Nilakantha); c. Bonynge, p. Ross; Seattle: 10, 13, 15, 19, 22 Apr.

Orfeo ed Euridice Euridice*; Gedda (Orfeo), Malas (Creonte); c. Bonynge, p. Hartmann, d. Ludwig; Theater an der Wien, Vienna: 21, 25, 29 May, 2, 6 June; Edinburgh: 25, 29 Aug., 1, 4, 6, 9 Sep.

La fille du régiment Marie; Pavarotti (Tonio), Malas (Sulpice), M. Sinclair (Marquise); c. Bonynge, p. Sequi, d. Anni/Escoffier; Covent Garden: 24, 27 June, 7, 11, 15 Jul.

Opera Gala mad scene (*Lucia*); c. Bonynge; Covent Garden: 4 Jul.

Messiah other soloists: M. Sinclair, Baillie, R. Myers; c. Bonynge; Royal Festival Hall, London: 29 Oct.

Norma Norma; Tagliavini (Pollione), Horne/Elkins (Adalgisa), Rouleau (Oroveso); c. Bonynge, p. Sequi, d. Pizzi; Covent Garden: 30 Nov., 4, 8†, 12, 16, 21, 28 Dec., 1 Jan. 1968

1968

Les Huguenots (concert performance) Marguerite de Valois; Raoul (Vrenios), Cossa (de Nevers), Tourangeau (Urbain), Arroyo (Valentine), Ghuiselev (Marcel), El Hage (St Bris); c. Bonynge; London Opera Society, Royal Albert Hall, London: 7 Jan.

Recital (appendix 5); P. Bonynge; Theatre Royal, Drury Lane, London: 14 Jan.; Newark, NJ: 13 Feb.; Philadelphia: 16 Feb.; Toronto: 28† Apr.; Florence: 12 June

Orfeo ed Euridice (concert performance) Euridice; Gedda (Orfeo), Malas (Creonte); c. Bonynge; American Opera Society, Carnegie Hall, NYC: 7, 10 Feb.

Concert *Al tua seno fortunato (Orfeo ed Euridice)*, *O beau pays (Les Huguenots)*, mad scene (*Lucia*); c. Bonynge; Salt Lake City: 21 Feb.

Lucia di Lammermoor Lucia; Molese (Edgardo), Cossa (Enrico), Malas

(Raimondo); c. Bonynge; New Orleans: 29 Feb., 2 Mar.

La traviata Violetta; Vrenios (Alfredo), Hedlund (Germont); c. Bonynge, p. Zeffirelli, d. Hall; Boston: 9, 11, 13 Mar.

Opera Gala *O beau pays (Les Huguenots)*, final scene (*Faust*): Marguerite, Shirley (Faust), Macurdy (Mephistopheles); c. Bonynge; Metropolitan, NYC: 16 Mar.

Norma Norma; Marti (Pollione), Elkins (Adalgisa), Malas (Oroveso); c. Bonynge, p. Frusca, d. Brooks van Horn; Philadelphia: 26, 29 Mar.

Concert *Care selve (Atalanta), Da tempesta (Giulio Cesare), Ombre pallide, Di cor mio, Tornami a vagheggiar (Alcina)*, Soft complaining flute (Ode to St Cecilia's Day: Handel), With plaintive note (*Samson*); Hunter College, University of NY: 6, 8 Apr.

Don Giovanni Donna Anna; Bacquier (Don Giovanni), Gramm (Leporello), Murphy (Donna Elvira), Tourangeau (Zerlina), Vrenios (Don Ottavio); c. Bonynge; Seattle: 16, 18, 20, 24 Apr.

Semiramide Semiramide; M. Sinclair (Arsace), Cappecchi/Ganzaerolli (Assur), Ferrin (Oroe); c. Bonynge, p. Sequi, d. Samaritani/Hall; Florence: 1, 4, 6, 9 June

Semiramide (Italian Radio broadcast) Semiramide; Sinclair (Arsace), Petri (Assur), Mazzoli (Oroe); c. Bonynge; 28 June

Messiah other soloists: M. Sinclair, Baillie, Noble, Woolf; c. Bonynge; Royal Albert Hall, London: 10 Jul.

Lakmé Lakmé; Tourangeau (Mallika), Vrenios (Gerald), Bacquier (Nilakantha); c. Bonynge/Suppa, p. Frusca, d. Brooks van Horn; Philadelphia: 19, 22 Nov.

La sonnambula Amina; Alexander/Shirley (Elvino), Giaiotti (Rodolfo), Pearl/Forst (Teresa), Boky/Clements (Lisa); c. Bonynge, p. Butler, d. Gerard; Metropolitan, NYC: 2, 6, 12, 18, 21†, 24, 27 Dec., 1, 4, 9 Jan. 1969

Concert with Vrenios; With plaintive note (*Samson*), Da tempesta (*Giulio Cesare*), duet *E il sol dell'anima (Rigoletto)*, duet *Tornami a dir che m'ami (Don Pasquale)*, *Ah, non credea (La sonnambula)*; c. Bonynge; Boston: 15 Dec.

1969

Recital (appendix 5); P. Bonynge; Columbia, S. Carolina: 13 Jan.; Minneapolis: 29 Jan.; Portland, Oregon: 10 Jul.; San Francisco: 12 Jul.; Ottawa: 20 Jul.; St Johns, Smith Square, London: 6 Oct.

Concert *Non mi dir (Don Giovanni), Al tua seno fortunato (Orfeo ed Euridice), O beau pays (Les Huguenots), Ah, non credea (La sonnambula)*; c. Bonynge; Indianapolis: 19 Jan.; Wabash, Indiana: 21 Jan.

Semiramide (concert performance) Semiramide; Horne (Arsace), R. Myers (Assur), Grant (Oroe); c. Bonynge; London Opera Society, Theatre Royal, London: 9 Feb.

Alcina (concert performance) Alcina; Elkins (Ruggiero), O'Brien (Morgana), M. Sinclair (Bradamante), Gibbs (Melisso), Davies

(Oronte), te Kanawa (Oberto); c. Bonynge; Royal Festival Hall, London: 19 Feb.

La traviata Violetta; Cioni (Alfredo), Cappucilli (Germont); c. Bonynge, p. Sequi, d. Lumaldo/Lerchundi; Buenos Aires: 17, 21, 24, 29 May, 1 June

Norma Norma; Craig (Pollione), Cossotto (Adalgisa), Vinco (Oroveso); c. Bonynge, p. Sequi, d. Pizzi; Buenos Aires: 21, 24, 26, 29 June, 2 Jul.

Concert *Al tua seno fortunato (Orfeo ed Euridice), O beau pays (Les Huguenots), Casta diva (Norma)*; c. Bonynge; Hollywood: 8 Jul.

Concert *Al tua seno fortunato (Orfeo ed Euridice), O beau pays (Les Huguenots), Casta diva (Norma), Ah, fors'è lui (La traviata)*; c. Bonynge; Chicago: 17 Jul.

Concert *Piangero la sorte mio, Da tempesta (Giulio Cesare), Al tua seno fortunato (Orfeo ed Euridice), O beau pays (Les Huguenots)*, sleepwalking scene *(La sonnambula)*; c. Bonynge; The Hague, Holland: 11† Oct.

Giulio Cesare Cleopatra; Tourangeau (Giulio Cesare), Ahlin (Ptolemy), Boese (Cornelia), Popp (Sextus); c. Bonynge, p. Capobianco, d. Ming Cho Lee/Varona; Hamburg: 9, 12, 15, 19, 23, 27 Nov., 6, 10, 16, 21 Dec.

1970

Gala (further information unknown); Philadelphia: 24 Jan.

Recital (appendix 6); P. Bonynge; Ottawa: 27 Jan.; Ann Arbor, Michigan: 30 Jan.; Washington: 8 Feb.; London, Ontario: 30 Mar.; Pauley Pavilion, Uni. of Ca: 23 May; Winnipeg, Ontario: 25 May; Bristol, UK: 11 June

Norma Norma; Horne (Adalgisa), Bergonzi/Alexander/Tagliavini/Cioni (Pollione), Siepi/Vinco/Giaiotti/Macurdy (Oroveso); c. Bonynge, p. Deiber, d. Heeley; Metropolitan, NYC: 3, 6, 10, 14, 19, 23, 27 Mar., 4†, 9, 14, 18 Apr.; Metropolitan Opera House tour: Boston: 22 Apr.; Cleveland, Ohio: 1 May; Atlanta: 7 May; Memphis: 12 May; Dallas: 16 May; Minneapolis: 20 May; Detroit: 28 May

Richard Tucker's 25th Anniversary at the Met Opera Gala *La traviata* Act I: Violetta; Tucker (Alfredo); c. Bonynge; Metropolitan, NYC: 11 Apr.

Norma Norma; Tourangeau (Adalgisa), Lavirgen (Pollione), Flagello (Oroveso); c. Bonynge, p. Frusca, d. Brooks van Horn; Philadelphia: 27 Apr.

Lucia di Lammermoor Lucia; Domingo (Edgardo), Sereni (Enrico), Macurdy (Raimondo); c. Bonynge, p. Wallmann, d. Collonello; Metroploitan, NYC: 1, 5 June

Norma Norma; Alexander (Pollione), Horne (Adalgisa), Rouleau (Oroveso); c. Bonynge, p. Sequi, d. Pizzi; Covent Garden: 25, 29 June, 3, 7, 11 Jul.

Sir David Webster Opera Gala mad scene (*Lucia*): Lucia; Bryn Jones

(Enrico), Rouleau (Raimondo); c. Bonynge; Covent Garden: 30‡ June
Norma Norma; Horne/Cossotto (Adalgisa), Bergonzi/Tagliavini/
Alexander (Pollione), Vinco/Ruggiero Raimondi/Flagello (Oroveso);
Metropolitan, NYC: 7, 23, 28 Sep., 3, 7, 17 Oct., 10, 14, 19† Dec.
La traviata Violetta; Aragall/Pavarotti/Bergonzi/Kraus/Domingo
(Alfredo), Milnes/Merrill/Sereni (Germont); c. Bonynge, p. Lunt, d.
Beaton; Metropolitan, NYC: 12, 22, 27, 31 Oct., 2, 5 Dec.
Les contes d'Hoffman 4 soprano roles*; Alexander (Hoffmann),
Tourangeau (Nicklaus, The Muse, Mother's voice), Hecht (Lindorf,
Coppelius, Dappertutto, Dr Miracle), Thorson (Andres, Frantz,
Pitichinaccio, Cochenille), Rubes (Crespel, Schlemiel, Spalanzani); c.
Bonynge, p. Hebert, d. Klein/Mess; Seattle: 12, 14, 18, 21 Nov.

1971

Giulio Cesare Cleopatra; Tourangeau (Giulio Cesare), Ahlin
(Ptolemy), Boese (Cornelia), Popp (Sextus); c. Bonynge, p.
Capobianco, d. Ming Cho Lee/Varona; Hamburg: 28, 31 Jan., 9, 12, 17
Feb.
Lucia di Lammermoor Lucia; Domingo/Gianni Raimondi (Edgardo),
Tom Krause (Enrico), Moll (Raimondo); c. Bonynge, p. Beauvais, d.
Rose; Hamburg: 7, 11, 14, 18, 21, 24, 27, 30 Mar., 3, 6, 12, 15, 18 Apr.
Concert *trio Tu ne chanteras plus (Les contes d'Hoffman)*: Antonia;
Bacquier (Dr Miracle), Tourangeau (Mother's voice); c. Bonynge;
Geneva: 30 Apr.
Concert *Da tempesta (Giulio Cesare), Ah, fors'è lui (La traviata), O
beau pays (Les Huguenots)*, mad scene (*Lucia*); c. Bonynge; Madrid: 5
May
Recital (appendix 6); P. Bonynge; Liverpool: 9 May
Rodelinda (concert performance) Rodelinda; Tourangeau (Bertarido),
du Plessis (Garibaldo), Proctor (Eduige); c. Bonynge; Brighton: 14, 16
May
Concert with Remedios, Clement, Macdonell; *Regnava nel silenzio
(Lucia)*, duet *E il sol dell'anima (Rigoletto)*, trio *Tu ne chanteras plus
(Hoffmann); Ah, fors'è lùi (La traviata)*); c. Bonynge; Royal Albert
Hall, London: 23 May
Concert (further information unknown); c. Bonynge; Geneva: 25 Aug.
Semiramide Semiramide; Horne (Arsace), Malas (Assur), Ferrin
(Oroe); c. Bonynge, p. Sequi, d. Samaritani/Hall; Chicago: 24†, 27, 29
Sep., 2, 8, 11 Oct.
Maria Stuarda Maria Stuarda*; Tourangeau (Elizabeth I), Burrows
(Leicester), Berberian (Cecil), Opthof (Talbot); c. Bonynge, p.
Capobianco, d. Pizzi; San Francisco 12, 16, 21, 24, 27 Nov.
Concert *Regnava nel silenzio (Lucia)*, Operetta Airs (Leo Fall), *Ah,
fors'è lui (La traviata)*; c. Bonynge; Salt Lake City: 30 Nov.
Concert with Tourangeau; *Casta diva (Norma)*, Act III *Norma*; c.
Bonynge; New Orleans: 14 Dec.

Lucia di Lammermoor Lucia; Luchetti (Edgardo), Opthof (Enrico), del Bosco (Raimondo); c. Bonynge, p. Guttman, d. Peter Wolf, ass. Brooks van Horn; Philadelphia: 7, 10 Dec.
Recital (appendix 7); P. Bonynge; Washington: 17 Dec.

1972
Recital (appendix 7); P. Bonynge; Rome: 22 Jan.; Raleigh, N. Carolina: 17, 18 Mar.; Philadelphia: 11 Apr.; Michigan: 5 May; Columbus, Ohio: 8 May
La fille du régiment Marie; Pavarotti/Alexander/ di Giuseppe (Tonio), Corena/Gramm (Sulpice), Resnik/Sinclair (Marquise); c. Bonynge, p. Sequi, d. Anni/Escoffier; Metropolitan, NYC: 17, 23, 28 Feb.; 4, 9, 14, 22, 25†, 30 Mar., 7, 15, 18 Apr.; Metropolitan Opera House tour: Boston: 24 Apr.; Cleveland, Ohio: 2 May; Atlanta: 11 May; Memphis: 17 May; New Orleans: 20 May; Minneapolis: 23 May; Detroit: 3 June
Sir Rudolf Bing Opera Gala duet *Sulla tomba (Lucia)*, Pavarotti (Edgardo); c. Bonynge; Metropolitan, NYC: 22‡ Apr.
Rigoletto Gilda; Milnes/Manuguerra (Rigoletto), Pavarotti (Duke), Ruggero Raimondi/Vinco (Sparafucile), Grillo/Godfrey (Maddalena); c. Bonynge, p. Graf, d. Berman; Verdi Festival, Metropolitan, NYC: 10, 14, 19, 22 June
Concert with Horne; duets *Serbami ognor (Semiramide), Mira o Norma (Norma)*; c. Bonynge; NJ: 16 June
Concert P. Bonynge; *Sempre libera (La traviata)*, The last rose of summer (*Martha:* Flotow), San Francisco: 11 Sep.
Norma Norma; Tourangeau (Adalgisa), Alexander (Pollione), Grant (Oroveso); c. Bonynge, p. Capobianco, d. Varona; San Francisco: 15, 20, 24, 30 Sep., 6 Oct.
Lucrezia Borgia Lucrezia*; Alexander (Gennaro), Quilico (Don Alfonso), Tourangeau (Orsini); c. Bonynge, p. Guttman, d. Varona; Vancouver 26, 28 Oct., 1, 4, 8, 11 Nov.; Edmonton, Alberta: 17, 20, 22 Nov.

1973
La fille du régiment Marie; Pavarotti (Tonio), Corena/Gramm (Sulpice), Sinclair/Resnik (Marquise); c. Bonynge, p. Sequi, d. Anni/ Escoffier; Metropolitan, NYC: 31 Dec. 1972, 6†, 11, 15, 19, 22 Jan.
Recital (appendix 8); P. Bonynge; Ottawa: 27† Jan.; Atlanta: 31 Jan.; Long Island, NY: 3 Feb.; New Rochelle, NY: 6 Feb.; Cardiff, Wales: 18 Feb.
Opera Gala mad scene (*Lucia*): Manuguerra (Enrico), Macurdy (Raimondo); c. Bonynge; Metropolitan, NYC: 10 Feb.
Concert *Qui la voce (I puritani)*, Operetta Airs (Leo Fall), *Mon cher amant (La Périchole:* Offenbach*), Waltz (Robinson Crusoe:* Offenbach); c. Bonynge; Royal Albert Hall, London: 23 Feb.
Lucia di Lammermoor Lucia; Pavarotti (Edgardo), Quilico (Enrico), Howell (Raimondo); c. Bonynge, p. Anderson (rehearsed only), d.

Zeffirelli; Covent Garden: 16, 19, 22, 25, 28, 31 May; 5, 9 June
Rodelinda Rodelinda; Tourangeau (Bertarido), van Bruggen (Garibaldo); c. Bonynge, p. Capobianco, d. Varona; Holland Festival: Scheveningen: 24 June; Rotterdam: 27 June; Amsterdam: 30 June, 3 Jul.
Die Fledermaus Rosalinde; van Way (Eisenstein), Blegen (Adele), Ulfung (Alfred), Yarnell (Dr Falke), Tourangeau (Orlofsky); c. Bonynge, p. Mansouri, d. Smith/Roth; San Francisco: 8†, 11, 14, 19, 30 Sep., 2 Oct.
Recital (appendix 9); P. Bonynge; Cuppertino, San Francisco: 22 Sep.; Claremont, California: 26 Sep.; Fresno, California: 5 Oct.; Brooklyn College, NYC: 16 Dec.
La fille du régiment Marie; Alfredo Kraus (Tonio), Malas (Sulpice), Resnik (Marquise); c. Bonynge, p. Sequi, d. Anni/Escoffier; Chicago: 20, 24, 26 Oct., 2, 5, 7 Nov.
Les contes d'Hoffman 4 soprano roles; Domingo/Alexander/Theyard (Hoffmann), Tourangeau (Nicklaus, The Muse), Stewert (Lindorf, Coppelius, Dappertutto, Dr Miracle), Velis (Frantz, Cochenille, Pitichinaccio, Andres), Morris (Crespel), Castel/Franke (Spalanzani), Harvuot/Holloway (Schlemiel), Munzer/Kraft (Mother's voice); c. Bonynge, p. Hebert, d. Klein; Metropolitan, NYC: 29 Nov., 3, 8, 11, 14, 19, 22 Dec., 17, 21, 25 Jan., 2† Feb. 1974

1974
Lucia di Lammermoor Lucia; Theyard (Edgardo), Opthof (Enrico), Morris (Raimondo); c. Bonynge, p. Stivenello, d. Bardon/Hall; Miami: 9, 16 Feb.; Miami Beach: 13 Feb.; Fort Lauderdale, Florida: 19 Feb.
Maria Stuarda Maria Stuarda; Alexander/Sandor (Leicester), Tourangeau (Elizabeth I), Corbeil (Cecil), Opthof (Talbot); c. Bonynge, p. Capobianco, d. Pizzi/Capobianco; Philadelphia: 26 Feb., 1 Mar., Hartford, Connecticut: 4 Mar.
La traviata Violetta; Alfredo Kraus (Alfredo), Zancanaro (Germont); c. Bonynge; Lisbon, Portugal: 18, 21, 24 Apr.
Les contes d'Hoffmann 4 soprano roles; Alexander (Hoffmann), Tourangeau (Nicklaus, The Muse), Stewert (Lindorf, Coppelius, Dappertutto, Dr Miracle), Velis (Franz, Cochenille, Andres, Pitichinaccio), Franke (Spalanzani), Morris (Crespel), Holloway (Schlemiel), Kraft/Munzer (Mother's voice); c. Bonynge, p. Hebert, d. Klein; Metropolitan Opera House tour: Detroit: 4 May; Atlanta: 7 May; Memphis: 13 May; Dallas: 16 May; Minneapolis: 20 May; Metropolitan, NYC: 27, 30 May
Recital (appendix 9); P. Bonynge; Birmingham, Alabama: 10 May; Kansas City: 23 May; Concert Hall, Sydney Opera House: 6 Jul.; Melbourne: 13 Aug.; Sacramento, California: 4 Nov.; Vancouver: 13 Nov.
Les contes d'Hoffmann 4 soprano roles; Wilden (Hoffmann), Tourangeau (Nicklaus, The Muse), R. Myers (Lindorf, Coppelius, Dappertutto, Dr

Miracle), Ewer (Frantz, Cochenille, Pitichinaccio, Andres), Maconaghie (Spalanzani), Eddie (Schlemiel), Dickson (Crespel), Connell (Mother's voice); c. Bonynge, p. Capobianco, d. Varona; Sydney Opera House: 13†, 16, 19, 24, 27, 30 Jul., 2, 6 Aug.
Recital (appendix 10); P. Bonynge; Concert Hall, Sydney Opera House: 9 Aug.; Melbourne: 17 Aug.
Esclarmonde Esclarmonde*; Aragall (Roland), Grant (Phorcas), Tourangeau (Perséïs), Kerns (Bishop); c. Bonynge, p. Mansouri, d. Montressor; San Francisco: 23, 26, 29 Oct., 2, 8† Nov.
Lucia di Lammermoor Lucia; Tagliavini (Edgardo), Darrenkamp (Enrico), Hale (Raimondo); c. Bonynge, p. Hebert, d. Bardon/Hall; Phoenix: 23, 26 Nov.; San Diego: 4, 6, 8 Dec.

1975
La traviata Violetta; Alfredo Kraus (Alfredo), Quilico (Germont); c. Bonynge, p. Visconti (reh. Rennison), d. Faria/Marzot; Covent Garden: 6, 11, 16, 21, 24, 27 Jan.
Recital (appendix 9); P. Bonynge/Holford; Manchester: 19 Jan.; Stratford-upon-Avon: 29 Jan.; Rochester, NY: 18 Feb.; Ithaca, NY: 18 Mar.; Pasadena, California: 5 Oct.
Darwin Gala: Midnight Matinée aria & cabaletta *Oh nube! Che lieve (Maria Stuarda)*, duet *Mira o Norma (Norma)* with Heather Begg; Covent Garden: 25‡ Jan.
La traviata Violetta; Little (Alfredo), Opthof (Germont); c. Bonynge, p. Capobianco, d. Wolf Ass./Mess; Philadelphia: 25, 27 Mar.
Lucrezia Borgia Lucrezia; Brecknock (Gennaro), Devlin (Don Alfonso), Tourangeau (Orsini); c. Bonynge, p. Mansouri, d. Varona; Houston: 8, 11, 13 Apr.
Maria Stuarda Maria Stuarda; Tourangeau (Elizabeth I), Little (Leicester), Rae Smith (Cecil), Opthof (Talbot); c. Bonynge, p. Capobianco, d. Varona; Las Palmas: 29 Apr., 2 May
La traviata Violetta; Alexander (Alfredo), Merrill (Germont); c. Bonynge, p. Lunt, d. Beaton; Metropolitan Opera House tour: Japan: 29 May, 3, 6, 9, 12 June
Il trovatore Leonora*; Pavarotti (Manrico), Wixell (di Luna), Obratsova/ Verrett (Azucena); c. Bonynge, p. Libby, d. Hager/Skalicki; San Francisco: 12, 17, 21, 27, 30 Sep., 3 Oct.
Recital with Tourangeau; P. Bonynge; duets *Sull'aria (Le nozze di Figaro), Regarde! (Pique Dame:* Tchaikovsky*), Barcarolle (Les contes d'Hoffmann), Viens Mallika (Lakmé), Mira o Norma (Norma), Tutti i fior (Madama Butterfly), Suvvia fuggiam perché (La bohème:* Leon-cavallo*), C'est le soir (Le roi de Lahore), Vivere io non potro (La donna del lago:* Rossini*), Serbami ognor (Semiramide)*, San Diego: 23 Sep.
Lucia di Lammermoor Lucia; Pavarotti/Theyard (Edgardo), Saccomani (Enrico), Ferrin (Raimondo); c. Bonynge, p. Copley, d. Bardon/Hall; Chicago: 12, 15, 18, 21, 24, 28 Nov., 1, 4 Dec.

1976

I puritani Elvira; Pavarotti (Arturo), Milnes/Opthof (Riccardo), Morris/Flagello (Giorgio); c. Bonynge, p. Sequi, d. Cho Lee/Hall; Metropolitan, NYC: 25, 28 Feb., 2, 5, 9, 13†, 17, 20, 25, 29 Mar.

The Merry Widow Anna Glavari*; van der Stolk (Danilo), Clark (de Rosillon), Shuttleworth (Valencienne), Rubes (Baron Zita); c. Bonynge, p. Mansouri, d. Varona; Vancouver: 22, 24, 27, 29 Apr., 1, 4 May.

Concert *Non mi dir (Don Giovanni), Casta diva (Norma)*, mad scene *(Lucia)*; c. Bonynge; New Zealand: Wellington: 19† May; Dunedin: 29 May; Christchurch: 4† June; Auckland: 13 June

Concert *Regnava nel silenzio (Lucia)*, Bell Song *(Lakmé), Qui la voce (I puritani);* c. Bonynge; Wellington, NZ: 22† May; Auckland, NZ: 10 June

Recital (appendix 10); P. Bonynge; Hamilton, NZ: 25 May; Wellington, NZ: 7 June

Recital (appendix 9); P. Bonynge; Napier, NZ: 1† June; Christchurch, NZ: 16 June

Lakmé Lakmé; Wilden/Austin (Gerald), Tourangeau/Elkins (Mallika), Grant (Nilakantha); c. Bonynge, p. Ayrton, d. Digby; Sydney Opera House: 10, 14, 17†, 21, 24, 26, 30 Jul., 2, 6, 13, 18‡ Aug.

Recital with Tourangeau, Wilden, Pringle; P. Bonynge; duet *Serbami ognor (Semiramide)*, trio *Tous les trois (La fille du régiment)*, quartet & excerpts *(Rigoletto)*, duet *Parigi o cara (La traviata)*, duet *Quanto amore (L'elisir d'amore)*, duet *Mira o Norma (Norma)*; Government House, Sydney: 8 Aug.

Recital (appendix 10); P. Bonynge; Adelaide: 21, 24 Aug.; Canberra: 27 Aug.; Seattle: 29 Oct.; Winnipeg: 31 Oct.

Esclarmonde Esclarmonde; Aragall/Alexander (Roland), Grant/Hines (Phorcas), Tourangeau (Perséïs), Quilico (Bishop); c. Bonynge, p. Mansouri, d. Montressor; Metropolitan, NYC: 19, 24, 27 Nov., 1, 4, 7, 11†, 17, 20 Dec.

United Nations Concert sleepwalking scene *(La sonnambula), Ah, fors'è lui (La traviata)*; United Nations, NYC: 12 Dec.

1977

Recital (appendix 9); P. Holford; Ames, Iowa: 22 Jan.; Buffalo, NY: 25 Jan.; Akron, Ohio: 27 Jan.; Danville, Kentucky: 29 Jan.; Sarasota, Florida: 1 Feb.; Miami: 3 Feb.

Lucia di Lammermoor Lucia; Aragall (Edgardo), Elvira (Enrico), Diaz (Raimondo); c. Bonynge, p. Ayrton; Puerto Rico: 9, 11 Feb.

Maria Stuarda Maria Stuarda; Tourangeau (Elizabeth I), Terranova (Leicester), Cunningham (Cecil), Bröcheler (Talbot); c. Bonynge, p. Capobianco, d. Heeley; Holland: Scheveningen: 10, 15 Mar.; Rotterdam: 12 Mar.; Utrecht: 18 Mar.; Amsterdam: 22, 27, 30 Mar.; Eindhoven: 25 Mar.

Recital with Tourangeau; P. Bonynge *Ah, non credea (La*

sonnambula), duet *Barcarolle (Les contes d'Hoffmann), Io non sono più l'Annetta (Crispino e la comare:* Ricci), duet *Viens Mallika (Lakmé)*, duet *Serbami ognor (Semiramide)*; Amsterdam: 13 Mar.

Lucrezia Borgia Lucrezia; Stevens/Ferris (Gennaro), Allman (Alfonso), Elkins (Orsini); c. Bonynge, p. Ogilvie, d. Fredrikson; Sydney Opera House: 7, 11†, 14, 18, 22, 25, 28 June, 5, 8‡ Jul.

Suor Angelica Suor Angelica*; Raisbeck (Princess); c. Bonynge, p. Ogilvie, d. Digby; Sydney Opera House: 16, 19, 22, 26 Jul.

Opera in Concert *Don Giovanni* quartet, Act I with Buchanan, Wilden, Yurisich; *Les contes d'Hoffmann* quartet, Epilogue with Bermingham, Wilden, R. Myers; *Esclarmonde* quartet, Act IV with Begg, Ferris, Grant; *Il trovatore* trio, Act I with Dowd, Shaw; *Bitter Sweet* (Coward) duet 'I'll see you again' with Pringle; *Three Little Maids* (Gilbert & Sullivan) with Raisbeck, Begg; *Lucia* sextet with Raisbeck, Byers, Ewer, Allman, Light; P. Bonynge/Kimmorley; Concert Hall, Sydney Opera House: 24 Jul.

Le roi de Lahore Sita*; Stevens (Alim), Tourangeau (Khaled), Opthof (Scindia), Morris (Timur); c. Bonynge, p. Sequi, d. Mariani; Vancouver: 23†, 25, 28 Sep., 1, 9 Oct.; Seattle: 27, 29 Oct., 2, 5 Nov.

Don Giovanni Donna Anna; Morris (Don Giovanni), Malas (Leporello), Cariaga (Donna Elvira), Tourangeau (Zerlina), Suarez (Don Ottavio); c. Bonynge, p. Ayrton, d. Prévost; Vancouver: 7, 12, 14, 16, 22 Oct.

Maria Stuarda Maria Stuarda; Tourangeau (Elizabeth I), Burrows (Leicester), van Allan (Cecil), Ward (Talbot); c. Bonynge, p. Copley, d. Heeley; Covent Garden: 15, 20, 23, 26, 29 Dec.

1978

The Merry Widow Anna Glavari; Stevens/van der Stolk (Danilo), Austin (Rosillon) Buchanan (Valencienne), Wilcock (Baron Zeta); c. Bonynge, p. Mansouri, d. Fredrikson; Concert Hall, Sydney Opera House: 19, 21, 23, 25, 26, 28†, 31 Jan., 2, 4, 6, 8, 9, 11 Feb.

Opera in Concert *Don Giovanni* quartet, Act I with Buchanan, Wilden, Germain; *Les contes d'Hoffmann* quartet, Epilogue with Bermingham, Wilden, R. Myers; *Esclarmonde* quartet, Act IV with Begg, Ferris, Grant; *Il trovatore* trio, Act I with Stevens, Shaw; *Bitter Sweet* duet 'I'll see you again' with Pringle; *Lucia* sextet with Raisbeck, Ferris, Ewer, Allman, Grant; P. Bonynge/Kimmorley; Concert Hall, Sydney Opera House: 18 Feb.

Don Giovanni Donna Anna; Morris (Don Giovanni), Bacquier (Leporello), Varady (Donna Elvira), Tourangeau (Zerlina), Brecknock (Don Ottavio); c. Bonynge, p. Graf, d. Berman; Metropolitan, NYC: 10, 16, 18, 21, 25†, 27, 30 Mar.

Recital (appendix 11); P. Bonynge; Kalamazoo, Michigan: 4 Apr.; Salt Lake City: 7 Apr.; Minneapolis: 9 Apr.; Memphis: 12 Apr.; Tulsa, Oklahoma: 14 Apr.; New Orleans: 16 Apr.; Tokyo, Japan: 7 June;

Nagoya, Japan: 10 June; Seoul, S. Korea: 13 June; Concert Hall, Sydney Opera House: 13 Aug.
Norma Norma; Elkins/Begg (Adalgisa), Stevens (Pollione), Grant/ Shanks (Oroveso); c. Bonynge, p. Sequi, d. Mariani; Sydney Opera House: 5, 8, 11, 14, 17, 20, 26, 29 Jul.; 1‡, 4, 10, 23, 26† Aug.
Concert *Casta diva (Norma)*, duet *Sulla tomba (Lucia)* with John Brecknock, Vilja (*Merry Widow*), mad scene (*Hamlet*), sextet (*Lucia*) with Brecknock, Kenny, Dempsey, Summers, King; c. Bonynge; Covent Garden: 26 Nov.
Norma Norma; Tourangeau (Adalgisa), van Limpt (Pollione), White (Oroveso); c. Bonynge, p. Capobianco, d. Hall; Holland: Amsterdam: 14, 17, 20 Dec.; Scheveningen: 23, 26 Dec.; Rotterdam: 29 Dec.; Utrecht: 1 Jan. 1979

1979

Recital (appendix 11); P. Bonynge; Philadelphia: 11 Jan.; Toronto: 14 Jan.; Opéra, Paris: 26 Apr.; Munich: 29 Apr.; Asolo, Italy: 14 May; Glasgow, Scotland: 16 Sep.; Ann Arbor, Michigan: 4 Oct.; Cincinatti: 7 Oct.
Concert with Pavarotti; duets *Libiamo, Un di felice, Parigi o cara (La traviata), Ernani, involami (Ernani)*, mad scene *(Hamlet)* I dreamt I dwelt in marble halls (*Bohemian Girl*), sleepwalking scene (*La sonnambula*), duet *Sulla tomba (Lucia)*; c. Bonynge; Avery Fisher Hall, Lincoln Centre, NYC: 22‡ Jan.
The Merry Widow Anna Glavari; Stevens/van der Stolk (Danilo), Austin (Rosillon), Furlan/Johnston (Valencienne), Wilcock (Baron Zita); c. Bonynge, p. Mansouri, d. Fredrikson; Concert Hall, Sydney Opera House: 9, 12, 14, 16, 19, 22, 24, 28 Feb.; 2 Mar.; Adelaide: 22, 26, 28, 30 Nov.; Melbourne: 6, 8, 10, 12, 13, 15 Dec.
La traviata Violetta; Austin (Alfredo), Allman (Germont); c. Bonynge, p. Copley (reh. Bremner), d. Bardon/Stennett; Melbourne: 10, 13, 16, 19, 24 Mar.
Norma Norma; Elkins (Adalgisa), Stevens (Pollione), Grant (Oroveso); c. Bonynge, p. Sequi, d. Mariani; Brisbane: 31 Mar., 3, 6, 9 Apr.
Lucia di Lammermoor (concert performance) Lucia; Clark (Edgardo), Cold (Enrico), Probst (Raimondo); c. Bonynge; Stockholm: 6 May
Idomeneo Electra*; Mitchell (Ilia), Elkins (Idamante), Stevens/ Baigildin (Idomeneo), Wilden (Arbace); c. Bonynge, p. Lovejoy, d. Truscott: Sydney Opera House: 4, 7 (performance unfinished), 14, 17, 20, 25†, 28 Jul.
La traviata Violetta; Austin (Alfredo), Allman (Germont); c. Bonynge, p. Bremner (rehearsed only), d. Bardon/Stennett; Sydney Opera House: 10 Jul.
Don Giovanni Donna Anna; Morris (Don Giovanni), Warren Smith (Leporello), Elkins (Donna Elvira), Moore (Zerlina), Wilden (Don Ottavio); c. Bonynge, p. Ogilvie, d. Colman/Fredrikson; Melbourne: 4, 7, 10, 13, 16, 18 Aug.

Concert with Horne; duet *Barcarolle (Hoffmann), Tornami a vagheggiar (Alcina), Ah, fors'è lui...Sempre libera (La traviata)*, duet *Serbami ognor (Semiramide)*, duet *Viens, Mallika (Lakmé)*, Vilja *(Merry Widow), Regnava nel silenzio ... quando rapita (Lucia)*, duet *Mira o Norma (Norma)*; c. Bonynge; Avery Fisher Hall, Lincoln Centre, NYC: 15‡ Oct.

1980

Opera in Concert *I puritani*: quartet, Act I with Austin, Germain, Grant; *Son vergin vezzosa (I puritani)* with Johnston, Austin, Pringle; *Maria Stuarda* duet, Act II with Donald Smith; *Pacific 1860* (Coward) duet with Ewer; *Bitter Sweet* duet with Germain; *Rigoletto* duet, Act I with Austin; duet *Serbami ognor (Semiramide)* with Begg; *Rigoletto* quartet with Moore, Donald Smith, Pringle; P. Bonynge/Kimmorley; Concert Hall, Sydney Opera House: 26 Jan.

Lucia di Lammermoor Lucia; Greager (Edgardo), Allman (Enrico), Grant (Raimondo); c. Bonynge, p. Copley, d. Bardon/Stennett; Concert Hall, Sydney Opera House: 6, 9, 12, 15, 20, 23, 26, 29 Feb.

Lucrezia Borgia Lucrezia; Alfredo Kraus (Gennaro), Dean (Don Alfonso), Howells (Orsini); c. Bonynge, p. Copley, d. Stennett/Pascoe; Covent Garden: 26, 29‡ Mar., 1, 5, 9, 12, 16 Apr.

Recital (appendix 12); P. Bonynge; Stuttgart: 21 Apr.; Staatsoper, Vienna: 24 Apr.

Lucrezia Borgia Lucrezia; Piero Visconti/Taund (Gennaro), Roni/Luccardi (Don Alfonso), Zilio (Orsini); c. Bonynge, p. Copley (reh. Renshaw), d. Pascoe/Stennett; Rome: 15, 18, 21, 24, 28, 31 May, 3 June

I masnadieri Amalia*; Donald Smith/Ferris (Carlo), Allman/Badcock (Francesco), Grant (Masimiliano); c. Bonynge, p. Beauvais, d. Lees/Stennett; Sydney Opera House: 2, 5, 8, 11, 17, 23, 26, 29 Jul., 2, 5, 9 Aug.

Lucia di Lammermoor Lucia; Greager/Ferris/Furlan (Edgardo), Allman/Badcock (Enrico), Grant/Shanks (Raimondo); c. Bonynge, p. Copley, d. Bardon/Stennett; Concert Hall, Sydney Opera House: 22, 25, 28, 31 Aug., 3, 6 Sep.; Melbourne: 5, 8†, 11, 14 Nov.; Adelaide: 19, 22, 26, 29 Nov.

Die Fledermaus Rosalinde; Titus (Eisenstein), Sills (Adele), Campora (Alfred), Gardner (Falke), Resnik (Orlofsky); c. Bonynge, p. Capobianco, d. Zack Brown/Oliver Smith; San Diego: 5, 8, 11, 16, 19 Oct.

1981

Otello Desdemona; Marenzi (Otello), Shaw/Allman (Iago), Ferris (Cassio); c. Cillario, p. Ogilvie, d. Girton/Fredrikson; Concert Hall, Sydney Opera House: 28, 31† Jan., 3, 6, 9, 12, 17, 20, 23, 28 Feb.; Melbourne: 20, 23, 26, 29 May, 1, 4 June

Concert with Pavarotti & Horne; trio, Act IV (*Ernani*); duet *O remembranza (Norma)*; trio, Act I (*Norma*); duet, Act II, trio, Act IV

(La gioconda); *Tu del mio Carlo (I masnadieri)*; duet, Act I *(Otello)*; final scene *(Il trovatore)*; c. Bonynge; Avery Fisher Hall, Lincoln Centre, NYC: 20, 23‡ Mar.

Concert with Pavarotti; duets *Libiamo, Un di felice, Parigi, o cara (La traviata), Tu del mio Carlo (I masnadieri), Tornami a vagheggiar (Alcina)*, scena & duet *Signor ne principe (Rigoletto)*, I dreamt I dwelt in marble halls *(Bohemian Girl)*, *O beau pays (Les Huguenots)*, duet *Sulla tomba (Lucia)*; c. Bonynge; Pittsburg: 27 Mar.

La traviata Violetta; Raffanti (Alfredo), Ryan Edwards (Germont); c. Bonynge, d. Karp; Memphis: 4 Apr.

Concert *Tornami a vagheggiar (Alcina), Tu del mio Carlo (I masnadieri)*, mad scene *(Lucia)*; c. Bonynge; Rock Hill, S. Carolina: 7 Apr.

Recital (appendix 12); P. Bonynge; Whitman Hall, Brooklyn College, NYC: 11 Apr.

Norma Norma; Troyanos (Adalgisa), Ortiz (Pollione), Diaz (Oroveso); c. Bonynge, p. Mansouri, d. Varona; Toronto: 28 Apr., 1, 4‡, 7, 10 May

La traviata Violetta; Austin/Greager (Alfredo), Summers (Germont); c. Bonynge, p. Copley (reh. Bremner), d. Bardon/Stennett; Sydney Opera House: 17, 20, 24, 27, 30 June, 4, 9 Jul.

Les Huguenots Marguerite de Valois; Zschau (Valentine), Austin/ Greager (Raoul), Pringle (de Nevers), Macdonald/Saliba (Urbain), Grant (Marcel), Martin (St Bris); c. Bonynge, p. Mansouri, d. Stoddart/ Stennett; Sydney Opera House: 24, 27, 31 Jul., 5, 8, 11, 15, 18, 22 Aug.

The Merry Widow Anna Glavari; Hagegard (Danilo), Austin (de Rosillon), Forst (Valencienne), Stark (Baron Zeta); c. Bonynge, p. Mansouri d. Laufer/Mess/Fredrikson; San Francisco: 3, 6, 9, 13, 16, 21, 25, 28, 31 Oct.

Concert *Ah, fors'è lui ... sempre libera, Addio del passato (La traviata)*; c. Bonynge; San Diego: 18 Oct.

George London Tribute Concert *O beau pays (Les Huguenots)*, c. Kohn; Washington: 4 Nov.

Concert with Bonisolli & van Allan; *Tirana gelosia...Tornami a vagheggiar (Alcina), O beau pays (Les Huguenots)*, duets *Libiamo, Parigi o cara (La traviata)*, *Io non sono più l'Annetta (Crispino e la comare:* Ricci), final trio *(Faust)*; c. Bonynge; Covent Garden: 29 Nov.

Il trovatore Leonora; Bonisolli (Manrico), Masurok (di Luna), Obratsova (Azucena); c. Bonynge, p. Renshaw, d. Sanjust/Stennett; Covent Garden: 10, 14, 18, 22† Dec., 1, 4 Jan. 1982

1982
La traviata (concert performance) Violetta; Austin (Alfredo), Shaw (Germont); c. Bonynge; The Domain, Sydney: 18 Jan.

Lucrezia Borgia Lucrezia; Furlan (Gennaro), Martin/Allman (Alfonso), Cullen (Orsini); c. Bonynge, p. Ogilvie, d. Fredrikson; Concert Hall, Sydney Opera House: 3, 6, 10, 17, 20, 23, 26 Feb., 1, 4 Mar.

Recital (appendix 12); P. Bonynge; Perth: 9 Mar.; Venice: 9 Apr.; Genoa: 12 Apr.

Lucrezia Borgia (concert performance) Lucrezia; Winbergh (Gennaro), Cold (Alfonso), Soffel (Orsini); c. Bonynge; Stockholm: 26 Mar.

Lucia di Lammermoor Lucia; Derksen (Edgardo), van Limpt (Enrico), ven den Berg (Raimondo); c. Bonynge/Challender, p. Copley, d. Bardon/Stone; Holland: Amsterdam: 29 Apr., 2, 5, 24, 27 May; Scheveningen: 8, 11 May; Utrecht: 14 May; Eindhoven: 17 May; Rotterdam: 20 May

Die Fledermaus Rosalinde; Gard/Stevens (Eisenstein), Brynnel/McGregor (Adele), Austin/Ferris (Alfred), M. Lewis (Falke), Begg (Orlofsky); c. Bonynge, p. Beshe, d. Stoddart; Sydney Opera House: 25, 28 June, 3, 6, 10‡, ¸3, 16, 19, 22, 28, 31 Jul., 4 Aug.

Concert Act II, Sc. 1 (*Lucia*) with Allman (Enrico), Grant (Raimondo); c. Challender; Sydney Opera House: 25 Jul.

Norma Norma; Mauro (Pollione), Horne (Adalgisa), Flagello (Oroveso); c. Bonynge, p. Mansouri, d. Varona; San Francisco: 11, 14, 17†, 21, 26, 29 Sep., 2 Oct.

Thirtieth Anniversary Concert with Summers, Soffel; *Com e bello (Lucrezia Borgia)*, duet *'Figlia!' – 'Mio padre' (Rigoletto)*, duet *Mira o Norma (Norma)*, duet *Dite alla giovine (La traviata)*, duet *Serbami ognor (Semiramide)*, *Czardas (Fledermaus)*, trio *Tu ne chanteras plus (Hoffmann)*, *Io son l'umile ancella (Adriana)*; c. Bonynge; Covent Garden: 17 Oct.

Richard Tucker Foundation Gala Concert *Casta diva (Norma)*, duet *(Hamlet)* with Milnes; c. Bonynge; Carnegie Hall, NYC: 24 Oct.

Lucia di Lammermoor Lucia; Alfredo Kraus/Raffanti (Edgardo), Elvira/Schexnayder (Enrico), Plishka/Morris (Raimondo); c. Bonynge, p. Donnell, d. Collonello; Metropolitan, NYC; 1, 5, 10, 13, 20, 24, 27†, 30 Nov., 4, 9, 13‡ Dec.

1983

Die Fledermaus Rosalinde; Stevens (Eisenstein), McGregor (Adele), Ferris (Alfred), Pringle (Falke), Begg, (Orlofsky); c. Bonynge, p. Besch, d. Stoddart; Sydney Opera House: 10, 18 Jan.; Concert Performance: The Domain, Sydney: 15 Jan.

Concert with Pavarotti; duet *Libiamo, Addio del passato (La traviata)*, *Qui la voce (I puritani)*, duet *Prendi l'anel ti dono (La sonnambula)*, *Io son l'umile ancella (Adriana)*, mad scene *(Hamlet)* duet *Sulla tomba (Lucia)*; c. Bonynge; Concert Hall, Sydney Opera House: 23‡ Jan.

Alcina Alcina; Elkins (Ruggiero), McGregor (Morgana), Elms (Bradamante), Wegner (Melisso); c. Bonynge, p. Helpmann, d. Pascoe; Sydney Opera House: 5, 9, 12†, 16, 19, 22, 26 Feb.

Concert duet *Mira o Norma (Norma)* with Elkins (Adalgisa), *Lucia* sextet with Raisbeck, Ferris, Ewer, Fulford, Shanks; c. Bonynge; Sydney Opera House: 27 Feb.

La traviata Violetta; Furlan (Alfredo), Montefusco (Germont); c. Bonynge, p. De Tomasi, d. Del Savio/D'Alessandro; Genoa: 17 Mar. (performance unfinished)

Adriana Lecouvreur Adriana*; Bröcheler (Michonnet), Moldoveanu (Maurizio), Silva (Princess de Bouillon); c. Bonynge, p. Capobianco, d. O'Hearn/Mess; San Diego: 22, 26, 29 May, 1 June

Concert *Deh vieni non tardar (Figaro)*, With plaintive notes (*Samson*), When William at eve, Light as thistledown (*Rosina*), *Sediziose voce. . . Casta diva (Norma)*, sleepwalking scene (*La sonnambula*); c. Bonynge; Sydney Opera House: 12 June

Il trovatore Leonora; Collins (Manrico), Summers (di Luna), Elms (Azucena); c. Bonynge, p. Moshinsky, d. Nolan/Arrighi; Sydney Opera House: 25, 28 June, 2‡, 5, 8, 13, 16, 19, 22 Jul.

Semiramide Semiramide; Elms (Arsace), Martin (Assur), Mavridis (Oroe); c. Bonynge, p. Oxenbould, d. Clark; Sydney Opera House: 5, 8, 13†, 17, 20 Aug.

La fille du régiment Marie; Alfredo Kraus (Tonio), Berberian/Malas (Sulpice), Resnik (Marquise); c. Bonynge, p. Sequi, d. Anni/Escoffier; Metropolitan, NYC; 27 Sep., 1, 5, 8, 11, 14, 19, 24 Oct.

Met Centenary Concert *Bel raggio (Semiramide)*; c. Bonynge; Metropolitan, NYC: 22 Oct.

Esclarmonde Esclarmonde; Veronelli (Roland), Howell/Rea (Phorcas), Montague (Perséïs), Summers (Bishop of Blois); c. Bonynge, p. Mansouri, d. Montressor; Covent Garden: 28 Nov., 6, 10, 13, 16 Dec.

1984

Lucia di Lammermoor (concert performance) Lucia; Greager (Edgardo), Fulford (Enrico), Grant (Raimondo); c. Bonynge; The Domain, Sydney: 14 Jan.

Adriana Lecouvreur Adriana; Shaw (Michonnet), Austin (Maurizio), Begg (Princess de Bouillon); c. Bonynge, p. Copley, d. Lees/Stennett; Sydney Opera House: 27, 30 Jan., 2, 7, 11, 14, 18‡, 22, 25, 29 Feb.

Anna Bolena Anna Bolena*; Morris (Enrico), Forst (Seymour), Stubbs/ Segar (Smeton), Michael Myers (Percy); c. Bonynge, p. Mansouri, d. Pascoe/Stennett; Toronto: 22, 25, 28‡, 31 May, 3 June; Detroit: 6, 9 June

I masnadieri Amalia; Zanazzo (Massimiliano), Greer (Carlo), Salvadori (Francesco); c. Bonynge, p. Capobianco; San Diego: 21, 24, 30 June

Les contes d'Hoffmann 4 soprano roles; Hoffmann (Hoffmann), Cullen (Nicklaus, The Muse), Summers (Lindorf, Coppelius, Dappertutto, Dr Miracle), Ewer (Andres, Cochenille, Pitichinaccio, Frantz), Warlow (Spalanzani), Eddie (Schlemiel), van der Stolk/Grant (Crespel), Price (Mother's voice); c. Bonynge, p. Capobianco, d. Varona; Sydney Opera House: 20, 23, 26, 30 Jul., 4, 7†, 11, 15 Aug.

Musicians for World Peace Concert *Casta diva (Norma)*, mad scene (*Lucia*); c. Bonynge; Sydney Opera House: 19 Aug.

The Carmelites Mme Lidoine; Chard (Marquis de la Force), Ferris (Chev. de la Force), Buchanan (Blanche), Begg (Mother Marie); c. Bonynge, p. Moshinsky, d. Bury; Sydney Opera House: 1, 4, 8, 11, 15‡, 19, 22, 24, 26 Sep.

Anna Bolena Anna Bolena; Langan (Enrico), Budai/Forst (Seymour), Gettler (Smeton), Blake (Percy); c. Bonynge, p. Mansouri, d. Pascoe/Stennett; San Francisco: 25, 28 Oct., 3, 6, 9, 13 Nov.

1985

Les contes d'Hoffmann (concert performance) 4 soprano roles; Austin (Hoffmann), Cullen (Nicklaus, The Muse), Yurisich (Coppelius), Lewis (Dappertutto), Swan (Dr Miracle), Ewer (Andres, Cochenille, Pitichin-accio, Franzt), Warlow (Spalanzani), van der Stolk (Crespel), Price (Mother's voice), Eddie (Schlemiel); c. Bonynge; The Domain, Sydney: 12 Jan.

Norma Norma; Hoffmann (Pollione), Hahn (Adalgisa), Shanks (Oroveso); c. Bonynge, p. Renshaw, d. Rowell; Concert Hall, Sydney Opera House: 22, 26, 29 Jan., 2, 9, 12†, 16 Feb.

Concert with Pavarotti; duet *Libiamo, Parigi o cara (La traviata), Io son l'umile ancella (Adriana), Son vergin vezzosa (I puritani)*, duet Act II *(Rigoletto)*, The Doll Song *(Hoffman)*, Vilja *(Merry Widow)*, *Regnava nel silenzio*, duet *Sulla tomba (Lucia)*; c. Bonynge; Phoenix: 27 Mar.; Atlantic City, NJ; 30 Mar.

Lucia di Lammermoor Lucia; Bergonzi (Edgardo), Rawnsley (Enrico), Howell (Raimondo); c. Bonynge, p. Sutcliffe, d. Zeffirelli: Covent Garden: 13, 16, 19, 23, 26 Apr.

Norma (concert performance) Norma; Hoffmann (Pollione), Soffel (Adalgisa), Appelgren (Oroveso); c. Bonynge; Stockholm: 24 May

Concert with Horne; *Tornami a vagheggiar (Alcina), Vorrei spiegarvi (La cambiale di matrimonio*: Rossini), duet *Serbami ognor (Semiramide)*, duet *Viens Mallika (Lakmé)*, The Doll Song *(Hoffmann), Ne craignez rien (Fra Diavolo:* Auber), duet *Mira o Norma (Norma)*; c. Bonynge; Melbourne: 9 June; Concert Hall, Sydney Opera House: 12‡ June

I puritani Elvira; Austin (Arturo), Shanks (Giorgio), M. Lewis (Riccardo); c. Bonynge, p. Helpmann, d. Bardon/Stennett; Sydney Opera House: 24, 28 June, 1†,6,10,13,16 Jul.

Hamlet Ophélie*; Bröcheler (Hamlet), Shanks (Claudius), Richards (Gertrude); c. Bonynge, p. Mansouri, d. Skalicki/Digby/Stennett; Toronto: 4, 7, 10, 13, 16, 19 Oct.

Anna Bolena Anna Bolena; Plishka (Enrico), Toczyska (Seymour), Zilio (Smeton), Merritt (Percy); c. Bonynge, p. Mansouri, d. Pascoe/Stennett; Chicago: 30 Oct., 2, 5, 8, 11, 14, 19 Nov.

Anna Bolena (concert performance) Anna Bolena; Yurisich (Enrico), Forst (Seymour), Clarey (Smeton), Hadley (Percy); c. Bonynge; Avery Fisher Hall, Lincoln Centre, NYC: 25‡ Nov., Boston: 1 Dec.; Washington: 6 Dec.

1986

Concert with Bernadette Cullen; *Casta diva ... bello a me ritorna (Norma)*, mad scene *(Hamlet)*, duet *Alle piu care imagini (Semiramide)*, duet *Mira o Norma (Norma)*, *Io sono l'umile ancella (Adriana)*, mad scene *(Lucia)*; c. Bonynge; Perth: 10 Jan.

Rigoletto (concert performance) Gilda; M. Lewis (Rigoletto), Greager (Duke), Shanks (Sparafucile), Gunn (Maddalena); c. Bonynge; The Domain, Sydney: 20 Jan.

Lucia di Lammermoor Lucia; Greager (Edgardo), Donnelly (Enrico), Grant (Raimondo); c. Bonynge, p. Wregg (rehearsed only), d. Bardon/Stennett: Concert Hall, Sydney Opera House: 28 Jan., 1, 8‡, 14, 19 Feb.

Concert *Io son l'umile ancella (Adriana)*, *Sediziose voce ... Casta diva ... bello a me ritorna (Norma)*, *Qui la voce (I puritani)*, mad scene *(Lucia)*; c. Bonynge; Wellington, NZ: 5‡ Mar.

Concert *Vorrei spiegarvi (La cambiale de matrimonio)*, *Non temete, Milord, Or son sola (Fra Diavolo:* Auber*)*, *Regnava nel silenzio (Lucia)*, mad scene *(Hamlet)*; c. Bonynge; Wellington, NZ: 8‡ Mar.

Norma Norma; Soffel (Adalgisa), Pinto (Pollione), Surjan (Oroveso); c. Bonynge, p. Calusso, d. Villagrossi; Barcelona: 21, 24, 27, 30 Apr.

La fille du régiment Marie; Blake (Tonio), Corbeil (Sulpice), Griffin (Marquise); c. Bonynge, p. Capobianco, d. Malabar Ltd; Pittsburgh: 5, 7, 10 June

Anna Bolena Anna; Ghiuselev (Enrico), Mentzer (Seymour), Hadley (Percy), Bunnell (Smeton); c. Bonynge, p. Mansouri, d. Pascoe/Stennett; Houston: 19, 22, 25, 28 June

La fille du régiment Marie; Austin (Tonio), Yurisich (Sulpice), Begg (Marquise); c. Bonynge, p. Sequi, d. Bardon/Stennett; Sydney Opera House: 22, 26, 30 Jul., 2, 9‡, 16, 23 Aug.

I puritani Elvira; Fisichella/Blake (Arturo), Milnes (Riccardo), Ramey (Giorgio); c. Bonynge, p. Sequi, d. Cho Lee/Hall; Metropolitan, NYC: 14, 18, 22, 25, 29, Nov., 3, 6, 9, 13, 18 Dec.

APPENDICES

APPENDIX 1

Aure soavi e liete ombre (Handel), *Il mio bel foco* (Marcello), *Pieta Signore* (Stradella), *Les Troquers* (Dauvergne), *Divinités du Styx!* (*Alceste*: Gluck), *Or sai chi l'onore* (*Don Giovanni*: Mozart), *Non mi dir* (*Don Giovanni*: Mozart), *Die Lorelei* (Liszt), *Verborgenheit* (Hugo Wolf), *Der Gartner* (Hugo Wolf), *Anakreons Grab* (Hugo Wolf), *En einem Garten* (Erich Wolf), *Erhebung* (Erich Wolf), Song of the Girl at the Window (Szymanowsky), *Pastorale* (Stravinsky), My Native Land (Gretchaninov), Lullaby (Gretchaninov), The Harvest of Sorrow (Rachmaninov), Spring's Return (Rachmaninov), *Qui la voce* (*I puritani*: Bellini).

APPENDIX 2

Care selve (*Atalanta*: Handel), *Qual Farfallette* (*Partenope*: Handel), When daisies pied (Arne), Where the bee sucks (Arne), O ravishing delight (Arne), *Ridente la Calma*: K152 (Mozart), *Un moto di Gioja*: K579 (Mozart), *An Chloe*: K524 (Mozart), *Ch'io mi scordi di te?.. Non temer amato bene*: K505 (Mozart), *Lied de Mignon* (Schubert), *Liebe Schwarmt auf aller Wegen* (Schubert), *An den Frulig* (Schubert), *Rastlosie Leibe* (Schubert), *La promessa* (Rossini), *La gita in gondola* (Rossini), *La pastorella delle Alpi* (Rossini), *Ernani involami* (*Ernani*: Verdi).

APPENDIX 3

Care selve (*Atalanta*: Handel), She never told her love (Haydn), The Shepherd's Song (Haydn), Light as thistledown (*Rosina*: Shield), *Gran dio che regoli* (Bianchi), *Tre giorni son che Nina* (attrib. Pergolesi), *Quand le bien-aimé reviendra* (*Nina*: Dalayrac), *Un moto di Gioja*: K579 (Mozart), *Or sai chi l'onore* (*Don Giovanni*: Mozart), The Bitterness of Love (James Dunn), I came with a song (Frank La Forge), Song of the Open (Frank La Forge), I dreamt I dwelt in marble halls (*The Bohemian Girl*: Balfe), *Mattinata* (Leoncavallo), *Parla* (Arditi), Recit, aria & cab: *Regnava nel silenzio* (*Lucia di Lammermoor*: Donizetti).

APPENDIX 4

Selection from: *Ritorna o cara* (*Rodelinda*: Handel), *Care selve* (*Atalanta*: Handel), As when the dove (*Acis & Galatea*: Handel), *Tornami a vagheggiar* (*Alcina*: Handel), *Ombre pallide* (*Alcina*: Handel), *Di cor mio* (*Alcina*: Handel), With plaintive note (*Samson*: Handel), *Quand le bien-aimé reviendra* (*Nina*: Dalayrac), *Nel cor più non mi sento* (*La molinara*: Paisiello), When daisies pied (Arne), *L'amero, saro Costante* (*Il rè pastore*: Mozart), *Tre giorni son che Nina* (attrib. Pergolesi), *Gran dio che regoli* (*Ines di Castro*: Bianchi), The traveller benighted (*Love in a Village*: Arne), When William at eve (*Rosina*: Shield), Light as thistledown (*Rosina*: Shield), Recit. & aria:

Surta la notte. . . Ernani, involami (*Ernani*: Verdi), Recit, aria & cab: *Care compagne. . . come per me sereno. . . sovra il sen* (*La sonnambula*: Bellini), *Regnava nel silenzio* (*Lucia di Lammermoor*: Donizetti), Voices of Spring (J. Strauss), *Qui la voce* (*I puritani*: Bellini), Songs My Mother Taught Me (Dvorak), *Solvejg's Lied* (Grieg), Spring's Return (Rachmaninov), The last rose of summer (*Martha*: Flotow), *Mattinata* (Leoncavello), *Serenata* (Tosti), *Parla* (Arditi), I dreamt I dwelt in marble halls (*The Bohemian Girl*: Balfe), *La pastorella delle Alpi* (Rossini), *La gita in gondola* (Rossini), Serenade (Gounod), *Si mes vers avaient des ailes* (Hahn), The Gypsy and the Bird (Benedict), Tell me lovely shepherd (Boyce), *Oh, mon cher amant* (*La Périchole*: Offenbach), *Les filles de Cadiz* (Delibes), mad scene (Hamlet: Thomas), Lo hear the gentle lark (Bishop).

APPENDIX 5

Selection from: *Quand le bien-aimé reviendra* (*Nina*: Dalayrac), *Care selve* (*Atalanta*: Handel), *Per la gloria d'adoravi* (*Griselda*: Bononcini), With plaintive note (*Samson*: Handel), *Dolente immagine* (Bellini), *Malinconia* (Bellini), *La pastorella delle alpi* (Rossini), *La gita in gondola* (Rossini), *Pastorale* (Stravinsky), *Ici bas* (Cui), Lullaby (Gretchaninov), *La canari* (Tchaikovsky), The Nightingale (Alabiev), *Allegro: Concerto for coloratura* (Gliere), *Ah, non credea* (*La sonnambula*: Bellini), I dreamt I dwelt in marble halls (*The Bohemian Girl*: Balfe), *Seitdem dien Aug'in meines schaute* (R. Strauss), *Weigenlied* (R. Strauss), *Der Kuckuck* (Abt), *Au printemps* (Gounod), Serenade (Gounod), *Pastorale* (Bizet), *Ouvre ton coeur* (Bizet), *Oh! si les fleurs avaient des yeux* (Massenet), *Le papillon et la fleur* (Fauré), *Le rossignol* (Delibes), *Les filles de Cadiz* (Delibes).

APPENDIX 6

Selection from: *Plaisir d'amour* (Martini), *Tre giorni son che Nina* (attrib. Pergolesi), *Venere bella* (*Giulio Cesare*: Handel), *Non desperare* (*Giulio Cesare*: Handel), When daisies pied (Arne), Tell me lovely Shepherd (Boyce), The Shepherd's Song (Haydn), She never told her love (Haydn), Light as thistledown (*Rosina*: Shield), *La promessa* (Rossini), *L'invito* (Rossini), *Adieux à la vie* (Rossini), *Il sospiro* (Donizetti), *Heimkehr* (Delius), *Abendstimmung* (Delius), *Solvejg's Lied* (Grieg), *Ein traum* (Grieg), Scottish folk songs (Annie Laurie, On the Banks of Allan Water, My Love is Like a Red, Red Rose, Ye Banks and Braes, Bonny Mary of Argyle), *La mélodie des baisers* (Massenet), *Crepuscolo* (Massenet), *Si mes vers avaient des ailes* (Hahn), *Oh, mon cher amant* (*La Périchole*: Offenbach), *Eclat de rire* (*Manon Lescaut*: Auber).

APPENDIX 7

Care selve (*Atalanta*: Handel), Soft complaining flute (*Ode to St Cecilia's Day*: Handel), As when the dove (*Acis & Galatea*: Handel),

Music for a While (Purcell), The Shepherd's Song (Haydn), She never told her love (Haydn), When daisies pied (Arne), *Guide au bord ta nacelle* (Meyerbeer), *Chanson de Zora* (Rossini), *Il sospiro* (Rossini), *Auf flugeln des Gesanges* (Mendelssohn), *Fruhlingslied* (Mendelssohn), *Der Kuckuck* (Abt), *O quand je dors* (Liszt), *Berceuse* (Chaminade), *Bleus* (Chaminade), *La mélodie des baisers* (Massenet), *Pastorale* (Bizet), *Oh, mon cher amant* (*La Périchole*: Offenbach), *Les filles de Cadiz* (Delibes), The Gypsy and the Bird (Benedict).

APPENDIX 8

O quand je dors (Liszt), *Die Lorelei* (Liszt), *L'esclave* (Lalo), *Berceuse* (Chaminade), *Puisqu'elle a pris ma vie* (Massenet), *Aimons-nous* (Saint-Saëns), *Aimons-nous* (Hahn), *Guide au bord ta nacelle* (Meyerbeer), *Chanson de Zora* (Rossini), *A mezzanotte* (Donizetti), *Ernani, involami* (*Ernani*: Verdi), Lament of Isis (Granville Barker), Love's Philosphy (Roger Quilter), The Unforeseen (Cyril Scott), Oh, that it were so (Frank Bridge), The Gypsy and the Bird (Benedict), *Il trovatore* (Ponchielli), *La tua stella* (Mascagni), *Stornello* (Cimera), *Serenata* (Tosti), *Ah, que les hommes sont bêtes* (*La Périchole*: Offenbach), *Tu n'es pas beau, tu n'es pas riches* (*La Périchole*: Offenbach).

APPENDIX 9

Selection from: *Dolente immagine* (Bellini), *Malinconia* (Bellini), *A mezzanotte* (Donizetti), *Lungi dal caro bene* (Sarti), *Quand le bien-aimé reviendra* (*Nina*: Dalayrac), *Morrai, si!* (*Rodelinda*: Handel), *Chanson de Zora* (Rossini), *Garde la couronne des Reines* (*Le tribut de Zamora*: Gounod), Recit. & aria: *O Roland . . . Regarde-les, ces yeux!* (*Esclarmonde*: Massenet), *Io non sono più l'Annetta* (*Crispino e la comare*: Ricci), *Chanson de Chérubin* (*Chérubin*: Massenet), *Je suis Titania* (*Mignon*: Thomas), *Chanson de Florian* (Godard), *Le papillon et la fleur* (Fauré), *Puisqu'elle a pris ma vie* (Massenet), *O, si les fleurs avaient des yeux* (Massenet), *Pensée d'automne* (Massenet), *La tua stella* (Mascagni), *Stornello* (Cimera), *Malia* (Tosti), *Serenata* (Tosti), *Oh, mon cher amant* (*La Périchole*: Offenbach), *Ah! que les hommes son bêtes* (*La Périchole*: Offenbach), *Tu n'es pas beau, tu n'es pas riches* (*La Périchole*: Offenbach), *Ah! quel dîner* (*La Périchole*: Offenbach), *Bolero* (*Le coeur et la main*: Lecocq).

APPENDIX 10

Selection from: *Tre giorni son che Nina* (attrib. Pergolesi), *Quand le bien-aimé reviendra* (*Nina*: Dalayrac), The Shepherd's Song (Haydn), She never told her love (Haydn), With plaintive note (*Samson*: Handel), *Guide au bord ta nacelle* (Meyerbeer), *Les hirondelles* (David), *Chanson de Chérubin* (*Chérubin*: Massenet), *Adieux à la vie* (Rossini), *Il sospiro* (Donizetti), The Gypsy and the Bird (Benedict), *Ah, non credea* (*La sonnambula*: Bellini), *Ernani, involami* (*Ernani*:

Verdi), Lullaby (Gretchaninov), *Wiegenlied* (Reger), *Ici bas* (Cui), *Der Kuckuck* (Abt), *Le rossignol* (Delibes), *Pastorale* (Bizet), *Il trovatore* (Ponchielli), *Berceuse* (Chaminade), *Bleus* (Chaminade), *Les filles de Cadiz* (Delibes), Waltz Song (*Robinson Crusoe*: Offenbach), Recit. & aria: *Ah, tardai troppo... O luce di quest'anima* (*Linda di Chamounix*: Donizetti).

APPENDIX 11

Selection from: *Ch'io mi scordi di te?... Non temer amato bene*: K505 (Mozart), *An Chloe*: K524 (Mozart), *Un moto di Gioia*: K 579 (Mozart), The Shepherd's Song (Haydn), She never told her love (Haydn), *Care selve* (*Atalanta*: Handel), With plaintive note (*Samson*: Handel), *Tornami a vagheggiar* (*Alcina*: Handel), *Le Serate Musicale*: *La promessa, Il rimprovero, La partenza, L'orgia, L'invito, La pastorella delle Alpi, La gita in gondola, La danza* (*Rossini*), Songs My Mother Taught Me (Dvorak), *Die Lorelei* (Liszt), *Der Kuckuck* (Abt), *La tua stella* (Mascagni), *Stornello* (Cimera), *Pastorale* (Bizet), *Ah, non credea* (*La sonnambula*: Bellini), *Puisqu'elle a pris ma vie* (Massenet), *Oh! si les fleurs avaient des yeux* (Massenet), *Pensée d'automne* (Massenet), *Oh, mon cher amant* (*La Périchole*: Offenbach), *Les filles de Cadiz* (Delibes), Recit. & aria: *Ah, tardai troppo... O luce di quest'anima* (*Linda di Chamounix*: Donizetti).

APPENDIX 12

Selection from:*Deh vieni non tardar* (*Figaro*: Mozart), *Non mi dir* (*Don Giovanni*: Mozart), *Tornami a vagheggiar* (*Alcina*: Handel), With plaintive note (*Samson*: Handel), Cherry Ripe (Charles Edward Horn), When daisies pied (Arne), Where the bee sucks (Arne), Tell me lovely shepherd (Boyce), Light as thistledown (*Rosina*: Shield), *Guide au bord ta nacelle* (Meyerbeer), *A mezzanotte* (Donizetti), *Chanson de Zora* (Rossini), *Dolente immagine* (Bellini), Twas in a garden beautiful (*Siege of Rochelle*: Balfe), *Garde le couronne des Reines* (*Le tribut de Zamora*: Gounod), *Chanson de Chérubin* (*Chérubin:* Massenet), *Com'è bello* (*Lucrezia Borgia*: Donizetti), *Tu del mio Carlo* (*I masnadieri*: Verdi), *Addio del passato* (*La traviata*: Verdi), *Tacea la notte* (*Il trovatore*: Verdi), *O beau pays* (*Les Huguenots*: Meyerbeer), *Berceuse* (Chaminade), *Ici bas* (Cui), *Aimant la rose* (Rimsky-Korsakov), *Le rossignol* (Delibes), Songs My Mother Taught Me (Dvorak), *Serenata* (Leoncavallo), *Le beau page* [Teatro Malibran, Venice, 9 Apr. 1982] (Malibran), When William at eve (*Rosina*: Shield), *Oh! si les fleurs avaient des yeux* (Massenet), Scottish folk songs (Annie Laurie, My Love is Like a Red, Red Rose, Ye Banks and Braes, Bonnie Mary of Argyle), The Gypsy and the Bird (Benedict), I dreamt I dwelt in marble halls (*The Bohemian Girl*: Balfe), sleepwalking scene (*La sonnambula*: Bellini), *Bel raggio* (*Semiramide*: Rossini), *Casta diva* (*Norma*: Bellini), *O nube che lieve* (*Maria Stuarda*: Donizetti).

APPENDIX 13

Wiegenlied (Reger), *Wiegenlied* (R. Strauss), *Das Theure Vaterhaus* (F. Gumbert), *Der Kuckuck* (Abt), Tell me lovely shepherd (Boyce), *Tre giorni son che Nina* (attrib. Pergolesi), When William at eve (*Rosina*: Shield), *Tornami a vagheggiar* (*Alcina*: Handel) *La tua stella* (Mascagni), *Stornello* (Cimera), *Malia* (Tosti), *Serenata* (Tosti), Bonnie Mary of Argyle (Trad.), The Unforeseen (Cyril Scott), The Bitterness of Love (James P. Dunn), I came with a song (Frank La Forge), Midsummer (Amy Worth), *Oh! si les fleurs avaient des yeux* (Massenet), *Oh! quand je dors* (Liszt), *Le papillon et la fleur* (Faure), *La mélodie des baisers* (Massenet), *Oh, mon cher amant* (*La Périchole*: Offenbach), *Addio del passato* (*La traviata*: Verdi), *O luce di quest'anima* (*Linda di Chamounix*: Donizetti)

DISCOGRAPHY

The following abbreviations are used: LP—long-playing record; MC—music cassette; CD—compact disc.

In the case of excerpts, composers are noted when not indicated in the text. Sutherland sings the lead role except where indicated.

'Compilation' indicates that all items have been previously released; in these cases arias are not specified. Recordings on which Sutherland sings one item are not noted here.

All recordings by Decca except where indicated. The year refers to year of release.

1958
Bach: Cantata 147 Herz und Mund und Leben, with Watts, Brown, Hemsley, Geraint Jones Choir & Orchestra, c. Geraint Jones; HMV CSD 151–2.

1959
Recital La fioraia fiorentina (Rossini), Rose softly blooming (*Zemire and Azore*: Spohr), cavetina & rondo finale from *Emilia di Liverpool*; P. Bonynge; Belcantodisc B LR 1, reissued: Ember GVC 45(LP).
Music of Handel arias from *Alcina: Tornami a vagheggiar, Ah! Ruggiero crudel...Ombre pallide*, with Philomusica of London, c. Anthony Lewis; Oiseau Lyre SOL 60001.
Operatic Arias Ancor non giunse!...Regnava nel silenzio, mad scene (*Lucia di Lammermoor*); Ah! tardai troppo...O luce di quest'anima (*Linda di Chamounix*); Surta la notte...Ernani, involami (*Ernani*) Merce, dilette amiche (*I vespri Siciliani*), with the Paris Opera Chorus & Paris Conservatoire Orchestra, c. Santi; SDD 146 (LP), KSDC 146 (MC)
Beethoven: Choral Symphony No 9 in D Minor, op. 125 with Proctor, Dermota, van Mill, Chorale du Brassus, Choeur des Jeunes de L'Eglise Nationale Vaudoise & Suisse Romande Orchestra, c. Ansermet; SDD108, reissued: SPA 328 (LP), KCSP(MC)

1960
Handel: Acis and Galatea with Pears, Brannigan, Galliver, St Anthony Singers & Philomusica of London, c. Boult; Oiseau Lyre SOL 60011–2, reissued: 414 310 1 ZM2(LP), 414 310–4ZM(MC)
Johann Strauss: Die Fledermaus inc. gala performance in which Sutherland sings Arditi's *Il Bacio* with orchestral accompaniment; SET 201–3, reissued: D247D 3(LP), K247K 32(MC)
The Art of the Prima Donna The soldier tir'd (*Artaxerxes*), Let the bright seraphim (*Samson*), Sediziose voce...Casta diva...Ah! bello a me (*Norma*), Son vergin vezzosa (*I puritani*), Bel raggio (*Semiramide*),

Care, compagne, e voi...come per me sereno...Sovra il sen (La sonnambula), O Dieu, que de bijoux...Ah! je ris. (Faust). Je veux vivre (Roméo et Juliette), Mia madre aveva una povera ancella... piange cantando (Otello), Martern aller Arten (Die Entführung aus dem Serail), E strano...Ah, fors'è lui..., Sempre libera (La traviata), mad scene *(Hamlet),* Bell Song *(Lakmé), O beau pays (Les Huguenots), Gualtier Malde...Caro nome (Rigoletto),* with the Chorus and Orchestra of the Royal Opera House, Covent Garden, c. Molinari-Pradelli; SXL 2256–7(LP), reissued: 414 450–1 DG2 (LP), 414 450–2 DHR (CD), 414 450–4 DH2 (MC)

1961

Mozart: Don Giovanni with Waechter, Taddei, Schwarzkopf, Sciutti, Alva, Philharmonic Choir & Orchestra, c. Giulini; SAX 2369–72 (Columbia), highlights: SAX 2559

Donizetti: Lucia di Lammermoor with Cioni, Merrill, Siepi, Chorus & Orchestra of the Accademia di Santa Cecilia, Rome, c. Pritchard; SET 212–4, reissued: GOS 663–5

Handel: Messiah with Bumbry, McKellar, Ward, London Symphony Chorus & Orchestra, c. Boult; SET 218–20, reissued: D1O4D 3(LP), K1O4K 33(MC), highlights: JB 80(LP), KJBC 80(MC)

1962

Verdi: Rigoletto with MacNeil, Cioni, Siepi, Malagu, Chorus & Orchestra of the Accademia di Santa Cecilia, Rome, c. Sanzogno; SET 224–6, reissued: GOS 655–7(LP), 411 880–1 DO2(LP), 411 880–4 DO2(MC)

Handel: Alcina with Berganza, Sinclair, Alva, Sciutti, Freni, Flagello, London Symphony Chorus & Orchestra, c. Bonynge; SET 232–4, reissued: GOS 509–11(LP)

Operatic Recital (compilation), inc. arias from *Die Entführung aus dem Serail, I vespri Siciliani, Les Huguenots, Artaxerxes, Lucia di Lammermoor,* with various orchestras and conductors; BR 3112

1963

Bellini: La sonnambula with Monti, Corena, Elkins, Stahlman, Chorus and Orchestra of the Maggio Musicale, Fiorentino, c. Bonynge; SET 239–41(LP), highlights: SXL 6128(LP)

Bellini: I puritani with Duval, Capecchi, Flagello, Chorus and Orchestra of the Maggio Musicale, Fiorentino, c. Bonynge; SET 259–61(LP), highlights: SXL 6154, reissued: SET 619

Wagner: Siegfried Woodbird, with Windgassen, Nilsson, Stolze, Neidlinger, Hotter, Boehme, Hoeffgen, Vienna Philharmonic Orchestra, c. Solti; SET 242–6 RING 1–22(LP), reissued: 414 110–1 DHA4(LP), 414 110–2 DH4 (CD), 414 110–4 DHA3(MC)

Verdi: La traviata with Bergonzi, Merrill, Chorus and Orchestra of the Maggio Musicale, Fiorentino, c. Pritchard; SET 249–51(LP); K19K

32(MC), highlights: SXL 6127(LP), reissued 411 877–1 DO2(LP), 411 877–4 DO2(MC)

Bizet: Carmen Micaela, with Resnik, del Monaco, Krause, The Grand Theatre Chorus, Geneva and Suisse Romande Orchestra, c. Schippers; SET 256–8(LP), reissued: 411 630–1 DO3(LP), 411 630–4 DO3(MC), highlights: SPA 539(LP), KCSP 539(MC)

Command Performance Volume I Ocean! thou mighty monster (*Oberon*: Weber), *De cet affreux... Pleurez mes yeux (Le Cid), Dieu! comme cette nuit... ombre légère. (Dinorah*: Meyerbeer), *Qual fiamma avea nel guardo (I pagliacci), Tu del mio Carlo... Carlo viva (I masnadieri), Che! e segnar questa mano... Tu puniscimi (Luisa Miller), Come tacer... Vorrei spiegarvi (La cambiale di matrimonio), Eccomi pronta... Deh, se un' urna (Beatrice di Tenda)*, with the Ambrosian Singers, the London Symphony Orchestra and Chorus, c. Bonynge. Volume II The Gypsy and the Bird (Benedict), *Parla, Il Bacio* (Arditi), *Io non sono più l'Annetta (Crispino e la comare), Ideale, La Serenata* (Tosti), *Mattinata* (Leoncavallo), Lo! hear the gentle lark (Bishop), Home Sweet Home (*Clari*: Bishop), The last rose of summer (*Martha*: Flotow), Scenes that are brightest (*Maritana*: Wallace), I dreamt I dwelt in marble halls. (*The Bohemian Girl*), with the London Symphony Chorus and Orchestra, c. Bonynge; SET 247–8 (LP)

Joan Sutherland Sings Verdi (compilation), inc. arias from *La traviata, Rigoletto, I vespri Siciliani, Ernani, Otello*, with various orchestras and conductors; SWL 8506(LP)

1964

Handel: Giulio Cesare in Egitto (excerpts), with Elkins, Sinclair, Conrad, Horne and New Symphony Orchestra, c. Bonynge; SDD 213(LP), reissued: SDD 574 (LP)

The Age of Bel Canto Furia di donna *(La buona figliuola)*, With plaintive note *(Samson)*, Mio caro ben *(Astarto*: Bononcini), Light as thistledown, When William at eve *(Rosina: Shield)*, O zittre nicht *(Die Zauberflöte)*, Ma Fancette est charmante *(Angela*: Gail and Boieldieu), Serbami ognor *(Semiramide)*, Und ob die Wolke *(Der Freischütz)*, Angiol di pace *(Beatrice di Tenda)*, Tornami a dir *(Don Pasquale)*, Santo di patria... allor che i forte corrono *(Attila*: Verdi), with Marilyn Horne, Richard Conrad, London Symphony Orchestra Chorus and the New Symphony Orchestra, c. Bonynge; SET 268–9(LP)

1965

Bellini: Norma with Alexander, Horne, Cross, London Symphony Chorus and Orchestra, c. Bonynge; SET 424–6(LP), K21K 32(MC), highlights: SET 456

Joy to the World Joy to the World (Handel/Watts, arr. Gamley), It came upon a midnight clear (Willis/Sears, arr. Gamley), O Holy Night (Adam, arr. Gamley), O Divine Redeemer (Gounod, arr. Gamley), Adeste fideles (trad., arr. Gamley), The Twelve Days of Christmas

(trad., arr. Gamley), Good King Wenceslas (trad., arr. Gamley), Hark! the herald angels sing (Mendelssohn, arr. Gamley), The Virgin's Slumber Song (Reger), Ave Maria (Schubert, arr. Gamley), The Holly and the Ivy (trad., arr. Gamley), Angels we have heard on high (trad., arr. Gamley), Deck the Hall (trad., arr. Gamley), with Valda Aveling, Patricia Clark, Ambrosian Singers and New Philharmonic Orchestra, c. Bonynge; SXL 6193(LP), KSXC 6193(MC)
Joan Sutherland Sings Handel (compilation), inc. arias from *Alcina, Giulio Cesare, Samson* and *Messiah*, with various orchestras and conductors; SXL 6191(LP)

1966
Rossini: Semiramide with Horne, Rouleau, Malas, Ambrosian Opera Chorus and London Symphony Orchestra, c. Bonynge; SET 317–9(LP), highlights: SET 391(LP)
Bellini: Beatrice di Tenda with Pavarotti, Veasey, Opthof, Ambrosian Opera Chorus and London Symphony Orchestra, c. Bonynge; SET 320–2(LP), highlights: SET 430(LP)
Graun: Montezuma (excerpts), with Elms, Ward, Harwood, Woodland, Sinclair, Ambrosian Singers and London Philharmonic Orchestra, c. Bonynge; SET 351(LP)
Bononcini: Griselda (excerpts), with Elms, Sinclair, Elkins, Malas, Ambrosian Singers and London Symphony Orchestra, c. Bonynge; SET 352, reissued: 411 719–1 DS(LP)
Gounod: Faust with Corelli, Ghiaurov, Massard, Elkins, Ambrosian Opera Chorus and London Symphony Orchestra, c. Bonynge; SET 327–30(LP), K127K 43 (MC), highlights: SET 431
Beethoven: Choral **Symphony No 9 in D minor, Op. 125** with Horne, King, Talvela, Vienna State Opera Chorus and Vienna Philharmonic Orchestra, c. Schmidt-Isserstedt; SXL 6233(LP), reissued: JB 1(LP), KJBC 1(MC)
Joan Sutherland Sings the Songs of Noël Coward I'll follow my secret heart, Never more, Melanie's aria, Charming, charming (*Conversation Piece*); I'll see you again, Zigeuner (*Bitter Sweet*); Dearest love, Where are the songs we sung, Countess Mitzi (*Operette*); I knew that you would be my love (*After the Ball*); Bright was the day, This is a changing world (*Pacific 1860*), with Noël Coward, Elkins, Wakefield, Ambrosian Singers and National Philharmonic Orchestra, c. Bonynge; SXL 6255
Joan Sutherland Sings Bellini (compilation), inc. arias from *Beatrice di Tenda, I puritani, Norma, La sonnambula*, with various orchestras and conductors; SXL 6192 (LP)
Joan Sutherland Sings Verdi (compilation), inc. arias from *Ernani, I masnadieri, Luisa Miller, Attila, Rigoletto, La traviata, I vespri Siciliani*, with various orchestras and conductors; SXL 6190 (LP)

1967
Love Live Forever – The Romance of Musical Comedy Students' Chorus,

Deep in my heart (*The Student Prince*: Romberg), Desert Song (*The Desert Song*), Falling in love with love (*The Boys from Syracuse*: Rogers), And love was born (*Music in the Air*: Kern), Make believe (*Show Boat*: Kern), Indian love call (*Rose Marie*: Friml), When you're away (*The Only Girl*: Herbert), Love will find a way (*Maid of the Mountains*: Fraser-Simson), Waltz Song (*Tom Jones*: German), *O mon cher amant, Mon Dieu! Ah! que les hommes sont bêtes, Ah! quel dîner*, (*La Périchole:* Offenbach), *Air de Nina (Cherubin), Schenkt man sich Rosen in Tirol (Der Vogelhändler*), The Dubarry (*The Dubarry*), *Kind du kannst tanzen Schlafcoupé Lied* (*Die Geschiedene Frau*: Fall), *Heute Nachte (Die Spanische Nachtigall:* Fall), *Dollarprinzessin (Die Dollarprinzess:* Fall), *Heut könnt' einer sein Glück (Madame Pompadour:* Fall), *Und der Himmel hängt (Der Lieber Augustin:* Fall), *Wär'es auch nichts als ein Traum von Glück* (*Eva*: Lehár), *Da draussen im duftigen (Der Walzertraum:* O. Strauss), *My hero (The Chocolate Soldier*: O. Strauss), *Im Chambre séparée (Der Opernball*: Heuberger), Nuns' Chorus (*Cassanova*: J. Strauss), Vilja (*The Merry Widow*). Love live forever (*Paganini*), Stars in my eyes (*The King Steps Out*: Kreisler), *Cossacks' Song, At the balalaika (Balalaika*: Posford), with the Ambrosian Light Opera Chorus and National Philharmonic Orchestra, c. Bonynge; SET 349–50(LP)

1968

Russian Rarities Concerto for Coloratura and Orchestra (Gliere), *Pastorale* (Stravinsky), *Ici bas* (Cui), Lullaby (Gretchaninov), with London Symphony Orchestra, c. Bonynge; SXL 6406

Mozart: Don Giovanni with Bacquier, Krenn, Lorengar, Horne, Monreale, The Ambrosian Singers and English Chamber Orchestra, c. Bonynge; SET 412–5 (LP), highlights: SET 496

Donizetti: La fille du régiment with Pavarotti, Malas, Sinclair, Chorus and Orchestra of the Royal Opera House, Covent Garden, c. Bonynge; SET 372–3(LP), K23K 22(MC), highlights: SET 491

Verdi: Requiem Mass with Pavarotti, Horne, Talvela, Vienna State Opera Chorus and Vienna Philharmonic Orchestra, c. Solti; SET 374–5(LP), K85K 22(MC), 411 944–2 DH2(CD)

Delibes: Lakmé with Vanzo, Bacquier, Berbie, Monte-Carlo Opera Chorus and L'Orchestre National de L'Opéra de Monte Carlo, c. Bonynge; SET 387–9(LP), highlights: SET 488

1969

Meyerbeer: Les Huguenots with Arroyo, Tourangeau, Vrenios, Bacquier, Cossa, Ghiuselev, The Ambrosian Opera Chorus and National Philharmonic Orchestra, c. Bonynge; SET 460–3(LP), highlights: SET 513

1970

Handel: Messiah with Tourangeau, Krenn, Krause, The Ambrosian

Singers and English Chamber Orchestra, c. Bonynge; SETA 485–7(LP), highlights: SXL 6540(LP), KSXC 6540(MC)

Romantic French Arias *Conduisez-moi vers celui qui j'adore (Robinson Crusoe), Bellah! ma chèvre chérie! (Dinorah:* Meyerbeer), *Depuis le jour (Louise), Dites-lui qu'on l'a remarqué (La Grande-Duchesse de Gérolstein:* Offenbach), *C'est l'histoire amoureuse (Manon Lescaut:* Auber), *Non temete milord. . . . Or son sola (Fra Diavolo:* Auber), *Me voilà seule. . . . Comme autrefois (Les pecheurs de perles:* Bizet), *Les oiseaux dans la charmille (Les contes d'Hoffmann), Ah! que mes soeurs sont heureuses (Cendrillon:* Massenet), *O légère hirondelle (Mireille:* Gounod), *Vous aimez le danger. . . Ah! que j'aime les militaires (La Grand-Duchesse de Gérolstein), C'est bien lui (L'étoile du nord:* Meyerbeer), *Ce Sarrasin desait (Le tribut de Zamora:* Gounot), *En vain j'espère. . . Idole de ma vie (Robert le diable:* Meyerbeer), *Un soir Perez le capitaine (Le coeur et la main:* Lecocq), *Au bord du chemin qui passe à ma porte (Les noces de Jeannette:* Massé), *Si le bonheur (Faust), La marguerite a fermé. . . Ouvre ton coeur (Carmen), Veille sur eux. . . Vaisseau que le flot balance (L'étoile du nord),* with the Grand Theatre Chorus, Geneva and Suisse Romande Orchestra, c. Bonynge; SET 454–5(LP), highlights: KCET 454 (MC)

The World of Joan Sutherland (compilation), inc. arias from *Faust, La fille du régiment, Rigoletto, La traviata, Norma, Louise*, etc, with various orchestras, c. Bonynge; SPA 100 (LP), KSP 100(MC)

Operatic Duets with Marilyn Horne (compilation), inc. duets from *Norma, Semiramide* with the London Symphony Orchestra, c. Bonynge; SET 456(LP)

1971

Donizetti: L'elisir d'amore with Pavarotti, Cossa, Malas, The Ambrosian Singers and English Chamber Orchestra, c. Bonynge; SET 503–5(LP), 414 461–2 DH2(CD), K154K 32(MC), highlights: SET 564

Verdi: Rigoletto with Milnes, Pavarotti, Talvela, Tourangeau, The Ambrosian Opera Chorus and London Symphony Orchestra, c. Bonynge; SET 542–4 (LP), 414 269–2 DH2(CD), K2A 3(MC), highlights: SET 580(LP), KCET 580(MC)

Donizetti: Lucia di Lammermoor with Pavarotti, Milnes, Ghiaurov, Chorus and Orchestra of the Royal Opera House, Covent Garden, c. Bonynge; SET 528–30 (LP), 410 193–2 DH3(CD), K2L 22(MC), highlights: SET 559(LP)

1972

Offenbach: Les contes d'Hoffmann with Domingo, Tourangeau, Bacquier, Cuenod, Plishka, Lilowa, combined choruses of the Radio Suisse Romande, Pro Arte of Lausanne and Du Brassus and Suisse Romande Orchestra, c. Bonynge: SET 545–7 (LP), K109K 32(MC), highlights: SET 569(LP), KCET 569(MC)

The Art of Bel Canto (compilation), inc. arias from *Rosina, Griselda,*

Montezuma, Die Zauberflöte, etc, with Horne, Conrad, various orchestras, c. Bonynge; SDD 317 (LP)

1973

Puccini: Turandot with Pavarotti, Caballé, Ghiaurov, Krause, Pears, John Alldis Choir, Wandsworth School Boys' Choir and London Philharmonic Orchestra, c. Mehta; SET 561–3(LP), 414–274 2 DH2(CD), K2A 2(MC), highlights: SET 573(LP), KCET 573(MC)

Songs My Mother Taught Me Songs My Mother Taught Me (Dvorak), *Auf Flugeln des Gesanges* (Mendelssohn), Homing (Riego), *Oh! Si les fleurs avaient des yeux, Crépuscule* (Massenet), Serenade (Gounod), Mary of Argyll (S. Nelson), *Le rossignol, Les filles de Cadiz* (Delibes), I came with a song (Frank La Forge), I was dreaming (Augustus Juncker), *Si mes vers avaient des ailes* (Hahn), *Der Kuckuck* (Abt), *Solvejg's Lied* (Grieg), Midsummer (Amy Worth), *Oh! Quand je dors* (Liszt), with the New Philharmonia Orchestra, c. Bonynge; SXL 6619(LP)

1975

Bellini: I puritani with Pavarotti, Ghiaurov, Luccardi, Chorus of the Royal Opera House, Covent Garden and London Symphony Orchestra, c. Bonynge; SET 587–9(LP), highlights: SET 619

Darwin: Song For a City recorded from the stage of the Royal Opera House, Covent Garden in aid of Flood Disaster Appeal, with other artists and Royal Philharmonic Orchestra, c. Bonynge; SXL 6719

1976

Massenet: Esclarmonde with Aragall, Grant, Tourangeau, Quilico, John Alldis Choir, Finchley Children's Music Group and National Philharmonic Orchestra, c. Bonynge; SET 612–4(LP)

Donizetti: Maria Stuarda with Pavarotti, Tourangeau, Morris, Soyer, Chorus and Orchestra of the Teatro Comunale, Bologna, c. Bonynge; D2D 3(LP), K2A 33(MC), highlights: SET 624

1977

Leoni: L'oracolo with Gobbi, Tourangeau, van Allan, John Alldis Choir and National Philharmonic Orchestra, c. Bonynge; D34D 2(LP), K34K 22(MC)

Verdi: Il trovatore with Pavarotti, Wixell, Horne, London Opera Chorus and National Philharmonic Orchestra, c. Bonynge; D82D 3(LP), K82K 32(MC), highlights: SET 631(LP), KCET 631(MC)

Operatic Duets with Pavarotti; *Brindisi, Parigi, o cara (La traviata), Perdona, o mia diletta. . . Prendi, l'anel ti dono (La sonnambula), Da quel di che t'incontrai (Linda di Chamounix) Gia nella notte densa (Otello), La fatal pietra. . . O terra, addio (Aida)*, with the London Opera Chorus and National Philharmonic Orchestra, c. Bonynge; SXL 6828(LP), 400 058–2DH (CD), KSXC 6828(MC)

The Voice of the Century (compilation), inc. arias by Handel, Weber, Bizet, Offenbach, Rossini, Bellini, etc. and *Vissi d'arte* from *Tosca*, with various orchestras and conductors; D65D 3(LP)

1978

Lehar: The Merry Widow (highlights), with Krenn, Masterson, Brecknock, Ewer, The Ambrosian Singers and National Philharmonic Orchestra, c. Bonynge; SET 629(LP), KCET 629(MC)
Donizetti: Lucrezia Borgia with Aragall, Wixell, Horne, London Opera Chorus and National Philharmonic Orchestra, c. Bonynge; D93D 3(LP), K93K 32(MC)

1979

Puccini: Suor Angelica with Ludwig and full cast, London Opera Chorus and National Philharmonic Orchestra, c. Bonynge; SET 627 (LP), KCET 627(MC)
Joan Sutherland Sings Wagner Gerechter Gott... *In seiner Blüte*, (*Rienzi*), Senta's ballad (*Die Fliegende Holländer*), *Dich teure Halle*, Elizabeth's prayer (*Tannhäuser*), *Einsam in trüben Tagen* (*Lohengrin*), *Du bist der Lenz* (*Die Walküre*), *O Sachs, mein Freund* (*Die Meistersinger*), *Liebestod* (*Tristan und Isolde*), with the National Philharmonic Orchestra, c. Bonynge; SXL 6930(LP), KSXC 6930(MC)
Joan Sutherland Sings Mozart Allelujah (*Exultate Jubilate*), *L'amerò, sarò costante, (Il rè pastore)*, *Vorrei spiegarvi, oh Dio; Porgi amor, Voi che sapete, Dove sono, Deh vieni non tardar* (*Le nozze di Figaro*), *Ch'io mi scordi di te?... Non temer amato bene Ach ich fühl's* (*Die Zauberflöte*), with the National Philharmonic Orchestra, c. Bonynge; SXL 6933(LP)

1980

Massenet: Le roi de Lahore with Lima, Tourangeau, Milnes, Morris, the London Voices and National Philharmonic Orchestra, c. Bonynge; D210D 3(LP), K210K 33(MC)

1981

Verdi: La traviata with Pavarotti, Manuguerra, London Opera Chorus and National Philharmonic Orchestra, c. Bonynge; D212D 3(LP), 410 154–2 DH3(CD), K212K 32(MC), highlights: SXDL 7562(LP), 400 057–2DH(CD), KSXD 7562(MC)
Serate Musicale – Songs, Melodies, Lieder La promessa, Il rimprovero, La partenza, L'ogia, L'invito, La pastorella delle alpi, La gita in gondola, La danza; Adieux a la vie!, Chanson de Zora, Arietta all'antica (Rossini); *Serenata francese* (Leoncavallo); *Il sospiro, A mezzanotte, J'attends toujours* (Donizetti); *I tempi assai lontani* (Respighi); *Dolente immagine, Vaga luna, che inargenti* (Bellini); *Il poveretto* (Verdi); *Stornello* (Cimara); *Il trovatore* (Ponchielli); *La tua stella* (Mascagni); *L'ultima speme* (Campana); *Au printemps* (Gounod);

Chanson de Florian (Godard); *Pensée d'automne, Oh! Si les fleurs avaient des yeux, Puisqu'elle a pris ma vie* (Massenet); *Quand le bien-aimé reviendra* (Dalayrac); *L'esclave* (Lalo); *Le soir* (Thomas); *Aimons-nous* (Saint-Saëns); *Le papillon et la fleur* (Fauré); *Pastorale* (Bizet); *Guide au bord ta nacelle* (Meyerbeer); *Hirondelles* (David); *Berceuse* (Chaminade); *Les filles de Cadiz* (Delibes); *Aimons-nous* (Hahn); *Mariquita* (Adam); p. Bonynge; D125D 3, K255K

Live from Lincoln Centre Arias, duets and trios from *Ernani, Norma, La gioconda, I masnadieri, Otello, Il trovatore* etc., with Pavarotti, Horne and New York Philharmonic Orchestra, c. Bonynge; D255D2(LP) K255K 22(MC), CD (number unavailable)

Grandi Voci – Joan Sutherland *Per la gloria d'adoravi* (*Griselda*: Bononcini), *Nel cor più non mi sento* (Paisiello), *Furia di donna (La buona figliuola*), The traveller benighted (*Love in a Village*: Arne), The soldier tir'd (*Artaxerxes*), When William at eve, Whilst with village maids, Light as thistledown (*Rosina*), with the Philomusica of London, c. Granville Jones. NB: the above were recorded during the 1950s and never released; the following (side 2) have been previously released. Ye verdant plains, Heart, the seat of soft delight (*Acis and Galatea*), with the Philomusica of London, c. Boult; *Tornami a vagheggiar, Ombre pallide* (*Alcina*), with the Philomusica of London, c. Anthony Lewis; GRV 1 (LP), KGRC1 (MC)

1982

Bellini: La sonnambula with Pavarotti, Ghiaurov, Jones, Buchanan, London Opera Chorus and National Philharmonic Orchestra, c. Bonynge; D23OD 3(LP), K23OK 33(MC)

Gay: The Beggar's Opera Lucy Lockit, with te Kanawa, Resnik, Morris, Clarke, Dean, Warren Mitchell, Michael Hordern, Alfred Marks, Angela Lansbury, London Opera Chorus and National Phil-harmonic Orchestra, c. Bonynge; D252D 2(LP), K252K 22(MC)

Operatic Duets with Pavarotti (compilation), inc. duets from *Lucia di Lammermoor, Rigoletto, L'elisir d'amore, La fille du régiment, I puritani*, with various orchestras, c. Bonynge; SXL 6991(LP), KSXC 6991(MC)

1983

Verdi: I masnadieri with Bonisolli, Ramey, Manuguerra, Chorus and Orchestra of the Welsh National Opera, c. Bonynge; D273D 3(LP), K273K 32(MC)

1984

Thomas: Hamlet with Milnes, Morris, Conrad, Chorus and Orchestra of the Welsh National Opera, c. Bonynge; 410 184–1 DH3(LP), 410 184–4 DH2(MC)

Grandi Voci – Joan Sutherland (compilation), inc. arias by Handel, Mozart, Bononcini, Graun, etc, with various orchestras and conductors; 410 147–1 DG (LP), 410 147–4DG(MC)

1986

Handel: Athalia with Rolfe-Johnson, Kirkby, Thomas, Bowman, Alcd Jones, Choir of New College, Oxford and the Academy of Ancient Music, c. Hogwood; 417 127–1(LP), 417 127–2(CD), 417 127–4(MC)

Bel Canto Arias Par che mi dica ancora. . . Fuggi l'immagine (Il castello de Kenilworth: Donizetti), *Liberamente or piangi. . . Oh! nel fuggente nuvolo (Attila*: Verdi), *Eccomi in lieta vesta. . . Oh! quante volte, oh! quante (I Capuleti e i Montecchi:* Bellini), *In questo emplice modesto asilo (Betly:* Donizetti), *L'ai-je bien entendu? . . . O mon Fernand (La favorita*: Donizetti), *Sur mes genoux (L'africaine*: Meyerbeer), *Sombre foret (Guillaume Tell*: Rossini), *Una voce poco fa (Il barbiere di Siviglia*: Rossini), with the Welsh National Orchestra, c. Bonynge; 417 253–1(LP), 417 253–2(CD), 417 253–4(MC)

1987

Handel: Rodelinda with Tourangeau, Ramey and the Welsh National Orchestra, c. Bonynge; 414 667–1 DH2(LP), 414 667–2DH(CD), 414 667–4DH2(MC)

For future release: *Norma* with Caballé, Pavarotti, Ramey, Chorus and Orchestra of the Welsh National Opera, c. Bonynge.

La sonnambula (CD transfer from D230D 3)

Romantic French Arias (re-release from SET 454)

I puritani (CD) transfer from SET 587–9

SELECTED BIBLIOGRAPHY

ASBROOK, William, *Donizetti*, London, Cassell, 1965

BING, Rudolf, *Five Thousand Nights at the Opera*, London, Hamish Hamilton, 1972

CULSHAW, John, *Putting the Record Straight*, London, Secker & Warburg, 1981

GALATOPOULOS, Stelios, *Callas, La Divina*, London, J.M. Dent & Sons, 1966

GISHFORD, Anthony, *Grand Opera*, London, Weidenfeld & Nicholson, 1972

HALTRECHT, Montague, *The Quiet Showman*, London, Collins, 1975

HARDING, James, *Massenet*, London, J.M. Dent & Sons, 1970

HETHERINGTON, John, *Melba*, London, Faber & Faber Ltd, 1967

HORNE, Marilyn, *My Life*, New York, Atheneum, 1983

MAY, Robin, *A Companion to the Opera*, London, Lutterworth Press, 1977

OSBORNE, Charles, *The Complete Operas of Verdi*, London, Victor Gollancz Ltd, 1967

PAVAROTTI, Luciano, *My Own Story*, London, Sidgwick & Jackson, 1981

PORTER, Andrew, *Music of Three Seasons, 1974–1977*, New York, Farrar Strauss Giroux, 1978

Report to the Australia Council by the Committee of Inquiry into Opera and Music Theatre in Australia, Sydney, May 1980

WEINSTOCK, Herbert, *Vincenzo Bellini, His Life and his Operas*, London, Weidenfeld & Nicholson, 1971

VON WESTERMAN, Gerhart, *Opera Guide*, London, Thames & Hudson, 1964

Index

Catalogue references are indicated by italic page numbers. Joan Sutherland and Richard Bonynge have not been indexed, as they appear on almost every page.